The Pictorial
in Modernist Fiction
from Stephen Crane to Ernest Hemingway

Studies in Modern Literature, No. 93

The Pictorial
in Modernist Fiction
from Stephen Crane to Ernest Hemingway

by
Deborah Schnitzer

U·M·I Research Press

Ann Arbor / London

Produced and distributed by
UMI Research Press
an imprint of
University Microfilms Inc.
Ann Arbor, Michigan 48106

Library of Congress Cataloging in Publication Data

Schnitzer, Deborah, 1950-
The pictorial in modernist fiction from Stephen Crane to Ernest
Hemingway / by Deborah Schnitzer.
p. cm.—(Studies in modern literature ; no. 93)
Bibliography: p.
Includes index.
ISBN 0-8357-1876-X (alk. paper)
1. American fiction—20th century—History and criticism.   2. Art
and literature—History—20th century.   3. Picturesque, The, in
literature.   4. Realism in literature.   5. Mimesis in literature.
6. Description (Rhetoric)   7. Modernism (Literature)   8. English
fiction—20th century—History and criticism.   I. Title.
II. Series.
PS374.A76S36   1988
813'.52'09357—dc19   88-11091
                                                                                        CIP

British Library CIP data is available.

To Mendel, the Polish prince,
and the laughter of our lovely young sons, Ben and Zachary

Contents

List of Figures   *ix*

Acknowledgments   *xiii*

Introduction   *1*

1   "Ocular Realism": The Impressionist Effects of an "Innocent Eye"   *7*
    Crane
    Woolf
    Matthiessen

2   Conceptual Realism: "Monadic Perspectives" and "Mackerel Eyes"   *63*
    Woolf
    Hemingway
    Lawrence

3   "Total Representation": "Cubification" and Cubist Effects   *159*
    Joyce
    Stein

Conclusion   *247*

Notes   *251*

Bibliography   *271*

Index   *279*

Figures

1. Claude Monet, *The Grenouillère*, 1869   *12*

2. Camille Pissarro, *Place du Théâtre Français*, 1898   *16*

3. Claude Monet, *The Garden, Giverny*, 1902   *21*

4. Edgar Degas, *Orchestra of the Paris Opera*, 1868   *35*

5. Claude Monet, *Rue St. Denis, Festival of June 30, 1878*, 1878   *37*

6. Edgar Degas, *Place de la Concorde*, 1872–1873   *41*

7. Claude Monet, *Boulevard des Capucines*, 1873   *44*

8. Edgar Degas, *Spartan Youths Exercising*, 1860   *46*

9. Claude Monet, *Rouen Cathedral: The Façade at Sunset*, 1894   *49*

10. Edgar Degas, *At the Theatre*, 1880   *53*

11. Peter Matthiessen, *Far Tortuga*, 1975   *56*

12. Claude Monet, *Poplars*, 1891   *71*

13. Vincent van Gogh, *Cornfield at Sunrise*, 1890   *79*

14. Vincent van Gogh, *Madame Roulin*, 1889   *80*

15. Paul Cézanne, *Mont Ste. Victoire, Seen from Bellevue*, 1885– 1887   *83*

16. Paul Cézanne, *Still Life with Fruit Basket*, 1888–1890   *84*

17. Paul Gauguin, *Self-Portrait, Les Misérables*, 1888   *85*

18. Vincent van Gogh, *Self-Portrait, Saint-Rémy*, 1889   *88*

19. Vincent van Gogh, *Starry Night*, 1889   *92*

20. Georges Seurat, *The Lighthouse at Honfleur*, 1886   *110*

21. Georges Seurat, *A Sunday Afternoon on the Island of La Grande Jatte*, 1884–1886   *112*

22. Xavier Mellery, *The Soul of Things*, 1890   *116*

23. Paul Cézanne, *The Boundary Wall*, 1872   *125*

24. Pieter Brueghel, the Elder, Active 1551–1569, *The Harvesters*   *127*

25. Paul Cézanne, *Chestnut Trees at Jas de Bouffan*, 1885–1887   *131*

26. Paul Gauguin, *The Poor Fisherman*, 1896   *137*

27. André Derain, *The Bathers*, 1908   *149*

28. Vincent van Gogh, *Crows over the Wheat Field*, 1890   *154*

29. Vincent van Gogh, *The Olive Orchard*, 1889   *156*

30. Georges Braque, *Violin and Palette*, 1909–1910   *161*

31. Pablo Picasso, *Still Life with Chair Caning*, 1912   *164*

32. Juan Gris, *Glasses and Newspaper*, 1914   *165*

33. Juan Gris, *Portrait of Picasso*, 1912   *168*

34. Pablo Picasso, *Portrait of Monsieur Kahnweiler*, 1910   *169*

35. Marcel Duchamp, *Nude Descending a Staircase, No. 2*, 1912   *170*

36. Georges Braque, *Houses at L'Estaque*, 1908   *172*

37.   Georges Braque, *Fishes*, 1910   *174*

38.   Pablo Picasso, *Bottle of Pernod*, 1912   *176*

39.   Pablo Picasso, *Ma Jolie*, 1910   *178*

40.   Pablo Picasso, *Les Demoiselles d'Avignon*, 1907   *180*

41.   Pablo Picasso, *Seated Female Nude*, 1910   *182*

42.   Georges Braque, *The Portuguese*, 1911   *184*

43.   Pablo Picasso, *Girl with a Mandolin* (Fanny Tellier), 1910   *195*

44.   Juan Gris, *The Open Window: Place Ravignan*, 1915   *199*

45.   Pablo Picasso, *Portrait of Gertrude Stein*, 1906   *219*

46.   Pablo Picasso, *Woman with Mandolin*, 1909   *222*

47.   Juan Gris, *The Table*, 1919   *224*

48.   Pablo Picasso, *La Suze*, 1912–1913   *226*

49.   Pablo Picasso, *Still Life with Calling Card*, 1914   *230*

50.   Pablo Picasso, *Student with a Pipe*, 1913   *231*

51.   Juan Gris, *Man in a Cafe*, 1914   *242*

Acknowledgments

I delight in this opportunity to express my appreciation to those who have helped to see this project through to fruition: to Dr. Evelyn J. Hinz, whose energy, insight, and continuing advocacy helped to shape this book; to Dr. John J. Teunissen, who offered his acumen, encouragement, and support; to the Faculty of Graduate Studies at the University of Manitoba, whose financial assistance helped to defray the cost of redaction; to Nancy McKinnell whose enthusiasm, friendship, and skill made the researching of permissions and the preparation of the manuscript a fine adventure; to Merv Henwood, whose attention to detail and clarity of focus held compulsivity at bay; to David Rozniatowski of the Winnipeg Art Gallery, whose interest, expertise, and kindness are well remembered; to Charlotte Elson and Taliza "e," who cared for all at 1069; to the special people who listened to my "arguments" over the phone and never put the receiver down until I did; and to Inez and Frank Richardson for their initial and generous collaboration.

The author gratefully acknowledges permission to quote from the following works: *A Different Language: Gertrude Stein's Experimental Writing* by Marianne DeKoven, copyright 1983, reprinted by permission of The University of Wisconsin Press. *Islands in the Stream* by Ernest Hemingway, copyright © 1970 by Mary Hemingway. Reprinted with the permission of Charles Scribner's Sons, an imprint of Macmillan Publishing Company. "Big Two-Hearted River" from *In Our Time* by Ernest Hemingway, copyright 1925, Charles Scribner's Sons; copyright renewed 1953 by Ernest Hemingway. Reprinted with permission of Charles Scribner's Sons, an imprint of Macmillan Publishing Company, and with the permission of Jonathan Cape, Ltd., London, and the Executors of the Ernest Hemingway Estate. *The Old Man and the Sea* © 1980 by Mary Hemingway. Reprinted with the permission of Charles Scribner's Sons, an imprint of Macmillan Publishing Company, and with the permission of Jonathan Cape, Ltd., London, and the Executors of the Ernest Hemingway Estate. *The Sun Also Rises,* copyright 1926 by Charles Scribner's Sons; copyright renewed

1954 by Ernest Hemingway. Reprinted with the permission of Charles Scribner's Sons, an imprint of Macmillan Publishing Company, and with the permission of Jonathan Cape, Ltd., London, and the Executors of the Ernest Hemingway Estate. *A Farewell to Arms* by Ernest Hemingway, copyright 1929 by Charles Scribner's Sons; copyright renewed 1957 by Ernest Hemingway. Reprinted with the permission of Charles Scribner's Sons, an imprint of Macmillan Publishing Company, and with the permission of Jonathan Cape, Ltd., London, and the Executors of the Ernest Hemingway Estate. *The Plumed Serpent* by D. H. Lawrence, copyright 1926, 1959 by Alfred A. Knopf. Reprinted by permission of the publisher. *The Rainbow* by D. H. Lawrence, copyright 1915 by David Herbert Lawrence; copyright renewed 1943 by Frieda Lawrence. Reprinted by permission of Viking Penguin. *Cezanne's Composition: Analysis of His Form with Diagrams and Photos of His Motifs* by Erle Loran, copyright 1946, reprinted by permission of The University of California Press. *Virginia Woolf: The Echoes Enslaved* by Allen McLaurin, copyright 1973, reprinted by permission of Cambridge University Press. *Far Tortuga* by Peter Matthiessen, copyright 1975 by Peter Matthiessen. Reprinted by permission of Random House. *As for Me and My House* by S. Ross. Used by permission of the Canadian Publishers, McClelland and Stewart, Toronto. *Tender Buttons* by Gertrude Stein, copyright 1914 by Gordon Press; copyright 1967 by Peter Owen, Ltd., London. Reprinted by permission of the publisher. *The Complete Letters of Vincent van Gogh.* Reprinted by permission of Little, Brown, and Company in conjunction with the New York Graphic Society. All rights reserved. *To the Lighthouse* by Virginia Woolf, copyright 1927 by Harcourt Brace Jovanovich, Inc.; renewed 1955 by Leonard Woolf. Reprinted by permission of the publisher. *A Writer's Diary* by Virginia Woolf, copyright 1953, 1954 by Leonard Woolf; renewed 1981, 1982 by Quentin Bell and Angelica Garnett. Reprinted by permission of Harcourt Brace Jovanovich, Inc. *Jacob's Room* by Virginia Woolf, copyright 1923 by Harcourt Brace Jovanovich, Inc.; renewed 1951 by Leonard Woolf. Reprinted by permission of the publisher. *The Waves* by Virginia Woolf, copyright 1931 by Harcourt Brace Jovanovich, Inc.; renewed 1959 by Leonard Woolf. Reprinted by permission of the publisher. *A Haunted House and Other Short Stories* by Virginia Woolf, copyright 1944, 1972 by Harcourt Brace Jovanovich, Inc. Reprinted by permission of Harcourt Brace Jovanovich, The Hogarth Press, and the Estate of Virginia Woolf.

Introduction

Of the many intriguing points raised in John Keats's "Ode on a Grecian Urn," one that is particularly relevant to a study of the pictorial in Modernist narratives involves the persona's advocacy of the superiority of the temporal over the spatial arts. In dramatizing this argument, the speaker's comparative strategy would seem to violate one of the basic principles of interartistic analysis: The quality of the urn's silent art is evaluated in terms of its ability to perform a narrative task that is incompatible with the reality of both the intent and the material resources of its medium. The point is raised here for the "Ode" so effectively demonstrates (possibly without intending to) that respect for the basic conventions that determine the nature of a particular art form must inform any Sister Arts perspective.

A second and related point concerns the use of the period concept itself, whose implementation Ulrich Weisstein counsels against, for this *Geistesgeschichte* method of analysis tends to "treat analogies as parallels by maintaining that all works created in a given period, regardless of medium or provenance, share essential features." In his discussion of how interartistic analogies might function more successfully, Weisstein observes that a comparative method can be fruitful if the focus is "specific," the relations "tangible," and the parameters for the study precisely delineated and vigorously controlled.[1] In her essay on the Sister Arts tradition as it is developed in the nineteenth century through Baudelaire's response to Delacroix's art, Elizabeth Abel similarly recommends that period concepts be abandoned in favor of more "modest claims and goals" that focus on "particular relationships within a given style or period."[2] The value of specificity is one Alastair Fowler also defends in his discussion of "Periodization and Interart Analogies": "The notion of a universally valid systematic correspondence between the arts must be regarded as chimera. Real correspondences exist and may be worth analyzing. But they change with time, and change so fundamentally as to make diachronic investigation a necessary preliminary to discussing them, if full rigor of method is to be achieved."[3]

One of the major problems that attends discussions of the potential relatedness of nineteenth- and twentieth-century visual and verbal art forms derives from the fact that many theorists have failed to conduct the kind of preliminary investigation Fowler defines as prerequisite to the discovery and analysis of "real correspondences." The second engages the establishment of a clearer understanding and appreciation for the differences that obtain between diachronic and synchronic modes so that the merit of one form is not placed in jeopardy by assessments that originate in the conventions of the other. This study attempts to solve these problems by recovering authentic and viable definitions for the various pictorial movements whose strategies are repeatedly cited by critics as plastic correlatives for similar features in Modernist literature, by being consistently aware of the fact that there is nothing in the plastic arts comparable to lexical meaning in language and by respecting the essential differences that obtain between the illusion of simultaneity a diachronic convention can sustain and the actuality of the optical synthesis a synchronic convention exhibits.

To this end, this study consists of three chapters, each dealing with one of the major art movements of the nineteenth and twentieth centuries: Impressionism, Post-Impressionism, and Cubism. These movements are chosen as the area of investigation for a variety of reasons. The first relates to their historical continuity and their shared focus on the issue of mimesis and its implications for the two dimensions of the plastic medium. This continuity highlights not only the characteristics that are maintained as one moves from Impressionism through Post-Impressionism to Cubism, but also the significant departures in envisioned reality and attendant technique that are demonstrated as the preoccupations of the parent group are modified and extended by the unique circumstances of the movement that follows. The second reason concerns the idiosyncratic nature of an Anglo-American comprehension of French art within this period. While it is hoped that the methodology applied and the care with which these correspondences are established can extend to other verbal-visual comparisons, my primary obligation will be to explore the implications of this comprehension for theorists who have perceived the relatedness of these movements to English literature. To meet this obligation, I have followed, wherever possible, the various arguments that have been developed by estheticians in both media and by reviewing journalists and art historians who responded to the emergence of the plastic movement itself. In England, for example, Roger Fry's preference for Post-Impressionist principles of composition and the metaphysic engaged therein led him to devalue the significance of Impressionism's "ocular realism" by comparison, and to associate the Impressionist artist's commitment to the appearance of the object as evidence of a certain degree of nonintellectual passivity. So too, Albert Gleizes and Jean Metzinger's enthusiasm for what both believed would be Cubism's ultimately nonobjective form generated a series of misconceptions about the nature of abstraction in Cubist compositions by theorists who amplified what they too considered was Cubism's nonreferentiability. This attitude often leads to an evasion of the array of techniques Cubist artists develop to maintain the picture's attachment to material reality.

To achieve as much clarity in presentation as possible for an audience that will come from both art historical and literary, as well as comparative, frames of reference, each chapter is divided into two parts. In the first section of each chapter, through an examination of pictorial works, statements by artists, and commentary by art historians, I have attempted to provide clear and precise definitions for the distinguishing philosophy and technical objectives of each movement. In the second section of each chapter, I examine passages from specific literary works with a view to determining the extent to which respective pictorial techniques can take verbal form.

Specifically my examples are chosen from prose fiction since narrative art presents the greatest challenge in this area. My principle of selection here generally involves a combination of literary status, an avowed interest on the part of the author in pictorial art, and a variety of critical perspectives that encourage interartistic approaches to individual writers. In chapter 1, for example, I trace the origin of misconceptions with respect to the actual nature of Impressionistic effects in the verbal medium to Stephen Crane himself, who perceived Impressionist realism in terms of subjective and meditative values that are incompatible with the naivety of Impressionism's recording eye. Having established in the first section of the chapter a more accurate sense of the techniques that pictorial Impressionism engages, I then locate what in fact might be comparable achievements in Crane's own *Red Badge of Courage* and therefore clarify the way in which the Impressionist moment functions in his prose.

This sense of the Impressionist moment has equal applicability to Virginia Woolf's *Jacob's Room,* a novel that has also been defined as Impressionist in orientation and form but that—consistent with Woolf's own discussions of the distinctions between an Impressionist and Post-Impressionist perspective in literature—reveals the extent to which Impressionist effects fail to disclose the kind of inimitable realities that Woolf chooses to pursue and which exist beyond the parameters of Impressionism's outdoor commitment. I conclude this chapter with an exploration of the kind of Impressionist technique that is at work in a post-Modernist novel like Peter Matthiessen's *Far Tortuga,* whose introductory chapter particularly achieves a verbal parallel for the serial approach of Impressionist art, the approach that deliberately maintains the attachment to the surface aspect under changing atmospheric conditions.

In the second chapter, my choices are guided primarily by the esthetics of those Modernist writers who had discovered affinities between the problems they had set out to solve in the narrative medium and those addressed by major Post-Impressionist artists themselves. In attempting to achieve enclosed space, for example, Ernest Hemingway's experience of Paul Cézanne's landscapes confirmed his own feeling for the autotelic integrity of the narrative medium. That sense of enclosure and the space experience it communicates is firmly established in the opening chapter of *A Farewell to Arms* and in the verbal techniques that Hemingway uses to abridge atmospheric and linear perspective articulation in *The Sun Also Rises* and in short stories like "The Big Two-Hearted River."

D. H. Lawrence's own enthusiastic response to the haptic and mural dimensions of the forms that both Vincent van Gogh and Cézanne create (a response clearly documented in an essay like "Introduction to His Paintings") finds its complement in *The Rainbow,* where the protagonist's grasp of the nonhuman is visualized by the realization of landscape configurations through sensibilities that play a subordinate role in the actualization of more naturalistic forms. By challenging the supremacy of the visual imagination that a naturalistic perspective engenders, and by allowing for the reintegration of the senses that had been segregated by an allegiance to optical truth alone, Lawrence realizes his sense of how a disindividualized perspective might function in narrative art. Woolf's own preference for the penetrative eye within the Post-Impressionist esthetic finds expression in *To the Lighthouse,* not only in terms of the strategies she develops to establish structures of enclosure, but also in terms of her awareness of the way in which graphic forms can operate as conceptions of reality. The tension that exists between these forms allows Woolf to approximate in verbal form the multiperspectival experience of Post-Impressionism's parallax view.

My literary selections in chapter 3 were determined to a large extent by the critical tradition that has assumed that viable correspondences exist between the Cubist esthetic and technique and James Joyce's *Ulysses* and Gertrude Stein's portraiture of people and objects. My own researches into the actual nature of Cubist art indicate the extent to which these assumptions are based, in part, upon false premises.

Those who insist upon a parallel between Joyce and Cubism, for example, tend to overlook the essential distinctions that hold between diachronic and synchronic modes of realization. In failing to observe these distinctions, critics advocate that Cubism's optical synthesis can be reconstructed in narrative terms and that the illusion of simultaneity that Joyce's multiplication of views approximates in *Ulysses* achieves actual synchronic effects. Both assumptions, however, justify modes of analysis which depend upon strategies of temporal sequence and cinematic form, diachronic values that do not respond to the way in which three-dimensional forms are displayed by the flat plane in Cubist art. Those who assert a correlation between Steinian portraiture and Cubist art often base their analogies upon a belief in their shared nonreferentiability, when in fact Stein's still lifes in a work like *Tender Buttons* demonstrate the verbal medium's capacity to sustain a dialogue between two- and three-dimensional values that parallels the tension between constructive and destructive means in Cubist art. While the Cubist analogy offers an exciting correlative for Stein's linguistic experimentation, all too often that affinity is conditioned by false premises. In establishing a more viable basis of comparison, it becomes apparent that Stein's etymological researches, manipulation of grammatical and syntactical patterns, and collaboration with alternate modes of reference all work to achieve effects that are analogous to the concept and technique of "total representation" in Cubist art.

Three additional points should be made at the outset. First, I am of course aware that the three major movements are not without overlap, yet sufficient essential differences do exist to make it possible to determine a basic distinguishing thrust for each. Second, in demonstrating the presence of a pictorial technique in a literary work, I am not attempting either to provide a full-scale reinterpretation of the work nor to argue that the work as a whole may therefore be labelled "Impressionist" or "Cubist." On the contrary, I am concerned with specific passages, and thus frequently I will use a single work to illustrate more than one pictorial technique. Third, the reader should be aware of the nonconventional or art history sense in which I use the terms *representational* and *nonrepresentational*.

In moving from Impressionism to Cubism the term *representation* is revaluated by practicing artists and estheticians. Nineteenth-century estheticians often conceived of mimesis as the accurate representation of surface realities. In "Of the Pathetic Fallacy," for example, John Ruskin suggests that the artifact created from this perspective offers an objective standard of truth by recreating "the very plain and leafy fact[s]" of the visible world.[4] This notion of mimesis can be adequately embraced by the term *enargia,* which Jean Hagstrum defines in his analysis of correlative rhetorical and pictorial strategies in the seventeenth and eighteenth centuries as the capacity of the artist to duplicate the "actual": the descriptive power that would set "before the hearer the very object of scene being described."[5]

The highly naturalistic sense of mimesis or of representation as the faithful reflection of familiar surface realities is transformed during the nineteenth and twentieth centuries by conceptions of mimesis that move beyond optically derived notions of resemblance. Such revaluations are generated by reconsiderations not only of what "reality" in fact might be, but also of where "reality" might in fact reside. Accordingly, the shift from surface to in-depth revelation, from exterior to interior processes of apprehension, can be defined as a shift in conception from *enargia* to *energia.* The term *energia* refers to the basic principle that superintends the creation of autotelic structures, which do not derive their authenticity from analogies with nature's exterior appearance, but rather are valued as self-reflexive entities that exhibit the kind of organic coherence intrinsic to the "dynamic and purposive life of nature" (Hagstrum, 12). Both verbal and plastic artists increasingly commit themselves to explorations of their media's capacity to support conceptions of *energia* as well as *enargia,* and the term *nonrepresentational* is meant to indicate this shift in perspective as alternate notions of the correspondence between art and reality are developed. The term is not meant to indicate that art loses its referentiability or abrogates its connection with lived realities and functions in an "abstract" realm. Rather, in moving beyond techniques that embody only the visual facts, artists develop strategies that extend the concept of iconicity (or referentiability) by bringing into being intellectual and emotional modes of apprehension that may elude the grasp of representational structures.

The real value of a comparative method lies precisely in its capacity to define accurately not only the extraliterary context that is to be invoked in the analogy, but also to appreciate the qualitative differences that obtain between disparate media. Thus, the critic is led to the "mutual illumination" (Weisstein, 258) of the arts, rather than to assertions of equivalence between art forms or to the advocacy of one medium's supremacy over another. It is this sense of reciprocal relation that my study attempts to foster.

1

"Ocular Realism":
The Impressionist Effects of an "Innocent Eye"

One gains some sense of the confusion that attends discussions of Impressionism in the verbal medium by examining the assumptions that establish the terms of debate in Maria Kronegger's *Literary Impressionism*. Kronegger is well aware of the tendency among literary critics to associate Impressionism with a variety of other literary movements including naturalism, imagism, symbolism, stream of consciousness, and decadent literature.[1] Sensitive to the misconceptions that are engendered by this tendency, Kronegger questions the validity of the generalization Helmutt Hatzfeld endorses in *Literature through Art:* "From a philosophical point of view any form of modern realism can be called impressionism."[2]

Kronegger notes as well the limitations of Hermann Bahr's definition of Impressionism as "subjective naturalism" where man becomes "a completely passive victim of his senses."[3] She supports Michel Décaudin's appreciation of the incompatibility of Symbolist and Impressionist esthetics. Décaudin observes, for example, that Impressionism "holds to the real, stabilizes the ephemeral" while Symbolism "is turned toward the absolute, the dream and the ideal," that transcendent reality the Impressionist shuns.[4] Yet despite Kronegger's awareness of the importance of Décaudin's careful distinction, she concurs with the prevailing Hatzfeldian trend toward generalizations: "Despite all the vagueness of what may be called an impressionist tendency in literature, it is a critical commonplace that all impressionists are to a certain extent expressionists" (28).

Not only does Kronegger accept this "critical commonplace," she herself tends to focus only on the "change from impressionism to expressionism" within a specific novel as the basis for her own analysis of literary Impressionism. Thus, though she defines literary Impressionism in terms of the Impressionist artist's fidelity to the "appearance of reality" or to what Lionello Venturi in *Painting and Painters* defines as sensation as free as possible from "reasoning and will,"[5] Kronegger increasingly conceives of that fidelity through the terms of the "plunge into the consciousness," where the individual consciousness is fused with the external world (38). The phrase "plunge into the consciousness" comes from the critic R.-M. Albérès, who suggests in his *Histoire de roman moderne* that "far from being an objective vision, impressionism is in effect a plunge into the consciousness."[6] Such an immersion Kronegger defines in phenomenological terms: "The objects which each work contains are the successive contents of the consciousness, that of the narrator. There is no separation between the narrator and the objects: there is a narrator seeing the objects and without objects there can be no self, and without a self there can be no objects." Accordingly, Kronegger feels "an object is not important *per se*" in literary Impressionism, but rather has significance "only in its relationship to the consciousness in which it has appeared" (40–41).

Interestingly, the quality of depersonalization and detachment which characterizes the Impressionist artist's objective and scientific fidelity to the optical sensation becomes, for Kronegger, an either/or situation. To her, he is either a "vitalist" whose happiness lies in "a state of fervent passivity" (60), or he is a "nihilist," a victim of his own passivity, "estranged from his social environment" and "alienated from himself" (89). As Kronegger seems to ignore that this nihilistic vision occurs "more often in literature" than it ever does in Impressionist art (60), she continues to use an Impressionist pictorial tradition as a correlative for the "passive impressionist protagonist" in literature whose redemption is possible only when he shifts from "an impressionist to an expressionist attitude toward the world": "If that same protagonist, however, not only sought the mirror of his self in things, but used these things to convey messages from his innerworld, and at the same time, felt free to deform natural appearance to express feelings in accord with his inner necessity, then he no longer perceived the world as phenomenon. As an emotional reaction to the outside world, such art becomes a symbol of the protagonist's emotions," and of his attempt to "return to an awareness of himself" and escape his "impressionistic state" of dissolution and self-destruction (28).

Kronegger's discussion of the "passive impressionist protagonist" reveals a prejudice toward Impressionist art, a prejudice that often prevails in literary criticism and one that involves, on the one hand, the devaluing of Impressionism's commitment to the mimesis of sensation and, on the other, the exalting of the subjective appropriation of that sensation in Expressionist art. Clearly in accepting Hatzfeld's sense of the legitimacy of that biased response, the critic is incapable of perceiving the nature, function, and significance of the Impressionist esthetic and technique, which cannot be defined merely as a stepping stone to an Expressionist vision.

Correctly used, the term *Impressionism* designates a movement that found its moment of fullest fruition in a group exhibition, *Exposition des Impressionistes,* held in an empty Paris apartment on rue Le Peletier in the spring of 1877. The group included five or six renegade artists who first exhibited together on April 15, 1874, under the title *Société Anonyme*. The important originators within the group were Auguste Renoir, Alfred Sisley, Edgar Degas, Claude Monet, and, for a time, Camille Pissarro and Paul Cézanne. Historically the movement covers the period from 1874 to 1882, when these painters exhibited together and shared the context of each other's stylistic developments.

Among the members of the group a common approach to external reality is evident, an approach which E. H. Gombrich describes as a "return to the unadulterated truth of natural optics."[7] This approach, however, does not constitute the persistent view of any one artist throughout his career. Rather, Impressionism, as Lionello Venturi explains in "Impressionist Style," should be understood as "that convergence of taste which had its consecration in the exhibition of '77"; "It is necessary to establish clearly that neither Monet, nor Pissarro, nor Sisley, were completely Impressionists after '80. No painter was an impressionist all his life; impressionism is a *moment* of taste of some painters" (110–11). The title of the group itself originates with Louis Leroy, a reviewing journalist in 1874, who took his impulse from a Monet entitled *Impressionism, Sunrise* and used the word "impressionism" with the intention of highlighting derisively what he considered to be the inconsequential and the incomplete in the group's treatment of external reality. By 1877, the time of the third Group Exhibition, the artists themselves had accepted the term coined somewhat facetiously on their behalf.

The 1877 exhibit is significant in that it represents the last time the original group was complete; hence Impressionism can be defined as a manifestation that represents the collective force of a specific group of artists who battled the influence of the Official Salon. The juries of the Salon, the art exhibition held annually in Paris sponsored by the Académie des Beaux-Arts, quite literally dictated what French art was supposed to be. The Impressionists challenged the limitations imposed by the Salon's definition of suitable subject matter by broadening the repertory of paintable subjects because of their commitment to the outdoor and the commonplace. Further, Impressionism shifted the emphasis from the pictorial subject to its treatment by the artist. Georges Rivière, an art critic at the time of the Impressionist exhibits, describes the shift in this way: "To treat a subject for its tones and not for the subject itself, that is what distinguishes impressionists from other painters."[8] The serial approach allows Monet, for example, to focus on what he defines as a "true impression of a certain aspect of nature and not a composite picture." Accordingly, canvases within his Rouen Cathedral series, like the *Rouen Cathedral: Full Sunlight*, reveal the kind of tension between two- and three-dimensional values that develops within Impressionism generally, that rich and voluble interplay of the space illusion and the surface effect that characterizes the dynamism of its realism.

Impressionism's fascination with surface appearance divests painting of the literary associations that had typically defined the polemical manner, polished character, and scenographic stability of Salon art.

In general terms the Impressionist return to the "truth of natural optics" meant that "the form[s] of reality," forms that were determined to a large extent by habits and conventions of seeing, were replaced by "the form[s] of appearance"[9] as observed by the artist at the moment of perception. Wylie Sypher uses the term "ocular realism" to define Impressionism's "astonishingly accurate study of a human field of vision."[10] In *Landscape into Art,* Kenneth Clark suggests that Impressionism's advocacy of "normal, factual vision" derives from the artist's "unquestioning belief in the natural vision as the basis of art."[11] Clark takes Camille Corot's note in an 1856 sketchbook as his point of departure for a definition of the Impressionist esthetic. In the note Corot advises the student to trust his first sensation above all else: "Let us not abandon this, and in searching for the truth and the exactitude never forget to give him this entirety which has had an impact on us. No matter what the situation, what the object; submit yourself to your first impression. If we have been truly touched, the sincerity of our emotions shall be passed on to others" (160–61 [translation mine]). Corot's admonition, when coupled by Clark with an 1861 statement by Gustave Courbet, provides the most viable context within which one can appreciate the idealism of Impressionism's scientific naturalism:

> The beauty lies in nature and is seen in reality through the most diverse of forms. Once we have found it, it belongs to art, or rather to the artist who understands it. Once the beauty is real and visible, it has in itself an artistic impression. But the artist does not have the right to amplify this expression. He cannot manipulate this expression in risk of taking away qualities of its beauty and in the end weakening the expression. The beauty given by nature itself is superior to all artists' impressions. (161–64) (translation mine)

Courbet's sense that nature's beauty "is superior to all artists' impressions" is borne out in the Impressionist esthetic which moves one from a conceptual or schematic approach to reality toward a preconceptual or perceptual approach that stresses the impartiality or innocence of the observing eye. The concept of an impartial eye was itself introduced by Ruskin in his 1857 *The Elements of Drawing,* where he pursues a distinction between seeing and knowing in John Turner's landscapes: "The whole technical power of painting depends on our recovery of what may be called the *innocence of the eye;* that is to say, a sort of childish perception of these flat stains of color, merely as such, without consciousness of what they signify,—as a blind man would see them if suddenly gifted with sight."[12] Though as Gombrich illustrates, there is really no such thing as an absolutely innocent eye—for that kind of passivity demands that one renounce the "'conceptual habits'" that are "necessary to life" (298) as well as the entire repertory of techniques art has developed to create or induce a convincing semblance of reality (11)—the kind of objectivity Impressionist artists struggle to achieve, in their realization of the thing as it *is,* favors the suppression of what is *known* in order to render what is *seen.*

That which appears quixotic and idiosyncratic in Impressionist art is simply not amenable to the subjectivist terms a phenomenological reading of the canvas would impose, for Impressionism's "discovery of appearances," as Gombrich suggests, means the "discovery of the ambiguities of vision" (314). The Impressionist artist's fidelity to "the unadulterated truths of the natural optic" encourages him to eschew the conceptual habits one traditionally relies upon to organize and classify the given. Impressionism therefore takes a Ruskinian notion of the innocence of the eye to its logical conclusion, inviting the artist to paint as if he "had been born blind and were suddenly endowed with sight": "For instance: when grass is lighted strongly by the sun in certain directions, it is turned from green into a peculiar and somewhat dusty looking yellow. . . . We always supposed that we *see* what we only know, and have hardly any consciousness of the real aspect of the signs we have learned to interpret. Very few people have any idea that sunlighted grass is yellow" ("E of D," 27–28). Impressionism becomes the exploration of the way the object appears in nature, not as we know it to be in any absolute sense, but as it is apprehended as phenomenon.

This naturalistic spirit is borne out in the techniques developed by Impressionist artists to record the visual impression, as sensations of light and color, in a variety of *plein air* or outdoor motifs. Impressionism begins with the work of Monet and Renoir at Bougival in 1869 where both realize their responsiveness to the play of reflections upon moving water, using a rainbow palette to explore the interdependence of light and color. Monet's *The Grenouillère* of 1869 (fig. 1) reflects throughout the kind of vitality and luminosity the Impressionist faith in the truth of the optical sensation can inspire. It is also indicative of the features which will distinguish Impressionist art as a whole, features that expand to include a preference for both the distant and close-up views, where contours dissolve and objects become blurred as artists render the vibrations of the air itself through delicate and hazy atmospheric effects. The commitment to the preconceptual conditions of the naive eye in Impressionist art asks that local colors and recognizable forms give way to the truths of the perceptual moment *sur le motif.*

In a parallel way the usual logic of subordination no longer obtains. Monet's figures, whether on the dock or in the water, share the quality of fragmentation and insubstantiality that is diffused throughout the entire canvas. In affirming the natural vision, Impressionism celebrates the very ambiguities its fidelity to the optic makes manifest. Space becomes a function of the interdependence of color and light. Traditional scenographic perspectives, which allowed artists to place objects in clearly defined and stable relations in a three-dimensional spa-

Figure 1.   Claude Monet, *The Grenouillère*, 1869
Oil on canvas, 29⅜″ × 39¼″.
*(The Metropolitan Museum of Art, the H. O. Havemeyer Collection; bequest of
Mrs. H. O. Havemeyer, 1929)*

tial illusion, are challenged by the Impressionist's fascination with the way in which atmospheric conditions alter and often deny illusions of density and gravity, and with the way in which the selective focus of a particular angle of vision displaces details. Finally, Impressionism's fidelity to the perceptual experience finds fruition in a serial approach to the same motif from a variety of angles of vision under changing atmospheric conditions where the unfinished and indeterminate insinuate moods of reverie and mystery, which have nothing to do with the metaphysics of mind but a great deal to do with the accuracy with which the recording eye realizes its first sensation. If, as Bernard Dunstan observes, the "direct visual stimulus" is of absolute importance to the Impressionist artist, he is enjoined to confront a subject which "must be seen—not imagined, remembered or invented—and seen as a whole, with no leaving out or re-composing in the studio."[13]

In discovering plastic equivalents for the process of perception itself, the object becomes an aspect rather than an isolate entity, an agent for the absorption and reflection of light rather than an indivisible whole. The artist becomes aware, Dunstan observes, that the sun of necessity empties yellow into the sky, that a green wood's illuminated and shadowed surfaces declare the colors of the spectrum, that outlines quiver and dissolve, and that shadows explore the complementary colors of the local color of the light which cast them. These principles of composition are strikingly present in Monet's *The Grenouillère* where a delicate and unitary brushwork suffuses objects with a quality of light that allows for the kind of "prismatic decomposition" Jules Laforgue enthused over in his descriptions of Impressionist art in 1883.[14] In surrendering himself to the object as it appears, the artist, Monet suggests, endeavors to realize the vision as given in the moment of perception, to convey "'instantaneity,' above all, the envelopment of the same light spread over everywhere" (qtd. in Nochlin, 34).

While the serial approach dramatizes the fact that the real subject of an Impressionist painting becomes light itself, it is important to note that the Impressionists are preoccupied with the physical properties of light and with its style-forming implications. Light does not function as a metaphysical or symbolic entity in their canvases, but is rather divested of any Platonic significance. So, too, the concept of change integral to the research into the artist's immersion in fugitive moment[15] does not engage any clearly defined philosophical position. The Impressionist artist does not pursue the implications of his concern with naturalistic effects under changing conditions beyond the accidents of colored illumination and the decomposition of color by light. The techniques developed to handle these effects provide stylistic coherence for the movement as a whole, while the belief in the natural vision encourages the artist to affirm his trust in both his oeuvre and "the beauty given by nature." There is little to suggest that the Impressionist canvas declares the transience of human life or the ephemerality of the visible world as its theme, for even though the Impressionist works with the random or the accidental scene, the moment chosen is devoid of any dramatic or didactic intention. As such their work lends itself to being described as unfinished and incomplete. This affair of the moment deals exclusively with the impermanent and shifting aspects of a particular time and place rather than with the immutable or immobile aspects of nature. It avoids themes which would emphasize man's yearning for permanence and order. In fact the Impressionist celebrates that evanescence in nature and glories in the potential harmonies of color and light that the various moods of nature engender. The very titles of the individual paintings that constitute the temporal sequence of Monet's Rouen Cathedral series emphasize the artist's preoccupation with the way in which the atmosphere creates the object itself: *Harmony in Blue; Harmony in White, Morning Effect; Harmony in Blue, Morning Sunshine; Harmony in Blue and Gold, in Full Sunlight; Harmony in Gray, Gray Weather; Harmony in Brown, Evening.*

The favored motifs in Impressionist art record processes of transmutation and metamorphosis that are engaged *en passage,* whether through the fluctuating twilight conditions of the boulevard, the varying density of the atmospheres that envelop riverbanks, marines, and harbor fronts, or the surface effects of melting snow and breaking ice. These motifs of transition manifest an ambient of ease and tranquility that is characteristic of the Impressionist moment. Dunstan notes that the Impressionists "did not attempt to capture rapidly changing effects of light nearly as much as earlier painters such as Turner and Constable, or for that matter their immediate forerunners Millet and Rousseau." There are, he notes, "no rainbows and no storms in Impressionism." The Impressionists focus primarily upon "overcast but bright spring days, or calm summer sunshine, or snow under gray skies." Contrary to what many art historians suggest, the Impressionist method "is not really suited to momentary effects in the way that Constable's sketching procedure certainly was; the scale is a little large for that, and the Impressionist insistence on doing the whole thing in front of the subject as far as possible demanded a relatively unchanging light." The Impressionist method, Dunstan concludes, offers "an altogether more objective analysis of visual facts" as they appear under relatively unchanging conditions (43). I emphasize Dunstan's point because it restores the Impressionist sense of the moment to its original meaning. The Impressionists were not trying to record the fantastic light effects of storm or shadow, nor were they interested in dealing with the human drama that a landscape so revealed might inspire. The Impressionist moment does not function in any epiphanic or symbolic sense.

In recording the conditions of a particular time and place, Impressionist artists exhibit those qualities of depersonalization and detachment that are consistent with the imperatives of an innocent eye. Technically this concept is manifest in the Impressionist artists' preference for distant or close-up views that would facilitate this process of defamiliarization. In Pissarro's *Place du*

Théâtre Français (fig. 2), the artist uses a second- or third-story aerial view to help realize the depersonalized perspective the full title of the painting endorses. In Alfred Sisley's *Floods at Port-Marly,* it is the interchange of tonal values between the sky and water rather than the human predicament that absorbs the artist, just as in his *Effect of Snow, The Hunter,* it is the infinite variety of gray-green tonal modulations rather than the anecdotal or associative potential of the motif itself that concerns him.

The concept of the innocent eye also finds its stylistic correlative in terms of the indeterminate and the incomplete where contours dissolve, the usual boundaries between volumes no longer obtain, and local colors give way to particular atmospheric effect. It is within this context that one speaks of the unexpected in Impressionism's treatment of the familiar and the commonplace. Color changes are recorded without preconception. The technical implications of this kind of patient and exact observation *sur le motif* include the building of compositional entities through the juxtaposition of small opaque touches of paint which accumulate and overlap to challenge stable outlines. Impressionism's "improvised technique,"[16] however, is an empirical rather than a theoretical one at this point. The rules that would continue and extend its passion for exactitude were established later by artists like Georges Seurat and Paul Signac, Neo-Impressionist Pointillists and Divisionists who provided a scientific basis for Impressionism's improvisations. Their application of Chevreul's laws of color composition, as well as the division of color—the unmixed color placed in patches on the canvas with the intention of allowing them to "merge"—belong to these Neo-Impressionists of a later date than the 1870s.

In his own admonition to aspiring artists, Monet emphasizes the significance of the unexpected in composition that results when the artist remains faithful to the first impression and tries "to forget what objects you have before you—a tree, a house, a field of water. Merely think, here is a little square of blue, here an oblong of pink, here a streak of yellow, and paint it just as it looks to you, the exact color and shape, until it gives you your own naive impression of the scene before you."[17] In attempting to articulate objects through color abstracted and given geometric definition, Monet anticipates the experiments of Seurat and Cézanne, who sought an architectonic formality; but more importantly, Monet's notion of the naive or innocent eye implies that the artist exorcises personal preconceptions about how objects look. He advises that the artist inhibit the flow of literary, experiential, or emotional associations that usually accompany perception of objects. In a very similar way Pissarro instructs a young painter, Le Bail, in a letter written about 1881, asking his student to "paint what you observe and feel. Paint generously and unhesitatingly, for it is best not to lose the first impression." Pissarro advocates that the artist ignore those conceptual habits which usually mediate experience:

Figure 2.   Camille Pissarro, *Place du Théâtre Français*, 1898
Oil on canvas, 29" × 36".
(The Minneapolis Institute of Arts, William Hood Dunwoody Fund)

Work on everything simultaneously. Don't work bit by bit, but paint everything at once by placing tones everywhere. . . . Use small strokes and try to put your perceptions immediately. The eye should not be fixed on one point, but should take in everything, while observing the reflections which the colors produce on their surroundings. Work at the same time on sky, water, branches, ground, keeping everything going on an equal basis and unceasingly rework until you have got it.

The innocent eye which Pissarro's preferred method actively solicits conveys a clear sense of the kind of direct translation Impressionism makes its medium capable of: "The motif should be observed more for shape and color than for drawing. . . . Precise drawing is dry and hampers the impression of the whole, it destroys all sensations" (qtd. in Dunstan, 44). A remark recorded by critic G.-Albert Aurier on the Impressionist method confirms my sense of the process of disassociation Pissarro's impartial and plastic vision engenders. Impressionism "is another imitation of matter, no longer perhaps in its accustomed form but as form seen, as color seen, a translation of sensation with all its impromptu of immediate notation, with all the distortions of a quick subjective synthesis" (qtd. in Sypher, 172).

In an effort to present a truer picture of the way objects appear under natural conditions, the artist resists the impulse to make the adjustments we are trained to make because of inherited and consensus schematizations of external reality. The initial public and critical response to the Group Exhibition of 1877 was one of censure, because the handling of pictorial subjects did not coincide with preconceived notions based on conventional iconographic representations of reality. Hence, many saw the distortions of Impressionist canvas as the expression of a purely subjective perception, whereas the kind of alteration that took place was in fact the result of attending to the visual sensation directly by resisting the mediation of either inherited schemata or personal feelings for the object.

In Impressionist art the viewer is disoriented, and that effect is intended by the artist insofar as he himself remains detached in his role as observer. At the same time, the concept of the innocent eye does not preclude the existence of a personalized vision, nor does it negate acts of intellection. The personality of the artist is at work even when he thinks he is working with total objectivity in representing what Ruskin defined as the "plain and leafy fact." Thus any notion of verisimilitude must be responsive to the intuitive as well as to the empirical judgments the artist makes in contact with the motif. His very selection of focus moves him beyond the indiscriminate detail and arbitrary pattern of the camera eye. Jean-Luc Daval in *Journal de l'impressionnisme* explores the way in which the Impressionist artist handles *les grandes boulevards* of Paris—using slightly elevated physical angles of vision, as in Pissarro's *Place du Théâtre Française,* or alternatively placing the spectator "directly involved with life" to convey the sensations of movement and of light, as evident in the dynamics of Renoir's *Place Clichy.* Daval's analysis of Pissarro's choice of perspective and emphasis provides a sense of the way in which the artist can discover particular patterns within a scene and render them emphatic without losing contact with the facts of vision. Even though Pissarro's ill health prohibited composing out-of-doors and he had to "duplicate the scenery from his windows," he still retained his sensitivity to the urban place and the "dynamics of vision."[18]

The Impressionist artist remains true to the naturalistic effect, analyzing the stimuli his eye receives from the scene without imposing those preconceptions that would temper or modify the way the object appears. At the same time, this kind of "ocular realism" allows for qualities of personality and feeling, for the very selection of the focus and the devotion to the scene as perceived fosters the sense of intimacy indigenous to the revelation of the felt quality of sensation. This combination of objectivity and personal vision is particularly compelling in Monet's *Haystack at Sunset near Giverny,* one of a series of works Monet composed in an effort "to get a true impression of a certain aspect of nature" as revealed under particular conditions. A kind of lyricism attends the quality of light that saturates this canvas and generates the variety of hues determined by the quiescent local color of the haystack itself. At the same time, this lyricism quite naturally originates in Monet's ability to discover pictorial equivalents for the optical sensations created by the appearance of things at sunset. The contour of the haystack's peak dissolves in an aura of heat whose vibrations are embodied in the prismatic decomposition that radiates from its partially melted edge.

The idiosyncratic in Impressionist works refers to both the notion of relativity or ambiguity in vision and the question of an individual style, which provide, of course, the context within which the creative processes, regardless of movement affiliation, takes place. The Impressionist balance between fidelity to nature as master and the subjectivity of the visual response, between a scientific approach to the model before the artist and personality or felt sensation, is addressed by Pissarro in the letter to Le Bail when he advises his student to "paint what you observe and feel," or to "look for the kind of nature that suits your temperament." Pissarro's statements embrace concepts of feeling and detachment, of interpretation and accuracy, that are integral to Impressionism's mimesis of things as they appear to be: "Don't be timid in front of nature; one must be bold, at the risk of being deceived and making mistakes. One must always have one master—nature, she is the one always to be consulted" (qtd. in Dunstan, 44).

While the notion of the innocent eye in Impressionist art encourages the artist to ignore conventions of seeing that authorize familiar standards of authenticity and verisimilitude, the concept also relies on the observer's conceptual habits to restore some measure of familiarity. In other words, the qualities of incompleteness and indefiniteness that characterize the Impressionist artist's commitment to his "first impression" also foster what Gombrich defines (in his discussion of Impressionism's relation to the illusionist tradition) as the "mechanism of projection" that allows the viewer to complete the image as given in the canvas. I use the term *illusionist* here to suggest the traditional repertory of techniques that plastic artists have developed to create and sustain a convincing illusion of a three-dimensional reality within the two dimensions of the picture plane—techniques that transform the easel into the open window. These include, for example, the use of linear and atmospheric perspective to convey sensations of recession and depth, which encourage the picture to function as an extension of actual space.

The *incomplete* can be defined as the power of indeterminate forms to create the illusion of reality by stimulating the imagination of the beholder to complete the image and to resolve ambiguities. Gombrich advises that there are two conditions which must obtain if the mechanism of projection is to function: "One is that the beholder must be left in no doubt about the way to close the gap; secondly, that he must be given a 'screen,' an empty or ill-defined area onto which he can project the expected image" (208). The indefinite evokes our instinct for mimesis, our need to "reconstitute the three-dimensional form in our minds" (16). The very contemporaneity of the Impressionist subject encourages the viewer to rely on his own knowledge and experience of similar motifs, to energize the visual and tactile sensations that facilitate the trompe l'oeil illusion of bodies in space. The "greatest protagonist of the naturalistic illusion in painting," Leonardo da Vinci, Gombrich observes, is also the inventor of the deliberately blurred image, or veiled form, that cuts down the information on the canvas to "stimulate" the mechanism of projection and encourages the observer to reveal what the artist partially obscures. Walter Pater's response to the provocative background effects of da Vinci's *Gioconda* illustrates how that mechanism might work. It is the enigmatic in the painting, that which changes and departs from Pater's view of nature "as it is" to become evocative of what Pater will define as the painter's soul, that disturbs the critic. Pater refers, for example, to "the strange veil of sight" in da Vinci, and notes that things are illuminated not in ordinary daylight, but rather in a strange half-light, a "faint light" of "eclipse," which Pater feels goes "too far below the outside of things in which art really begins and ends." Pater's final judgment is that da Vinci simply "attaches too much of his own meaning to things that will not bear it." Clearly Pater's agitated response is set within the continuing critical debate between eighteenth-century notions of verisimilitude and emerging expressive theories of art which challenge the possibility of an exact transcription or accurate reproduction of natural phenomena. What is significant in Pater's discussion here is the way in which, as Gombrich suggests, partial illumination and indeterminate forms engage the beholder's participation. It is perhaps the meanings that Pater himself attaches to the background effects that he cannot bear.[19]

While the "mechanism of projection" may run the risk of allowing acts of appropriation to take place, such that the incomplete is transformed into a vehicle for the observer's private preoccupation (hence the contemporary critical indignation which led Joris-Karl Huysmans to attempt to establish a causal link between the Impressionist artists' violet tinting and mental disorders),[20] that risk is checked by our understanding of and respect for the preconceptual nature of Impressionism's absorption with the interdependence of color and light. The incomplete in Impressionist art simultaneously fosters the three-dimensional illusion of objects in space even while it emphasizes the surface aspect of volumes whose presences are evoked rather than articulate. Monet's blurring of forms in *The Garden, Giverny* (fig. 3) asks that the viewer enter into a reciprocal relationship with the canvas. Objects are intelligible even though their forms are tentative. Monet's adherence to the atmospheric conditions within which they appear or disappear creates an illusion whose integrity the observer affirms, for she discovers that nature is in fact capable of being perceived in this way. In this painting, the artist explores the sensation of light as it is diffused by the arches of the overhanging trees, absorbed and redirected by the underlying foliage, and described in the chromatic shadows that document the alternating horizontal bars emphasizing the painted surface even as they lead the eye into space toward the cottage, which appears through random apertures within the trellis itself.

I began this chapter by noting the misconceptions generated by Kronegger's tendency to define Impressionism's fidelity to the natural vision as a state of passivity that must be renounced or overcome if the protagonist is to achieve a vital sense of identity. In a parallel way, Jean Guiguet in *Virginia Woolf and Her Works,* while acknowledging the dangers attending any critic's effort to unite Impressionism, Post-Impressionism, and Expressionism under a single general heading, nonetheless suggests that there "does not seem, in retrospect" to be "a basic opposition" between Impressionist and Post-Impressionist styles. Rather "we see therein nowadays only modalities of style, all directed towards a single goal: the integral expression of the artist's vision, of his impression—a formula which includes both impressionism and expressionism."[21]

The misunderstanding that encourages literary critics to reduce Impressionism to a notion of impression conceived of in Expressionistic terms is perhaps fostered by art historians like Sheldon Cheney, whose terms implicate a subjectivist quality that is incompatible with the scientific basis of Impressionist naturalism: "If they caught the atmospheric condition of the moment, in color, the goal was won. A fleeting impression—that had something to do with the sticking of the name 'Impressionists,' if not with its origin."[22] This notion of a

Figure 3.   Claude Monet, *The Garden, Giverny,* 1902
Oil on canvas, 89 × 92 cm.
(Osterreichische Galerie, Vienna)

fugitive moment subjectively apprehended is central to Jack Stewart's discussion of the analogy between Woolf and Impressionism, which is grounded upon Stewart's Expressionistic notion of a "plunge into the consciousness" in his analysis of what he terms Woolf's Impressionist techniques: "As the painters record evanescence in nature . . . Woolf records the shifting tides of consciousness and reverie."[23] Accordingly, Stewart deals with landscape correlatives for the perceptual moment in *Jacob's Room* in symbolic terms and finds them symptomatic of a general syndrome variously defined as the restlessness and instability of the age, the "atomization" of nineteenth-century culture, the loss of the self, and the isolation of the individual. Though Stewart refers repeatedly to the mystical and cosmic properties of Woolf's lighting techniques, he still uses the term "Impressionistic" to define their character: "As a 'spiritual' writer concerned with 'innermost flame' of consciousness . . . Woolf, like Impressionist painters, stresses the *activity* of light," its "symbolic overtones" (263–64). Stewart does not recognize the kinds of problems he creates when he suggests that "Woolf's Impressionism verges at times on lyrical Expressionism," or that her "Impressionist perspectives" contribute to themes of alienation, that they operate as focuses through which protagonists project their "own disordered feelings" or detached angles of vision, realizing "large-scale city impressions" that symbolize "the 'City of Dreadful Night'" (255–58). Following Kronegger's lead, Stewart tends to define the Impressionist fascination with the ephemeral in terms of an Expressionist dream of lost wholeness, maintaining that the form of *Jacob's Room* is Impressionistic because the novel emphasizes the "elusiveness, rather than fulfillment of being" (250–52).

Ironically, the validity of Stewart's interpretation of Woolf's techniques, a validity which is borne out by the way in which Woolf does in fact often saturate the "colorful surface" with "inner significance," demonstrates that Woolf is not dealing with an Impressionist technique and esthetic at all in many of the passages he analyzes. Though critics repeatedly define the way light functions in Woolf's novels in Impressionistic terms, it becomes progressively apparent, from a pictorial point of view, that Woolf is not so much interested in the physics of light, and the sensation of lighted surfaces received by the retina, as she is concerned with the metaphysics of light, or with the way light functions as symbolic chiaroscuro to define nonhuman analogues for man's condition in the cosmos.

What has happened in literary criticism especially is that Impressionism has been defined in terms of etymology, whereby it is infused with an expressive and metaphysical significance incompatible with the imperatives of "ocular realism" itself. Studies that seek to establish Impressionist frames of reference for Willa Cather and Joseph Conrad, for example, invariably assert that it is the interpretative dimension of perception that provides the common ground for literary and pictorial Impressionism. In "Conrad's Impressionism and Watt's

'Delayed Decoding,'" Bruce Johnston argues that the "optical integrity" of Monet's innocent eye expresses an "equivalent integrity," defined as the concern with the moral "problems of perception and signification that are central to historic impressionism." Accordingly, for Johnston, the "unrehearsed perception" becomes an antidote that finds its genesis in the primitive consciousness working to offset the decadence of the civilized eye in *The Heart of Darkness.*[24] In "Willa Cather and the Impressionist Novel," David Stouck argues that the term "impressionism" expresses Cather's desire "to convey a sensuous appreciation of life, to seek 'truth' not through intellectual discovery but responsive emotions, through temperament." This Zolaesque position is borne on the wings of the basic assumption that Cather's art, like pictorial Impressionism, declares a general "contempt for verisimilitude."[25]

At the same time, the misuse of the term can be traced to conditions associated with the birth of Impressionism itself. John Rewald, in *The History of Impressionism,* reprints the article written by Louis Leroy and published under the title "Exhibition of the Impressionists" in *Charivari* April 25, 1874, following the opening of the first Group Exhibition. Leroy not only coins the term "Impressionism" within that article, he also sets the negative tone which characterizes many subsequent discussions of Impressionist art. Group members, for example, are subject to criticisms of their technical and compositional skills and accusations of superficiality, insincerity, and immorality. In applying the prevailing canons of classical realism venerated by the official Salon, in looking for gallery tone, polish, rhetoric, and romantic ornament, Leroy and his public seemed incapable of understanding the significance of the plastic problems Impressionist artists had set out to confront. Leroy's response to Monet's *Impressionism, Sunrise* ran as follows: "*Impression*—I was certain of it. I was just telling myself that, since I was impressed, there had to be some impression in it . . . and what freedom, what ease of workmanship! Wallpaper in its embryonic state is more finished than that seascape" (qtd. in Rewald, 323). Leroy equates the creative process with the rendering of a personal impression of sunrise and, in doing so, unwittingly fathers the confused mixture of the subjective and the objective that allows the literary critics to adopt pictorial Impressionism as the sister of the phenomenological novel, the novel concerned with the illusion of things as they appear to be interpreted by the individual sensibility.

The misuse of the term Impressionism in literary criticism is further explained by the critical reception of Post-Impressionist painting in England by estheticians like Roger Fry and Clive Bell. Fry not only organized the first Post-Impressionist exhibit in London in 1910, invented the name for the movement, and prepared the preface for the 1912 catalogue to the second exhibit, he also set the tone for the depreciation of Impressionist realism that was part of the general Post-Impressionist reaction against Impressionist art. One cannot underestimate Fry's sphere of influence both in Britain and in North America, where he was the director of New York's Metropolitan Museum of Art from 1905 to 1910. His fascination with and preference for Post-Impressionist values led him to misrepresent Impressionist art by comparison. He championed the Post-Impressionists because, to him, they represented a return to first principles—a return to formal structure in art. The Impressionist's "extreme preoccupation with atmospheric effects," he argued in *Transformations*, "tended to destroy any clear and logical articulation of volumes within the picture space."[26] In *Vision and Design*, he presents the Impressionist artist as "a mere recording instrument of certain sensations."[27]

Bell, a practicing esthetician and artist who shared Fry's biased response, also welcomed Post-Impressionism as an affirmation of the irrelevancy of representational values in art. Both perceived Cézanne's formal achievement as radically opposed to the aims of Impressionism. While Cézanne himself intended to express his admiration for Monet's poetic response to the moods of nature with the remark that Monet is "only an eye, but . . . what an eye!" the observation was interpreted by estheticians as confirmation of a Post-Impressionist indictment of Impressionist shallowness. Thus Monet, as Dunstan explains, was often described as "a sort of machine for painting, a brilliant transcriber of the appearance of whatever happened to be before his eye" (46).

The literary criticism shaped by the legacy of Leroy's poorly conceived response, and Fry's and Bell's interpretation of the "antidote" to Impressionism offered by a Post-Impressionist esthetic, continued to misrepresent Impressionist aims and techniques accordingly. Critics who focused on the etymological derivation of the term "impression" hoped to elevate the meaning of the Impressionist optic—to "legitimize" Impressionism by emphasizing the optic's role as a precursor of the expressive tendencies actualized in Post-Impressionist art. Arguments directed by this critical impulse suggest that transcriptions of naturalistic effects somehow betray Impressionism's ultimate concern with subjective and meditative values. Literary critics who were directed by the Fry-Bell hypothesis (which recurs throughout early twentieth-century esthetic theory) tend to view literary impressionism as an approach that involves some sense of intellectual wanness, and of a desultory fragmentation of the forms of identity and coherence.

Together, these perceptions are clearly linked to faulty notions about the role of illusion, the incomplete, and the unexpected within Impressionism; they are linked further by the failure to appreciate the difference between Expressionist subjectivism and Impressionist visual subjectivity where feeling is placed in a subordinate role with "Nature" as "master." As the role of the artist's personality as observer has been misunderstood in Impressionist art, so too the conception of impression as subjective-response prepares the way for the inappropriate analogy between stream-of-consciousness techniques in Modernist fiction and pictorial Impressionism.

It is in this sense that Virginia Woolf's vision of the subject matter of the novelist in modern fiction is mistakenly regarded as the corollary literary manifesto of pictorial Impressionism: "The mind receives a myriad impressions—trivial, fantastic, evanescent, or engraved with the sharpness of steel. From all sides they come, an incessant shower of innumerable atoms; and as they fall, as they shape themselves into the life of Monday or Tuesday, the accent falls differently from of old. . . . Life is a luminous halo, a semi-transparent envelope surrounding us from the beginning of consciousness to the end."[28] The discontinuous, the indefinite, the realization of plot through the architectonics of discrete concretizations of the moment advanced through leitmotif, these are traits that become characteristic of Virginia Woolf's novels in her search for the convention that would embody the truth about human beings, a method "deeper and more suggestive, for conveying not only what people say, but what they leave unsaid; not only what they are, but what life is."[29] The task of the novelist, as she sees it, is therefore to "record the atoms as they fall upon the mind in the order in which they fall, let us trace the pattern, however disconnected and incoherent in appearance, which each sight or incident scores upon the consciousness" ("Modern Fiction," 107). The above clearly represents what many define as the stuff of the Impressionist method; yet the kind of penetration that Woolf sought in conveying the life of the mind has little to do with the objectives of Monet and Pissarro.

Woolf relies on Impressionist, Post-Impressionist, and Expressionist techniques of visualization in her novels, but her focus centers on those "dark places of psychology" that lie beyond the very surface view of things with which Impressionism is concerned. More often than not, she relies on surface only insofar as it reveals depth, the interior "life of spirit, truth or reality this, the essential thing" ("Modern Fiction," 105). Woolf's terms indicate the extent to which the concern has shifted from Impressionism—the representation of an optic by attending to the visual impression of surface reality—to the notion of impressionism in its original etymological sense as that which bears the impress of personality, the stamp of sensibility, the representation of emotions felt for reality through natural forms.

When I refer to Monet's innocent or naive eye, I emphasize his concerted effort to submit to the impression and restrain the tendency to plagiarize the object by humanizing the visual phenomenon such that the external expresses an interior state. It is in this context of restraint that we are dealing with the subjectivity of the visual impression as objective vision. Further, the kind of anonymity or detachment the observing eye struggles to maintain in Impressionist painting cannot be defined through nascent existential statements about uncertainty, self-alienation, and nothingness which critics advance when they interpret Impressionist technique as a statement about the condition of the protagonist who is the "passive victim of his senses."[30] As Impressionism is a vision of reality conceived in terms of sensations of light and color, one must resist the temptation to infuse this method with attenuated metaphysical implications.

In his opening address for the 1968 "Symposium on Literary Impressionism," Michel Benamou observed: "Along with phlegmatic Naturalism, choleric Wagnerism and splenetic Decadentism, Impressionism is one of the four cardinal humors governing fin-de-siècle literature. It is Sanguine and thrives on good air, sunshine and things as they are."[31] Stewart's article on Woolf's Impressionist technique demonstrates the kinds of problems that evolve if one defines Impressionism as a period concept, "a direct signifier of life-values" (251) that are generated by a Modernist anxiety over the Heraclitean flux. Happily, however, Herbert Howarth, in a paper delivered at this 1968 Symposium, carefully distinguishes between Naturalism and Impressionism in literature, noting that while the Impressionist simultaneously "examined the 'object'" and "seemed to be doing the same thing," "the outcome of the Impressionist analysis was pure pleasure," while the outcome of the realist tradition which generated Naturalism in literature involved a "protest against the world," against the very vitality of things as they are which the Impressionist pays tribute to. For Howarth, Woolf's protest "is a legacy not of Impressionism but of a counter-force, Naturalism" and the tension in her work reflects the confrontation between "two attitudes to existence: pleasure and horror" that is "central to British literature of the period 1890–1930."[32]

The validity of Howarth's discussion of this particular tension is borne out in a variety of Modernist works where the Impressionist moment is itself subservient to a larger method in which, as in Woolf's *Jacob's Room,* the very naivety of the Impressionist vision and its fidelity to a surface view of life is examined and found wanting. In his discussion of the techniques of verbal Impressionism Calvin Brown suggests that as Impressionism "is essentially an art of fragments, sketches and small forms generally . . . the novel, as a whole, can never be an impressionistic work either in its essential techniques or in its primary impact on the reader."[33] There are certain generic restrictions, intrinsic to the Impressionist vision, that are not compatible with the novel form itself: "The determined Impressionist who undertakes a large work must go outside his aesthetic theories in order to give it some coherence, and hence it follows not only that the work will not be a purely impressionistic production, but that the artist's expressed intentions will probably not be carried out" (58).

There is a second qualitative difference between the two media that must be acknowledged, for, very simply, words are not paint. There is nothing in the resources of plastic elements equivalent to lexical meaning in language. Accordingly, the conceptual basis of language itself would seem to be incompatible with the preconceptual and perceptual basis of Impressionist art. Impressionism means the immediate apprehension of sensation. Every effort is made to retain the spontaneity and purity of that first sensation, and though the incomplete allows the "mechanism of projection" to function, the primary emphasis rests with the duplication without mediation of the form as it appears to the eye in the moment of perception. It would seem, therefore, that it is more difficult to achieve that kind of spontaneity and naivety in the verbal medium, for language alters sensation by infusing it with meaning in the process of translation.

This is a problem Paul Ilie considers in his discussion of literary Impressionism. He notes that while there is no such thing as an inherently Impressionistic language,[34] the verbal artist can nonetheless rely upon a set of features that will evoke an Impressionistic surface. In an effort to create the illusion of a preconceptual and yet subjective synthesis of a visual impression, verbal artists rely on techniques such as ellipsis and verb omissions to evoke a sense of immediacy. There is as well a tendency to eliminate connectives, to break up syntactical rhythms, and move disconnectedly through descriptive passages to convey a sense of the fragmentary nature of the momentary perception. At the same time, verbal artists can sustain a sense of naivety by keeping their forms indeterminate, by resisting the impulse to define spatial relations, and by discarding the larger perspective in which the smaller units function. Rather than the usual logic of subordination, there is a tendency to fuse unlike perceptions through synesthesia and to invent neologisms or new compounds through which delicate nuances in color and vibrations of tone can be registered. Impressionist prose also exhibits a general preference for impersonal verbs and passive constructions to emphasize the receptive condition of the observing eye. These idiomatic elements allow the verbal artist to discover equivalents that encourage the verbal medium to duplicate in kind Impressionism's loyalty to the first impression.

These strategies are implemented when Woolf deliberately sets out to create Impressionist "effects" in "Kew Gardens," for example, where the initial scene is actualized by a depersonalized observer enamored by the accidents of time and atmosphere. Throughout the short story, landscape and human forms share the common tonality and unpredictable duration this fascination with surface illumination entails. The petals of the flowers within an oval-shaped flowerbed are "marked with spots of colour raised upon the surface." When "stirred by the summer breeze," "red, blue and yellow lights passed one over the other, staining an inch of the brown earth beneath with a spot of the moist intricate colour."[35] The physical conditions of a particular angle of vision are faithfully recreated. The light, which randomly activates the surface aspect, falls into a raindrop and expands it "with such intensity of red, blue and yellow . . .

that one expected" the "thin walls of water . . . to burst and disappear" (32). The observing eye is absorbed by single objects which take shape under varying degrees of exposure and thus the larger perspective is deliberately abridged. The "figures" of the men and women who straggle past the flowerbed in Kew Gardens in July momentarily occupy the narrator's attention and their fragments of conversation and gesture are dutifully recorded. However, these forms appear and disappear according to their proximity to the flowerbed itself and the exigencies of the light conditions that operate at that vantage point.

When the first couple move beyond the field of vision, they "soon diminished in size among the trees and looked half transparent as the sunlight and shade swam over their backs in large trembling irregular patches" (34). Snatches of dialogue are equally elliptical and are capable of being perceived as running patterns "of falling words" estranged by the sun-drenched atmosphere within the garden and the unstable perceptual conditions that determine reality for the observing eye:

> "My Bert, Sis, Bill, Grandad, the old man, sugar,
>   Sugar, flour, kippers, greens,
>   Sugar, sugar, sugar."
> The ponderous woman looked through the pattern of falling words at the flowers standing cool, firm, and upright in the earth, with curious expression. She saw them as a sleeper waking from a heavy sleep sees a brass candlestick reflecting the light in an unfamiliar way, and closes his eyes and opens them, and seeing the brass candlestick again, finally starts broad awake and stares at the candlestick with all his powers. (36)

While the narrator provides clues that will allow the reader to reconcile ambiguities through the "mechanism of projection" (the candlestick analogy functions to restore a familiar context in this way), the primary focus rests on the unexpected way in which objects—human words, natural forms—are realized when perception is not evaluated. Illusions of density and outline are challenged: "One couple after another . . . were enveloped in layer after layer of green blue vapour, in which at first their bodies had substance and a dash of colour, but later both substance and colour dissolved in the green-blue atmosphere" (38). Butterflies contextualized by the interdependence of color and light become "white shifting flakes" that "make the outline of a shattered marble column above the tallest flowers." The juxtaposition of human "shapes" of "colour" and treed shade becomes an interchange of color values: "the yellow and green atmosphere" stained "faintly with red and blue." The blurring of contours and categories of meaning serve to advance the larger theme of generation and decay in both human and nonhuman orders and thus the Impressionist "effect" is always evaluated as the story values accumulate. However, the observing eye's deliberate effort to "forget what kind of a scene you have before you" by attaching itself to a "now" that exists without presupposition confers upon the optical reality of the scene so revealed a convincing example of the kinds of techniques Woolf relies on when she too sets out to solve the problems Impressionist artists confront because of a shared outdoor commitment.

Crane

The misconceptions which result when Impressionism is used as a period concept, or as a term to define a literary work that engages the very criticism of life that Impressionist art shuns, are particularly evident in discussions of Stephen Crane's *The Red Badge of Courage*. In a letter to Crane dated December 1, 1897, Joseph Conrad writes of his fascination with Crane's method: "You are a complete impressionist. The illusion of life comes out of your hand without a flaw."[36] *Impressionism* was the term to which Conrad returned in a 1919 discussion of Crane in "A Note without Dates," where he observes that Crane's "impressionism of phrase went really deeper than the surface."[37] Yet the very concept of a surface that discloses a deeper meaning, or of what Conrad describes in "His War Book" as Crane's ability as "a seer with a gift for rendering the significant on the surface of things,"[38] infuses the notion of Impressionism with a symbolic and visionary character that is absolutely incompatible with both its esthetic and method.

Conrad's position encouraged the kind of subjectivist approach to Impressionism that has been perpetuated through John Berryman in his 1950 biography of Crane, and by R. W. Stallman in his 1952 *Stephen Crane: Omnibus*. It is a misconception deriving as well from Crane's own use of the term in "War Memories," where he defines Impressionism as the revelation of "mental light and shade, something which the French impressionists do in colour, something meaningless and at the same time overwhelming, crushing, monstrous."[39] This kind of misconception informs James Nagel's discussion of what he perceives to be the Impressionist method, in *Stephen Crane and Literary Impressionism*. Referring to Crane's use of third-person limited points of view, Nagel argues that the kind of unreliability fostered by the use of perspectives that seemingly duplicate the uncertainty of the protagonist is the "natural expression of Literary Impressionism."[40] Nagel cites Crane's letter to Northern Hilliard to corroborate his sense of the naive eye in Crane's fiction: "I try to give readers a slice out of life; and if there is a moral or lesson in it, I do not try to point it out. I let the reader find it for himself. . . . As Emerson said, 'There should be a long logic beneath the story, but it should be kept carefully out of sight.'" The very presence of this kind of indirection in Crane's prose, the oblique methods he relies on to create a deceptive illusion of naivety, moves one beyond an art of surfaces, for even while the recording intelligence argues for the truth of the moment, he exposes the deficiencies of the character's naive response.

More often than not, the moment of vision in Crane's fiction is both psychological and moral. Symbolic and, as Nagel suggests, "self-projected images" expose the flawed perception of the protagonists themselves. Further, in *The Red Badge of Courage* for example, the protagonist's heroic idealism and Romantic enthusiasm are directly as well as covertly undercut by the recording intelligence. The narrative irony which consistently exposes the shortcomings of Henry's distorted perceptions of war, shortcomings articulate in the mock heroic figures Henry relies on to deal with "the red animal-war, the blood-swollen god,"[41] reaches its most accusative form in chapter 7: "He had been a tremendous figure, no doubt. . . . He had slept and, awakening, found himself a knight" (81). In her analysis of the ironic distance Crane uses to dramatize the failure of his protagonist's ability to see, Milne Holton suggests that one can use the term *dramatic impressionism* to define the paradoxical combination of the seeming fidelity to and the censoring of the perceptual experience,[42] though I find the term misleading insofar as it blurs the distinction between Impressionism and Naturalism central to an understanding of Impressionist art.

It would seem impossible to reconcile Crane's use of dramatic irony in a narrative medium with the kind of natural vision in Impressionist art where the artist never intrudes to refer the illusion itself to moral, ethical, or conventional frames. Because Nagel invokes the very cognitive and interpretative faculties that Impressionism's innocent eye attempts to render inoperative, his definition of verbal Impressionism is not viable.

This point is nowhere more apparent than in Nagel's own discussion of the formative and evaluative role of the intermediary intelligences who record the protagonist's perceptions in *The Red Badge of Courage*. Though Nagel defines Crane's method as a "basic Impressionist narrative stance," he does acknowledge that the "problem" of the "qualifying variable of the mind that perceives the sensations . . . did not affect Impressionistic painting because there was no presumed creation of human consciousness, only of the scene being perceived: the assumption is that what is depicted is rendered as the *painter* saw it, in *plein air,* in a *vistazo*" (36). Because, as Nagel emphasizes, this "assumption is not present" in Crane's fiction, one is not dealing with an Impressionist esthetic and method. The presence of the recording intelligence who explores the veracity of the protagonist's internalization and interpretation of the sensory data means that the naive perception has become a conceptual experience. Nagel evades the crucial distinctions between Naturalism and Impressionism that Howarth underlines. In doing so, he fails to recognize that an Impressionist method must serve an Impressionist vision. If it does not, then the notion of an Impressionist method in Crane's fiction has little validity.

This is precisely, furthermore, the kind of confusion that is part of Charles Walcutt's discussion in "Stephen Crane: Naturalist and Impressionist." Walcutt allies Crane's method with Impressionism because Crane expresses a Naturalistic theme. Crane's style, for example, fractures experience into "disordered sensation in a way that shatters the old moral 'order' along with the old orderly processes of reward and punishment."[43] Walcutt defines Naturalism as the exposure of the sham present in accepted or inherited concepts of social morality, and he sees the kind of alteration of conventional schematizations of reality as an Impressionistic visual correlative of the Naturalist manifesto he discovers in Crane's work.

In a parallel way, Sergio Perosa in "Naturalism and Impressionism in Stephen Crane's Fiction" consistently defines Impressionism as an art form which pursues the "underlying secret" or the "fundamental, lasting and essential" truths "in the fleeting aspects of life."[44] Though initially Perosa attempts, like Nagel, to distinguish between objective and subjective forms of Impressionism (though the distinction is itself superfluous, for subjective Impressionism is really part of the expressive emphasis in both Post-Impressionist and Expressionist art), he increasingly endorses the view, inherited from Conrad, that defines Impressionism as "an instrument for the representation of the moral and psychological inner life of the protagonist" (271).

This fact is borne out by the way in which Perosa relies upon the distinction Conrad makes in his 1897 preface to *The Nigger of the "Narcissus"* between impression and sensation. Conrad notes that fiction appeals because it is "an expression conveyed through the senses." It holds up "the rescued fragment before all eyes" and shows "its vibration, its colour, its form; and through its movement, its form and its colour reveal[s] the substance of its truth—disclose[s] its inspiring secret and passion within the core of each convincing moment."[45] Perosa applies Conrad's essentially Post-Impressionist sense of the impression as epiphany to Crane's method in *The Red Badge of Courage:* "By faithfully recording [Henry Fleming's] sensations, Crane gives substance and shape to the dramatic scene or the evoked picture, and the gradual unfolding of the meaning coincides with the slow process of perception" (272). So too, Rodney Rogers in "Stephen Crane and Impressionism" ignores the vital fact that there is a fundamental difference between the kind of realism achieved by those who consider impression to mean a psychological datum and those who, like the Impressionists, define it in terms of a physical sense datum. Rogers, therefore, works with a conception of literary Impressionism based on the erroneous assumption that pictorial Impressionists are fascinated by the way in which "a person's psychology affects the way he *conceives* the world."[46]

The paradigm for Perosa's method seems to derive from R. W. Stallman's assessment of Crane in "Stephen Crane: A Revaluation," for in this essay, Stallman, like Perosa, invokes Conrad's preface as the most viable context within which one can discuss the Impressionist method in Crane. Not only is the fragment to be defined as an Impressionist moment of discovery, but Impressionist colors and atmospheric effects are to function in symbolic terms where it would seem that "the precision of vision is equated, symbolically, with revelation or spiritual insight."[47] The paradigm established as the tradition of literary Impressionism in terms of Crane specifically is one Michael Fried accepts as well in *Realism, Writing, Disfiguration: On Thomas Eakins and Stephen Crane,* though Fried does indicate that, while he is following the "classically conceived" tradition, "in speaking of Crane as an 'impressionist,' by placing the term between quotation marks" he means "to indicate that" his "use of the term will be heuristic."[48] "Impressionism" in Fried's text, therefore, will express the critic's conception of a tension between "manifest" and "latent" content in Crane's work (144), which declares the text's "double consciousness" (205 n. 70). If one accepts this heuristic use of the term, however, one is led unwittingly at times to devalue the pictorial tradition that is assumed as the basis of correlation. Further, meaningful analogies based upon interartistic methods that comprehend an actual Impressionist method and technique fail to materialize.

My analysis of the critical response to Crane's Impressionism clearly demonstrates the need for a reconsideration of the term *Impressionism* in literature generally. Donald C. Yelton's analysis of verbal iconography in Conrad, in *Mimesis and Metaphor: An Inquiry into the Genesis and Scope of Conrad's Symbolic Imagery,* contributes to that end, for here Yelton notes that Conrad's "ostensibly sensory and impressionist imagery" often tends to merge its identity with the expressionistic imagery of inner states."[49] Though Yelton suggests that Conrad's use of the term Impressionism to define Crane's "surface rendering" has applicability, he does acknowledge that "Conradian 'impressionism' assumes its own distinctive character—a character which, in accord with current terminology, contains as much of *ex*pressionism as of *im*pressionism" (130).

In "Hanging Stephen Crane in the Impressionist Museum," Bert Bender further explores the extent to which the use of the term *Impressionism* in discussions of Crane is inappropriate. As Crane's "primary interest" rests with "dramatizing" the inability of his characters "to see," the kind of realism he attains has nothing in common with that achieved in Impressionist canvases: "Crane is concerned with a subjective, psychological realism that is both a response to and an interpretation of his surrounding world. The impressionists, on the other hand, are concerned with the reality of their sensations, a reality which is inextricably involved with their techniques of rendering it."[50] Bender suggests that the confusion evolves because "discussions of literary impressionism are based mainly on false comparisons of techniques in painting rather than on comparisons of envisioned realities" (49). The presence of sensual words, of disconnected fragments, of verbal indefiniteness and depersonalized and detached perspective can, as Ilie suggests, "advance the purpose of many kinds of styles" (47), and therefore the set of features in literature that are commonly defined as Impressionist are in fact only so when they serve the creation of an Impressionist "envisioned reality."

Though Bender argues à la Lessing that an interdisciplinary approach focusing on technical correlations between the two media raises more problems than it can ever hope to solve (49), he himself is led to posit a series of analogies between Crane and Post-Impressionist and Surrealist artists in terms of stylistic affinities.[51] Bender's sense of correspondence is viable because, though he does not seem aware of the process, he is referring to the style-forming implications of an esthetic and metaphysical approach to reality that Crane shares with artists who do not work within the parameters of Impressionism's "envisioned reality." While Bender argues that the term *Impressionism* in literary criticism is a "meaningless concept," and that interartistic analogies are untenable, his own inspired use of non-Impressionist contexts demonstrates the extent to which an interartistic method is a fruitful one. *Impressionism* can be a viable term in literary criticism when its original meaning is recovered, for the term is in fact responsive to a particular stylistic mode that verbal artists rely on when they wish in fact to stop at the surface and attend to the truths of the natural and factual vision integral to Impressionist realism.

The Red Badge of Courage is the story of Henry Fleming, who discovers during his first trial by fire in a Civil War battle that there are no moral absolutes and that one's untested notions of honor and courage must be more responsive to actual experience. Though Crane is concerned with visualizing, through an expressive and often symbolic chiaroscuro, the "mental light and shade" of his young protagonist, there are times within the novel that Crane works to achieve an objective rather than a subjective correlative for the perceptual moment.

At the opening of chapter 3, for example, just prior to Henry's first contact with the enemy, Crane's recording intelligence is absorbed by the effect of firelight on the landscape, and both the tone and mode of the piece are consistent with the detachment and anonymity of Impressionism's observing eye: "When another night came the columns, changed to purple streaks, filed across two pontoon bridges. A glaring fire wine-tinted the waters of the river. Its rays, shining upon the moving masses of troops, brought forth here and there sudden gleams of silver or gold. Upon the other shore a dark and mysterious range of hills was curved against the sky. The insect voices of the night sang solemnly" (20).

Despite the fact that the insects sing "solemnly," and the fire glares, the reader experiences the calculated effect of Crane's choice of an anonymous third-person point of view. Crane's prose exhibits the kind of condensation that is amenable to recording the volubility of atmospheric effects. The verb forms themselves are visually descriptive of the very processes of transmutation that the firelight generates as it wine-tints the waters or randomly animates the silver and gold accents of the massed troops. The indefiniteness of "another night" when conjoined with "the columns" fosters a sense of the depersonalized eye that disassociates itself from the potential poignancy and drama of the human dimensions of the scene it simply surveys. Crane insinuates a mood of mystery that is not particularly prophetic, for it is a mystery that is perfectly consistent with perceived atmospheric effects where, for example, the local color of the columns gives way to the accidents of colored illumination just as they do in Monet's *The Grenouillère,* and where spatial relations are either ignored or flattened to a certain extent as with the hills "curved against the sky" to sustain the emphasis upon the surface aspect and effect.

Often, to balance Fleming's tendency to project feelings into the landscape, Crane will present a striking visual image that recovers a sense of the essential neutrality of the landscape. In the midst of the clamor of an early skirmish, for example, the authorial observer notes: "A cloud of dark smoke, as from smouldering ruins, went up towards the sun now bright and gay in blue, enameled sky" (82). In restraining the realization of a visual scene to a consideration of color and line alone, Crane is able to avoid familiar verbal terms and habits of association, an avoidance much like that of the Impressionist artist who frees the optic from ordinary visual modes of schematization. To underscore Henry's dislocation in the midst of battle, he observes:

> It seemed to the youth that he saw everything. Each blade of the green grass was bold and clear. He thought he was aware of every change in the thin, transparent vapor that floated idly in sheets. The brown or gray trunks of the trees showed each roughness of their surfaces. And the men of the regiment, with their starting eyes and sweating faces, running madly, or falling, as if thrown headlong, to queer, heaped-up corpses—all were comprehended. His mind took a mechanical but firm impression so that afterward everything was pictured and explained to him, save why he himself was there. (86–87)

In this passage Crane is struggling to find the objective visual correlative that will approximate those moments in the novel when Henry is dispossessed of the conventional romanticized notions of war that compelled him to enlist. Crane describes the process of the random illumination of objects that strike the eye with unusual microscopic clarity as Henry's taking of a "mechanical but firm impression." He is suggesting both the naivety and receptivity of Impressionism's observing eye. The scene realizes a momentary halt in the action in which the "new appearance of the landscape" in a "clearer atmosphere" comes as a "revelation." Crane makes the observer aware of the way in which objects lose their distinction in the shift from a close to a distant view, an effect that is faithfully recreated by Degas through his preferred oblique angle of vision in *Orchestra of the Paris Opera* (fig. 4), where the exquisite and minute attention to foreground detail is gradually lost as one moves into the canvas toward the diffuse pink and blue forms on the stage.

Crane also uses a naive eye to record processes of dislocation by attending to the directional force and dynamism of lines and the shape of colors. Early in the novel, Henry, indifferent to his own emotions and compelled by curiosity rather than self-interest, scrambles up a bank "to observe everything" before he

Figure 4. Edgar Degas, *Orchestra of the Paris Opera*, 1868
(Musée d'Orsay, Paris; cliché des Musées Nationaux)

characteristically "wonder[s] about himself" and "probe[s] his sensations" for meaning. The frenzy of the conflicting battalions is visualized in terms of "knots and waving lines of skirmishers who were running hither and thither. . . . A dark battle line lay upon a sunstruck clearing that gleamed orange color. A flag fluttered" (22). Points of contact between the two lines are realized as "commotions . . . woven red and startling into the gentle fabric of softened greens and browns. It looked to be a wrong place for the battlefield" (22). The kind of abstraction achieved by a depersonalized point of view is equally a part of the effect that Monet works toward in *Rue St. Denis, Festival of June 30, 1878* (fig. 5).

Crane will often visualize the configuration in terms of a conjunction or interchange of blue and red tonal values as part of a process of reification or equanimity of eye that does not abide by the conventional distinctions between human and nonhuman forms in the landscape. At a particularly bleak moment during the battle, for example, the observer notes that "the regiment bled extravagantly. Grunting bundles of blue began to drop" (182). During the same skirmish a "collection of men" execute a "blind" and "despairing rush" in "dusty and tattered blue, over a green sward . . . under a sapphire sky" (103). The conception of an isolate human identity gives way to the perception of patterns of color, in sketches where the focus momentarily centers on blue men and gray men, where "the sunlight made twinkling points of the bright steel" (83) and where the natural landscape, unperturbed by the pandemonium of the battlefield, offers its "red sun . . . pasted in the sky like a wafer" (50).

Crane also underwrites Henry's temptation toward the pathetic fallacy by having his protagonist register the indifference of the landscape at crucial moments of battle: "As he gazed around him the youth felt a flash of astonishment at the blue, pure sky and the sun gleamings on the trees and fields. It was surprising that Nature had gone tranquilly on with her golden process in the midst of so much devilment" (34). Henry is of course taken by surprise because the landscape's appearance does not coincide with the set of expectations he brings with him into battle. The undercutting of the familiar or the expected, the dislocation achieved by attending to the optic alone, provides Crane with visual modes that expose the inapplicability of themes of heroism to the landscape action.

Woolf

Whereas Crane uses the Impressionist perspective to temper his protagonist's tendency to dramatize the landscape, Virginia Woolf, in *Jacob's Room* especially, relies upon the Impressionist method to expose what she considers to be the deficiencies of its surface view, which fails to grasp the essentials of life and character, the underlying patterns of reality, and the rich interior life of mind

Figure 5.   Claude Monet, *Rue St. Denis, Festival of June 30, 1878*, 1878
(*Musée des Beaux-Arts, Rouen*)

wherein her novelistic interest lies. In "Mr. Bennett and Mrs. Brown" Woolf observes that the novelist penetrates his character and moves beyond the surface changes to grasp the essential and definitive force of that character's human nature, "the spirit we live by" (*Collected Essays* I: 337). It is clear that she wishes to solve, for the most part, problems the Impressionist artist does not address.

In *Jacob's Room,* Woolf creates the illusion of an Impressionistic technique to demonstrate the way in which its vision fails to disclose the inner reality that her narrator attempts to embrace: "It is this that we live by, they say, driven by an unseizable force. They say that novelists never catch it; that it goes hurtling through their nets and leaves them torn to ribbons. This, they say, is what we live by—this unseizable force."[52] It is Woolf's capacity "to apprehend processes of thought and feeling as though they were pictorial shapes"[53] that constitutes her greatest achievement. In so doing, she penetrates beyond the surfaces that so captivated Impressionist artists, and in fact finds in the subjective deformation of natural forms the symbolic equivalents for the interior region, the twilight vision that is indigenous to the "dark places of psychology." In "Street Haunting: A London Adventure," Woolf distinguishes between two worlds the novelist may inhabit: the one rendered by the "unprofessional eye" content with "surface only"—the one she sees capable of reflecting the volubility and changeability of external reality, of recording "the atoms as they fall"—and the other rendered by the "professional eye" trained to bring out the more obscure angles and relationships."[54] Like many artists who came after the impressionists, Woolf saw Impressionism itself as the product of the casual eye, lacking in form and stability. In "Phases of Fiction," she observes that the novel in "its immense power to imitate surface reality" endangers itself by becoming obsolete and lifeless if it simply equals the verisimilitude of the photograph (*Collected Essays* II: 100). Though the notion of Impressionism as photographic realism ignores the role of the unexpected and the incomplete that is integral to its concept of visual naivety and selective focus, Woolf's disdain for "surface only," and her tendency to define a preoccupation with surface reality as an indictment of intellectual superfluidity, predisposes her toward Post-Impressionist techniques which could, she felt, circumscribe that "true reality." In this sense, the "professional eye" can then be defined as the "mind's eye"—that which for Woolf could disclose the immaterial or the unseen.

As a consequence of Woolf's affinity with both Post-Impressionist and Expressionist esthetics, it is important to note that often, in her exploration of scene under varying conditions of light and dark, it is the symbolic value of light rather than the scientific which is most significant.[55] She explores color and light not only to produce delicate Impressionistic effects, but also to create structures that visualize states of mind. It is in this sense that the abstract core of her mature works, like *The Waves,* involves an architectonic structure of linked images that operate as the signature of character in pictorial terms. The novel, then, evolves as a sequence of emotions felt for reality that is given pictorial definition.

Jacob's Room, a novel set in pre–World War I London, traces the fortunes of one Jacob Flanders as he moves from childhood through to manhood with a stint at Cambridge, an aborted affair, and a walking tour of Greece and Italy— episodes which occur prior to his premature and tragic death in the war itself. In the novel, as Jean Alexander suggests, one has but a "shadowy sense" of the central character,[56] but that effect is intentional. Woolf yields her omniscience as narrator but retains a relatively impersonal external point of view, using a multiplicity of physical angles of external events and objects in an attempt to release the inner processes of the central character. The naive eye, when joined with a cinematic process, allows Woolf to detach her meditative intelligence from the immediate surroundings and shift from one consciousness to another insofar as they arrange themselves around the central character. Jacob Flanders, visualized as "a young man alone in his room," is the magnetic force that provides the underlying cohesiveness for disparate scenes. Because a deliberately sustained detached tone almost consistently accompanies that external point of view, the emotional resonance of the novel is intentionally low-pitched. One has the sense of the observing eye moving from a panorama of the whole, passing in and reducing the field of vision, disclosing through the random or accidental scene a casual yet revealing juxtaposition of objects or persons that epitomize the surface quality of life that an anonymous eye can render.

This is not to suggest that Woolf does not explore the expressive possibilities of physical perspectives, nor that she does not experiment with the symbolic potential of the reflecting surfaces that will constitute the abstract core of *The Waves;* but just as part of the thematic significance of the novel is the fugitive and ephemeral nature of that "true reality," so too the Impressionist methods she works with demonstrate that theme by demanding that she stop bravely at the surface. Through both "direct" and "indirect mirror modes,"[57] Jacob's personality is diffused through objects, scenes, and the reactions of other people. He is, then, obliquely present through various pictures that attempt to disclose his subjective reality—visible forms that operate as metaphoric equivalents for the unseen. However, Woolf's tendency to suggest the essentials of character in a few bold strokes, the creation of caricature by canvasing the most telling gesture or pose, coupled with a reliance upon sequences of rapidly dissolving sense impressions, often make the general atmosphere of the novel Impressionistic.

The theme of inaccessibility is emphasized in the novel by the recurring references to the inadequacy of traditional narrative techniques that "sum people up." The various pictures of reality that the narrator visualizes, those "rude illustrations, pictures, in a book whose pages we turn over as if we should at last find what we look for" (97), underline the irrevocable otherness of people and things. The scene, for example, immediately following Jacob's sighting of Florinda walking up Greek Street "upon another man's arm," provides a clearer sense of the way in which Impressionistic values sustain the illusion of an impenetrable surface. The empirical quest—those observations which "lace our days together and make of life a perfect globe" (93)—cannot concretize the ineffable quality which somehow lies embedded in surface appearance: "And yet, and yet . . ." as we "'try to penetrate,' . . . as we lift the cup, shake the hand, express the hope, something whispers, Is this all? Can I never know, share, be certain?" (93). The pictorial forces of this interlude are directed toward the light-drenched character while the visual effects, which attend the street lamp as the source of illumination, send chequered shadows encroaching upon the street. Anonymous forms, "single and together," obliterate Jacob's view of his mistress. Various aspects of his form are randomly illuminated: "the pattern of his trousers; the old thorns on his stick" (94). Extended verbal similes emphasize startling light effects: "It was as if a stone were ground to dust; as if white sparks flew from a livid whetstone." They serve as visual equivalents for Jacob's decomposure: "as if the switchback railway, having swooped to the depths, fell, fell, fell. This was in his face" (94). The narrator undercuts this final fanciful conceit with the following admonition, advising that "whether we know what was in his mind is another question" (94). Her awareness of the perils of the process of sympathetic identification that her analogies initiate culminates in a tongue-in-cheek plumbing of possible clichéd romantic associations: "Surely there's enough light in the street at this moment to drown all our cares in gold!" (95).

The narrator repeatedly emphasizes the seemingly unalterable fact that all one can, in fact, know is the surface view. This sense of shallowness is fostered by the way in which bodies are decomposed to undermine illusions of mass, density, stability, and gravity. The narrator may, for example, emphasize the two-dimensionality of the image to create the kind of flat playing-card effect Degas achieves in *Place de la Concorde* (fig. 6): "The women in the streets have the faces of playing cards; the outlines accurately filled in with pink or yellow, and the line drawn tightly round them" (115). During a tête à tête between Jacob and Florinda over dinner, the narrator chooses to animate Florinda by attending to the surface details of her partially dissolving form in a manner reminiscent of the delicate atmospheric effects Renoir creates to disclose his female figure in *The Lodge:* "Florinda leant the points of her elbows on the table and held her chin in the cup of her hands. Her cloak had slipped behind her. Gold and white with bright beads on her she emerged, her face flowering from her body, innocent, scarcely tinted, the eyes gazing frankly about her, or slowly setting on Jacob and resting there" (79–80).

The decomposition and metamorphosis of the figure through the interplay of color and light is central to Jacob's view of Clara as she stands on the ladder

Figure 6.   Edgar Degas, *Place de la Concorde*, 1872–1873
79 × 118 cm.
(Archives Durand-Ruel)

above him in her family vineyard: "She looked semi-transparent, pale, wonderfully beautiful up there among the vine leaves and the yellow and purple bunches, the lights swimming over her in coloured islands" (62). In fact the afternoon at the Durrants is drenched with the kind of light that characterizes the intoxication of Renoir's *Dancing at the Moulin de la Galette:* "Opposite him were hazy, semi-transparent shapes of yellow and blue. Behind them again, was the grey-green garden, and among the pear-shaped leaves of the escallonia fishing-boats seemed caught and suspended. A sailing ship slowly drew past the women's backs. Two or three figures crossed the terrace hastily in the dusk. The door opened and shut. Nothing settled or stayed unbroken" (57).

The novel, as a whole, consistently highlights the evocativeness of the surface illusions, which tempts the narrator-observer to read into the scene's apparent reality emotions and intentions that simply may not be there. This disjunction between the possible contents of the interior life and their relationship, if any, to surface detail dramatizes the dual consciousness of the meditative voice. During the scene in which Jacob catches sight of Florinda "turning up Greek Street upon another man's arm" (94), for example, the perceiving eye registers the animation of the street-lit scene, fascinated, in a very impersonal manner by the way in which the lamplight bathes Jacob's figure and patterns the street itself. At the same time, however, this observer, who is ten years older than her subject, female, and certainly not immune to Jacob's sense of betrayal at this moment, is equally aware that she is absorbed by her own desire to penetrate the very surface she so impersonally records. Significantly, it is the question of penetration which determines the shape of the novel itself, and thus the reader is continually aware, through the observer herself, of the dialectic between the surface view delivered by the naive eye, and the in-depth revelation which absorbs the mind's eye that "all the while" has for its "centre," for its "magnet, a young man alone in his room" (95). In this sense one is encouraged to describe the novel as an exploration of the tension that develops when an Impressionist technique is used to try to realize the kind of Post-Impressionist and penetrative vision Impressionism's absorption with apparent realities does not intend to bring into being.

As if to underline this duality of focus, the narrator aborts her pursuit of the central character in this episode, and stops before his door to present a series of seemingly discontinuous visual responses to the street scene itself:

> It was January and dismal, but Mrs. Wagg stood on her doorstep, as if expecting something to happen. A barrel-organ played like an obscene nightingale beneath wet leaves. Children ran across the road. Here and there one could see brown panelling inside the hall door. . . . The march that the mind keeps beneath the windows of others is queer enough. Now distracted by brown panelling; now by a fern in a pot; here improvising a few phrases to dance with the barrel-organ; again snatching a detached gaiety from a drunken man; then altogether absorbed

by words the poor shout across the street at each other (so outright, so lusty)—yet all the while having for centre, for magnet, a young man alone in his room. (95)

In her correspondence with painter Jacques Raverat, Woolf states that the novelist, like the painter, wants "to catch and consolidate and consummate" those "splashes" that Raverat had defined as the simultaneity of the moment of vision: "There are splashes in the outer air in every direction, and under the surface waves that follow one another into dark and forgotten corners" (Bell, *Virginia Woolf: A Biography,* vol. 2, 106). She understood that the linearity of the "formal railway line of sentence" inhibited the novelist's ability to achieve the simultaneity of the visual moment of perception. In this scene it is precisely that sense of spatiality that Woolf tries to visualize by emphasizing the radial possibilities of her medium.

Syntactically, through ellipses and parataxis, Woolf simulates the very kind of prose rhythm that offers a verbal equivalent for Impressionism's improvised technique. Further, by attending to the way in which details are registered in the moment of perception, Woolf also creates the illusion of the in medias res vitality sustained in Renoir's *Place Clichy*. We move from the clearly delineated foreground figure in an attitude of expectancy ("Mrs. Wagg stood on her door-step") to the partially visible barrel-organist obscured beneath wet leaves, to the indifferentiated mass of children running across the road in the far distance. The sporadic glimpses of random details that strike the eye allow us to shift our vision from the fern pot to the brown panelling as if we were, in fact, responding to surface stimuli alone. We have a sense of the successive receding planes of the panelled interiors of row housing. The evocativeness of this seemingly haphazard arrangement accentuated by its quality of improvisation and blurred outline provides a verbal correlative for the incomplete in Impressionist art.

The compositional focus of the scene is of course the road itself, to which every detail refers. Within the context of the journey initiated by the mediative eye the scene dramatizes the elusiveness of Jacob as subject, which consistently undermines our expectations. Of itself, the scene represents Woolf's mastery as an illusionist artist and her relatedness to Impressionism. It is not surprising, therefore, to discover that Woolf's street scene in *Jacob's Room* shares, in effect and tone, an interesting affinity with the apprehensive qualities of Monet's *Boulevard des Capucines* (fig. 7) with its oblique angle of vision, and touches of thin paint that create a suggestion of figures increasingly decomposed in planar recession.

Woolf presents the linguistic equivalent of an open-window pictorial tradition by using both linear and atmospheric perspective to achieve a three-dimensional spatial illusion. If the street scene situates the narrative eye poised "beneath the window," Woolf also places her behind the eyes of the central charac-

Figure 7.   Claude Monet, *Boulevard des Capucines*, 1873
Oil on canvas, 31¼″ × 23¼″.
*(The Nelson-Atkins Museum of Art, Kansas City; acquired
through the Kenneth A. and Helen F. Spencer Foundation
Acquisition Fund)*

ter in front of a window that operates much like a picture frame opening out on the scene below. The novel presents a recurring tableau of its subject so conceived, gazing out to capture the rhythms of daily life through an Impressionistic rendering of scene to simulate an actual space experience. Parts of these scenes are repeated to maximize the reverberation of the reality of the suburb throughout the novel, while the tableau itself has, of course, expressive potential in that it conveys the observer's sense of alienation from her subject.

In one sense one can see a parallel between Woolf's composite portrait of Jacob through the sequence of visual complexes—"those pictures in a book"—and Degas's technical method in his early portraits. Dunstan observes that Degas put his composition together from a number of separate drawings, yet his unique contribution to this academic method was his decision "to correct and alter the drawings at all stages, even quite late in the execution of the canvas." Degas said of his work that it "proceeded by a series of operations," or a "series of restatements of the drawings on canvas," and this process is particularly evident in an early composition *Spartan Youths Exercising* (fig. 8), where the redrawing of the legs is left untouched. Woolf's meditative intelligence approaches her subject in the same kind of tentative and insistent way, attempting to get him right: "Every face, every shop, bedroom window, public-house, and dark square is a picture feverishly turned—in search of what? It is the same with books. What do we seek through millions of pages? Still hopefully turning the pages— oh, here is Jacob's room" (97). When this kind of portraiture pentimento is combined with the filter, the doorway, and the window, all work together to deepen the psychological and emotional resonances of the failure of surface to disclose depth.

In terms of the Impressionistic significance of the open-window technique, it is important to note that the window both encloses space and opens up upon reality so that, as with the street scene in *Jacob's Room*, the rhythms of life are viewed in perspective and create the illusion of spatial depth. The moment of perception becomes stabilized and more durable. In *Jacob's Room*, Woolf consistently recreates the view beyond Jacob's window, following his angle of vision, duplicating his perceptual experience to recreate the world as closely as he must see it from his room on Holborn Street: "At Mudie's corner in Oxford Street all the red and blue beads had run together on a string" (64). The scene opens up through a sequence of loosely outlined, rapidly dissolving sense impressions that duplicate the way in which the eye momentarily focuses on objects in a wide and often aerial perspective that creates the incessant stream of traffic over the bridge of the Serpentine or "the hordes crossing Waterloo Bridge" (112–13). Woolf's Holborn Street pictures find their correlative in Pissarro's *Place du Théâtre Français*, a series which was begun in 1897. The idea of painting the impression of a crowd in its weaving and diverse patterns of buildings and human movement was an innovation of the Impressionists. In

Figure 8. Edgar Degas, *Spartan Youths Exercising*, 1860
(*Reproduced courtesy of the Trustees of the National Gallery, London*)

Théâtre Français Pissarro chooses a second-floor view of the corner, a view which often defines the point of departure for Woolf's observing eye, which moves off from this position into the crowd. Thus, for example, for the scene at Mudie's corner she moves into the omnibuses, identifying her characters in cipher form as "a man with a red moustache" or "a young man in grey smoking a pipe," duplicating the kind of perceptual naivety and impersonality that Pissarro's study of human forms as tonal values is intended to achieve.

The meditative intelligence, which patterns events and arranges scenes, often provides explicit set direction in *Jacob's Room* in order to align the reader and bring objects into focus: "If you look closer you will see . . . three elderly men at a little distance" (66). She presents Scarborough from varying perspectives, moving from Mrs. Flanders positioned on Dods Hill and a panoramic sweep of the sea edged toward the city skyline, panning in to capture the variety of everyday rhythms ("Banjoes strummed; the parade smelt of tar" [18]), contracting the field of vision to register a mood through the quick cataloguing of types in bold outline: "Triangular hoardings were wheeled along by men in white coats. Captain George Boase had caught a monster shark. One side of the triangular hoarding said so in red, blue, and yellow letters; and each line ended with three differently colored notes of exclamation" (18). This sense of visual naivety is sustained by the observer's method of resisting those familiar terms which one usually relies on to identify objects. Rather, objects become abstract geometric shapes, or are registered only in terms of vivid splashes of color. The entire seasonal motif is traced through color changes alone, effected by the absorption and refraction of light:

> The entire gamut of the view's changes should have been known to her; its winter aspect, spring, summer and autumn; how storms came up from the sea; how moors shuddered and brightened as the clouds went over; she should have noted the red spot where the villas were building; and the criss-cross of lines where the allotments were cut; and the diamond flash of little glass houses in the sun. Or, if details like these escaped her, she might have let her fancy play upon the gold tint of the sea at sunset, and thought how it lapped in coins of gold upon the shingle. (17)

Interestingly, Woolf places the entire passage within the subjunctive mood to indicate the way in which the view would appear if one were simply aware of it as it appears. This is the kind of detachment Monet achieves in *The Garden, Giverny,* for example, where the interest rests with the way in which wind and sunlight combine forces to impose a common tonality and pattern. Mrs. Flanders, preoccupied with her children's needs and mourning her own bereavement, simply cannot respond in this kind of depersonalized way. Her more prosaic and pragmatic eye, trained to find direction through space, ignores the very conditions of the landscape that can absorb the more disinterested eye of the authorial observer.

Woolf is capable of this kind of Impressionist evocation in *The Waves* as well, where, as in the seventh interlude, the narrator fixes a carefully designed track of vision which allows the reader to identify points of reference on the horizon that stabilize our entry into the pictorial space. The illusion of depth is achieved through the perspective line secured by both a brilliant reflecting surface and a single dominating vertical: *"The round-headed clouds never dwindled as they bowled along, but kept every atom of their rotundity. Now, as they passed, they caught a whole village in the fling of their net and, passing, let it fly free again. Far away on the horizon, among the million grains of blue grey dust, burnt one pane, or stood the single line of one steeple or one tree."*[58] Woolf reinforces the illusion of depth through atmospheric perspective by attending to the decomposition of color under changing conditions of light and dark.

By observing the diffuseness of color, Woolf is able to texture the atmosphere and thereby achieve a purer apprehension of the naturalistic effects of seemingly intangible qualities such as the conditions of sky and light. In the King's College Chapel, Cambridge, of *Jacob's Room*, the narrator attends to the way in which refracted light metamorphosizes the wall's surface, finding a verbal equivalent to register the delicate meteorological effects that Monet devotes himself to in *Rouen Cathedral: The Façade at Sunset* (fig. 9): "An inclined plane of light comes accurately through each window, purple and yellow even in its most diffused dust, while, where it breaks up stone, that stone is softly chalked red, yellow, and purple" (32). To concretize the reader's illusion of inhabiting space, Woolf relies on synesthetic effects that will render external light sources palpable in interior spaces: "The door opened; in came the roar of Regent Street, the roar of traffic, impersonal, unpitying; and sunshine grained with dirt" (169).

In *The Waves* as well, Woolf visualizes atmosphere by giving the sky texture and depth approximating the diffuseness of color at sunrise: "The burning bonfire . . . lifted the weight of the woollen grey sky on top of it and turned it into a million atoms of soft blue" (179); or through twilight haze: "the million grains of blue grey dust" (303); and midday heat: "The sun made the hills grey as if shaved and singed in an explosion, while, further north . . . hills smoothed into slabs as with the back of a spade had a light in them as if a warder, deep within, went from a chamber to chamber carrying a green lamp. Through atoms of grey-blue air the sun struck at English fields and lit up marshes and pools, a white gull on a stake, the slow sail of shadows over blunt-headed woods and young corn and flowing hayfields" (278–79). Often, Woolf achieves striking effects by the close observation of light's ability to impose a unifying tonal value. The atmosphere of interlude 7 in *The Waves,* for example, is never wholly transparent but realized in a gradation of hues according to conditions of light that give us the sense of what Woolf defines in *Jacob's Room* as the

Figure 9.   Claude Monet, *Rouen Cathedral: The Façade at Sunset*, 1894
Oil on canvas, 39½″ × 26″.
(National Gallery of Art, Washington; Chester Dale Collection)

"gauze of the air" (163): "The islands of cloud had gained in density and drew themselves across the sun so that the rocks went suddenly black, and the trembling sea holly lost its blue and turned silver, and shadows were blown like grey cloths over the sea" (302).

Woolf's acute sensitivity to the alteration of shape and color, the reciprocity between light and objects through colored shadows and luminous tints, is evident in both *Jacob's Room* and *The Waves*. Like the Impressionists, Woolf is a seismographer of change, using the landscape as a foil for the dramatic interchange of wind, sunlight, and cloud. The continuous movement of cloud formations in *Jacob's Room* is mirrored through the effects of shadow: "The moors shuddered and brightened as the clouds went over" (17). Intrigued by the play of light on the water's surface, Woolf composes a delicate sea piece and follows the swift transformation of color filtered through sunlight with a rich scale of transitional hues: "The Scilly Isles were turning bluish; and suddenly blue, purple and green flushed the sea; left it grey; struck a stripe which vanished. . . . The whole floor of the waves was blue and white, rippling and crisp, though now and again a broad purple mark appeared, like a bruise; or there floated an entire emerald tinged with yellow" (48).

The characteristic perspective line chosen in *Jacob's Room*—a view from the sea to the mainland or vice-versa—works toward the realization of spatial depth as Timmy and Jacob approach the Scilly Isles. The scene itself is published through varying time periods as the observer follows the descent of the sun, while the illusion of space is achieved with Timmy's face highlighted in the foreground with the lantern lights behind him, the rocks and the Isles articulate in the middle distance, and finally the lighthouse and stars annotating the ten o'clock sky (52). Perceptual depth is intensified by the way in which the narrator attends to the gradations of color values under the changing incidence of luminosity reflected on the sea's surface as we move from insistent to retiring shades—from purple to gold to applegreen and pale yellow. In the modulating of forms, according to degrees and quality of reflected illumination, one observes the beginnings of Woolf's techniques of color abstraction. The simplification of shape through color, geometrically defined, begins in *Jacob's Room* with "wedges of applegreen" and "plates of pale yellow" and the distorted colors of elongated and squat waves. In a very similar way, *Façade at Sunset* transforms the cathedral façade into a study of the rectangles created by verticals and horizontals.

One recalls as well Monet's advice to young painters and his deliberate cultivation of perceptual naivety to inhibit the kinds of visual adjustments our color expectations usually impose upon outdoor scenes, when the accidents of color illumination alter our preconceptions about the way things look while paradoxically presenting a closer approximation of the way things actually appear in natural light. This is Monet's objective as he duplicates the way the umbrella veils his figure in the flowered hat in *On the Beach, Trouville,* and it is exactly the kind of accuracy Woolf achieves in this scene through the conjunction of twilight conditions and lamp light: "Durrant's face, as he sat steering . . . the colour of a red lacquer box polished for generations" (52). We can also anticipate in this early sequence the formal and architectonic dimension of Woolf's work in *The Waves,* where the abstract geometric definition of color functions as a compositional force in the interludes. In *Jacob's Room* Durrant's face is abstracted to a red rectangle, sky reflections to wedges of light, lantern lights to fluctuating long and flat shapes, such that color works as a structural element of design as in the manner of Monet's compositions.

In restricting the discussion at this point to color alone, it is apparent that Woolf is capable of the rich color-play of the Impressionists. The profusion of compound epithets in *Jacob's Room* and *The Waves* such as "pink-feathered," "just-reddened," "water-colored," and "diamond-tipped" provide evidence of her desire to expand the possibilities of color expression and attain greater truth in the transcription of naturalist effects. In *Jacob's Room,* the atmosphere is semitransparent to render the diffuseness of objects through color and light such that contours and outlines are always on the verge of dissolution. The moth becomes "something yellow-tinted and sulphurous in the darkness," or "that pale-clouded yellow" Jacob caught on the moors "the night the tree had fallen." She also works with Post-Impressionist values to visualize Jacob's obvious resentment toward the world of the elderly and their social convention: Lady Miller's picnic party becomes "a flaw in the column of air between two trees round which curled a thread of blue" (37). In rendering a psychological state of mind as an anomaly of design, Woolf foreshadows the way in which the theme of *To the Lighthouse* will be conceived in visual terms through the conjunction of abstracted forms in Lily Briscoe's painting.

Woolf is also able to place the reader firmly behind the eyes of the character's perceptual experience by observing the physical sensations that attend a chosen perspective. She describes the effect of Jacob's oblique angle of vision as he lies in the boat moored to the shore: "The meadow was on a level with Jacob's eyes as he lay back; gilt with buttercups, but the grass . . . stood juicy and thick. Looking up, backwards, he saw the legs of children deep in the grass, and the legs of cows. . . . In front of him two white butterflies circled higher and higher" (37). She introduces a secondary angle in order to simulate the rhythms of the rocking boat: "the boat rocked, and the trees rocked, and the white dresses and the white flannel trousers drew out long and wavering up the bank" (37). The two aspects of this single position work to embody the felt qualities of perception, that aspect of visual subjectivity so important to Impressionist painting. This is not a symbolic distortion, for we do not transcend a purely physical sensation, just as in *At the Theatre* (fig. 10) Degas concerns himself with pictorial equivalents for the observed effect the physical angle of vision induces.

In *L'Impressionniste* Rivière stresses the objective nature of Degas's correlatives: "He is an observer; he doesn't exaggerate: the effect is always obtained by nature itself, without change. This is what makes him the most precious historian by the visions that shows us."[59]

In exploring the child's perspective in terms of the alteration of spatial relationships of an object to its surroundings, Woolf attends to physical sensations determined by natural conditions, as well as to symbolic overtones. Significantly, she conveys a sense of the vividness and unfamiliarity of objects seen for the first time, using a naive eye that is consistent with the kind of innocence Degas achieves in *At the Theatre*, where his extreme fidelity to a close range view transforms the fan into an exotic organism. In *Jacob's Room*, Woolf demonstrates the way in which the child's physical angle of vision contributes to his sense of being merged with the landscape. To do so, she resists the imposition of an adult corrective, and so we encounter an unexpected configuration that is paradoxically more true to the actual conditions of perception. The alteration through magnification gives the masses on the beach exaggerated dimensions: "The rock was one of those tremendously solid brown, or rather black, rocks which emerge from the sand like something primitive." Those primitive shapes, as Jacob approaches, are differentiated according to gender, species, and color: "he saw, stretched entirely rigid, side by side, their faces very red, an enormous man and woman" (9). Ironically, the child's attempt to delineate the forms in conventional terms—"A large black woman was sitting on the sand" (10)—is reversed, for the Nanny is the rock "covered with the seaweed which pops when it is pressed" (10).

In presenting the same visual data from an adult angle of vision, familiarity is restored, objects lose the child's distortion, and distances contract: "Mrs. Flanders, coming around the rock and covering the whole space of the beach in a few seconds." The juxtaposition of these two points of view illustrates that the articulation of a single scene must vary according to the physical conditions of perception. Certainly the full emotional and psychological complexity of the subjective deformation of objective reality is, as I suggested earlier, Woolf's primary concern, but what one does see here in the novel is evidence of the author's continuing fascination with otherness, which, insofar as it is visualized in her work, resists the humanizing impulse. These attempts at anonymity, to describe the world seen without the mediation of the self before the individual has appropriated it as carrier of his vision and record of his condition, provide the verbal correlative for the naive realism of Impressionist art; both media concretize the apprehension of the surfaces of things, surfaces often concealed by our habit of seeing and by our imposition of inherited schemata.

This kind of detachment is borne out in those scenes in *Jacob's Room* where the meditative intelligence focuses on the physical properties of light in the landscape, intrigued not by their potential metaphysical or symbolic dimen-

Figure 10.   Edgar Degas, *At the Theatre*, 1880
55 × 68 cm.
(Archives Durand-Ruel)

sions but rather absorbed by the way in which light composes or decomposes forms. Significantly, those effects are recorded during the eclipse of the individual light where the personality of the observer is held in abeyance, and the emphasis is placed on the disinterested quality of the eye. In the storm sequence in *Jacob's Room,* for example, the observer explores the sheer physicality of light as life-giver. When Mr. Pearce extinguishes the lamp, "the garden went out." Using the subjunctive mood again to indicate the transition from a subjective to an objective point of view, the observer records the way in which things appear when they are not altered by the pathetic fallacy: "The garden went out. It was but a dark patch. Every inch was rained upon. Every blade of grass was bent by rain. Eyelids would have been fastened down by the rain. Lying on one's back one would have seen nothing but muddle and confusion—clouds turning and turning, and something yellow-tinted and sulphurous in the darkness" (13–14). The very plainness of the prose style itself sustains the sense of the observer's fidelity to a normal and factual vision, just as the indefiniteness of the forms discovered under these conditions emphasizes the depersonalized character of Impressionism's scientific naturalism.

At the same time one is increasingly aware of the provisional nature of external reality, an emphasis which is borne out in the miraculous revelation of the illusion of actuality under the increasing exposure of light, as the observer explores the ephemerality of solid objects at the birth of day:

> But colour returns; runs up the stalks of the grass; blows out into tulips and crocuses; solidly stripes the tree trunks; and fills the gauze of the air and the grasses and pools. . . . And the light mounts over the faces of all the tall blind houses, slides through a chink and paints the lustrous bellying crimson curtains, the green wine-glasses; the coffee-cups, and the chairs standing askew.
>
> Sunlight strikes in upon shaving glasses; and gleaming brass cans; upon all the jolly trappings of the day, the bright, inquisitive, armoured, resplendent summer's day, which has long since vanquished chaos. . . . (163)

In an abbreviated and accelerated way Woolf parallels in her own medium the disembodied quality of forms that characterizes Monet's series view, bringing this sense of contingency to bear upon interior spaces, just as Renoir in *Young Girl at the Window* and *Madame Choquet Reading* explores the implications of outdoor principles of composition through the exchange of interior and exterior light values.

Though Woolf relies on Impressionist techniques to evoke surface in *Jacob's Room,* the narrator as artist clearly demonstrates that Impressionist principles cannot visualize the unseen and make articulate the inner reality of the "silent young man," which is deliberately mute insofar as the narrator remains faithful to the exigencies of an external point of view.

Matthiessen

Whereas *Jacob's Room* as a whole dramatizes the inability of the Impressionist method to disclose Jacob's "true reality," the opening chapters of Peter Matthiessen's *Far Tortuga*, a novel that records the luckless venture of a motley crew of Caymanian turtle men, demonstrate its success in realizing landscape as landscape freed from the pursuit of any inner significance. Like Woolf, Matthiessen experiments with a variety of technical styles to visualize his subject, relying on both Impressionist and Expressionist methods of concretization. He incorporates into the text figural approximations of landscape conditions as epigraphs for chapters and events (fig. 11), architectural drawings, maps, charts, a ship's manifest, and documentary, symbolic, and theatrical modes of visual presentation, all of which work toward the realization of the pictorial.

As an Impressionist artist in a verbal medium, Matthiessen depends upon those techniques that we have discovered in Woolf's novels, and that create illusions of depth through linear and atmospheric perspective. Matthiessen sustains a sense of space by attending to the texture of the air itself: "As the burlap sacks tumble together, motes of dust arise in the sun shaft of the hold."[60] He experiments with a variety of physical angles of vision, preserving in his presentation of the multiple view the anonymity and detachment of the observing eye. In visualizing that eye's sensitivity to fluctuating conditions of illumination, especially in terms of water as a reflecting surface, the observer discovers verbal equivalents for the tonal variations that are induced by the interaction of wind, water and sunlight: "The wind rises as the morning grows, to twenty knots or better, blowing crests off the big seas that cross the small bows of the *Eden*. The broken blues are flecked with torn sargassum" (56).

While the crewmen pit their wits against unexpected weather changes and read aberrations in climatic patterns as portents and symbols, the observer is consistently impartial in his own response, bringing that depersonalized quality to bear on both the landscape and the human configuration. Thus when Wodie Greaves, the vessel's visionary and part-time obeah worker, emerges from the hatch, he is simply "a figure" whose "hair and skin are whitish": "In the twilight he looks silver"; "He laughs a high sweet laugh. In the dry whiteness of his face, which has caked where he has sweated, his mouth looks raw and wet. He is barefoot, in clownish pants too small for him and a bright checkered vest cut from coarse sacking. One eye is blind" (39).

Matthiessen preserves the distinction between depersonalized and human points of view by using two contrasting idioms, one for the recording intelligence who simply registers human and natural events as they occur, and one for the Caymanian sailors themselves, a rich Caribbean dialect that captures the energy and emotion of their very human response to their increasingly futile predicament. Following the destruction of the *Eden*, for example, one after the

Figure 11. Peter Matthiessen, *Far Tortuga*, 1975
(*Courtesy of Random House; copyright © 1975 by Peter Mathiessen*)

Noon.

Dis de bad time of de day. Oh, yes.

Huh?

Oh, yes. Mon got no shadder. Very dangerous time. Cause de shadders of de dead is flyin round, lookin for people dat don't have no shadder.

Afternoon.

De old people, dey taught me. I was just a boy dat loved to keep old people company. I loved to know something about de old people and de old ways. I loved . . .

Wodie sits up smiling, starts to speak again, sees Byrum, stops. He lies back again beside the turtle.

I dyin, Speedy.

Not Speedy, mon. Not dis year, anyways. I goin home.

Speedy winks at Byrum, but Byrum turns away.

Yah, mon. Been goin home all of my life, seem like, and dis time I meanin to remain.

Dark.

Byrum?

Course in de night, if you cotch a spider web across de face, or if you might hear an old cow lowin where no cow belongin, den you know dat dey are dere . . .

Face forward into de bow, Byrum. And stay dat way.

Fuckin black Honduran!

Dass me, okay. I nigger to de bone. (*sighs*) Wodie mon? Shut up, okay? I got to sleep a little, so lay down all across de thwart, 'tween me and Byrum.

Maybe he get me in de night!

No, mon. He get *you*, den he know I get *him*. De only way he gone get you is if he get me first.

other of the remaining crew members perishes. With only two left, and the rhythm of an inevitable doom upon them, Wodie confides to his mate that he has dreamed his own death; yet the observer, apparently immune to the poignancy of this revelation between them, simply records a fugitive meteorological effect: "Daybreak. High in the west, a lone cloud following the night is caught by the sun still under the horizon. The cloud turns pink" (399).

In exploring the landscape during the sunrise of the opening chapters, Matthiessen achieves a kind of Impressionist indefiniteness through verbal abbreviation and ellipses. Perhaps the finest example of this kind of verbal Impressionism as one dimension of Matthiessen's multiple styles is achieved here through the elimination of connectives, to underline the zones of silence between the image sequences that realize this process. Unlike the interlude sequences of *The Waves*, where light primarily functions thematically and the growth and decline of the phenomenal world operates as symbolic content for the drama of the six characters, Matthiessen's interlude light, which establishes place, is absolutely material. He restrains the impulse toward humanistic analogies and context by giving us surfaces only. To create a verbal illusion of stasis and simultaneity, Matthiessen uses only present tense verbs, or eliminates verbs entirely through infinitives and participial phrases—decelerating movement by compressing images, discarding subordinate conjunctions completely, and relying on simple connectives to inhibit linearity and deprive the verbal medium itself of its usual temporal conditions. The reader has a sense of advancing through the space that the longitudinal notations suggest, and yet of absorbing randomly illuminated details, simulating the conditions of normal binocular vision in a panoramic sweep of the sea from the bow of a moving schooner:

Daybreak

At Windward Passage, four hundred miles due east, the sun is rising. Wind east-northeast, thirty-eight knots, with gusts to forty-five: a gale.

Black waves, wind-feathered. White birds, dark birds.

The trade winds freshen at first light, and the sea rises in long ridges, rolling west.

Sunrise at longitude 76, 19 degrees north latitude.

Sunrise at longitude 77.

Sunrise at the lesser Caymans. Horizon rises from horizon. To the westward, Grand Cayman is gray; its high cumulus, visible to migrant birds a hundred miles away, is a gray-pink.

The sun, coming hard around the world: the island rises from the sea, sinks, rises, holds. (5)

Not only does Matthiessen's verbal rhythm approximate the movement of the boat during the gale winds, it also stresses the provisional nature of the forms themselves during daybreak conditions. Especially significant are the planes of color which articulate transitions in the seascape: "Daybreak at Gun Bay Village, at East End. Parted, the Antilles Current caroms on the reef. The new light turns the sea from black to blue, the surf from gray to white, the hulks high on the reef from rust to black. Sunrise at Old Isaacs. . . . The sun kindles the thatch of hip-roofed cottages, built at East End since early days. Sand road, white pickets, periwinkle; white sand yards bordered with pink conchs" (6). The observer revels in the synesthesia created by undifferentiated shapes and colors at Sunrise: "Sunrise at Meagre Bay and Bodden Town, on the white road of coral marl that trails along the emerald sounds of the south shore. Fringing the sounds is the long reef and beyond the reef, cold deep blues of the abyss" (6). The second passage also provides a particularly effective instance of the appeal to tactile and auditory memories that, along with the visual sensations, enable the beholder to reconstitute the three-dimensional form in her mind. At the same time, the nautical abbreviations interjected through the image motif give us the balance of precision, through the scientific and the indefinite, through the diffuseness of objects, that characterizes Monet's *The Grenouillère,* where the figure's profile is lost in the reflections on the water, and where the glittering sky, shore, and river seem suspended through the perforated screen of cool shadow in the foreground. In *The Grenouillère* the observer enjoys the truth of sensations that accord with the perceptual moment experienced through half-closed eyes, even while she absorbs the suggestion of spatial relation that allows her to reconstitute the third dimension, which is evoked rather than fully articulate.

If we understand that Matthiessen is concerned with making an art of surfaces, we can perhaps appreciate his insensitivity to the usual who-what-why-where questions that are traditionally provided for in the exposition of a narrative. In one sense his evasion of those questions, whose answers would integrate the disparate passages, approximates the kind of emphasis upon two-dimensionality that is intrinsic to Monet's exploration of the façade of his Rouen Cathedral. It is an emphasis that is concretized pictorially throughout the novel in images that stress the flatness of the painted surface: "In the port boat, the two stiff figures are black sticks on the white sky" (380); "The harbor, no more than a shallow bight on the western shore, flattens out against the islands as the pastels of Georgetown drop away" (38). This evocation of shallowness is of course central to the surface effects of Impressionist art and implicit in its resistance to sculptural completeness.

Matthiessen makes no effort to integrate the historical synopsis provided in his introduction into the scenic method that follows in chapter 1 of the novel. They appear as two discrete linguistic modes to represent the same place. So, too, he emphasizes the relativity of vision that any Impressionist serial approach endorses. We are made aware of how our sense of the realities that they appear to embody is contingent upon point of view. Though Matthiessen uses multiple points of view, their quality of depersonalization is consistent throughout, and therefore the scientific exactitude of his nautical shorthand, the brief visual footnotes that are rich in color architectonics that annotate them, and the historical preview itself occur together without creating any sense of disparity or dramatic irony.

The observing eye, regardless of linguistic mode, is as equivocal and as unprejudiced as the new sun which actualizes color and form in the landscape. In remaining faithful to the perceptual present, Matthiessen repudiates continuity and the accumulated sense of what a thing is that a concern with continuity would uphold. His "pictures" disappoint expectations set up by the conventional plotting of objects, for by a particular defect of narrative memory his observing eye fails to make connections and relate details, a failure that allows him to perceive the human combatants in the actual story as patterns in the landscape. The inherited meanings of things are continually called into question by descriptions whose meanings are partial, provisional, and often contradictory, or at least true only for a particular moment of time.

In the scenic passages of the opening chapter, the observing eye moves freely through the landscape from the panoramic to the microscopic, absorbed by randomly illuminated details or arrested by particularly effective color contrasts: "Green parrots cross the sunburst to the mango trees. Light polishes gray-silver cabin sides, glows the bolls of the wild cotton, shines the dun flanks of a silken cow in pastures of rough guinea grass; a gumbo limbo tree, catching up the sun in red translucent peels of shedding bark, glows on black burned-over ground between gray jutting bones of ocean limestone" (7).

By repeating parallel grammatical structures ("Sunrise at") to introduce each image, Matthiessen achieves a gallery effect as if the reader, as beholder, were walking through an exhibition of seascapes, each titled to indicate the specific locale of the visual impression, while the composite effect on the viewer would alert him to the fact that the actual subject is "Sunrise" itself. We are reminded immediately of the controversial work by Monet, *Impression, Sunrise,* which initiated those basic misconceptions about pictorial Impressionism. Significantly, with Matthiessen, each visual impression works to achieve the single esthetic impression of sunrise, such that any individual object has significance only in terms of its capacity as a reflecting surface. At the same time, Matthiessen purposely delays the story values by introducing the rhythms of the sea inaudibly in the penultimate paragraph: "the roof of the church is wind-slotted, battered by gales. Lizards scatter in the leaves and sun-spots that stray in the church door, and a hermit crab, snapped shut, rocks minutely in the silence" (7). In the final paragraph, those rhythms are more forcefully articulate as a prelude to the sea story which begins with the dedication to William Parchment and the emergence of the "three walking figures and a dog" in the next chapter: "In the graveyard behind the falling church grows oleander and white frangipani. On the ironstone below, incoming seas burst through black fissures in the rock, and black crabs scutter" (7).

Certainly in terms of the staging of Matthiessen's Jonah story, the juxtaposition of this final sequence of objects—the decaying church, the graveyard behind it, the black crabs scurrying to evade the bursting sea and the dedication to William Parchment—contributes to our sense of the inevitability of the ensuing action. Read retrospectively, the Impressionistic rendering of the sunrise series emphasizes the disparity between the eternality and neutrality of the nonhuman order, and the fugitive and futile ephemerality of human existence. On the other hand, one can suggest that this sequence, which helps to orchestrate the opening of the novel, is perhaps one of the finest examples of literary Impressionism in Modernist fiction and, as such, clearly demonstrates that the kind of viable correspondence between verbal and visual Impressionism that does exist is dramatically different from that which our prevailing critical assumptions would have us believe.

This revaluation is especially significant for the literary critic, because it allows her in discussing Sinclair Ross's *As for Me and My House,* for example, to temper the usual critical classification of Philip's work as modernist-abstractionist[61] with the recognition of the applicability of Impressionist principles of design. The recurrence of the same Main Street scene with its "false fronts" or the prairie landscape as pictorial subject becomes indicative of Philip's interest in phenomena exposed to almost unchanging conditions of drought and wind rather than with the drama of the human condition lived within that landscape. It is precisely Philip's scientific detachment as artist and his concern with purely esthetic emotions—"in art, memories and associations don't count. A good way to test a picture is to turn it upside down. That knocks all the sentiment out of it, leaves you with just the design and form"[62]—that elude or bewilder Mrs. Bentley's romantic and literary temperament. Insofar as she interprets the artist's objectivity as an indictment of her husband's insensitivity or domestic frustration, she misreads his esthetic intention. And, conversely, if we examine the recurrent landscape pieces that she as a verbal artist executes, we become aware that the subject of this series is the weather itself, while her inability to resist the imposition of the pathetic fallacy allows us to see her as an Expressionist artist using landscape forms to express herself more completely: "It's an immense night out there, wheeling and windy. The lights on the street and in the house are helpless against the black wetness, little unilluminating glints that might be painted on it. The town seems huddled together, cowering on a high, tiny perch, afraid to move lest it topple into the wind" (5).

In Impressionist art one accepts the dislocation and disorientation that attends the loss of the traditional response or familiar vision of the landscape, not as a new kind of subjective or psychological realism, but rather as an extension of the principles of scientific naturalism that had begun with Courbet and Corot in the middle of the nineteenth century. The transformation of the known into the unknown that is effected by Impressionism's detached and disinterested approach to its subject is the result of the Impressionists' concern with the reality of their sensations, a reality that is objectively verifiable by attending to the lighted surface. It is a concern which has style-forming implications, to generate a series of techniques capable of rendering the interdependence of light and color, the diffuseness of outlines, and the ephemerality of the object's appearance whose illusion of solidity is contingent upon the transfiguring power of light and the quality and texture of the atmosphere informed by this reciprocity.

These are techniques which find their verbal counterpart in depersonalized and detached third-person points of view, in preferences for distant or close-up views, and in the development of color lexicons that will make the medium exquisitely responsive to delicate gradations in tonal values, and to the diffuseness of forms under varying atmospheric conditions. The incomplete and the indefinite in the plastic medium find their verbal correlative in linguistic surfaces, which achieve comparable effects through omission and ellipses, through parataxis and the alteration of usual syntactical patterns—effects that attempt to create the illusion of a random and momentary perception of the accidents of time and place.

While the Impressionist, as Charles Gauss suggests in *The Aesthetic Theories of French Artists*, "records the perceptual surface of the world, its lighted visual surface," the Post-Impressionist artist undertakes an exploration beneath those very surfaces, inquiring into the "metaphysical constituents" of its interior.[63] The Post-Impressionist artist sees himself capable of realizing a more profound vision by throwing off the obligation to recreate the surface aspects of the tangible world. He chafes at the restraints imposed by the emphasis upon the notion of verisimilitude, which had shaped Impressionism's fidelity to the given.

On the one hand, the Post-Impressionist perception of Impressionist art encouraged critics to accuse the Impressionist artist of a certain kind of superfluity and formlessness. On the other hand, the Impressionist's commitment to an accurate rendering of the external scene, a commitment that resulted in the alteration or transformation of conventional modes of presentation, seemed to sanction the subjectivist emphasis intrinsic to the expressive theories of art that followed Impressionism. In Post-Impressionism, the imaginative and penetrative eye of the artist seeks to discover patterns of significance the Impressionist artist never felt the obligation to pursue.

In allowing a Post-Impressionist prejudice against Impressionist art to define Impressionism in general, literary critics conceive of notions of passivity and alienation that simply do not coincide with the actual nature and function of perceptual naivety in Impressionist art. By recovering a clearer sense of the way in which surface, moment, and point of view operate within Impressionist art, it is possible to discover correspondences within the verbal arts where correlative techniques realize in kind the perceptual realism that Impressionist art embodies.

2

Conceptual Realism:
"Monadic Perspectives" and "Mackerel Eyes"

First used in 1910 by Fry in reference to the exhibition he entitled "Manet and the Post-Impressionists," the term *Post-Impressionism* was used to describe all art following the decline of Impressionism after the Group Exhibition in 1877. Thus, Post-Impressionism has been burdened with the all-but-impossible task of consolidating a number of diverse styles and theories of art that were incubating within the artistic community and first made public in 1884, the year of the foundation of the *Salon des Indépendants* in Paris. Through the one-man exhibitions and group shows which culminated in the creation of the *Salon*— notable for its exhibition that year of Seurat's *Bathing at Asnières,* which had earlier been refused by the official Salon—Post-Impressionism extended and intensified the debate between official and unofficial art which had engulfed Monet's *Impression, Sunrise* ten years before.

Fry's 1910 exhibit, which included representative works by Paul Cézanne, Paul Gauguin, and Vincent van Gogh, as well as by younger artists like Henri Matisse, Georges Rouault, Pablo Picasso, André Derain, and Maurice de Vlaminck, created its own turbulence. As Richard Shone observes in *The Post-Impressionists,* "the public came to laugh, the newspapers published caricatures and lampoons and the battle over Post-Impressionism had begun."[1] The words "anarchist," "degenerate," and "madmen" expressed reviewing critics' indignation, while to counter this assertion of a Post-Impressionist pathology, the theme of the embattled artist became a favorite motif of the Post-Impressionist artist himself.

There were, however, champions of the movement, like Fry, who saw in Post-Impressionism a return to tradition after what he considered the aberrant experimentation of Impressionism, and, in *Vision and Design,* Fry attempted to clarify the structural principles he felt operative within Post-Impressionist art. So too, Bell celebrated the movement as a return to order, an affirmation of the first commandment of art, "Thou shalt create form."[2] For these estheticians, Post-Impressionism's architectonic character renewed interest in the constructive power of the plastic medium. In addition, since the penetrative eye of the artist could disclose an order or harmony beneath the manifold of surface appearance, discussions of Post-Impressionist art also involved speculations as to the nature and impact of the personality of the artist in the creation of form.

To describe this synthesis of formal and expressive values Bell coined the phrase "Significant Form," a concept which depended upon his belief in the evocative value of form: "In each [work of art] lines and colours combined in a particular way, certain forms and relations of forms, stir our aesthetic emotions. These relations and combinations of lines and colours, these aesthetically moving forms, I call 'Significant Forms'" (22). In turn, Bell's esthetic hypothesis of Significant Form became inextricably bound up with a metaphysical one: art expresses through pure form the "essential reality," the "God in everything," the "universal in the particular," "the all-pervading rhythm" (54). This marriage of the Classical (i.e., formal) and the Romantic (i.e., emotive) values in Post-Impressionist esthetics opened the door once again to a critical consideration of the redemptive, indeed hieratic, function of art.

Within a Post-Impressionist canvas, there is always the paradoxical and enigmatic interplay between the appearance of the object as it is perceived by the conventionally trained eye, and the object as it exists on the canvas transformed by the penetrative eye of the creative artist. This tension between "appearance" and "reality" is engendered by both the subjective alteration of external forms occasioned by the nature and intention of the artist, and by the objective alterations necessitated by the laws of color and line and the two dimensions of the picture plane. The axis of Post-Impressionism, therefore, involves a symbiotic relation between the artist and his subject expressed through the deformation of landscape and human form, and any viable definition of Post-Impressionism must guard against the temptation to overemphasize either the subjective or the objective nature of the deformations so conceived.

The critical tendency to focus exclusively on subjective values in Post-Impressionist art is exemplified by Cheney, who, in *Expressionism in Art,* endorses the tendency in the 1920s to assimilate Post-Impressionism generally into Expressionist Art. Alternately, the tendency to stress objective values is exemplified by R. H. Wilenski, whose *Modern Movement in Art* rules out van Gogh and Gauguin because their subjectivity is incompatible with his emphasis upon the formal dimensions of Post-Impressionism's return to "the severely classical idea of architecture as the mother of the arts."[3]

Any valid definition of Post-Impressionism must, moreover, accommodate the variety of roles assigned to nature by the Post-Impressionist artists, and discover those key technical developments that allowed them as a group to concretize their collective sense of the basic convention of their medium, i.e., its two dimensions, and hence the nonrepresentational character of their art. In *Post-Impressionism from van Gogh to Gauguin,* Rewald traces the development of the period from the incomplete and final 1886 Impressionist exhibition through the next twenty years. Within this relatively short period of time, Rewald observes, groups composed of artists who "did not follow each other or exist simultaneously in clearly defineable form" "assembled and dispersed with great fluidity" and "with no particular homogeneity."[4] Rewald concludes his historical exposition by quoting the Belgian poet Emile Verhaeren who, after his first visit to the *Salon des Indépendants* exhibit, exclaimed with some measure of frustration: "There is no longer any single school, there are scarcely any groups, and those few are constantly splitting. All these tendencies make me think of moving and kaleidoscope geometric patterns, which clash at one moment only to unite at another, which now fuse and then separate and fly apart a little later, but which all nevertheless revolve within the same circle, that of the new art."[5] The "new art" above all else implies Post-Impressionism's fascination with processes of abstraction through which the pictorial space is achieved, where abstraction implies the freedom to alter the surface aspect of nature according to both the conditions of the medium and the vision of the artist.

The Post-Impressionist reaction against Impressionism's scientific naturalism does not, however, imply a total rejection of the stylistic developments that had taken place under the Impressionists' hand. Post-Impressionist artists absorbed Impressionism's new discoveries in composition, specifically the influence of Japanese prints and photography, extended the liberation of subject matter initiated by the outdoor tradition, and continued and expanded experiments in the use of an unadulterated color. They explored the deeper implications of the naivety of Monet's innocent eye and the optimism of Renoir's sun-drenched boulevards. Further, they fostered interest in the naive or primitive art form and the potentially salutary and revelatory role of instinct and intuition in the creative act.

Yet they had objections. Because light was the prevailing interest of Impressionist artists, forms dissolved and the expression of volume became elusive at best. For many Post-Impressionists that interest was of itself indicative of both a technical and philosophical superficiality and "woolliness," and led often to the charge that there was "a danger of too much eye and not enough mind" (Shone, 16).

Fry's response to Impressionism becomes characteristic of those artists who saw themselves returning to pure art, to the recovery of form and the conceptual basis of the created image. Though the Impressionist artist sought to create life, and arouse this within the observer through the sharing of the visual experience, he never spoke of the sharing of feeling; thus, for many Post-Impressionists, the expressive, as well as the formal, value of their medium was ignored by Impressionist artists. Further, an increasing emphasis on the act of intellection in the artistic process—the conception that art was an act of mind and not of eye alone—led to charges of insufficiency, not only of form and feeling, but of meaning as well. Disenchanted with what was defined as "looseness of design" and triviality of thought, Post-Impressionist artists questioned the validity and significance of an artistic process that seemed to measure its worth on the basis of eighteenth-century standards of fidelity to external nature.

In questioning the validity of the innocent eye and the issue of exact transcription in Impressionist art, the Post-Impressionists were in fact confronting pictorially the philosophy of doubt that had gained currency in the Post-Romantic Chiliasm of the late nineteenth century. As Hans Hess notes in *Pictures as Arguments,* "what was placed in doubt at the beginning of the twentieth century was exactly the unchanging stable nature of material reality."[6] Part of the Post-Impressionist disenchantment with Impressionist art is based on the former's intuitive understanding of the way in which the new physics would challenge established assumptions with respect to the supposedly stable nature of space and time. The personal optic of Impressionism's innocent eye inadvertently demonstrated the way in which objective reality could be altered by individual perception and angle of vision. The world of objective observation was therefore placed in doubt by virtue of an artistic process that, while endeavoring to render the thing as it appeared, revealed rather the elusiveness of the surface aspect and the transformative power of individual eye. While Impressionist naturalism expressed a positivist conception of nature, the Post-Impressionist emphasis upon the penetrative eye and absorption with "real" significance clearly confirmed that the so-called facts of vision were not absolute. As Carol Donnell-Kotrozo observes in *Critical Essays on Postimpressionism,* it became increasingly apparent to Post-Impressionist artists that the "observed nature of external 'objective' phenomena" was "a product of human consciousness" and depended "upon the method of observation of the perceiving subject."[7] The technical means that Renaissance masters had developed to accomplish the illusion of three-dimensional space, of volume and texture, and of an "accurate" reproduction, included linear or single-point perspective, which in itself was the logical expression of fourteenth-century naturalism. The means that foster this kind of naturalism are possible, Hess suggests, only in a "social and spiritual climate which made the acceptance and observation of the material world possible" (17). The Impressionist artist accepted the spatial convention of the Renaissance tradition of illusionist art, and part of that acceptance was based upon his faith that the appearance of material reality and the "fact" of reality were one and the same. In questioning the sufficiency of the Renaissance creed, Post-Impressionist artists were acknowledging their sense of this potential discrepancy.

Once the plastic medium was no longer charged with the task of recreating the three-dimensional spatial illusion, artists were free to explore the medium's two-dimensionality. To declare the reality of the picture plane, Cézanne, for example, challenges the dominance of linear and atmospheric perspective techniques, while van Gogh explores their expressive and symbolic possibilities. In forsaking the principles of construction integral to Renaissance art, or in adapting them to serve other ends, the Post-Impressionist dramatically alters the relationship between the observer and the canvas. In his examination of the Renaissance space conception, Hess describes its open-window convention in terms of a continuum between the picture space and the space of the observer: "The spectator stood outside the frame at an appropriate distance calculated by the artist and could look into and become part of that spatial organization. . . . Whatever the artist painted was painted from one point of view and the spectator could enter the picture. The more realistic art became, the easier it was made for the spectator to enter a world he knew" (35). Without a fixed position, a clearly articulate external point of view, and the assurance that the pictorial space was coextensive with the observer's, the conventionally trained eye had to adapt to the ambiguities that attend the construction of multiple and internalized points of view in Post-Impressionist art.

Although the effort to reveal the subject from within necessitates a certain loss of security and certainty for the observer, that loss is compensated for to the degree that the observer is allowed to participate in the lived perspective of the perceiving consciousness. Cézanne, in both his still lifes and landscapes, eliminates the fixed standing ground of the observer and brings the spectator into the picture space on more than one exclusively visual level. The spectator is assailed by the sum of disparate perspectives that the artist introduces to give a composite view of the object; thus he must adjust his trained set of expectations, and experience the object both visually and tactually.

In his discussion of the space conception within Cézanne's canvases, André Lhote observes that Cézanne "gives to each object the place and the size that its expressive quality assigns to it [a kind of 'depth, perceived through feeling'] rather than that which results from distance [*éloignement* or the application of classical perspective] and which the absurd work of the academies pitilessly fixes." Lhote's conception of *perspective vécue* provides a most adequate analysis of the difference between depth illusion generated by classical perspective and that created by Cézanne's systematic application of overlapping planes. "With each field pushing the other," Lhote observes, "the eye is maneuvered in front, then behind, is forced to realize a third dimension": "Genius consists in knowing how to compensate, through constant repetition of each phenomenon, for every thrust into depth, by an *equal* advance or return. Without this ruse, the eye would immediately find the horizon, the distance, without being excited by the successive oppositions, which retard its quest for space, and procure for it a subtle pleasure." For Lhote "this depth, perceived through feeling, is of a different quality, of a different essence, if one may say it, from that physical depth which, offered to the guilty eye, seems to create a hole in the picture, and takes away from it *the mural character which so many generations of painters have so virtuously respected.*"[8]

Finally, the flat plane that conditioned Post-Impressionism's approach to nature established a profound appreciation for the enclosed and organic nature of the pictorial illusion. For the Post-Impressionist the picture becomes, above all, a flat painted surface on which the artist can create spaces and dimensions which heretofore did not exist. As such the Post-Impressionist canvas explores the paradoxical relation between art and reality fostered by its sense of art as penetrative, transformative, and revelatory.

The Post-Impressionist feels himself capable of realizing a more profound vision of the mind's experience of the essential character of external reality. Though in its positive aspect Impressionism meant a return to the sun, to diffused light and freedom of composition, it was perceived retrospectively, by Gauguin, for example, as merely the perpetuation of the "shackles of verisimilitude."[9] In eschewing surface verisimilitude, which seemed to suggest the passive, acquiescent, and nonintellectual character of Impressionist art, the Post-Impressionist accent was placed upon what Donnell-Kotrozo defines as the "felt apprehension of the value-laden external world" (111–12). The Post-Impressionist artist sought to imbue the moment of perception with far greater authority, for he felt it contained within it the basic motifs of existence. We move therefore from the Impressionist optic—the pure optical response to reality—to perception as conception which acknowledges the complexity of the perceptual act and the fusion which takes place between external object and perceiving subject. This distinction between conception and perception parallels Immanuel Kant's differentiation between sensation and perceptual experience in his analysis of the relation between sensation and perceptual experience in the *Prolegomena*. Throughout Post-Impressionist discussions, the absorbing interest rests with hidden realities beyond sense data as part of the thrust to penetrate life as surface and discover the integrating structures of a more permanent order.

This reappraisal of the role of the painted surface in art brings with it the recognition of the autonomy of the picture space. In his discussion of Seurat and Neo-Impressionism, for example, Fry notes that for all its decorative flatness, for all its theoretical and abstract coloring, the canvas is intensely real, "but for all its reality, nothing of the original theme, of the thing seen, remains untransformed, all has been assimilated and remade by the idea." Perhaps, Fry suggests, "the complete transformation of the theme by the idea is the test of great art," for "it means that in proportion as a picture attains to this independent reality and inherent significance, the element of illustration drops out altogether and becomes irrelevant" (*Transformations*, 194–95). Though Seurat's optical mixture is based on the artist's systematic and analytical observations of the nuances of light and shade in nature, his canvases, rather than providing a transcription of natural effects, may exaggerate the difference between art and reality. Meyer Schapiro defines that difference by observing that Seurat's dots move beyond transcription to create a "special kind of order": "the visual world is not perceived as a mosaic of colored points, but this artificial micro-pattern serves the painter as a means of ordering, proportioning and nuancing sensation beyond the familiar qualities of the objects that the colors evoke."[10] Post-Impressionism engages the outdoor commitment of van Gogh and Cézanne— outdoor insofar as both felt nature played a determining role in their pursuit of its essential character. When Gauguin questions the necessity of requiring a model, of painting from nature or even producing after her, he is not referring to any desire to abandon nature, but is rather expressing his need to move beyond naturalistic imitation so that, as Donnell-Kotrozo observes, the canvas becomes an "equivalent" or "symbol" of the artist's profound experience of visual reality (44). One can, therefore, describe the transition from Impressionist to Post-Impressionist principles in terms of a shift from *enargia* to *energia,* from the mimesis of an optic to the mimesis of a perceptual experience, from the mimesis of the first sensation to the mimesis of the way in which the evaluative eye of the artist interacts with matter.

Monet's development becomes indicative of this new attitude toward the painted reality, an attitude embryonic in the Etretat and Belle-Isle paintings of 1886. In their discussion of Monet's Giverny canvases, Charles Moffett and James Wood observe that at this time subjective factors begin to play an even greater role in his work: "he had begun to paint his experience of certain phenomena rather than the phenomena themselves."[11] The primary motivation for undertaking a serial approach rests with the fact that in fragmenting the subject into a succession of observed moments the objective accuracy of the record is increased. Ironically, as Robert Goldwater points out, as the greater accuracy in fact depends upon an acute sensibility in the artist, the degree of subjectivity is also increased. Goldwater writes in *Symbolism* that even in the Etretat paintings "Monet had gone beyond naturalistic accuracy," and he shows that through a process of concentration and reduction—the "simplification of design, purification of rhythm, elimination of contrasting detail, lessening of perspective, dominance of a single hue"[12]—Monet moves beyond the very principles of Impressionism that motivated him initially. Goldwater describes the paradox in the following way: "The exacerbation of the impressionist method has led to a work that stands for rather than represents the object" (2).

Thus Monet's *Poplars* (fig. 12), with its decorative simplicity and delicate nuance, is more evocative than representational, reflecting not so much a change in the repertory of objects depicted as a changing interpretation in the significance that those objects possess for the artist. If we take Monet's *Poplars* as indicative of the movement beyond scientific realism, we can describe the transition from Impressionism to Post-Impressionism generally as the movement from Monet's "innocent eye"—the naivety of vision suggested in his paintings before these later serial pictures—to the individual eye, from detachment to involvement, from acquiescence to transformation, from transcription to interpretation, from rendering a corner (the slice of life) to suggesting totalities, and from the celebration of change to the pursuit of permanence.

The conception of art as an independent creation that is not descriptive of a material reality becomes Gauguin's absorbing theme. Gauguin is fascinated with the quality of abstraction involved in the creative process, and he advises his friends: "do not paint too much after nature. Art is an abstraction; derive this abstraction from nature while dreaming before it, and think more of the creation which will result than of nature. Creating like our Divine Master is the only way of rising toward God."[13] Gauguin wished to avoid any impulse that would provide the illusion of a photographable reality. In affirming the creative eye, he asked that the artist not expend his energies competing with the *trompe l'oeil* of the sun as the Impressionists had done, but rather appropriate its effects to serve his own pictorial ends: "I will get as far away as possible from that which gives the illusion of a thing, and since shadows are the *trompe l'oeil* of the sun, I am inclined to do away with them. . . . put in shadows if you consider them useful, or don't put them in. It's all the same thing, if you consider yourself not a slave to shadow; it is, as it were, the shadow which is at your service" (letter 75, *Lettres de Gauguin,* 149–50).

In "Notes Synthetiques," which was published in 1910, Gauguin elaborates upon the position of the artist more fully: "Yet you have fewer means than nature, and you condemn yourself to renounce all those which it puts at your disposal. Will you ever have as much light as nature, as much heat as the sun? And you speak of exaggeration—but how can you exaggerate since you remain below nature?"[14] Art was, for Gauguin, above all a freeing from what he felt was the "tyranny" of the eye. Writing ten years after the letter to Schuffenecker in "Diverses Choses, 1896–1897," Gauguin's own symbolist tendencies occupy the foreground as "the mysterious centres of thought" neglected by Impressionists who "heed only the eye." With respect to technique, he observes that he does not have one, "or rather I do have one, but it is very fugitive, very flexible, according to my disposition when I arise in the morning; a technique which I apply in my own manner to express my own thought without any concern for the truth of the common exterior aspects of Nature" (qtd. in Chipp, 65).

In much the same way, van Gogh, in an 1888 letter to Bernard, refers to the imagination as that "faculty which we must develop, one which alone can lead us to the creation of a more exalting and consoling nature than the single brief glance at reality . . . can let us perceive."[15] For van Gogh this "exalting and consoling nature" is one which manifests a fundamental truth that is revealed by persistent observation of the same spot: "this corner of the garden is a good example of what I was telling you, that to get at the real character of

Figure 12. Claude Monet, *Poplars*, 1891
32½″ × 32⅛″.
(The Metropolitan Museum of Art, the H. O. Havemeyer
Collection; bequest of Mrs. H. O. Havemeyer, 1919)

things here, you must look at them and paint them for a long time" (letter 541, *Letters of van Gogh* 3:48). Cézanne's discussion of the thinking eye most fully embodies the middle ground of Post-Impressionist thought: "There is a logic of color; the painter owes obedience to this alone, and never to the logic of the intellect. He must always follow the logic of his eyes. If he feels accurately, he will think accurately. Painting is primarily a matter of optics. The matter of our art lies there, in what our eyes are thinking" (qtd. in Dunstan, 122).

The concept of transformation implied by both Cézanne and van Gogh gained currency through Maurice Denis's 1909 article "Subjective and Objective Deformation," a statement that helps clarify the way in which the artist deforms sensation into meaning through personal apperception, where apperception implies the operation of both the imagination and the intellect. The term "subjective deformation" was first used by Jean Moreas, whose Symbolist and Literary Manifesto of 1886 attacked the Naturalist school of literature. It was subsequently paraphrased by Dujardin in his definition of Louis Anquetin's Cloisonism, an innovative technique that, like the stained-glass window that influenced Gauguin's decorative emphasis, focused on simplicity of design, strong outlines surrounding each vibrant flat tone, and the avoidance of modeling. Calling the depiction of objects as they appear in nature a chimera, Dujardin said the aim of painting was to employ special means, line and color vigorously defined, to express not the appearance, but rather the sentiment and character of objects. This artistic ideal therefore emphasized the symbolic dimension of Post-Impressionist principles of construction. The concept of deformation absorbed by both Bernard and Denis, members of the *Nabis* who exaggerated the symbolism inherent in Gauguin's esthetic, obliged the artist to distort natural appearance. Denis's discussion, in particular, brings into focus the notion of plastic or formal equivalence, which is expressive throughout of a synthesis of subject and object. It is in this context that the Post-Impressionist canvas itself functions as a correlative for the artist's conception of reality.

Taking as his point of departure Gauguin's statement that instead of "working with the eye, we search in the mysterious centre of thought," Denis writes: "Art is no longer only a visual sensation which we record, only a photograph, however refined it may be, of nature. . . . Art, instead of being a *copy*, becomes the *subjective deformation* of nature."[16] Denis's article accentuates the significance of equivalence, as opposed to representation or copy, to underline the difference between style and nature that the nineteenth-century academicians ignored:

> The Masters never distinguished between reality, as an element in art at least, and the interpretation of reality. Their drawings and their studies from nature have just as much style as their paintings. The word ideal is misleading; it dates from an era of materialistic art. One does not stylize artificially, after the event, a stupid copy of nature. "Do what you like, so long as it is

intelligent," Gauguin said. Even when he imitates, the genuine artist is a poet. The technique, the content, the aim of his art warn him well enough not to confuse the *object* that he creates with the spectacle of nature which is the subject of it. The Symbolist viewpoint asks us to consider the work of art as an equivalent of sensation received; thus nature can be, for the artist, only a state of his own subjectivity. And what we call subjective distortion is virtually style. (107)

In emphasizing the primacy of technique and the autonomy of the canvas, Denis is also underlining the ambiguity that naturally attends the artist's recognition of the subjectivity of vision and the provisional nature of epistemology. The Renaissance tradition that sustained a consensus of meaning with respect to conventional stylistic and iconographic elements loses its power in the course of the nineteenth century, so that one moves from collectively sanctioned to highly individualized symbols that provide meaningful equivalents for an idiosyncratic experience of external reality. Denis's famous definition of art, which was inspired by Gauguin's own sense of title as signature, effectively summarizes the Post-Impressionist position: "It is well to remember that a picture—before being a battle horse, a nude woman, or some anecdote—is essentially a plane surface covered with colors assembled in a certain order."[17] Denis's definition was derived from Gauguin's pronouncement from Pont-Aven in 1880, a pronouncement which was transmitted by Paul Sérusier and Denis himself who, with others, formed the *Académie Julian* in Paris and absorbed Gauguin's principles into their more pronounced Symbolist esthetic: "How do you see this tree," Gauguin had said, standing in one of the corners of the *Bois d'Amour*. "Is it really green? Use green then, the most beautiful green on your palette. And that shadow, rather blue? Don't be afraid to paint it as blue as possible."[18]

As with Cézanne and van Gogh, it becomes increasingly apparent that a personal and intuitive standard of truth replaces any scientific notion of accuracy. The emphasis is placed not on the thing as it is as natural fact, but rather on the thing as it is apprehended and felt by the penetrative eye. Fry recognized the paradoxical relation between art and reality through his own experience of the 1910 Post-Impressionist Exhibition. He observes that "it is not the object of those artists to exhibit their skill or proclaim their knowledge, but only to attempt to express by pictorial and plastic form certain spiritual experiences. . . . By that I mean that they wish to make images which by the clearness of their logical structure, and by their closely-knit unity of texture, shall appeal to our disinterested and contemplative imagination with something of the same vividness as things of actual life appeal to our practical activities. In fact they aim not at illusion but at reality."[19]

The canvas becomes, therefore, the formal plastic equivalent for apperception of reality. For those like Bernard and Denis who, as members of the *Nabis*, sought through symbolic painting an alternate religion, the concept of deformation is couched in the language of communion. Thus Bernard, in discussion with Cézanne, speaks of art "as a union of the universe and the individual."[20]

In Post-Impressionist esthetics there is the continuing sense that the artist's fidelity both to nature and to the two dimensions of the canvas leads to the revelation of the essential structure of the landscape form. Lhote translates Denis's statement about the primacy of the flat plane and the creative act into his own terms, suggesting that "in the midst of the modern deliquescence" the Post-Impressionists offer "the only landscapes which express depth by means of stepped-up planes, without attaining it in a stupid sense; the only landscapes in which one can experience an idealistic promenade, not by foot, but with the spirit. These constructions offer us a monumental succession of natural elements, held together somehow by the steps of an imaginary stairway, which rises from the ground and opens up into the sky, but with the last step returning wisely to the level of the first" (qtd. in Loran, 33).

In his discussion of the differences between our experiences of the spatial illusion in perspective and Post-Impressionist art, Marshall McLuhan in *the Gutenberg galaxy* argues that the rediscovery of the mural character of art during this period allowed for a reintegration of the senses. The traditional three-dimensional illusion of Renaissance perspective with its fixed visual point of view depended for its success upon their separation: "It is the three-dimensional world of pictorial space [which, according to Gombrich in his analysis of illusionist art, is a conventionally acquired mode of seeing rather than the normal mode of human vision] that is, indeed, an abstract illusion built on the intense separation of the visual from the other senses."[21] The Renaissance spatial illusion not only violates the two-dimensional convention of the medium but, because of its exclusive emphasis upon the sense of sight in deliberate isolation from the other senses, especially the sense of touch, denies to the observer the kind of "tactile synesthesia" (17) or interplay among the senses that is integral to normal vision. McLuhan notes that "men have 'since Cézanne' abandoned the visual" three-dimensional world of Renaissance pictorial space "in favor of the audile-tactile modes of awareness and organization." It is the multidimensionality of primitive two-dimensional art that the modern space conception rediscovers.

Cézanne respects the flat surface by integrating two- and three-dimensional elements through the interstructural resonances of stepped-up planes. Rather than allowing the observer to participate within the pictorial space on anything but a visual level, Cézanne assaults the eye through multifaceted planes, which maximizes the interplay among visual and tactile sensations. These planes, which construct the pyramid that provides the illusion of a penetration into deep space, also, by their powerful horizontality, assert the reality of the picture plane. They create, as McLuhan suggests, the illusion that one paints as if one "held" rather than simply "saw" the object (42). It is in this way that Cézanne's objective deformations, which accommodate the object to the picture plane, provide a closer approximation of the dynamic and organic nature of the perceptual experience, and duplicate that process for the observer. One does not enter a Post-Impressionist canvas in the same manner that one does a work of art that depends upon the rules of linear and atmospheric perspective to create what Gombrich defines as an "acquired illusion" (16), an illusion which tricks the eye into believing that the space created is but an extension in visual terms of actual space. Rather, one enters a pictorial space that engages the complete sensibility of the observer, where the forms caress the eye and one feels the volumes in high relief.

The desire to discover plastic equivalents for apperceptions of reality unites the disparate styles of Post-Impressionist artists. In a letter to Maurice Beaubourg in 1890, Seurat reveals his fascination with discovering correspondences for emotional states through composition and color. He writes, for example, of the "gay, calm, or sad combinations" of tonal values: "Gaiety of *tone* is given by the luminous dominant; of *color,* by the warm dominant; of *line,* by lines above the horizontal." In contrast he suggests, "sadness of *tone* is given by the dominance of dark; of *color,* by the dominance of cold colors; and of *line,* by downward directions."[22] Seurat's sense of the analogies between form and feeling is borne out in his last large figure painting, *The Parade,* where the monumental calm is achieved, as he suggests, through the "equivalence of light and dark . . . of warm and cold . . . and by horizontals" (qtd. in Rewald, *Post-Impressionism,* 128).

Equally intrigued by the notion of an objective correlative, van Gogh writes of the "terrible" greens and reds of his *Night Cafe at Arles,* through whose complementary color contrasts he wishes to express the atmosphere of a sinful place where a man might lose his soul. In a letter to his brother Theo from Arles in 1888, van Gogh explains: "I have tried to express the terrible passions of humanity by means of red and green. The room is blood red and dark yellow with a green billiard table in the middle; there are four citron-yellow lamps with a glow of orange and green. Everywhere there is a clash and contrast of the most disparate reds and greens in the figures of the little sleeping hooligans, in the empty, dreary room, in violet and blue" (letter 533, *Letters of van Gogh* 3: 28–29).

The Hegelian notion of the musical (i.e., nonrepresentational and suggestive) tendency of all art abounds in the artistic theory of the time, even when the particular bias is scientific, as in Seurat's more analytical and deliberate approach to abstract formal equivalents, or mystical, as in Gauguin's sense of the expressive power of line and color. In a letter to Emile Schuffenecker in January 1885, Gauguin speaks of the intrinsic qualities inherent in objects and the intuitive nature of artistic perception. He concludes his letter by observing that "there are lines which are noble, false, etc. The straight line indicates the infinite, the curve limits the creation, without taking into account the fatality of numbers. . . . There are noble tones, ordinary ones, tranquil harmonies, consoling ones, others which excite by their vigor. In short, you see in graphology the features of honest men and liars" (letter 11, *Lettres de Gauguin,* 44–47).

Gauguin's own enthusiasm for the decorative (i.e., art as design or abstraction rather than copy) is engendered by his appreciation for the evocative power and deliberate ambiguity of plastic elements. In a letter to Daniel de Montfried he writes that he was "born to do decorative art": "The simple stained-glass window, attracting the eye by its divisions of colors and forms, that is still the best. A kind of music" (letter 132, *Lettres de Gauguin,* 232), while in "Diverses Choses" he speaks of the "mysterious and enigmatic interior force" of color itself (qtd. in Chipp, 66). Gauguin sees his esthetic as an antidote to the corruption of his time. His love of line, of simplified stylizations, and the "honesty" of flat planes of color is motivated by his appreciation for primitive art, and his distrust or subtlety generally. Ironically, though Gauguin objects to modeling on moral grounds (because, as Goldwater suggests, "its vagueness permits deceit"), his simplifications of method and visual appearance were intended to highlight the ambiguities of his model: "Representation, which had in one sense ceased to be representation, took on symbolic overturns going far beyond the 'corner of nature' that has provided his point of departure."[23]

The paradoxical relation between the actual and the created subject in Post-Impressionism applies equally to portraiture and still life. The transformation of familiar topographies and faces by the thinking eye, the alteration of the given to disclose essential structures and characters, becomes of paramount interest. While Cézanne remains faithful to his motif, rarely detaching his eyes from it while he worked, he nonetheless speaks of the way in which "nature *reveals* herself . . . in very complex forms,"[24] and of expressing himself according to his "personal" temperament: "Time and reflection, moreover, modify little by little our vision, and at last comprehension comes to us" (letter 183, *Paul Cézanne: Letters,* 250). Van Gogh, in contrast, seems to have attached himself to nature in fear of abstraction. In an 1889 letter to Bernard he reveals: "I found danger in these abstractions. If I work on very quietly, the beautiful subjects will come of their own accord; really above all, the great thing is to gather new vigor in reality" (letter B21, *Letters of van Gogh* 3: 522–25). Yet even as van Gogh advises Bernard to paint "your garden just as it is," he is not asking that one transcribe exactly what is seen, but rather that one free from the model or the motif "the real character of things" (letter 541, *Letters of van Gogh* 3: 48).

Not only does van Gogh reveal the need of the Post-Impressionist to discover formal (i.e., structural) correlatives for conceptions of reality, he also expresses the Post-Impressionist longing for stability and order, a longing borne out in van Gogh's own desire for contact with nature. He looks forward to the time when the "socialists" will "construct their logical social edifice" and thus reincarnate a stable Golden age. Within his work one senses his attachment to solid objects, that faith in nature that is often an ideal whose realization is frustrated by the profundity of his need. This tension is borne out in the combination of distortion and naturalism in his canvases. In the October 1888 letter to Bernard he speaks simultaneously of both his fidelity to, and departure from, the given: "I exaggerate, sometimes I make changes in the motif" and yet "my attention is so fixed on what is possible and really exists that I hardly have the desire or the courage to strive for the ideal as it might result from my abstract studies." For van Gogh the balance between the seen and the unseen is possible because "I do not invent the whole picture; on the contrary, I find it all ready in nature, only it must be disentangled" (letter B19, *Letters of van Gogh* 3: 518).

Van Gogh's sense of the strengthening effect of contact with nature is borne out in the tangibility and concreteness of his landscape forms and in his homological treatment of human and phenomenal figures. The tension between objective and subjective values in his work materializes in his expressive as well as representational use of perspective line and angle of vision. Schapiro observes that "for van Gogh perspective was a dramatic element in vision, the carrier of infinity, a means of intensifying movement into depth."[25] Both nearness and remoteness electrify van Gogh's canvases. Early in his career he writes that "the peculiar effects of perspective intrigue me more than human intrigues" (qtd. in Schapiro, *Vincent van Gogh,* 29) and, as Schapiro observes, perspective becomes "a quality of the landscape that he is sighting":

> This paradoxical device—both phenomenon and system—at the same time deformed *things* and made them look more real; it fastened the artist's eye more slavishly to appearances, but also brought him more actively into play in the world. While in the Renaissance pictures it was a means of constructing an objective space complete in itself and distinct from the beholder, even though organized with respect to his eye, like the space of a stage, in many of van Gogh's first landscape drawings the world seems to emanate from his eye in a gigantic discharge with a continuous motion of rapidly converging lines. (29)

In van Gogh's later work, Schapiro notes, "the flight to a goal is rarely unobstructed or fulfilled." One encounters "counter goals" or "diversions" which van Gogh visualizes as in *Cornfield at Sunrise* (fig. 13), where the imbalance in the choice of the path of vision is partly achieved by two competing centers of rest. There is a struggle in the canvas, as Schapiro observes, between the "re-centering of the view" (*Vincent van Gogh,* 98) that is suggested through the succession of curved darker patches in the middle of the enclosed field leading to the solitary tree atop the mountain, and the pallid, anorectic sun which hovers beyond it—a form brought to the surface though no path of vision prepares for its realization. The struggle between the two centers restrains the illusion of infinite depth that is usually suggested by a perspective line, for the sun inhibits

its thrust toward a vanishing point. In this way, van Gogh provides a sense of deep space while at the same time managing to close the recessed field. In other words, he brings the two-dimensionality of his canvas to bear upon the three-dimensional illusion and uses both to dramatize the theme of inaccessibility. Portraits such as *Madame Roulin* (fig. 14) demonstrate a parallel integration of representational and nonrepresentational values, for van Gogh creates power-fully molded characterizations of specific individuals who function as emblematic folk types as well.

While Gauguin represents the most violent Post-Impressionist reaction to the Impressionist ocular realism, and van Gogh suffers the duality of his allegiance to the real and the force of his own temperament, Cézanne strikes an equipoise in his process of realization. Under his penetrative eye, the naive vision of Impressionism is transformed into what he describes in a letter to Louis Aurenche as a "strong experience of nature" (letter 165, *Paul Cézanne: Letters*, 232) which depends upon "contact with nature" (letter 160, *Paul Cézanne: Letters*, 228) to extract an underlying essence. Cézanne's realization is the optic based in conceptions of nature. It is an effort, he suggests, that allows one to "see nature as no one has seen it before,"[26] a statement that, by implication, suggests the revelatory capacity of the innocent eye. "The artist," he explains, "creates a reality, he does not depict an already existent one."[27] In a 1904 letter to Bernard, Cézanne offers the most concentrated statement of his artistic intention: "Literature expresses itself by abstractions, whereas painting by means of drawing and color gives concrete shape to sensations and perceptions. One is neither too scrupulous nor too sincere nor too submissive to nature; but one is more or less master of one's model, and above all, of the means of expression. Get to the heart of what is before you and continue to express yourself as logically as possible" (letter 169, *Paul Cézanne: Letters*, 236–37).

The paradox of the Post-Impressionist, whose faithfulness to direct observation inevitably transforms the given, is discussed by Erle Loran, who explains how his own method, "a comparative study of Cézanne's paintings in relation to the actual motif in the countryside of Aix," led him to the following conclusion: "At the time the photographs were taken, the primary objective was to show how closely Cézanne followed nature, because at first it seemed an astounding revelation that the paintings were so much like the subjects. But now, after many years of thinking about the problems of space organization, it seems to me that the most significant facts are those revealing differences between Cézanne's space and the space in nature" (5).

Though Cézanne "always worked from nature," Loran emphasizes that he is not the kind of "objective painter" that such an approach would imply. Loran's diagrammatic analyses stress, in fact, the kinds of alterations of the given that Cézanne effects in transposing the three-dimensional configuration in nature to the two-dimensional reality of the picture plane. It is primarily

Figure 13.   Vincent van Gogh, *Cornfield at Sunrise*, 1890
Oil on canvas, 72 × 92 cm.
(Rijksmuseum Kröller-Müller)

Figure 14.   Vincent van Gogh, *Madame Roulin*, 1889
(Stedelijk Museum, Amsterdam)

Cézanne's consideration of the "space function of line" (Loran, 15) which allows him to control and organize three-dimensional spatial illusions that are balanced by the picture plane, which Loran defines as the "architectural absolute" (3) in the visual medium. In this way Cézanne's spatial illusion "holds to the wall" and differs dramatically from an open window's infinite recession. Superimposed upon this basic linear structure rests a system of color-plane modulations which also have a form-building function. "Color-plane modulation" simply means the systematic breaking up of color into a counterpoint of stepped-back, overlapping planes that tend to follow forms in their roundness.

The technique, known as the parallax effect, allows the artist to use the color plane to compensate for the picture plane, or, as Dunstan explains it, to allow the artist to discover plastic equivalents for the multidimensional experience of form in normal binocular vision: "we can see more than one contour at a time, even when the head is held still. With the slightest movement, the effect known as 'parallax' comes into operation: every contour, or plane seen on edge, shifts slightly in relation to what is behind it" (122). Whereas Cézanne achieves the parallax effect through overlapping, continuously restated contours, creating the illusion of form without violating the picture plane, Seurat and the Neo-Impressionists use the juxtaposition of multicolored spots to realize the complicated dialectic of surface and depth that distinguishes Post-Impressionist art generally. In his discussion of Seurat's method, Schapiro observes: "Seurat's dots may be seen as a kind of *collage*. They create a hollow space within the frame, often a vast depth; but they compel us also to see the picture as a finely structured surface made up of an infinite number of superimposed units attached to the canvas" (102).

Cézanne's control of space does not depend upon chiaroscuro or modeling through tonal gradations, nor does it depend upon aerial and linear perspective (the traditional techniques of illusionist art); but rather it depends upon the firmness of his basic linear structure. Like the Impressionists, Cézanne realized that line was an abstract element but, unlike the Impressionists, he used line to serve nonnaturalistic ends: he "disregards the logic of external appearance for the sake of the inner logic of design."[28]

In his diagrammatic analysis of the distinctions that emerge between Renoir's and Cézanne's handling of the mountain called Saint Victoire, Loran explores the differences that obtain between the stereoscopic or open-window illusion Renoir sustains through linear and mechanical perspective and the sensation of both depth and enclosure Cézanne achieves by using bold outlines and a series of overlapping planes to declare both the location of the mountain in deep space and its relation to the picture plane. Cézanne's *Mont Ste. Victoire, Seen from Bellevue* (fig. 15) demonstrates how the artist is able to create that "satisfying illusion of nature" by methods that deliberately distort, alter, condense, exaggerate, or transform the motif as it is found in the landscape. Rooted in naturalistic observation, Cézanne's method nevertheless leads to its opposite. It is the abstract element—in this case the artist's use of line—which achieves an illusion of space. Thus painting, as a constructed reality, is both like and unlike the motif which in some sense inspired it.

This paradox is central to his use of multiple perspectives in still life as well, where he achieves a prepossessing sense of weight, solidity, and actuality through drawing distortions, which incorporate several eye levels into one picture. The technique, which Loran defines as universal perspective (76), allows Cézanne in *Still Life with Fruit Basket* (fig. 16), for example, to increase the illusion of space or of feeling the object in the round while coextensively emphasizing the nonnaturalistic nature of the illusion by relating it clearly to the flat plane of the picture. For Cézanne, "painting is not a servile copying of objects, but the discovery of a harmony among numerous relationships" (qtd. in Venturi, *Impressionists and Symbolists,* 136), a harmony that parallels the organic wholeness of nature. Cézanne's method develops inductively from his observation of phenomena rather than deductively as a system that is imposed upon it. Venturi's discussion of the "parallel between artistic and natural vision" in a Cézanne still life helps us to understand the principle of *energia* that informs this correspondence: their "celebrated beauty . . . depends precisely on the authority with which he succeeds in convincing us that his 'distorted' vision is truer, more self-evident, more vital than the common mortal's vision of real objects" (134).

In an important and unique exchange of self-portraits among Gauguin, Bernard, and Charles Laval, instigated by van Gogh around mid-September of 1888, Post-Impressionist artists demonstrate the way in which, just as in Cézanne's landscapes and still lifes, the alterations of the given culminate in the disclosure of essential character. Gauguin's *Self-Portrait, "Les Misérables"* (fig. 17), completed at Pont-Aven for van Gogh, becomes representative of the Post-Impressionist drive to move beyond scientific realism to psychological realism in the revelation of character by discovering plastic equivalents for inner states rather than superficial appearances. Gauguin writes to Schuffenecker speculating on the implications of the stylistic transformations he feels his portrait reveals:

> I believe it is one of my best things: absolutely incomprehensible (for example) it is so abstract. Head of a bandit in the foreground, a Jean Valjean (*Les Misérables*) personifying also a disreputable Impressionist painter shackled always to this world. The design is absolutely special, a complete abstraction. The eyes, mouth, and nose are like the flowers of a Persian carpet, thus personifying the symbolic aspect. The color is far from nature; imagine a vague suggestion of pottery contorted by a great fire! All the reds, violets, striped by flashes of fire like a furnace radiating from the eyes, seat of the struggles of the painter's thought. The whole on a chrome background strewn with childish bouquets. Chamber of a pure young girl. The Impressionist is pure still unsullied by the putrid kiss of the Ecole des Beaux Arts. (letter 71, *Lettres de Gauguin,* 140–41)

Figure 15.   Paul Cézanne, *Mont Ste. Victoire, Seen from Bellevue*, 1885–1887
25¾″ × 32⅛″.
(The Metropolitan Museum of Art, the H. O. Havemeyer Collection; bequest of Mrs. H. O. Havemeyer)

Figure 16. Paul Cézanne, *Still Life with Fruit Basket*, 1888–1890 (Musée d'Orsay, Paris; cliché des Musées Nationaux)

Figure 17.   Paul Gauguin, *Self-Portrait, "Les Misérables,"* 1888
(*Stedelijk Museum, Amsterdam*)

The letter encapsulates themes special to Gauguin—his appreciation for the naivety and purity of the Impressionist vision[29] (Gauguin was fond of styling himself as both child and savage) coupled with a new sensitivity to the decorative possibilities of the picture space, an increased smoothness of surface and broadness of color, and an emphasis on continuous outline—techniques which would become the mark of his more revolutionary canvases.

With color "far from nature," and forms that are suggestive rather than photographic, Gauguin initiates his exploration of private and interior regions. By exaggerating and distorting facial topography to dramatize the dialectic of his own sensibility—"personifying the symbolic aspect of his personality through the 'image of myself'"—Gauguin's exotic and Edenic dream self is fully integrated within the plastic terms of the total decorative Persian motif. This equivocal treatment of the human figure absorbed within the rhythm of the background motif is characteristic of Post-Impressionist portraiture. As if to dramatize the nonnaturalistic direction of the Pont-Aven group, Gauguin includes a portrait of Bernard in the upper-right-hand corner of the canvas, the eyes shut to all exterior reality.

The self-portrait van Gogh selected and dedicated to Gauguin during this exchange is equally expressive of the Post-Impressionist emphasis upon the artist's conceptual response to his model. The canvas, van Gogh explains, allows him to "exaggerate" his "personality," to disclose that which is representative of his vision of the individual artist and of the artist "in general" (letter 545, *Letters of van Gogh* 3: 328). This portraiture of soul, van Gogh observes in another letter to Theo, actualizes the representation of "a *real* man. Ah! portraiture, portraiture with the thoughts, the soul of the model in it, that is what I think must come." Throughout the series of twenty-two self-portraits van Gogh executes from 1888 to 1890, he struggles to discover plastic equivalents for the "eternal" in himself: "I want to paint men and women with that something of the external which the halo used to symbolize, and which I seek to convey by the actual radiance and vibration of our coloring" (letter 531, *Letters of van Gogh* 3: 25).

This pursuit of the "eternal" is actualized in the pervading blueness of van Gogh's 1890 *Self-Portrait, Saint-Rémy* (fig. 18), which integrates costume and the abstract surroundings. Schapiro observes: "The live brushwork forming this environment follows in its interwoven traces the changing edges of the head like a halo around it; at the same time it conforms in its vehement flow to the impassioned rhythms of the strokes that model the costume and the hair. Out of a dark hollow in the center of this blue emerges the head with a glowing intensity—the crescent of the hair and beard is like the moon in *The Starry Night*" (*Vincent van Gogh,* 102). The tension between horizontals and verticals, between naturalistic detail and the impulsive rhythms of the more unstable elements, the stress visualized between the right and left sides of the face, provide evidence of what Schapiro defines as the "style of strain" in van Gogh's work. This emotional dynamism often compels the observer beyond the boundary of the visible and leads to confrontations with the archetypal dimensions of his forms. Further, this plasticity of line, conjoined with the interplay of blues and greens and the repetition with variation of the crescent motif, demonstrate the way in which the recurrence of large ornamental elements provides structural coherence within Post-Impressionist canvases.

Throughout esthetic discussions of major Post-Impressionist artists, there exists a tendency to perceive the movement toward abstraction inherent in the notion of an organic yet enclosed system of relations in quasi-mystical terms, and certainly the themes of penetration, possession, transformation, and revelation that dominate the period suggest this kind of supposition. In Cézanne's famous 1905 "Cylinder, sphere and cone" letter to Bernard, for example, he explains in the closing section how he sustains a compelling illusion of depth: "Lines parallel to the horizon give breadth, that is a section of nature or, if you prefer, of the spectacle that the *Pater Omnipotens Aeterne Deus* spreads out before our eyes. Lines perpendicular to this horizon give depth. But nature for us men is more depth than surface, whence the need of introducing into our light vibrations, represented by reds and yellows, a sufficient amount of blue to give the impression of air" (letter 167, *Paul Cézanne: Letters*, 234). The very provocative nature of Cézanne's spatial illusion, the paradoxical relationship between the completed painting and the actual motif, and Cézanne's own feelings for depth rather than surface, emphasize the conceptual nature of Cézanne's approach to external reality. It is in this sense that Cézanne's austere and monumental forms are imbued with archetypal significance.

In conversation with Joachim Gasquet, Cézanne describes the process whereby plastic equivalent for the thinking eye is achieved by using a graphic gesture of interlocking fingers to symbolize the complex network of interlocking lines and planes that characterize his mature style. He states that it is this kind of motif which he must painstakingly achieve: "I bring together in the same spirit, the same faith, all that is scattered. All that we see disperses, vanishes; is it not so? Nature is always the same, but nothing remains of it, nothing of what comes to our sight. Our art ought to give the shimmer of its duration with the elements, the appearance of all its changes. It ought to make us taste it eternally. What is underneath? Nothing perhaps. Perhaps everything. You understand?"[30]

In submitting to the scene before him, and to a vision he intuitively feels, Cézanne's terms approximate an archetypal sense of possession. This approach entails the concept of symbolic art that Carl Jung endorses, where the artist in fact seems possessed of either demon or angel, and participates in a creative action in which he functions as amanuensis rather than primogenitor. The vision so given also underlines the tangible character of Post-Impressionism's nonrep-

Figure 18.   Vincent van Gogh, *Self-Portrait, Saint-Rémy,* 1889
Oil on canvas, 25½″ × 21¼″.
(Musée d'Orsay, Paris; cliché des Musées Nationaux)

resentational forms, the immanent as opposed to transcendent quality of their revelation of the noumena behind the appearance of the thing. In his discussion of Cézanne's "universal architectonics," Cheney discusses the way in which Cézanne's depersonalized and multiple perspectives discover "behind each contemplated landscape in his beloved Provence some hint of a cosmic structure, an architectonic rhythm": "It is not so much *personal* feeling that controls here, as cosmic feeling, a consciousness of great impersonal forces underlying the order of the universe—to be revealed, if he is lucky, through an artist freed from the obsession of 'naturalness.'"[31]

It is this same quality in Cézanne's mature landscapes to which Venturi responds—an order seems to prevail in Cézanne's works that possesses archetypal power. Venturi notes, for example, that the Mont Ste. Victoire is a recurring pictorial subject in Cézanne's art, one which was painted between 1885 and 1887 several times. In describing the effect of these paintings, Venturi speaks of the "spiritual values" Cézanne discovers in nature. In confronting the more abstract *Mont Ste. Victoire* painted between 1894 and 1900, he describes the sense of "struggle," of "battle" articulate through the simplified rock forms that dominate the summariness of the foreground, an effect that, for Venturi, allows one to "hear the cry of forces unleashed by the earth" (*Impressionists and Symbolists*, 132).

The artists participating in the Post-Impressionist movement may be grouped together because they all rejected the prevailing canons of realism that had held for the preceding generation. They share therefore a nonnaturalistic esthetic that remains intact despite the wide variation of personal styles. In fact, the corollary of their nonnaturalistic bias is that multiplicity must be tolerated insofar as the artist is encouraged to realize his personal vision. One sees, as well, a general synthesis of the diverse range of alternative artistic traditions. The work of these Post-Impressionist artists, accordingly, exhibits a wide range of adaptations, which results in a creative synthesis of Japanese, Egyptian, Greek, primitive, and late-Medieval styles. In widening the range of stylistic alternatives, Post-Impressionism becomes representative of the international spirit of Art Nouveau. This kind of eclecticism is especially evident in the multiplicity of reference in van Gogh and Gauguin, both literary and pictorial. Cézanne had expressed the wish to "make of impressionism something solid and lasting like the art of the museums."[32] This statement, rather than providing evidence of Cézanne's desire to enter the inner sanctums of officially approved art, confirms his own awareness of the contemporaneity of ancient styles: "In my thought, one does not substitute one's self for the past, one merely adds a new link to the chain." Thus, at the same time that Post-Impressionism represents a new movement, it may also be seen as a modern adaptation of principles of construction and concepts of art inherent in the nonnaturalistic emphasis of pre-Renaissance perspective art.

The Post-Impressionist search for abstract, plastic equivalents to adequately embody patterns of feeling conceived through nature assumes the dimensions of a quest to express the inimitable and the unseen. One places the Post-Impressionist fidelity to the external landscape within the context of a profound secular idealism that would allow for the liberation of meaning in that landscape. It is in this sense that art, no longer bound in service to a traditional theology or a particular ideology, becomes a religion unto itself. The drive to penetrate—where the essential is disentangled or disengaged from the given and where the canvas becomes the symbolic equivalent for the artist's conceptual experience of reality—expresses the need to discover something beyond the surface appearance, and coextensively to elevate painting itself to a level beyond that of base imitation. The question which Plato raised with respect to the legitimacy of an art thrice removed from reality had thus to be challenged by attacking the legitimacy of the mimetic basis Plato himself used to raise that question.

The most important features of Post-Impressionist art may therefore be summarized in terms of (*a*) the decorative symbolism, stained-glass effects, and use of recurring linear and color patterns in Gauguin's compositions; (*b*) the tendency toward abstraction and the deliberate adjustment of three-dimensional elements to the picture plane in theoretical formulations respecting the disposition of color in Seurat and in Cézanne's stepped-back planes; and (*c*) the use of multiple perspectives in van Gogh, particularly to dramatize his feelings for the landscape, and of formal correlatives generally to articulate conceptions of reality based on an increasing sensitivity to the emotional and symbolic value of color and line. These are techniques which emphasize the Post-Impressionist artist's sense of the nonrepresentational character of his medium and his belief in its capacity to reveal essential structures.

The close of the nineteenth century was characterized as "corrupt," "agonized," and "anarchic" by those most sensitive to change.[33] Post-Impressionist artists began the search for what van Gogh describes as "*only one thing*" valued by those "who love order and symmetry" (letter B14, *Letters of van Gogh* 3: 508). Whether in Arles, Pont-Aven, Aix, or Tahiti, that "*one thing*" symbolized for the isolate artist a recovery of meaning in an increasingly disturbed world. While light for the Impressionist painter was celebrated with all its romantic and traditionally conceived spiritual values intact, in Post-Impressionist art light becomes a more ambivalent force. It characteristically emanates from within the canvas rather than as a source of illumination from without. While in Impressionist art light effects are recorded joyfully because the source itself retains its beneficent and purposive aspect, in Post-Impressionist art light values function in a more enigmatic way as a symbolic rather than as a natural chiaroscuro. These are values that are defined by the artist himself rather than solely by a conventionally determined typology. With nature no longer the unambiguous model, light begins to function in correspondingly evocative terms. In van

Gogh's visionary *Starry Night* (fig. 19) an impassioned serpentine nebula and eleven verticil stars work in conjunction with a haunting radiating horn-shaped moon and agitated, spiraling flame-forked cypresses to dramatize the symbolic capacity of the artist's light and dark values. Together these configurations express van Gogh's generalized yearning for contact with cosmos, an upward sweeping drive that is countered by the more stable geometrized forms that articulate the village in the foreground. In this way tension is developed between the dynamic sky light and the rectangular blocks of illumination within the houses, just as a pattern of resistance is sustained by the opposition between the thin church spire, whose needle is pressed against the horizon, and the quivering cypresses, which cross the nebula and arc beside the adjacent exfoliating star.

Penetration, transformation, and revelation become as well the dominant thematic and technical preoccupation of Modernist verbal artists, whether through the adaptation of Cézanne's space conception implicit in Hemingway's concept of the "fifth dimension," through Lawrence's drive to reconnect with the cosmos by integrating man within the landscape expressed in his esthetic of the "fourth dimension,"[34] or through Woolf's communion theme realized as the need "to penetrate," or "lift the veil," to "know," "share," and be "certain" despite the otherness of people and things (*Jacob's Room*, 93). Coincident with Post-Impressionism's increasing awareness of painting as painting, Modernist writers free their medium from the representational role which had been imposed by inherited mimetic conventions, and explore the capacity of the medium to support a concept of *energia* as well as *enargia*.

The antipathy toward the descriptive and illustrative aspects of conventional modes of representation in the fictive medium is reflected in Fry. Recognizing the applicability of both the formal and metaphysical implications of nonrepresentational values in visual art for the verbal medium, he saw literature "suffering from a plethora of old clothes." Writers, he felt, could gain impetus and direction from the 1910 Post-Impressionist exhibition: they too "should fling representation to the winds and follow suit" (Woolf, *Roger Fry*, 172). The purpose of both art and literature, he therefore suggests, "is the creation of structures which have for us the feeling of reality," structures which are "self-contained, self-sufficient," are "not to be valued by their reference to what lies outside."[35]

Fry wanted literature to have the same kind of organic unity Cézanne had achieved in the plastic medium. The novelist, he suggests, could create "single perfectly organic aesthetic whole[s]" (qtd. in Johnstone, 60) by attending to the constructive aspect of the medium itself. The successive unity of design "depends on forms being presented to us in such a sequence that each successive element is felt to have a fundamental and harmonious relation with that which preceded it" (*Vision and Design*, 33). Organic unity in both visual and verbal

Figure 19. Vincent van Gogh, *Starry Night*, 1889
Oil on canvas, 29″ × 36¼″.
(*Collection, the Museum of Modern Art, New York; acquired through the Lillie P. Bliss Bequest*)

media was thus the result of clear and absolutely inevitable relationships set up between volumes.

Charles Mauron, Fry's contemporary, also emphasizes nonrepresentational values in his own study of *The Nature of Beauty in Art and Literature,* advising that "if one creates one must create a reality, and not, as painters, say, cardboard."[36] Cardboard in visual art finds its corollary in literature: "A 'living' novel is not the realistic mirror in which we find once more a too well-known face" (19).

Fry approves of Mauron's suggestion that there are "psychological volumes" in literature that correspond to plastic volumes in visual art. Plot then becomes interpreted as the significant relations constructed between these complexes: "As the painter creates a spatial being, the writer creates a psychological being" (66–67). The simplest psychological entities used in literature are "states of mind" or "moments of the spirit" through which the exterior and interior life are fused (74); the more complex are characters, facts, or situations and their complexes (78). Mauron suggests that the traditional chronology of plotted events be exchanged for a complex of psychological realities or volumes which model a spiritual whole (70).

As the denial of the reality of the two-dimensionality of the visual medium led to the fallacy of the copy and the open window in pictorial art, so too an evasion of the artificial character of the verbal medium led to the creation of narrative structures whose illusions of surface continuity and linear succession falsified the way in which the mind actually experiences external reality. Modernist writers emphasize that language need not be shackled by an inherited standard of verisimilitude, that the word and the thing do not of necessity coincide in any one-dimensional way, and that language is a convention which allows for the transmutation of sensation into meaning.

McLuhan argues the legitimacy of this analogy by noting that the Post-Impressionist recovery of the nonrepresentational character of the plastic medium maximizes the interplay among the senses that the three-dimensional space illusion in Renaissance art denied. In realizing the bodily character of sensations and the corporeality of forms by attending to both haptic and optic dimensions of the perceptual experience, Post-Impressionist artists achieve "depth, perceived through feeling" or *perspective vécue.* In a parallel way, McLuhan argues, "alphabet technology," like the three-dimensional spatial illusion, abstracts the visual from the ordinary sense interplay: "whereas speech is an outering (utterance) of all our senses at once, writing abstracts from speech" (43). The intense visual life fostered by the written character of the medium leads to the same kind of disassociation of the senses, or to what McLuhan defines as the "anguish of the third dimension" in perspective art.[37] To recover the actual organic, dynamic, and synesthetic character of our experience of form, Modernist writers endeavor to make language engage the whole temperament of the observer by embodying the tactile sensibilities that conventionally play a subordinate role in the creation of traditionally conceived mimetic spatial illusions.

Finally, in committing themselves to the creation of fictive realities, which are analogous to their conception of how the mind experiences external forms, Modernist writers, like Post-Impressionists, abdicate fixed, single, and external points of view in favor of an exploration of dynamic, multiple, and internalized perspectives within a single work. It is in this sense that the parallax effect, achieved by Cézanne through his use of multiple and discontinuous eye levels and by van Gogh through his exploration of the tension that can be created by using engaged and disengaged, near and far, perspectives and competing centers of rest, finds its verbal correlative in Modernist literature.

The dialectic between a surface view of external reality, one where conventional assumptions with respect to time and appearance remain intact, and an in-depth revelation where those assumptions are fragmented and transformed by the individual eye, is apparent, for example, in Stephen Crane's "The Open Boat." This short story is instructive because it so clearly anticipates similar technical experiments in Modernist fiction, which attempt to realize the full complexity of the object by duplicating in verbal terms the multidimensional experience of form that Cézanne and van Gogh achieve through split planes, shifting eye levels, and multiple perspectives. While James Nagel argues that the parallax view that Crane realizes through the ironic and dramatic juxtaposition of contrasting points of view is "another variation of Impressionistic narration" (27), the kind of tension that Crane's use of multiple perspectives actually realizes in this story has applicability only within a Post-Impressionist context.

In "The Open Boat," the facts themselves have little significance, while the various interpretations of those facts by a number of different characters with varying perspectives are of crucial importance. Just as symbolic chiaroscuro in *The Red Badge of Courage* annotates Fleming's idealistic propensity to be seduced by the seemingly beneficent effects of landscape configurations, so too "The Open Boat" presents various pictures of reality, which index the character's visions of landscape and seascape. These pictures, taken together, provide a composite view of the multiple aspects of a single scene.

The short story opens with a view of the sea as seen by the men at eye level with the horizon. Their precarious position transforms what would ordinarily be perceived as a "weirdly picturesque scene if viewed from a balcony" into something sinister and terrifying. Without the protective distancing effect of an Olympian perspective ("It was probably splendid, it was probably glorious, this play of the free sea, wild with lights of emerald and white and amber"[38]), and without the subsequent diffused ambience of an Impressionist seascape that accompanies an aerial view, the "anxious eyes" of the drifting crew experience something akin to the forest fears of the northern Gothic. Forms are exaggerated and deformed: the horizon "was jagged with waves that seemed thrust up in points like rocks"; "These waves were most wrongfully and barbarously abrupt and tall and each froth-top was a problem in small-boat navigation" (335).

The opposition between near and distant views is simultaneously present in the detached and engaged perspective of the correspondent, who is both participant and observer. The divergence, felt throughout the story, climaxes in the poignantly visualized antithesis of the shore as at once "lonely and indifferent"—with its tall wind-tower, a "giant, standing with its back to the plight of the ants" (351)—and strangely attractive, "like a bit of scenery on a stage . . . with its white slope of sand and its green bluff topped with little silent cottages" that spread "like a picture" (353). This tension is further delineated by contrasting views of the sea from human and nonhuman perspectives: "the serenity of nature amid the struggles of the individual—nature in the wind, and nature in the vision of man" (351). Realized from a bird's eye, the "canton-flannel gulls" sit comfortably upon the rolling waves that move "like carpets on a line in a gale" (337). From a crewmember's eye, the grace of the moving waters is "terrible," the crests of the waves "snarling," and the whole of the "broken sea" so "gruesome" that the birds become "uncanny and sinister" and look, from the oiler's point of view, as if they were crudely carved with a "jackknife" (338). The diversity visualized in these renderings of perspectival experience—symbolically condensed in the radical opposition of the horizontal and vertical, which delineates the wind-tower on the shore—adequately convey for Crane both the beauty and the terror of the sea. He senses the quality of unreality that attends the external point of view implicit both in an aerial Olympian perspective and in the rigidly enforced linear perspective that transforms the shore into the "stage" and "picture," and modifies this effect by bringing into play the internal points of view of the men in the boat to visualize the multidimensional nature of external reality.

Woolf

The kind of tension Crane's parallax effect creates and sustains in "The Open Boat" is central to Woolf's esthetic theory and practice as well. Her abdication of the received convention of authorial omniscience and her commitment to a multiperspectival approach is grounded on her understanding of the relative and partial nature of conceptions of reality. In response to Hugh Walpole's sense of unreality in *The Waves*, for example, Woolf invites him to acknowledge that reality has no single, definitive form: "Well—I'm very much interested about unreality & *The Waves*. . . . But unreality does take the colour out of a book, of course; at the same time, I don't see that it's a final judgment on either of us—You're real to some—I to others. Who's to decide what reality is?"[39] Woolf's frustration with an Impressionist method is based on her own expressed desire to penetrate beyond the surface realities and the illusion of homogeneity that attention to surface detail and fixed, external perspectives often generate.

Throughout her literary criticism Woolf distinguishes between the materialism of realistic Edwardian conventions and the antimaterialism of Georgians, suggesting that from a novelistic point of view "human nature changed" around about 1910 ("Mr. Bennett and Mrs. Brown," 320). The date is significant in that it coincides with the time of the Post-Impressionist exhibition in London and the revaluation of representational values in art that led to the revelation of unfamiliar terrain in landscape and portraiture. In "Evening over Sussex: Reflections in a Motor Car," two sides of Woolf's multiple self playfully debate the possibility of penetrating the surface of the scene before her. She advises at one point in the essay that the perspective which endeavors to master and illuminate the scene relinquish "these impossible aspirations; be content with the view in front of us, and believe me when I tell you that it is best to sit and soak; to be passive; to accept; and to not bother nature because nature has given you six little pocket knives with which to cut up the body of a whale" (*Collected Essays* 2: 291).

The Edwardians, Woolf argues in "The Novels of E. M. Forster," epitomize that state of acquiescence which she allies with surface representation, for they "have laid an enormous stress upon the fabric of things. They have given us a house in the hope that we may be able to deduce the human beings who live there." The Georgians, in contrast, endeavor to explore the way in which life is lived through and within the object insofar as they attempt to connect "the actual thing with the meaning of the thing": "Our business is not to build in brick and mortar, but to draw together the seen and the unseen." The novelistic method, which allows for this conjunction of surface and depth, enables the reader "at once to believe in the complete reality of the suburb and in the complete reality of the soul. In this combination of realism and mysticism . . . the paraphernalia of reality have at certain moments to become the view through which we see infinity" (*Collected Essays* 1: 345–46).

In "The Novels of E. M. Forster," Woolf asks as well that the novelist allow the object to function in realistic or conventional terms, and at the same time in symbolic terms: "the object which has been so uncompromisingly solid becomes, or should become, luminously transparent" (346–47). In "The Moment: A Summer's Night," Woolf suggests the way in which the wider circumference of the moment, the visual and sense impressions transcribed by the innocent eye, can be contracted "in the centre" to a "knot of consciousness": "a light is struck" and the external sense is reshaped by the quality of mind which experiences it (*Collected Essays* 2: 294–95).

Throughout Woolf's critical writings this image of the transfiguring power of the thinking eye, of the "windows . . . lit by our lamps" recurs to embody her sense of how the image, as the basic building block of the novel, provides a visual correlative for evaluative components of vision. Within this larger context, Woolf questions the viability of Forster's materialism, arguing that his own gift for observation "has served him too well. He has recorded too much and too literally. He has given us an almost photographic picture on one side of the page; on the other he asks us to see the same view transformed and radiant with eternal fires" (*Collected Essays* 1: 347). Because Woolf believes that Forster's overzealous attention to surface verisimilitude obscures the inner reality he wishes to disclose, the balance of representational and nonrepresentational values becomes a goal she attempts to realize in her own work.

Rather than creating a fictional reality shaped exclusively by the "unprofessional eye," Woolf focuses her attention on the realities disclosed by the "professional eye" and on methods of narration and presentation which will reveal how the mind shapes sensation into meaning. For her, "the method of writing smooth narration cannot be right; things don't happen in one's mind like that."[40] In *To the Lighthouse,* for example, Woolf uses a third-person point of view to register the disparate responses of the members of the Ramsay family and their assortment of house guests and friends at their summer retreat at the Isle of Skye just before and after the first World War. Though she uses the "objective" third person, Woolf also achieves the effects of the interior monologue by dramatizing the inner processes of her characters' responses to the tensions within the family. She abandons the "naturalistic" method, which would enforce the standard of verisimilitude that naturalism itself engages. Instead of sustaining the illusion of biographical completeness that an omniscient point of view can authorize in the text, Woolf's narrator often raises questions about the appearances she brings into being, or focuses on matters of reliability that traditional exterior points of view ask the reader to take for granted. She does not privilege events that are traditionally defined as the critical points of the character's individual destiny. Instead she chooses to allow them to function at subordinate levels, slipping them in unobtrusively during the transitional "Time Passes" interlude, for example, and elevating instead the often trivial and the mundane moments of consciousness to epiphanic levels of significance.

Thus Mrs. Ramsay's death is recorded parenthetically in the "Time Passes" interlude as simply a footnote to the larger action of generation and decay that is registered by the apprehending consciousness who is absorbed by the way in which time reclaims the deserted summer house during the family's absence. In a similar way, the exterior event which opens the novel, Mr. and Mrs. Ramsay's discussion of the projected outing to the lighthouse, functions, as Auerbach suggests, as a "framing occurrence,"[41] a background "occasion" which releases Mrs. Ramsay's perception of herself as a buffer between James and his father. Woolf's sense of the limitations of an Impressionist method, represented by the meditative intelligence in *Jacob's Room* as those "pictures in a book" that fail to disclose the central character's inner reality, is immediately asserted at the outset of *To the Lighthouse*. Its initial scene dramatizes the way Mrs. Ramsay hopes to draw James's attention to the "rude" illustrations in the Army and Navy Store's Catalogue so that she can insulate him from the complexity of the family relationships.

In exploring the discontinuity between exterior and interior modes of apprehending reality, Woolf emphasizes the way in which departure from conventional methods in presentation leads paradoxically to a closer approximation of the nature of one's experience of phenomena. In "Phases of Fiction" she explores the novel's potential to be responsive to the change in conceptions of human nature that the contemporary novelist must embody in his method of presentation: "It is the gift of style, arrangement, construction, to put us at a distance from the special life and to obliterate its features; while it is the gift of the novel to bring us into close touch with life. The two powers fight if they are brought into combination. The most complete novelist must be the novelist who can balance the two powers so that one enhances the other" (*Collected Essays* 2: 101).

In those works where the "professional" and the "unprofessional" eye interact, Woolf advises that the shaping power of the writer's conception is felt: "The barrier between us and the book is raised higher. We do not slip so instinctively and easily into a world that we know already. We feel that we are being compelled to accept an order and to arrange the elements of the novel—man, nature, God—in certain relations at the novelist's bidding" (100). This clear sense of the paradoxical relation between art and life is reformulated in "Mr. Bennett and Mrs. Brown," where Woolf suggests that the author must create, to borrow Mauron's term, a "psychological reality" that is "real." Woolf adds by way of explication that by using the term she does not "by that mean so lifelike" (325).

In the revelation and shaping of her character's human nature, Woolf consistently envisions her task as one that will penetrate surface changes to realize underlying essence. It is in this[1] context that "Mrs. Brown is eternal, Mrs. Brown is human nature, Mrs. Brown changes on the surface, it is the novelist who gets in and out" (330). As Woolf's first priority is to bring an in-depth Mrs. Brown to the surface, it is clear that she sets out to solve problems the Impressionists do not address. Possibly it is through Lily Briscoe, who is presented in *To the Lighthouse* as a Post-Impressionist artist, that Woolf best demonstrates her affinity with Post-Impressionist art, for it is Lily's task to bring into being, and make concrete, "the essential thing" in both Mr. and Mrs. Ramsay, and to discover in her canvas plastic equivalents for her conception of the relationship between them. That "essential thing" is further achieved through the multiple perspectives that Lily cultivates as artist, houseguest, friend, confidante, potential adversary, and detached observer. The tension among these disparate points of view leads Lily to exclaim in frustration that "one wanted fifty pair of eyes to see with. . . . Fifty pair of eyes were not enough to get round that one woman with,"[42] while her triumph is shaped by the way in which she brings the tension to equipose through plastic equivalents in her canvas.

Woolf consistently uses the window in the novel as a symbolic correlative for Lily's own commitment to a process that leads her beyond surface verisimilitude into an exploration of the symbiotic relationship between inner and outer modes of existence. The window, therefore, not only functions as an opaque surface that the artist must penetrate in order to release the essence of the characters, but also characterizes the thinking eye within Post-Impressionist art, the window of the soul, which, unlike the naive eye of the Impressionist artist, is endowed with the capacity to create rather than to transcribe. This is a power that Lily describes as "some secret sense, fine as air, with which to steal through keyholes" (294).

Early in the novel, while suffering William Bankes's cross-examination of her canvas, Lily despairs of her own ability to possess that sixth sense and to illuminate through "all those mounds of blue and green" on her palette "the spirit" in Mrs. Ramsay, "the essential thing, by which, had you found a crumpled glove in the corner of a sofa, you would have known it, from its twisted fingers, hers indisputably" (76). In pursuing the life that is lived through objects, Lily pursues the methods of Post-Impressionism, just as the novel as a whole pursues the fundamental metaphysical and epistemological dimensions of the various characters rather than their surface presentation. In his discussion of "Virginia Woolf and Our Knowledge of the External World," Jaako Hintikka points an analogy between Woolf and Post-Impressionism based on his sense of their shared conceptual response to external reality: "Novotny aptly called Cézanne's art *gemalte Erkenntnistheorie*, painted epistemology. With an even better right, large parts of Virginia Woolf's novels can be fictionalized epistemology."[43] The real drama of *To the Lighthouse* is conceived in terms of the tensions between various conceptions of reality, which Hintikka describes through a Leibnizian analogue as "monadic perspectives" (8). In his own discussion of this conceptual dimension in Woolf's art, Lee Whitehead suggests that *To the Lighthouse* as a whole may "be understood as one understands a picture or a landscape as a balancing of elements, a tension between opposing but mutually clarifying masses, colors and shapes."[44]

Through Lily, Woolf demonstrates her understanding of the way in which a particular point of view generates a particular kind of reality, a correspondence that Woolf materializes through her responsiveness to the expressive and architectonic power of color, light, and line. Lily, for example, sets in motion sequences of images that repeat basic geometric configurations, providing pictorial equivalents for her sense of the essential quality that defines husband and wife. Thus the dynamic balance between Mrs. Ramsay's intuitive irrationalism and Mr. Ramsay's scientific rationalism is given concrete definition through images that explore the tension between relaxed, curvilinear arabesques with their upward sweeping lines, and angular, hard-driving, downward-moving verticals.

Lily initially perceives Mrs. Ramsay sitting in the wicker armchair in the drawing room window as an "august shape; the shape of a dome" (80), a form successively imaged as both hive and shell, and which finds its graphic correlative as a "triangular purple shape" on Lily's canvas. In remaining faithful to the vision, intuitively grasped, Lily discards obsolete standards of verisimilitude, like the one Bankes uses to translate the abstract form into a commonplace symbolic iconographic representation of the Mother and Child: "Mother and Child then—objects of universal veneration, and in this case the mother was famous for her beauty—might be reduced, he pondered, to a purple shadow without irreverence" (81). Rather than acquiescing to the convention as conceived by Bankes, Lily replaces it with a personal vision "which she had seen clearly once and must now grope for among hedges and houses and mothers and children—her picture" (82). She wishes to show Bankes that "she had made no attempt at likeness," that the picture "was not of them . . . in his sense. There were other senses too in which one might reverence them. By a shadow here and a light there, for instance" (81).

Though Lily's picture is in fact a "picture" of Mrs. Ramsay reading to James, "no one could tell it for a human shape" (81). For Lily "it was a question . . . how to connect this mass on the right hand with that on the left" (82–83). So, too, Gauguin writes: "The sense of a picture lies not in its title or its subject, but in those visual elements of which it is composed; its true meaning, related only indirectly to representation, is found in the arrangement of its lines and shapes and colors whose musical qualities have the power of suggestion" (letter 170, *Lettres de Gauguin,* 286–90). Accordingly, Lily's picture has little to do either with Bankes's literalism or with the superficial realism of Mr. Paunceforte's popularized anemic Impressionism: "The jacmana was bright violet; the wall staring white. She would not have considered it honest to tamper with the bright violet and the staring white, since she saw them like that, fashionable though it was, since Mr. Paunceforte's visit, to see everything pale, elegant, semitransparent" (31–32). Lily remains faithful to her perceptual experience and, further, she, like her real life counterparts van Gogh and Cézanne, directs her attention not only to what she sees, but also to the structure which underlies the surface color: "Then beneath the colour there was the shape. She could see it all so clearly, so commandingly, when she looked: it was when she took her brush in hand that the whole thing changed. It was in that moment's flight between the picture and her canvas that the demons set on her who often brought her to the verge of tears and made this passage from conception to work as dreadful as any down a dark passage for a child" (32).

Lily discovers structural correlatives that will embody both her sense of Mrs. Ramsay's ability to protect and soothe, to create in fact sanctuaries within which her family can seek refuge, and Mr. Ramsay's philosophical impulse to penetrate the veil and perceive the object as it is. Significantly, the subject of Mr. Ramsay's philosophical inquiry concerns the "subject and object and the nature of reality" (38), which effectively defines the Post-Impressionist theme of the novel as a whole. His intellectual pragmatism, philosophical skepticism, and analytical detachment, however, commit him to a mode of perception that begins and ends in phenomenal reality. The object as it is, freed from the imposition of human need and value, is conceived by Lily in plastic terms as "this seeing of angular essences, this reducing of lovely evenings, with all their flamingo clouds and blue and silver to a white deal four-legged table," the kitchen table "when you're not there":

> So now she always saw, when she thought of Mr. Ramsay's work, a scrubbed kitchen table. It lodged now in the fork of a pear tree, for they had reached the orchard. And with a painful effort of concentration, she focused her mind, not upon the silver-bossed bark of the tree, or upon its fish-shaped leaves, but upon a phantom kitchen table, one of those scrubbed board tables, grained and knotted, whose virtue seems to have laid bare by years of muscular integrity, which struck there, its four legs in the air. (38)

The kitchen table lodged within the forked branches of the pear tree becomes paradigmatic of Ramsay's conceptual relationship to external reality. It is only when Lily "has" Mr. Ramsay at the novel's close that she is able to appreciate the standard of beauty which can evolve from his mode of vision. Defined physically and symbolically as "farsightedness," this realism offers a vision of "unornamented beauty." Lily explains: "The kitchen table was something visionary, austere; something bare, hard, not ornamental. There was no colour to it; it was all edges and angles; it was uncompromisingly plain" (232). Mr. Ramsay's "doubts about that table," "whether the table was a real table" or an idea in the mind—a sort of classic Berkeley versus Descartes dilemma—becomes the battle he wages intellectually on the terrace of the summer house, and wins, so it seems, just prior to his arrival at the lighthouse at the close of the novel. It is a commitment to objective reality, plain and unadorned, that is given graphic form in the clearly articulated, boldly outlined, depersonalized, and simplified forms of the kitchen table still life.

To counter this radical disjunction of subject and object created by Mr. Ramsay's detached and disindividualized perception of the fact dispossessed of human significance, there is Mrs. Ramsay's creative appropriation of objects as carriers of her integrating vision. Mrs. Ramsay's essentially Symbolist dream of sharing is borne out in her sense of a mysterious continuum between the isolate self and the world of things, a sense of contiguity that is abrogated by the disembodied intelligence that apprehends things in their irrevocable otherness in the "Time Passes" interlude. In the "Window" interlude, however, the synthesis of subject and object that she is capable of achieving balances the linearity and angularity of her husband's definition of the nature of reality and the depersonalized point of view it encapsulates. Her "daily miracles" are visualized in terms of curved and arabesque forms that express her capacity "to surround and protect" one from Ramsay's uncompromising empiricism. The image of the shawl draped over the skull in the children's room functions, as do the conventions of the dinner party, as a meaningful illusion, for Mrs. Ramsay "as a nurse carrying a light across a dark room" creates what Whitehead effectively describes as "magic mountains." She transforms the inert fact of our biological mortality into an "unreal universe" (406), which, like the work of art, conveys an imaginative fact as convincing as the biological one. Thus, though Mrs. Ramsay's skill in the art of lying enrages her husband—for "he had ridden through the valley of death, been shattered and shivered; and now she flew in the face of facts, made his children hope what was utterly out of the question, in effect told lies" (50)—her Berkeleian *esse est percipi* provides the necessary corrective for his scientific positivism. As the creator of consoling fictions, Mrs. Ramsay is consistently illuminated by the window, knitting the stocking for the lighthousekeeper's son (thereby sustaining the illusion of the morrow's journey that Ramsay's predictions would extinguish). Her mode of vision finds its formal equivalent in a kind of Symbolist blurring of outline, in which, commensurate with her symbolic and physical nearsightedness, forms dissolve and contours are vaguely stated, lost in a kind of luminous transparency.

Mrs. Ramsay is therefore realized through generically parallel visual images that accentuate the life-giving qualities that those illusions of stasis and security possess. These forms refer her creative power to organic processes—the fecundity of the sea, the fountain, and the fruit-bearing tree suggesting a vitality that is subterranean in origin. James's visualization of his mother affirms this Symbolist pattern: "Mrs. Ramsay who had been sitting loosely, folding her son in her arm, braced herself, and, half turning, seemed to raise herself with an effort, and at once pour erect into the air a rain of energy, a column of spray, looking at the same time animated and alive as if all her energies were being fused into force, burning and illuminating (quietly though she sat, taking up her stocking again)" (58). The image is strikingly evocative of the transformative energy of van Gogh's *Self-Portrait, Saint-Rémy* and boldly delineates James's responsiveness to his mother's procreative powers.

Syntactically Woolf conjoins realistic and lyrical impulses by using an extended series of phrasal constructions to adumbrate the way in which Mrs. Ramsay's human form partially dissolves in the transformative process, and a parenthetical insert to retain the conventional sense of her surface appearance. In *A Writer's Diary*, Woolf indicates the way in which parenthetical commentary might function in a verbal medium to create the illusion of simultaneous yet disparate perspective views of the same subject. In thinking through the last chapter of *To the Lighthouse* she attempts to solve the problem of bringing Lily and Mr. Ramsay together and observes:

> The last chapter which I begin tomorrow is In the Boat: I had meant to end with R. climbing on to the rock. If so, what becomes of Lily and her picture? Should there be a final page about her and Carmichael looking at the picture and summing up R.'s character? In that case I lose the intensity of the moment. If this intervenes between R. and the lighthouse, there's too much chop and change, I think. Could I do it in a parenthesis? So that one had the sense of reading the two things at the same time? (98)

In parallel plastic terms, van Gogh achieves polyphonic effects by fusing poetic and prosaic methods of presentation, methods he actualizes in the *Self-Portrait* and anticipates in his analysis of a projected portrait of an unidentified "artist friend": "Behind the head, instead of painting the ordinary wall of the mean room, I paint infinity, a plain background of the richest, intensest blue that I can contrive, and by this simple combination of the bright head against the rich blue background, I get a mysterious effect, like a star in the depths of an azure sky" (letter 520, *Letters of van Gogh* 3: 6).

James's sense of the opposition between his parents is expressed in terms of thrust and counterthrust, for the momentum of Mrs. Ramsay's rising force is aborted by the downward pull of Mr. Ramsay's overwhelming need: "and into this delicious fecundity, this fountain and spray of life, the fatal sterility of the male plunged itself, like a beak of brass, barren and bare" (58). Woolf manages the dynamics of their relationship as Cézanne manipulates the "thrust and return" (Loran, 88) of the linear content in his *Still Life with Fruit Basket*. These are distortions of photographic notions of verisimilitude, which Cézanne relies on to bring his feelings for the three-dimensional form to fruition on the canvas. In balancing the contrapuntal rhythms of rising and falling patterns that realize the essential spirit rather than external appearance of her characters, Woolf suggests that both Mr. and Mrs. Ramsay's modes of perception must be taken together adequately to comprehend the nature of reality. By realizing the still-life subject from disparate eye levels, Cézanne brings into being his sense of painting as "the discovery of a harmony among numerous relationships" rather than as "the servile copying of objects" (qtd. in Venturi, *Impressionists and Symbolists*, 136). In Woolf, one experiences in verbal terms the dynamic interaction of psychological figures that find their plastic correlative in the Post-

Impressionist tension between masses, colors, and shapes. It is Mrs. Ramsay's gift to bring her husband within the "charmed circle" of those "globed compacted things" (286) which make "life stand still": "In the midst of chaos there was shape; this eternal passing and flowing (she looked at the clouds going and the leaves shaking) was struck into stability" (241).

In conjunction with rising and falling directional lines, Woolf also explores the tension between the Ramsays through natural and metallic analogues in these signature images. Mrs. Ramsay is conceived by James as a "rosy-flowered tree laid with leaves and dancing boughs," a vital organic analogy which visualizes the life-giving properties that seem to be jeopardized by James's sense of the possessiveness of his father: "So boasting of her capacity to surround and protect, there was scarcely a shell of herself left for her to know herself by; all was so lavished and spent; and James, as he stood stiff between her knees, felt her rise in a rosy-flowered fruit tree laid with leaves and dancing boughs into which the beak of brass, the arid scimitar of his father, the egotistical man, plunged and smote, demanding sympathy" (60).

The concept of interpenetration and interdependence visualized through natural and metallic correspondences, and contrapuntal linear forces, is brought to fruition in purely plastic and equally nonrepresentational terms in Lily's final composition. Here the intricate surface pattern of running blue and green hedge-shaped lines is penetrated by the uncompromising and unnatural (straight lines, as Cézanne observed, do not exist in nature) vertical which intersects the center of the canvas:

> There it was—her picture. Yes, with all its greens and blues, its lines running up and across, its attempt at something. It would be hung in attics, she thought; it would be destroyed. But what did that matter? she asked herself, taking up her brush again. She looked at the steps; they were empty; she looked at her canvas; it was blurred. With a sudden intensity, as if she saw it clear for a second, she drew a line there, in the centre. It was done; it was finished. Yes, she thought, laying down her brush in extreme fatigue, I have had my vision. (309–10)[45]

Not only does Woolf create graphic verbal correlatives that dramatize the tension between Mr. and Mrs. Ramsay's conceptions of reality, she also understands the nature of the modern space effect, and attempts to find a literary equivalent for it in the novel. Lily's method of working is described as "tunnelling her way into the picture, into her past." In *The Echoes Enslaved,* Allen McLaurin points out that the term *tunnelling* is similar in intention to the phrase of Seurat's which Fry was fond of quoting.[46] Seurat defined the art of painting as "the art of hollowing out a canvas" (*Transformations,* 189), and this creation of enclosed space forms the basis of the Post-Impressionism sense of the nonrepresentational nature of art. This conception is intrinsic to Woolf's own sense of how the moment of vision functions within a narrative medium, to "symbolize" and "give us an epitome," which, through selection and arrangement, erects a barrier that inhibits us from "instinctively" and "easily" entering "a world that we know already" ("Phases of Fiction," 100–102).

McLaurin suggests that the space effect in Woolf's work is achieved by typographical tricks such as the use of the dots to suggest "disconnected movements within a landscape" (87–88). This observation forms part of his definition of the pictorial quality of *To the Lighthouse* generally in terms of the typographical rhetoric of square and round brackets. McLaurin, however, sabotages his analysis by suggesting that the novel as a whole should be perceived as if it were a painting: "Seeing the novel as a whole shape, the thin central section is like a vertical line, as well as an empty space bracketed by the first and last sections. . . . The curve is linked with the scythe of Father Time and also with the indirect method of achieving the truth, but a further intention is to make the novel approximate as nearly as possible to the visual effect of a painting" (199). The novel's typography is a descriptive narrative device which allows Woolf to eliminate those discursive passages which traditionally function to indicate changes in setting, tone, and point of view. Insofar as typographical rhetoric contributes through simplification and condensation to the overall dramatic quality of the narrative, by eliminating superfluities and tightening the tension between perspective shifts, it enhances the context within which Woolf's visual correlatives operate. However, it is clearly inadequate to define the visual character of the novel within typographical terms, and much more to the point to explore the way in which space effects are actually achieved through perspectival distortions and patterns of enclosure.

Woolf's sense of a Post-Impressionist conception of enclosure is nowhere more apparent than in her presentation of the effect of Rose's arrangement of fruit, for the still life "brought up suddenly into the light . . . seemed possessed of great size and depth, was like a world in which one could take one's staff and climb hills." Distortion through magnification, intensified by the effects of candlelight, heightens our sense of the corporality of the arrangement's elements. Woolf engages both the tactile and visual sensibility of the reader by insisting upon the eye's ability to grasp form: "she saw that Augustus too feasted his eyes on the same plate of fruit, plunged in, broke off a bloom there, a tassel here, and returned, after feasting, to his hive" (146).

Interestingly, Woolf's sense of taking possession of an object by creating an illusion of depth rather than surface forms the basis of her own appreciation of the distortions Cézanne uses to imbue the natural object with a saliency it would not possess in a purely visual illusion of its three-dimensionality. In recording her responses to Cézanne's *Pommes,* which was on exhibit at the National Gallery in April 1918, Woolf observes: "There are 6 apples in the Cézanne picture. What can 6 apples *not* be? I began to wonder. Theres their relationship to each other, & their colour, & their solidity." As she moves to another room in the Gallery, she is intrigued by Cézanne's ability to enter into a fullness of possession other artists cannot equal: "We carried it into the next room & Lord! how it showed up the pictures there, as if you put a real stone among sham ones; the canvas of the others seemed scraped with a thin layer of rather cheap paint. The apples positively got redder & rounder & greener. I suspect some very mysterious quality of potation(?) in that picture."[47]

The spatial illusion that Woolf achieves in the fruit bowl episode parallels what Lhote defined in Cézanne as a "promenade" "not by foot, but with the spirit" (33). Not only does Woolf enhance the sense of the relief of her volumes through distortion, she also dramatizes her notion of the moment's autotelic condition by framing the rectangular dinner table with the frieze-like immobility of the guests whose illuminated faces are "brought nearer by the candle light." Finally, the suggestion of enclosed space communicated by the dish of fruit and repeated by the human frame is echoed in the reversal effected by the night-darkened window panes that describe the outer limits of the gathering: "the night was now shut off by the panes of glass, which, far from giving any accurate view of the outside world, rippled it so strangely that here, inside the room, seemed to be order and dry land; there, outside, a reflection in which things wavered and vanished, waterily" (146–47).

Through a series of parallel patterns of enclosure, Woolf sustains the sense of stasis, depth, and substantiality that she feels the moment possesses. Further, in blackening the window and deliberately undermining our sense of the accessibility and tangibility of the external world, she returns our attention to the moment that, like a painting, discloses the "ultimate reality." Lily's understanding of Rose's "gift of style" anticipates her recognition of the fact that, in a parallel way, Mrs. Ramsay's creative power depends upon the image of "that woman sitting there writing under the rock" resolving "everything into simplicity," bringing together the discontinuous elements, "giving them a wholeness not theirs in life," and through acts of creative transmutation making "something," "affecting one almost like a work of art" (239–40).

In his discussion of what he feels to be the hermetic nature of the epiphany in twentieth-century British fiction, Daniel Schwarz argues that the moment of vision in Woolf's novels is achieved in isolation from the social community. He suggests that Lily's completion of her vision in the painting comes "at the expense of a social life," just as Mrs. Ramsay's victories are "more aesthetic than moral." Yet at the same time Schwarz observes that Lily's quest for order—to make, as does Mrs. Ramsay, "something permanent" of the moment, something which has the force of "revelation"—mimes Woolf's own "quest for values."[48] What Schwarz evades is that the achievement of stability, the disclosure of pattern and order, the very creation of enclosed space in Lily's canvas and in the proportions of the dinner scene, are indicative of the way in which moral and esthetic values complement each other in Post-Impressionist art.

Lily's capacity to create reality, to illuminate "this other thing, this truth, this reality" is born in her achievement of enclosed space: "she scored her canvas with brown running nervous lines which had no sooner settled there than they enclosed (she felt it looming out at her) a space" (236). Further "this form" becomes as valid a form of "intercourse" with social realities, as intellectually invigorating and as morally significant, as any other conception of the human community that Schwarz narrowly defines for Lily in terms of the "form of marriage" alone (293).

Not only does Woolf concretize the tension between Mr. and Mrs. Ramsay by attending to the expressive power of line and shape, she further adumbrates that opposition in terms of near and far perspectives, working like van Gogh to make perspective a "quality" of the landscape that is sighted. She is aware, as McLaurin suggests (91–92), of both the spatial and psychological effects that alterations in perspective can achieve. Her sensitivity to the reciprocal relation between them materializes in an entry in her diary, "Proportions changed":

> That in the evening, or on colourless days, the proportions of the landscape change suddenly. I saw people playing stoolball in the meadow; they appeared sunk far down on a flat board; and the downs raised high up and mountainous round them. Detail was smoothed out. This was an extremely beautiful effect: the colours of the women's dresses also showing very bright and pure in almost untinted surroundings. I knew also, that the proportions were abnormal—as if I were looking between my legs. (*A Writer's Diary*, 95)

In *To the Lighthouse,* Mr. Ramsay is consistently imaged standing erect at the edge of some promontory, leading a procession, moving from A to Z in an absolutely straight line: "Who then could blame the leader of that forlorn part which after all has climbed high enough to see the waste of years and the perishing of stars" (56). His consciousness of the ephemerality of human existence, of the preternaturality of the nonhuman order ("The very stone one kicks with one's boot will outlast Shakespeare"), the inevitability of human mortality ("Mr. Ramsay squared his shoulders and stood very upright by the urn" [56]), and the irrevocable isolation the human condition imposes ("we perish each alone") finds its perspectival correlative in the distant view. Walking with Mrs. Ramsay toward the close of the day on the terrace, it is Mr. Ramsay who looks toward the lighthouse revealed through "the gap between the two clumps of red-hot pokers," a view Mrs. Ramsay "will not herself look at." She turns back instead toward the view of the lights of the town, the harbor and the boats, lights which "seemed like a phantom net floating there to mark something which had sunk" (104). The net image is itself, by implication, suggestive of the protective fabric she weaves about the bare facts, a fabric, like the shawl about the skull, which creates illusions of security and continuity.

Ramsay, in contrast, looks "across the bay." He yearns for its solitude and contemplates communion with a world undisturbed by any human presence but his own: "That was the country he liked best, over there; those sand hills dwindling away into darkness. One could walk all day without meeting a soul. There was not a house scarcely, not a single village for miles on end. One could worry things out alone. There were little sandy beaches where no one had been since the beginning of time. The seals sat up and looked at you. It sometimes seemed to him that in a little house out there, alone—he broke off, sighing" (105). Recalled to the reality of his brood of eight and his domestic responsibilities, Ramsay infuses the distant scene with the pathos of his own perhaps histrionic, yet inveterate and preemptive, need for detachment: "They showed he did not damn the poor little universe entirely, for on an evening like this, he thought, looking at the land dwindling away, the little island seemed pathetically small, half swallowed up in the sea" (106).

It is Mr. Ramsay's gift in fact "to come out thus on a spit of land which the sea is slowly eating away, and there to stand, like a desolate sea-bird alone," "as a stake driven into the bed of a channel upon which the gulls perch and the waves beat inspires in merry boat-loads a feeling of gratitude for the duty it is taking upon itself of marking the channel out there in the floods alone" (68–69). The image of his uncompromising vertical, coupled with the manic downward imagistic thrust of that line driven into the channel (a rhythm which is repeated in the tattoo of his peripatetic soliloquies about the summer house punctuated by the stamping of his foot upon the stone step [50]), finds its perspectival complement in distant views.

Ramsay dominates the top of his own magic mountain looking from it "down the long waste of ages" (56). His Olympian perspective commensurate with his intellectual (though not emotional) detachment is realized in expansive vistas, which repeat the basic pattern articulated in the rise and fall of the waves. Significantly removed from the organic rhythm of his wife and family, he is perceived as an alien and disruptive force. Woolf demonstrates the kind of subjective deformation of objective reality that a particular perspective engenders, by emphasizing the psychological implications of both near and distant views. When Ramsay's meditative rhythm on the terrace is interrupted by Lily and Bankes, for example, the break is visualized through a shift in perspective: "Who shall blame him? Who will not secretly rejoice when the hero puts his armour off, and halts by the window and gazes at his wife and son, who, very distant at first, gradually come closer and closer, till lips and book and head are clearly before him, though still lovely and unfamiliar from the intensity of his isolation and the waste of ages and the perishing of stars" (57).

From the depersonalization of this distant view Ramsay moves within the orbit of his wife and son. Though he brings them more clearly into focus, he is still sufficiently detached and therefore perceives them esthetically—"he does homage to the beauty of the world"—rather than personally. Significantly the tableau is completed with James resentfully peering up at his father as Ramsay commandingly looks down upon the boy and his mother, who appears finally to rise as a column of spray to meet his insistent though unspoken appeal for consolation. In this way, Woolf maximizes the nondiscursive capacity of her medium. Through the carefully orchestrated and highly concentrated manipulation of perspective, she is able to explore the subtle distinctions in Ramsay's relationship to his family, as intellectual, esthete, husband, and rival.

This awareness of the expressive and constructive power of perspective line functions through Lily as well, as she begins to understand the immense power of the distant view which absorbs Ramsay: "The sea without stain on it, thought Lily Briscoe, still standing and looking out over the bay. The sea stretched like silk across the bay. Distance had an extraordinary power; they had been swallowed up in it, she felt, they were gone for ever, they had become part of the nature of things. It was so calm; it was so quiet. The steamer itself had vanished, but the great scroll of smoke still hung in the air and drooped like a flag mournfully in valediction" (279–80).

The theme of inaccessibility, absence, and ephemerality implied by the distant view is balanced by Lily's actual physical position in front of the summer house with brush in hand where she had "attacked that problem of the hedge" before the "instinctive need of distance and blue" had taken hold of her (270). The hedge itself is allied with Mrs. Ramsay's mode of perception, for in her nearsightedness she is acutely responsive to its intricate surface patterns. Her husband's farsightedness characteristically prompts him to peer through the break across the bay to the lighthouse in the far distance. In sharing Ramsay's perspectival experience, Lily begins finally to understand his character. Experiencing the conditions of landscape rendered from his point of view provides, she suggests, a "way of knowing people" (289). Thus, renewed by her contact with him in this way, Lily returns: "So coming back from a journey, or after an illness, before habits had spun themselves across the surface" (285), she is able to penetrate finally beyond her superficial and one-sided conception of Mr. Ramsay to "achieve that razor edge of balance between opposite forces; Mr. Ramsay and the picture" necessary to complete the canvas (287).

So too, James's instinct for harmony is realized in the juxtaposition of two views of the lighthouse itself. The first, rendered under his mother's protective influence, is visualized in a manner that parallels the charm and mysterious evocativeness of Seurat's *The Lighthouse at Honfleur* (fig. 20): "The Lighthouse was then a silvery, misty-looking tower with a yellow eye, that opened suddenly, and softly in the evening" (276). The second, rendered from his father's perspective, is visualized with the precision that parallels Ramsay's austere sense of the object as it is: "He could see the white-washed rocks; the tower, stark and straight; he could see that it was barred with black and white; he could see windows in it; he could even see washing spread on the rocks to dry" (276–77).

Figure 20. Georges Seurat, *The Lighthouse at Honfleur*, 1886
Oil on canvas, 26¼" × 32¼".
(National Gallery of Art, Washington; collection of Mr. and Mrs. Paul Mellon)

Woolf's choice of linguistic patterns heightens the tension between the two perspectives. The first "picture" is expressed simply in one rhythmic and graceful declarative sentence, while the second is visualized in a sequence of short grammatically parallel subordinate structures, halting in their rhythms and monotonous in their repetition, which exaggerate the visual effect of the series of horizontal planes, unmodulated and severe. Most significantly, James is able to absorb both pictorial definitions of the nature of reality: "No, the other was also the Lighthouse. For nothing was simply one thing. The other Lighthouse was true too" (277). Woolf's parallax view allows for the creative juxtaposition of these two versions of the lighthouse, both near and far, subjective and objective, a juxtaposition integral to the Post-Impressionist sense of the multidimensional nature of reality.

The kind of dynamic Woolf achieves by rendering a single scene from disparate points of view is equally central to the balance between surface and in-depth values that she sustains through the juxtaposition of two of Lily's visions of the Ramsay marriage. In an outdoor scene at twilight, Lily attempts to grasp the symbolic dimensions of what had always been the prosaic character of the conception of marriage Mrs. Ramsay seemed to advertise to her: "Mrs. Ramsay was wearing a green shawl, and they were standing close together watching Prue and Jasper throwing catches. And suddenly the meaning . . . came upon them, and made them in the dusk standing, looking, the symbols of marriage, husband and wife. Then after an instant, the symbolic outline which transcended the real figures sank down again, and they became, as they met them, Mr. and Mrs. Ramsay watching the children throwing catches" (110–11).

Seurat's stylizations in *A Sunday Afternoon on the Island of La Grande Jatte* (fig. 21) provide an interesting pictorial correlative for the dualistic nature of Lily's vision of the Ramsays in *To the Lighthouse*. While Seurat's stylizations render his figures representative, they do not sever the scene's relationship to actual conditions. Seurat's nonrepresentational focus is felt in the regularity of his forms, which is indicative of his own disaffection with the fashion of his day. The potential humor of that convention is also underlined by the stasis he achieves through precision in outline and clearly delineated contrasts of light and shadow. Woolf creates a parallel sense of the tension between the reality and unreality of prevailing norms through Lily's rather facetious affirmation of the convention of marriage itself. For a moment, a "spell" is cast by her own creative eye. Taking advantage of the twilight light values, which accentuate surface, she imbues the Ramsays with monumental significance: "In the failing light they all looked sharp-edged and ethereal and divided by great distances." In the next instant, "the spell" is "broken," and everyday conditions reassert themselves: "Then, darting backwards over the vast space (for it seemed as if solidity had vanished altogether), Prue ran full tilt into them and caught the ball

Figure 21. Georges Seurat, *A Sunday Afternoon on the Island of La Grande Jatte*, 1884–1886
Oil on canvas, 207.6 × 308 cm.
(Helen Birch Bartlett Memorial Collection; courtesy of the Art Institute of Chicago)

brilliantly high up in her left hand, and her mother said, 'Haven't they come back yet?' whereupon the spell was broken."

While Mr. Ramsay's distant view exaggerates the incompatibility of human and nonhuman worlds on any other than a biological level, Mrs. Ramsay's nearsightedness enables her to sustain a vital reciprocity between self and world. Woolf conceives the private, elusive, and amorphous self in geometric terms as a "wedge-shaped core of darkness, something invisible to others" (95), freed from ordinary physical and temporal limitations. The configuration provides a particularly rich example of the way in which the abstract, the unseen, and the inimitable can be given concrete definition in a verbal medium. The shape is repeated through a series of natural analogues such as the butterfly's wing, that vibrant reflecting surface, "color burning on a framework of steel," which insinuates itself as does the shawl about the skull, creating unity out of multiplicity, the first principle of design. In contrast, Mr. Ramsay's analogue is the "framework of steel," "this admirable fabric of the masculine intelligence, which ran up and down, crossed this way and that, like iron girders spanning the swaying fabric, upholding the world" (159). While he fixes his attention on the underlying linear order, which, as the second principle of design, provides direction through space, Mrs. Ramsay weaves those illusions of enclosure and stasis that transcend the linear but paradoxically depend upon that structure for their being. These verbal images, absorbed by Lily as "the light of a butterfly's wing lying upon the arches of a cathedral" (75), find their plastic equivalents in her canvas, as she resolves the "problem of space" by affirming the two dimensions of her medium:

> It glared at her. The whole mass of the picture was poised upon that weight. Beautiful and bright it should be on the surface, feathery and evanescent, one colour melting into another like the colours on a butterfly's wing; but beneath the fabric must be clamped together with bolts of iron. It was a thing you could ruffle with your breath; and a thing you could not dislodge with a team of horses. And she began to lay on a red, a grey, and she began to model her way into the hollow there. At the same time, she seemed to be sitting beside Mrs. Ramsay on the beach. (255)

One immediately recalls not only Cézanne's expressed intention "to make of Impressionism something solid and lasting," but also the various techniques he used to work out the interrelationships between surface modulation and linear content to balance representational and nonrepresentational values. Woolf's profound sense of this dynamic is particularly evident in the way she uses perspective, formal correlatives, and the spatial effects of the moment to explore the way in which surface can reveal depth.

I have suggested that Mrs. Ramsay's close-range vision complements her husband's distant view and, further, that because of her shortsightedness she is capable of communion with the object of contemplation. McLaurin defines that perspective, however, as the verbal counterpart of pictorial Impressionism, an "Impressionist blur," which he describes in the following manner:

> In *Jacob's Room* the natural scene becomes a kind of rudimentary impressionist painting when it is viewed through tears. In *To the Lighthouse* the equivalent everyday vision is the short-sightedness of Mrs. Ramsay. Perhaps this indicates her intellectual limitations as well, for the visual and psychological cannot be disentangled here. The shortcomings which Fry saw in the paintings of the Impressionists also apply to Mrs. Ramsay's short-sighted vision of the world. Like them, she sees the full mosaic of her visual field, but it is insufficiently articulated. This is necessarily so, for articulation involves the rejection of some of the elements which make up our immediate experience. Mrs. Ramsay does not want to relinquish any aspect of her immediate feelings and so she becomes absolutely identified with the thing she is looking at. (179)

McLaurin then documents Mrs. Ramsay's "all-embracing passivity," which he defines in terms of Impressionism (a correspondence that, I have shown in chapter 1, is clearly inappropriate) by analyzing the scene in which Mrs. Ramsay, as the "wedge-shaped core of darkness," meets the "long steady stroke" of the lighthouse beam:

> Often she found herself sitting and looking, sitting and looking, with her work in her hands until she became the thing she looked at—that light for example. . . . It was odd, she thought, how if one was alone, one leant to inanimate things; trees, streams, flowers; felt they expressed one; felt they became one; felt they knew one, in a sense were one; felt an irrational tenderness thus (she looked at that long steady light) as for oneself. There rose, and she looked and looked with her needles suspended, there curled up off the floor of the mind, rose from the lake of one's own being, a mist, a bride to meet her lover. (97–98)

It is clear, however, that the configuration here parallels the disposition of the earlier fountain of spray image in the novel and that, further, Woolf's visualization of Mrs. Ramsay's inner force shares many of the qualities of the works of Pre-Raphaelite and Symbolist artists within the Post-Impressionist movement who were similarly fascinated with the female figure. Woolf conceives of Mrs. Ramsay's malign and benign aspects in complementary iconographic forms. Bankes, on the one hand, transposes her into an etherealized Helen of Troy, a disembodied Madonna, in a manner congenial with the ideal creature of the Pre-Raphaelite mode evinced in the generalized spirituality of Dante Gabriel Rossetti's *The Blessed Damousel* or Giovanni Segantini's enigmatic *Goddess of Love*. Ramsay, on the other hand, is both threatened by and attracted to his wife's sublime self-sufficiency, and thus she possesses for him a sphinx-like quality in her sternness and remoteness. The sphinx is a predominant iconographic motif in Symbolist paintings ranging from Gauguin's *Tahitian Women*, through to Fernand Khnopff's enigmatic temptress in *The Sphinx* and Edvard Munch's more positive *Madonna*. The bride figure is equally popular, and especially effective in Xavier Mellery's 1890 *Evening Dream,* which explores the symbiotic relationship between the seated female figure and the vaguely stated interior which is bathed, as Goldwater suggests, in a "mystical liquor" to visualize the theme of interpenetration between mind and matter.

Clearly the Impressionists' visual subjectivity, which is based upon fidelity to the optic alone, is incompatible with the psychological realism Woolf explores pictorially through her character's myopia. Further, it is precisely because, as McLaurin suggests, one cannot "disentangle" the "visual and psychological" that one places Mrs. Ramsay's silent art within a Post-Impressionist context. Her attachment to the real simultaneously liberates the soul of objects and the essence of self. That creative synthesis is possible when the mind is freed from the exigencies of ego and social identity.

We recall, as well, the impersonal emotion Cézanne's landscapes communicate when, as in *Mont Ste. Victoire, Seen from Bellevue,* cosmic perspective techniques allow him to eliminate every subjective reference including the standing ground of the observer. We can also relate Woolf's abridgement of the personal self at the moment of vision to the kind of "osmotic participation" (*Symbolism,* 211) Mellery achieves in his *The Soul of Things* (fig. 22), where the artist's mysticism is oriented toward an intuition of the inner psychic dynamism of the world and things, where silent hypnagogic interiors are imbued with vibrations of shadowed light that play an almost pantheistic role.

At the same time, the "blurring of material delimitations," to use Douwe Fokkema's description of the kind of "subject-object blending" Woolf achieves in the scene under discussion, is different from those Expressionistic devices which objectify feelings and spiritualize inanimate objects. "The difference," Fokkema suggests, "may be that between detached but intense observation on the one hand [i.e., the kind of depersonalization both Cézanne and van Gogh achieve through cosmic perspective] and a voluntaristic effort of the committed subject on the other" [i.e., the externalization of private worlds through natural forms which function only as a means to that end].[49] The creative synthesis of subject and object that Woolf visualizes must then be received as confirmation of the applicability of Post-Impressionism's fascination with the reciprocal relation possible between external and internal realities.

One can then understand the meaning of Woolf's worship of solid objects not as evidence of what Marjorie Brace defines as Woolf's despair over the "unknowableness of people and the impossibilities of communion," which drives her "toward a pagan reanimation of objects."[50] Rather, Woolf's treatment of the object provides evidence of her belief in the redemptive power of a depersonalized perspective. The lighthouse beam in this context, "steady," "pitiless," "remorseless," "with its silver fingers" stroking "some sealed vessel in her brain," provides a sense of communion with the inner recesses of being that provokes "exquisite happiness": "it silvered the rough waves a little more brightly,

Figure 22.   Xavier Mellery, *The Soul of Things*, 1890
Black and white chalk, 93 × 67 cm.
(Koninklijk Museum voor Schone Kunsten, Antwerp)

as daylight faded, and the blue went out of the sea and it rolled in waves of pure lemon which curved and swelled and broke upon the beach and the ecstasy burst in her eyes and waves of pure delight raced over the floor of her mind and she felt, It is enough! It is enough!" (99–100). Rather than despair, the expressive vitality of those "waves of pure lemon" communicates a rhythm which is felt throughout the piece, paralleling in its effectiveness the dynamic energy of van Gogh's kinesthetic forms in *Starry Night*.

In "The Revolt against Language: Virginia Woolf and Clive Bell," Jan Heinemann files a number of Woolf's statements about the seeming inadequacy of the verbal medium to convey the "true reality," an attitude that he suggests is epitomized by an observation made in *Flush*, Woolf's biography of Elizabeth Barrett Browning rendered from her spaniel's perspective: "Not a single one of his myriad sensations ever submitted itself to the deformity of words."[51] Heinemann suggests that both Bell and Woolf suffer from logophobia or a "radical distrust of language," and that their "linguistic pessimism" provides evidence of their irrationalism. This skeptical attitude toward language (its inability to express "private phenomena") leads, he advises, to a belief in a special intuitive faculty which in itself is "irrational," "fallible" and a "superfluous" means "of acquiring knowledge."[52]

Not only does Heinemann ignore the Post-Impressionist conception of the provisional nature of reality that Woolf's affirmation of the multidimensionality of form endorses, but in his criticism of the intuitionalist position he ignores how linguistic patterns can in fact evoke the sense of fusion between the observer and the observed that Woolf is working with through Mrs. Ramsay. Woolf's desire to reshape the conventions of her medium is based, not upon an indictment of language's ability to express "private phenomena," but rather upon a belief in the medium's capacity to reveal the way in which the mind transmutes the conventional appearance of the object into significance. In "Notes on an Elizabethan Play," Woolf discusses the new breed of novel that would fuse the prosaic and the poetic, the realistic and the mystical, and she commissions the novelist to inaugurate "the creation of what may yet be devised to liberate us from the enormous burden of the unexpressed" (*Collected Essays* 1:59). That liberation, of necessity, involves the deformation of traditional narrative methods and notions of linguistic orthodoxy to embody the change in the perception of what human nature in fact is.

In order to realize Mrs. Ramsay's moment of "osmotic participation," Woolf relies on a set of linguistic features that will evoke the sense of interpenetration that is integral to Post-Impressionist art. She builds toward the actual moment of vision through an extended paratactic and periodic construction, allowing the protagonist to explore the psychological ambiguities that attend the parallax effect. She uses parenthetical insertions, as she did in the fruit-bowl epiphany, to restore a detached point of view even while the repetitive prose rhythms advocate a profound sense of being absorbed within, and at one with, the beam of light. And finally she allows oxymoronic images to adumbrate the way in which the barriers between the individualized psyche and the other are progressively dissolved:

> She saw the light again. With some irony in her interrogation, for when one woke at all, one's relations changed, she looked at the steady light, the pitiless, the remorseless which was so much her, yet so little her, which had her at its beck and call (she woke in the night and saw it bent across their bed, stroking the floor), but for all that she thought, watching it with fascination, hypnotised, as if it were stroking with its silver fingers some sealed vessel in her brain whose bursting would flood her with delight, she had known happiness, exquisite happiness, intense happiness. (99)

Hemingway

The precedent for arguing an affinity between Hemingway and Post-Impressionism generally, and Hemingway and Cézanne specifically, is provided by the author himself through a statement he made to Lillian Ross while both toured the Museum of Modern Art: "I can make a landscape like Mr. Paul Cézanne. I learned how to make a landscape from Mr. Paul Cézanne by walking through the Luxembourg Museum a thousand times with an empty gut, and I am pretty sure that if Mr. Paul was around, he would like the way I make them and be happy that I learned it from him."[53]

In proclaiming that he can "make a landscape like Mr. Paul Cézanne," Hemingway is alluding to his grasp of the way in which the modern space conception functions within Cézanne's canvas, a "secret" which he describes in *A Moveable Feast* in terms of compression and dimension:

> I went there [to the Luxembourg Museum] nearly every day for the Cézannes and to see the Manets and the Monets and the other Impressionists that I had first come to know about in the Art Institute at Chicago. I was learning something from the painting of Cézanne that made writing simple true sentences far from enough to make the stories have the dimensions that I was trying to put in them. I was learning very much from him but I was not articulate enough to explain it to anyone. Besides it was a *secret*.[54]

In an interview with George Plimpton, Hemingway provides a clearer indication of the kind of verbal techniques he is developing that will allow him in his own medium to duplicate the realism of Cézanne's achievement of *perspective vécue*. He states, for example, that "A writer, if he is any good, does not describe. He invents, or *makes* out of knowledge personal and impersonal," and that further this "invention" is "not a representation but a whole new thing truer than anything true and alive." So too, Cézanne argues for the nonrepresentational fidelity to the given, "from all the things you know," and from a belief of one's "strong experience of nature," "all those things you cannot know."[55]

In the same interview, Hemingway uses the term "dimensions" to explicate his sense of the shortcomings of the descriptive mode: "If you describe someone it is flat, as a photograph is, and from my standpoint a failure. If you make him up from what you know, there should be all the dimensions" (33). The sense of having "all the dimensions" is intimately related to the art of omission and involves, as is apparent in Cézanne's work, the elimination of extraneous surface details that would obscure the purity of lines and the integration of sensations that will actualize the depth sensation. Hemingway's admiration for Cézanne is based upon his understanding of the way in which tactile and visual sensations can cooperate in the construction of form. In conversation with Ross, he suggests that the illusion of solidity and saliency Cézanne achieves in *Rocks: Forest of Fontainebleu* is one he wishes to sustain in prose: "This is what we try to do in writing, this and this, and the woods, and the rocks we have to climb over" (36).

Just as the "hole" in the picture in perspective art undermines the self-sufficiency of the painting itself by ignoring the conditions of the medium, so too the "hole" in the story undermines the autonomy of the fiction and its ability to offer in its own terms a profound sense of the actuality of the protagonist's experience of the created landscape. Despite the simplification of the naturalistic surface in Cézanne's landscapes—for there is as Clark suggests "no attempt to delineate a leaf"—his forms are "remarkably true to nature" (223). The comment applies equally to Hemingway's art of compression and omission as well. The illusion of substantiality he creates is carefully prepared for by incorporating those details which possess the greatest expressive and architectonic power to convince the reader of the actuality of the *perspective vécue*. In *Death in the Afternoon*, Hemingway elaborates: "I was trying to write then and I found the greatest difficulty . . . was to put down what really happened in action; what the actual things were which produced the emotion that you experienced."[56] In attempting to create a depth experience that possesses the force of actuality, Hemingway, like Cézanne, makes the transition from paradigm to simulacrum, from *energia* to *energia,* from the mimesis of surface to the mimesis of a process that allows the created reality to function as a harmony that is parallel with but not an imitation of nature.

Hemingway's fidelity to this conception of the space experience leads him to discover linguistic equivalents that will manage the sense of enclosure that is integral to the sensation of depth and actuality in Cézanne. Unfortunately, the kind of linguistic style that is generated by Hemingway's Iceberg Theory is often perceived by critics as evidence of his passionate lyricism or latent Expressionism. Thus the kind of distortion of the naturalistic surface Hemingway achieves through omission and selection in his creation of landscape is defined by Raymond Nelson, in *Hemingway: Expressionist Artist,* in terms of an emotional intensity he suggests Hemingway shares with Cézanne. Taking his point of departure from esthetician John Willett—who suggests in *Expressionism* that Cézanne's "controlled mastery" predisposes us to underestimate the artist's emotional forcefulness[57]—Nelson extends the compliment to Hemingway. Within this context Nelson cites H. E. Bates's analysis in "Hemingway's Short Stories" to corroborate his position. Bates suggests that "the colder and harder a man writes, as Chekhov once pointed out, the more deeply and more movingly emotional is the result likely to be. Hemingway was in reality so deeply susceptible to emotion that he strove constantly for the elimination of himself, his thoughts and feelings, from the surface of the work."[58]

Nelson absorbs the Chekhovian less-is-more formula without question, and concludes that when Hemingway speaks of putting down what one saw, "what the actual things were which produced the emotion that you experienced," he is endorsing the Expressionistic esthetic that Nelson believes he discovered in Cézanne: "Hemingway 'objectifies' or represents his emotion-generating material, and little more."[59] In a parallel way, Nelson cites Richard Murphy's *The World of Cézanne 1839–1906* and argues that Cézanne "shifted the emphasis in painting from the things viewed to the consciousness of the viewer." Art becomes "an expression of the emotion evoked in the artist by the enduring forms and colors of the natural world."[60]

This tendency to define the compression and precision of both artists in terms of unrestrained or undeclared emotion is common throughout Hemingway criticism. In relying on this perspective, critics assume that the object exists simply as a pretext for self-expression in Hemingway, and in Cézanne as well.[61] Along with the tendency to define the Cézanne-Hemingway affinity in Expressionist terms, there is the predisposition to view distortion itself as an occasional lapse in technique, an obstacle Cézanne and Hemingway struggle to overcome in their realization of verisimilitude. In "Hemingway and Cézanne: A Speculative Affinity," E. T. Jones suggests, for example, that the two artists "worked to make their art solid and durable, representing the truth of life as they apprehended it through the expression of essential form. Both men, not withstanding instances of deliberate distortion in their works and a variety of contrary labels assigned to them, remain basically realists; their concern is to show the way things are in terms of representation which is clean and well-lighted."[62] Working within a narrow conception of realism which seems once again tied to conventional notions of verisimilitude, Jones fails to realize that actually those "deliberate distortions" form the very basis of the realistic effect in Hemingway and Cézanne.

The paradox of penetration-transformation-revelation that defines Post-Impressionist art means that the artist's fidelity to the actual motif does not preclude the possibility of making arbitrary changes according to the exigencies of *perspective vécue*. When Lhote defines *perspective vécue* as the perception of depth through feeling, he is using the term *feeling* to suggest not simply the expression of personal emotion but rather the eyes' sensual grasp of form, the fusion of visual and tactile dimensions integral to the Post-Impressionist dynamic space conception. Thus, in entering a Hemingway or a Cézanne landscape the observer is engaged at every level of being. Hemingway systematically imposes deliberate and unifying distortions that simplify and condense the naturalistic surface, and these simplifications are manifest in his drive to eliminate the superfluous at linguistic levels as well. Further, these distortions often impose a dominant shape or image, which is repeated with minor variations throughout the scene to integrate its disparate aspects into architectural wholes. Hemingway not only absorbs Cézanne's pyramid configuration, he also absorbs the dialectics of thrust and return, the tension between directional lines, and the abridgement of linear and atmospheric perspective integral to Cézanne's achievement of enclosure. His choice of perspective sustains in kind the impersonal quality of emotion that Cézanne's multiple or cosmic perspectives work toward, for points of reference that would personalize the standing ground of the observer are eliminated to accentuate the experience of depth and pattern in the landscape.

These techniques function together in the opening landscape in *A Farewell to Arms,* to achieve parallel effects of enclosure and actuality. The impersonal quality of the prose, a quality often perceived as evidence of the Hemingway protagonist's struggle to suppress emotions too painful to express, provides evidence of Hemingway's ability to create a vigorous spatial effect by eliminating a personalized point of view.

> In the late summer of that year we lived in a house in a village that looked across the river and the plain to the mountains. In the bed of the river there were pebbles and boulders, dry and white in the sun, and the water was clear and swiftly moving and blue in the channels. Troops went by the house and down the road and the dust they raised powdered the leaves of the trees. The trunks of the trees too were dusty and the leaves fell early that year and we saw the troops marching along the road and the dust rising and leaves, stirred by the breeze, falling and the soldiers marching and afterward the road bare and white except for the leaves.[63]

Venturi illustrates how Cézanne achieves that same impersonal quality by sustaining an objective relationship between the various aspects of the motif in *The Bay of Marseilles, Seen from L'Estaque.* Cézanne abstracts both background and foreground from their real positions, both to preserve the space relationship between near and far and to generate a tangible sense of the essential structures of his landscape forms. In doing so, Venturi observes, he elimi-

nates "every subjective reference" by organizing an "objective relationship between the village, the sea, and the mountain, objective not with respect to nature
but with respect to the picture, to art" (*Impressionists and Symbolists,* 132–33).

So, too, in this opening chapter of *A Farewell to Arms,* Hemingway chooses
to render the landscape from a detached and anonymous perspective. Further,
he deliberately avoids those factual details that would identify either the exact
location of the scene or the identity of the narrative voice. Thus, one experiences
an essentially flat and laconic journalistic presentation, which paradoxically
avoids any specific documentary reference. It is simply "a house" that "looked
across the river and the plain to the mountains" in the "late summer" of "that
year." Hemingway brings everything to the surface, for, though there is the
suggestion of linear perspective, no corollary attention is given to the diminution
of objects as they recede in the distance. Also avoided are those kinds of
adjectives that would evaluate the scene in human terms. The house may "look"
but it certainly is not an animated form. The surfaces are not disturbed by any
imposition of the pathetic. Rather, objects are equivocally delineated by an
impartial observer: the pebbles and boulders are "dry" and "white," the water
is "blue in the channels."

At the same time, one has a sense of a three-dimensional reality that is
feelingly perceived, an effect created by the incremental repetition of rhythms
and images that operate structurally to integrate phenomena and expressively
to amplify the sense of ennui the laconic tone suggests. What Hemingway thus
provides is the "sequence of motion and fact" that makes the "emotion," "the
real thing" (*Death in the Afternoon,* 10). Initially we grasp the fundamentals of
the scene in their entirety: house, river, plain, and mountains. Our gaze is then
fixed momentarily in the middle distance with the river and the road which runs
a parallel course, and then is led through a series of rising and falling rhythms
integrated by the repetition of dust. Initially used with respect to the troops who
"went by the house and down the road" where "the dust they raised powdered
the leaves of the trees," the sequence which follows directs the eyes first from
the surface detail that defines the picture plane, as it were—"The trunks of the
trees too were dusty and the leaves fell early that year"—then back to the middle
distance, expanding the depth illusion with the troops marching, the "dust
rising" and the leaves "falling." The configuration concludes with the kind of
precision and simplicity that accentuates the minor key within which the piece
is conceived: "and afterward the road bare and white except for the leaves."

Though the coordinates "that year" and "afterward" indicate a temporal
shift, the paratactic pattern, which is sustained syntactically and in the generalized past tense, conveys a sense of a dominant rhythm that unifies disparate
time zones, just as Cézanne's multiple eye levels cooperate together in the
construction of a single plastic whole. Hemingway is thus able to preserve a
sense of the difference between one moment and the next while at the same time

suggesting the underlying pattern that renders them continuous. His syntactical rhythms, repeated images, and verbal indefiniteness work together to suggest the extent to which the natural scene has been altered by the *perspective vécue* of the protagonist who is recreating the scene he has lived in.

In Cézanne's *The Bay of Marseilles, Seen from L'Estaque,* as in the *Mont Ste. Victoire, Seen from Bellevue,* the alterations of near and far exaggerate the depth illusion while at the same time acknowledging, as Venturi suggests, that "the illusion belongs to no particular world." Thus the observer is invited to respond to the verisimilitude of the depth sensation that his own binocular experience confirms as more true and enduring than any photographic reproduction might be. In a similar way, Hemingway evokes a sense of familiarity with the scene depicted, not by appealing to scientific standards of accuracy, but rather by focusing on dimensions in the landscape that the reader knows or can know in his own experience of space. The archetypal power of Cézanne's landscape configurations, their monumental and architectonic certainty, depend upon the unifying patterns of enclosure and stasis that Hemingway similarly achieves by exaggerating through simplification a dominant pattern that establishes clear and inevitable relationships between volumes. Certainly that pattern of inevitability, which is secured visually in the opening landscape of *A Farewell to Arms,* is borne out in the tragic action which ensues. The overall pattern of rise and fall finds its correlative in Frederic's and Catherine's retreat into the mountains and their necessary return to the plain with Catherine and the newborn child dying during the descent.

In a very real way, Hemingway's landscape invites the observer to reenact an actual space experience, and it is important to note that the invitation to enter his landscapes is different in kind from the "promenade by the foot" Lhote disparaged in traditional open-window perspectives. This distinction is often ignored by the literary critic. Robert Lair, for example, acknowledges the "indebtedness" between Hemingway and Cézanne for the wrong reasons. While Lair appreciates the "inner vitality of the landscape" that Hemingway creates in *A Farewell to Arms,* he speaks of enjoying the "illusion" of "entering" it, as one enters a Cézanne by "gliding from vantage to vantage." Lair explains that this illusion develops because "one is . . . never located in time or space to any fixed degree." Though Lair understands how Cézanne's alterations of near and far relations preserve and exaggerate the depth experience so that the observer has "the almost uncanny experience of perceiving the foreground of the painting to be behind him," he chooses to view this experience in epiphanic terms, as a moment of consciousness that "transcends conventional limitations of space and time" (167).

What Lair misunderstands is that Cézanne's use of multiple and depersonalized perspectives achieves two things simultaneously. The time period remains indefinite while the space experience, rather than a transcendent evocation, is indefinite while the space experience, rather than a transcendent evocation, is both immanent and tangible. The kind of depth sensation Cézanne achieves depends upon his abandonment of traditional perspectival techniques and not upon an etherealized space. Lair responds to what Clark defines as the "direct and frontal approach to nature" in Cézanne (218), the approach concretized by powerful horizontals running parallel to the picture plane to reinforce the two-dimensionality of the medium while simultaneously supporting the pyramid structures whose multifaceted planes provide the illusion of a penetration into deep space. He does not, however, see how this space effect functions both in Cézanne's own work and as part of Hemingway's deliberate transposition of this method of space construction.

Neither Hemingway nor Cézanne permit the viewer or the reader the complacency of external observation. Cézanne's fusion of tactile and visual sensations and his abridgment of perspective invite the observer to duplicate the *perspective vécue* of the artist himself. Using verbal techniques to achieve the same ends, the Hemingway protagonist in his role as observer invites the reader to share his perspectival experience. In *The Sun Also Rises,* there are times when the protagonist Jake Barnes is literally sight-seeing, momentarily free of his compulsive and almost fatal attraction to Brett. The landscape conceived during this hiatus in the main action demonstrates Hemingway's Cézanne-like powers of exact observation, the disinterested character of his beholder's eye, and the anti-Renaissance character of the spatial illusion.

To register Jake's approach to Pamplona, for example, Hemingway achieves an illusion of actuality by balancing a series of verticals against a horizon, using a distant architecture as nucleus, to emphasize the depth experience of his protagonist in terms which parallel Cézanne's techniques in *The Boundary Wall* (fig. 23). Hemingway introduces, with a vigorous horizontal, a succession of visualizations of the scene: the wide plain supporting the verticals of the pyramid structure that becomes Pamplona "rising out of the plain, and the walls of the city, and the great brown cathedral, and the broken skyline of the other churches." Beyond this architectural nucleus are the mountains, which seem to enclose the horizon line: "In the back of the plateau there were the mountains, and every way you looked there were other mountains."[64]

Spatial relations are suggested verbally in a generalized way: "there was a big river off on the right shining," and "away off you could see the plateau." The sense of deep space is more concretely realized by the way in which our path of vision through the sequence is directed from the broad plain up the series of elevations from the plateau to the walls of the cathedral to the mountains beyond; yet the thrust into space is countered by a return to the plain and the road "ahead" which now (because Hemingway has created the spatial illusion by suggesting near and far relations) cuts through the plain toward Pamplona. All the visual details contribute to this sense of balanced verticals and horizon-

Figure 23. Paul Cézanne, *The Boundary Wall*, 1872
69 × 65 cm.
(Archives Durand-Ruel)

tals that integrate two- and three-dimensional elements, from the plain/pyramid configuration, to the line of trees through which the river shines, to the road stretching across the plain.

In the Pamplona piece, the observer enjoys the sense of moving within a landscape that does not depend upon a carefully differentiated descriptive vocabulary to convey the tactile relief of volumes. Adjectives are restricted to "wide," "big," "great," "brown," "broken," and "white." Thus Levin is in error when he suggests that this deliberate simplification, and the very equivocal nature of the adjectives themselves, provide evidence of the nonpictorial quality of Hemingway's prose. Levin refers, for example, to the classical opening of *A Farewell to Arms:* "The town was very nice and our house was very fine," and notes that "such descriptions—if we may consider them descriptions—are obviously not designed for pictorial effect." "Like 'fine' and 'nice' or 'good' and 'lovely,'" Levin suggests, these terms do "not describe," they "evaluate"—they are in fact "projections" of the narrator's state of mind" (105–6). Nelson is equally misguided when he suggests that Hemingway's use of comprehensive or inclusive descriptive details, and Cézanne's restricted palette and the seemingly incomplete demarcation of individual forms that attends that restriction, both provide evidence of their interest in emotion rather than the "actual shape of things" (43).

Far from being indifferent to the "shape" of objects, however, both Cézanne and Hemingway are committed to revealing it by penetrating beyond surface detail. Because Hemingway is interested in the sequence of motion and fact which makes for the verisimilitude of *perspective vécue,* it is not so much the secondary and tertiary qualities of phenomena but rather their relations that will absorb his interest. Rather than being loaded with "subjective implication" as Levin advises, Hemingway's method of abstracting or purifying forms allows him to place the stress on the relations between volumes to exaggerate the sensation of enclosure. It is in this sense that surface details would distract the observer and diminish the spatial effect itself.

Meyly Chin Hagemann supports this response by noting the way Cézanne's simplifications contribute to the space experience. Specifically in an analysis of Cézanne's *Farmyard,* she observes that Cézanne's vertical shapes, which accentuate and enclose the sides of the picture box, are deliberately ambiguous so that the artist can stress their spatial function: "The entire painting would change if Cézanne had given these brown and yellow 'things' an identity that could be verbalized; they would have fronts and backs, and these in turn would convey directions, shifting the painting's movements."[65] To the same effect, by eliminating adjectival qualifiers, which would isolate the individual object within the landscape, Hemingway evades the limitations that a series of self-contained highly sculptured forms would impose upon a scene. He is thus better

Figure 24. Pieter Brueghel, the Elder, Active 1551–1569, *The Harvesters*
Oil on wood, 118 × 160.7 cm.
(The Metropolitan Museum of Art, Rogers Fund, 1919)

able to relate the disparate entities to the scene's format as a whole and to maintain the balance of motion and fact that he feels can delineate emotion.

Hemingway's own reference to Brueghel's *The Harvesters* (fig. 24) in the Ross interview substantiates my sense of his profound understanding of the modern space conception, and of how that space conception often functions in Renaissance masters "*in spite of,* rather than because of, their use of mechanical perspective" (Loran, 20). In Brueghel, flat colors, minimal modeling, and the absence of cast shadows accentuate the reality of the picture plane, while the saliency of the grain field, the way it is used "geometrically," makes, according to Hemingway, "an emotion that is so strong for" him that he "can hardly take it" ("An Interview with Ernest Hemingway," 35).

Emily Stipes Watts discusses the sensual physicality of Hemingway's prose in relation to the synesthetic character of Cézanne's own handling of geometric form and color. While Watts focuses on the symbolic dimension of Hemingway's "physical images," which "break down the purely visual quality of prose," and explores the "metaphysical and mythical relationships"[66] that the empirical situation embodies, her insight here into the relationship between the depth experience in both artists and the interplay of the senses that helps to actualize this experience can be more fully developed. The geometric quality of Cézanne's abstractions, like the geometrical disposition of Brueghel's simplifications, make an emotion not because they are geometrical but because they contribute to the construction of a spatial illusion so pervasive that one can feel the relief of the volumes within the picture space. Their aims perfectly coincide with Hemingway's desire "to write on the principle of the iceberg" by eliminating "everything unnecessary to conveying the experience to the reader so that after he or she has read something it will become part of his or her experience and seem actually to have happened" ("An Interview with Ernest Hemingway," 34).

In the Brueghel, for example, the artist experiments with competing centers of rest. The traditional perspective line, which directs the eye out beyond the edge of the grain field over the valley below to the vaguely stated shoreline where objects fade as they recede into deep space, is deliberately inhibited because Brueghel does not prepare for its advance at the picture plane. Further, this effect is underscored by the saliency of the grain field itself, especially in the sharp edges of the diagonals and the horizontals that define its shape toward the center of the canvas, and in the strong vertical provided by the tree just left of center (the kind of vertical Cézanne favored to enhance the stability of two-and three-dimensional elements). The almost continuous curvilinear shape that is articulated from left to right not only opens up a second movement path from the lower-left-hand corner into the bush at right angles to the partially harvested field, but also encloses the middle and foreground of the picture.

Just as the perspective line, which leads toward a vanishing point at the horizon, is abridged by the grain field, so too linear recession in this track of vision is blunted by the bush at the end of the field. The bush becomes the obstacle one must climb over to enter the homestead beyond, which in turn functions as an architectural nucleus to arrest further movement into space. Because Brueghel establishes a tension within the canvas between at least two distinctive perspectival directions, the standing ground of the observer is not fixed. In fact, if her position were fixed, she could not enjoy the deep spatial illusion, because the frontal horizontal places her in two positions simultaneously. The observer has the sense of being brought to an elevation beyond the grain field in order to experience the distant view which begins at the juncture of the serpentine line of the road and the further edge of the grain field. At the same time, the observer is led through the enclosed space, pulled toward its outermost edge by the succession of rectangular and vertical forms of thrashed and stacked grain—a configuration which in itself anticipates Cézanne's manipulation of stepped-back planar recession.

From Brueghel through Cézanne, this spatial convention is developed by multiple perspectives that allow for successive perceptual experiences of the same scene, the repetition of rhythmically parallel configurations, and the modification of aerial and linear recession to bring background and foreground into vital relation. Hemingway's presentation of Jake's approach to Burguette in *The Sun Also Rises* provides a convincing illustration of how these techniques find their verbal equivalent in his work. Interestingly, one of the points Watts makes to verify her sense of the parallel between Cézanne and Hemingway is raised within this context: "Hemingway has structured the vista in a traditional manner with his establishment of a foreground, middle ground and background" (144). If this were true, however, Hemingway's space illusion would be diametrically antithetical to Cézanne's, for the latter deliberately blunts or avoids traditional vistas.

Though Hemingway uses a number of phrases to suggest recession into space (i.e., "looking back we could see the country spread out below," "out ahead of us was a rolling green plain," "the green plain stretched off," "and away off" [108]), in each instance the perspective line is abridged by a conjoining form, so that one does not have the sense of the diffuseness of volumes in the far distance or of their diminution in size. On the contrary, the surface pattern is brought forward: "Far back the fields were squares of green and brown on the hillsides." The prepositions Hemingway selects to initiate movement emphasize the substantiality of the landscape forms: "the road . . . went into the forest," "rocks stuck up through the clay," "the road showed through the trunks of a double line of trees." Similarly, he delineates relations between volumes and emphasizes the interiority of the light source: "It was a forest of cork oaks, and the sun came through the trees in patches, and there were cattle grazing back in the trees." Finally, Hemingway uses multiple perspectives to animate the spatial dimensions of the landscape and to provide a sense of enclosure by focusing on the changing shape of the horizon line. Initially, for example, the "brown mountains," "strangely shaped" are envisioned as "making the horizon." One attends not only to their color—which, since it is undifferentiated, does not provide the illusion of fading out into the distance—but also to their architectonic power, for they *make,* they do not simply *mark,* the horizon, and therefore one does not move beyond them to unlimited space.

As the bus moves up the rise of land through a series of elevations (much like the pyramid effect in the Pamplona piece), Hemingway manipulates rising and falling rhythms to simulate the *perspective vécue* of his protagonist. One encounters a new set of mountains "coming up in the south," and then a second set, dark and wooded,which describe the end of the rolling green and which "have clouds coming down from them." Interestingly, the contrapuntal thrust of the verticals that hold the horizon is balanced by a connecting horizontal: "the road came over the crest, flattened out, and went into a forest"; in the second elevation, the road follows along a "rise of land" and is held by a green plain stretching off and the "dark mountains beyond it." Linear recession is modified once again by the cut in the plain by fences, and "the white of the road," which shows "through a double line of trees" crossing the plain toward the north. This complicated pattern of horizontals and verticals sustains the illusion of being within and among volumes.

The final prospect from the edge of the rise, which focuses on the pattern of red and white houses strung out on the plain, is enclosed by the "shoulder of the first dark mountain" and brought to rest by the "gray metal-sheathed roof of the monastery of Roncevalles." As one moves up and through the alternating sequence of rise and plateau, each expanse of vista is checked by the changing edge of the horizon, which is architecturally secure. Rather than Watts's sense of a landscape unfolding "in a traditional manner," Hemingway's landscape demonstrates the extent to which he departs from that tradition. It is constructed upon the dynamic principles of thrust and return, of rise and fall, that provide the synesthetic richness to which the mural character of Cézanne's art remains faithful.

Perhaps the best example of the way in which Hemingway achieves the sensation of enclosure through the abridgement of linear and atmospheric perspective and the reintegration of visual and haptic sensibilities is given in "Big Two-Hearted River," whose grove of pine trees exhibits technical parallels with Cézanne's *Chestnut Trees at Jas de Bouffan* (fig. 25). The story is simply about a young war veteran's returning to a favored fishing spot, yet the intensity with which the protagonist sets up camp evokes a sense of ritual that is consistent with the kind of consolation that contact with a natural setting can provide following the trauma of war. The feeling of enclosure and contact that Hemingway achieves is due to the simplified static and dynamic lines which delineate the scene: "The trunks of the trees went straight up or slanted toward each

Figure 25. Paul Cézanne, *Chestnut Trees at Jas de Bouffan*, 1885–1887
Oil on linen, 29 1/16″ × 36⅝″.
(The Minneapolis Institute of the Arts, William Hood Dunwoody Fund)

other." As in the Cézanne painting, where the tree trunks run parallel to the vertical picture plane, Hemingway's pines solidly frame the grove: "The trunks were straight and brown without branches." Instead of following a path of vision which would lead through the interlocking branches to the unlimited space above, both Hemingway and Cézanne modify the funnellike depth of the alleys they suggest.

Loran provides this analysis of the alterations of the given that Cézanne imposes to achieve a truer sense of the dynamics of the individual's perceptual experience of space and volume:

> (b) The plane of the alley between the trees has been "tipped up" to a position more nearly parallel to the picture plane. (c) The distance does not fade out in aerial perspective, and foliage interlaces the two sides of the picture. (d) Cézanne has reduced the number of trees, which can be counted in the photograph of the motif, thereby modifying the funnel-like depth and recession. (e) An important pattern of foliage is prominent in the upper right-hand fourth of the picture, and this light shape is carried into the central area of deepest recession; the most recessive area of the deep space is thus brought into relation with the most prominent plane of the foreground foliage. (50)

To achieve a similar dynamic in "Big Two-Hearted River," Hemingway counters the upward thrust by pulling the eye back to the horizontal: "The branches were high above. Some interlocked to make a solid shadow on the brown forest floor."[67] Further linear recession into the distance is inhibited by the sweet fern which commences "sharp at the edge" of the extended bare space that encircles the island of pine to exaggerate the sense of enclosed space. Certainly the sense of grove, as a form of the enclosed garden, intensifies the pastoral implications of Nick's return to the forest.

In recreating Nick's sensations as he lies upon the forest floor, Hemingway reinforces the feeling of enclosure by retracing the path of vision he establishes in the introductory paragraph. Though Nick looks "up into the pine trees" (like the upward thrust of the interlocking branches "high above"), he is simultaneously aware of the pressure of the earth beneath him which "felt good against his back." Hemingway then repeats the sequence twice more: "He looked up at the sky, through the branches, and then shut his eyes. He opened them and looked up again. There was a wind high up in the branches. He shut his eyes again and went to sleep." Through a sequence of parallel movements, Hemingway aborts an upward track of vision. He modifies the illusion of deep space by returning our eye to the horizontal, the solid brown shadow on the forest floor, or by having Nick open and shut his eyes so that we are not lost in an undifferentiated sky. Hemingway brings masses to a point of order and maintains equilibrium for the observer.[68]

Of equal importance to the spatial illusion Hemingway does engage is the way he tries to incorporate all the senses in his presentation. He writes, for example, that the bare space within the grove "was brown and soft underfoot," that the sweet fern grew "sharp at the edge" of the island of pines, and that the earth "felt good." When Nick does look up, the emphasis is tactile as well as visual: "There was a high wind up in the branches." Hemingway's synesthesia functions, as does his modified perspective, to encourage the eye to hold the object.

In a very similar way, Hemingway sustains the illusion of being within space by activating both tactile and visual sensations in his depiction of Nick fishing from the log: "He sat on the logs, smoking, drying in the sun, the sun warm on his back, the river shallow ahead, entering the woods, curving into the woods, shallows, light glittering, big water-smooth rocks, cedars along the bank and white birches, the logs warm in the sun, smooth to sit on, without bark, gray to the touch; slowly the feeling of disappointment left him" (175). The incremental repetition of sun images focuses on tactile rather than visual effects: "drying in the sun," "the sun warm on his back," "the logs warm in the sun." The two rhythmically parallel phrases enhance our sense of the substantiality of the river within the landscape: "entering the woods," "curving into the woods." The process of unification achieved through the repetition of a dominant tactile sensation integrates animate and inanimate forms by emphasizing the shape of a perception in terms of its sharp and smooth dimensions: the disappointment "that came sharply after the thrill" is diffused by the warmth of the sun and the smoothness of the forms—the curvilinear shape of the river, the "big-water-smooth rocks," the log "smooth to sit on." Hemingway is thus able to convince us of the actuality of the moment by making it possible for the observer to duplicate the perspectival experience of the protagonist.

So too, in the introductory landscape of *Islands in the Stream*, Hemingway positions his unnamed observer in front of the house "on the highest part of the narrow tongue of land between the harbor and the open sea," but his focus does not settle on the expansive vista of the Gulf Stream below him, but rather is directed into the water: "The water of the Stream was usually a dark blue when you looked out at it when there was no wind. But when you walked out into it there was just the green light of the water over the floury white sand and you could see the shadow of any big fish a long time before he could ever come in close to the beach."[69] Not only is an illusion of the infinite countered by placing the observer within the water to duplicate the conditions at eye level, there is the further suggestion that, taken alone, aerial perspective falsifies actual conditions. The water is not only deep blue but also light green. In choosing to juxtapose distant and close-range views of the same scene, to complement a disengaged perspective with one that is engaged and able to conjoin both visual and tactile sensations, Hemingway provides a fuller experience of the given.

Significantly, the artist-protagonist in *Islands*, Thomas Hudson, shares the Post-Impressionist esthetic Hemingway activates in his own landscapes. Hudson's sense of the actuality of the picture space, one that is "truer than a photograph" (139), is borne out in the waterfront picture he paints for the local bar. The painting presents an illusion of three-dimensionality so compelling that the bartender's terms of praise include the story of "some gentleman" who got "so excited" he attempted to "climb into the skiff" (142).

Hudson's artistic tastes run to Brueghel and Duchamp, to painters who emphasize the mural character of the visual medium. In his own casting about for pictorial subjects, he is absorbed by his conception of art as painted surface, and thus, when he sees flamingos from the flying bridge during an extended reconnaissance mission in the Gulf waters, he notes that if he could paint them, he would not want them through his field glasses "because he did not want details now. He wanted the roseate mass on the gray brown flat" (393).

The processes of simplification and condensation in Hemingway's land-scapes—which allow him to focus on a dominant pattern that will integrate the disparate aspects of a single scene and sustain the illusion of a unified vision—are techniques that Hemingway uses in *The Old Man and the Sea* to determine the overall structure of the work itself. The narrative simplicity of the novel finds its visual correlative in the repetition of graphically conceived cruciform configurations whose constructive and expressive power simultaneously purify or streamline the prose even while they enhance its emotional resonance and suggestiveness. Thus Hemingway is able to exploit our intuitional responsive-ness to the archetypal dimensions of this recurring iconographic detail without ever bringing it explicitly to the surface.

The novel opens with Santiago shouldering the mast and ascending the slope toward his shack, a tableau which articulates the essential theme of his story. This concretization of Santiago's unique Calvary is graphically presented through the intersection of the horizontal and the vertical, and is echoed visually at every stage in the story's development. Santiago holds his line "straighter than any other" as it descends from the rod into the depth of water. The rod is but an extension of the old man, an antenna that joins him to the sea, whose line not only penetrates the sea's surface, but also significantly crosses his shoulders as he leans against the bow of the skiff. The fish and the men are "joined together," in a sense reminiscent of the kind of osmotic participation integral to the Symbolist vision of the vital relation between man and nature. This conception of intercourse between man and nature is reinforced pictorially ("The line showed like a phosphorescent streak in the water straight out from his shoulders") as well as graphically ("Once he stood up and urinated over the side of the skiff").[70] Even the arm-wrestling contest of Santiago's youth, the contest that established a reputation commensurate with the intrepidity of his spirit, is conceived in terms of an unyielding vertical perpendicular to the horizontal contest mark on the table: "They had gone one day and one night with their elbows on a chalk line on the table and their forearms straight up and their hands gripped tight" (69).

Further, just as the line of the rod penetrates the horizontal plane of the sea's surface, and thus connects the old man with a life force whose depth he can feel though not visually perceive, so too Hemingway makes the reader feel the pressure of the axis of the lines which run at right angles to one another. The tension between the defiant vertical and the gravitational pull downward exerted on the rod functions as a paradigm for the structure of the tale that ensues as Santiago moves through space "beyond all people" (i.e., linearly) and, in doing so, endeavors to transcend the insurmountable obstacles that destroy both himself and the fish. This tension is concretized in the final image of the fish before it is caught, arching above the water in its final and relentless drive to free itself before it yields to the old man: "The fish came alive, with his death in him, and rose high out of the water showing all his great length and width and all his power and his beauty. He seemed to hang in the air above the old man in the skiff" (94).

In the final sequences of *The Old Man and the Sea*, as Santiago struggles to bring his fish to shore, Hemingway uses the vertical-horizontal configuration in a more sinister context: the fins of the sharks break through the water and Santiago, erect by the side of the bow, drives the harpoon, or rather the knife lashed to the oar, "onto the shark's head at the spot where the line between the eyes intersected with the line that ran straight back from his nose" (102). This compelling figure of intersecting lines, operating at every level, visualizes those dimensions of a tale where the mythical and the empirical coincide. Santiago's thinking eye penetrates the naturalistic surface to grasp the inimitable and unseen: "There were no such lines. There was only the heavy sharp blue head and the big eyes and the clicking, thrusting all-swallowing jaws. But that was the location of the brain and the old man hit it" (102).

Ironically and appropriately, at the story's close, Santiago—with the mast once more shouldered across his back—"stopped for a moment and looked back and saw in the reflection from the street light the great tail of the fish standing well behind the skiff's stern. He saw the white naked line of his back bone and the dark mass of the head with the projecting bill and all the nakedness between" (121). In cruciform position the wasted marlin is lashed to the skiff, just as the wasted Santiago is lashed to the mast. The fish's tail, the vertical that stands erect at the base of the naked white line of the backbone, functions as an inexorable fate, as the rudder that directs Santiago to the shore in triumph and defeat.

This powerful iconographic element is visually repeated in quick succession as the tale is completed, for once again Santiago struggles up the hill, with Hemingway choosing to underline the inevitable conclusion of that Calvary by closing with the final portrait of Santiago sleeping face down on the newspapers with his "arms out straight and the palms of his hands up" (122). It is in this sense that one shape dominates and unifies Hemingway's narrative, just as Cézanne's clearly articulated linear content—defined as the succession of rhythmic parallels (the stepped-back planes)—integrates surface and depth through the repetition of a unifying dominant shape.

Hemingway uses the principle of synesthesia to realize his sense of the dynamics of the natural vision, and he also sees its ability to concretize the archetypal dimensions of his protagonist's experience of the landscape. The Symbolist aspects of Hemingway's iconography in *The Old Man and the Sea* is determined by the simplicity of the narrative form, creating a kind of naivety that is very much a part of the primitivistic experience in Gauguin. It is within this context that one explores Santiago's dream of the lions, a motif that recurs and functions much like the cruciform configuration, both integrating surface details and amplifying underlying associations. Just as Gauguin's *The Poor Fisherman* (fig. 26) expresses the artist's inveterate longing for a prelapsarian world, which fuses Cytherean and Edenic motifs (in this way Gauguin extends the Christian typology of Puvis de Chavanne's painting of the same subject), Santiago's African landscapes function to visualize his dream of an unspoken harmony felt between man and nature in his youth.

As mystery and suggestion are key concepts of Gauguin's Symbolist forms, Hemingway's African landscape functions on a number of evocative levels. Santiago's memory of that scene has accumulated in significance just as it has been stylized in visual terms and becomes a symbolic episode, one that, of necessity, suggests more than is stated. As a metonymic image that functions enigmatically through the tale, the dream landscape alludes to a mystery that lies at the heart of man's racial experience. Commensurate with Hemingway's need to realize those concrete sensations that recreate for the reader the actual feel of one's perceptual experience, the image of "the lions on the beaches in the evening" appeals to the entire sensibility "of the observer": "he dreamed of Africa when he was a boy and the long golden beaches and the white beaches, so white they hurt your eyes, and the high capes and the great brown mountains. He lived along that coast now every night and in his dreams he heard the surf roar and saw the native boats come riding through it. He smelled the tar and oakum of the deck as he slept and he smelled the smell of Africa that the land breezes brought at morning" (24–25).

This archetypal recognition of the continuity and the relatedness of all things in the dream of the lions provides a visual context within which one comprehends the blood brotherhood of man and fish. Significantly, the dream, as an alternate mode of vision, occurs at night when one's vision of everyday present reality is obscured. In repeating the sequence, Hemingway signals Santiago's turning from a surface to an in-depth reality where the source of his being

Figure 26.   Paul Gauguin, *The Poor Fisherman*, 1896
(Museu de Arte de Sao Paulo, Brazil)

resides. In choosing to imbue that landscape with the force of actuality by integrating visual, tactile, auditory, and even olfactory sensibilities, Hemingway indicates that Santiago's conception of what is real has as much validity as any other conception of what reality might be. He gives to the experience of nature the kind of fifth-dimensional realism that is integral to the recognition of alternative modes of seeing in Post-Impressionist art.

Lawrence

Like Hemingway, Lawrence's sense of a "fourth dimension" in the verbal medium evolves from his own intuitive responsiveness to the "isness"—or, as he defines it in "Introduction to His Paintings," the "appleyness" of Cézanne's forms and the lumpiness of van Gogh.[71] This sense of "appleyness" and lumpiness refers to Lawrence's own dissatisfaction with the exclusively visual character of the Renaissance spatial illusion, which he felt was perpetuated in Impressionism's "glorious escape" from the world as "substance." In his view, the Post-Impressionists "admit" the existence of the world's body. They may "rage" against it, but they paint it: "Instead of being nice and ethereal and non-sensual," the landscape "was discovered by Van Gogh to be heavily, overwhelmingly substantial and sensual. Van Gogh took up landscape in heavy spadefuls. And Cézanne had to admit it" (323).

This is the kind of substantiality and tangibility, Lawrence suggests, that the narrative medium must recover, a fourth-dimensional "relation between man and his circumambient universe at the living moment," which is brought into being by attending to that relation as it is realized "with your blood and bones, as well as with your eyes."[72] Lawrence's appreciation of Cézanne, for example, derives from his sense that he restores the full complexity of the bodily character of his model by bringing his whole consciousness to bear upon it. Thus Cézanne is capable of a "complete truth, a complete vision or a complete revelation" because "the whole consciousness of man working together in unison and oneness; instinct, intuition, mind, intellect all fused into one complete consciousness" is brought into relation with external reality ("Introduction to His Paintings," 334). The fourth-dimensional capacity of Cézanne's thinking eye demonstrates the validity of one of Lawrence's major esthetic presuppositions: "Design, in art, is a recognition of the relation between various elements in the creative flux. You can't *invent* a design. You recognize it, in the fourth dimension" ("Art And Morality," 525). Lawrence's sense of the "fourth dimension" embraces both the concept of the creative and penetrative role that the eye of the artist is endowed with in Post-Impressionist art, and the sense that this eye discovers in nature, both human and nonhuman, underlying, unifying patterns that bring disparate elements into vital relation.

In "Art and Morality," Lawrence pursues the distinction between the naive and the thinking eye by discriminating between the "All-Seeing Eye of humanity" (524)—a convention of seeing that has been trained by the photographic impulse implicit in perspective art and the Ruskinian admonition to paint the object "as it is"—and Cézanne's penetrative and impersonal "mackerel eye." For Lawrence, the former is a convention that pretends to represent "the real objective reality" (522) but depends upon the tyranny of the eye alone. The object as picture, as a purely visual perception, falsifies Lawrence's sense of the way one actually experiences external forms. The egotistical and essentially anthropomorphic vision of the "All-Seeing Eye" begins with the "Kodak" idea of self: "Each man to himself is a picture. That is, he is a complete little objective reality, complete in himself, existing by himself, absolutely, in the middle of the picture. All the rest is just setting, background. To every man, to every woman, the universe is just a setting to the absolute little picture of himself, herself" (523). To oppose this perspective, Lawrence posits the vital polarity with nature that is felt by the child and the primitive, whose contact with otherness is sensory rather than merely visual (525), tactile rather than just optic, hieroglyphic rather than photometic (522).

Lawrence senses in the nonnaturalistic dimensions of primitive art a consummation of self and other that breaks through the inert conventions of seeing and is realized "in the place where no Kodak can snap it" (526): "Egypt had a wonderful relation to the vast living universe, only dimly visual in its reality. The dim eye-vision and the powerful blood-feeling of the Negro African, even today, gives us strange images, which our eyes can hardly see, but which we know are surpassing" (525). Etruscan art appeals to him because he recognizes the kind of model for a worldview that is both empathetic (i.e., vitalistic or corporeal) and impersonal (i.e., an empathy which differs from the kind of sympathy that reduces the landscape to human proportions). In chapter 4 of *Etruscan Places,* for example, Lawrence discusses the painted tombs of Tarquinia, delighting in the "wonderfully suggestive *edge* of the figures. It is not outlined. It is not what we call 'drawing'. It is the flowing contour where the body suddenly leaves off, upon the atmosphere. The Etruscan artist seems to have seen living things surging from their own centre to their own surface. And the curving and the contour of the silhouette-edge suggests the whole movement of the modelling within."[73]

For Lawrence, the Kodak convention creates the schism between body and spirit that he attempts to repair in his own medium. Conventional notions of verisimilitude, with their emphasis upon surface appearance, seem to be both abstractive and spiritualizing. What Lawrence is after is a reunification of both the haptic and optic dimensions of our apprehension of form that is integral to the primitive sense in Post-Impressionist art. This apprehension involves an intuitive state of awareness, an "at-one-ness," or the "state of being at one with the object,"[74] which means that the artist grasps the object from the inside:

"There is nothing to do but to maintain a true relationship to the things we move with and amongst and against. The apple, like the moon, has still an unseen side" ("Art and Morality," 525). From the Kodak point of view, Cézanne's forms are immoral: "Comes Cézanne with his pitcher and his apples, which not only are not life-like, but are a living lie. The Kodak will prove it" (523). From Lawrence's point of view, Cézanne's forms substitute "a finer morality, for a grosser" (525). The very nonrepresentational (i.e., nonnaturalistic, antiphotometic) character of Cézanne's still lifes, the iconoclasm of their antimimetic disposition, paradoxically brings Lawrence into vital relation with what he feels is the truth of the "living universe."

One sees immediately the affinity between Lawrence's response to Cézanne and his own major themes of connection and relatedness with the cosmos. It would be a mistake, however, to read his appreciation of Cézanne as simply the subsumption of the artist's vision within Lawrence's concept of blood consciousness. In "The Impact of Modernism on Lawrence," Jack Lindsay highlights the "profound" and revelatory character of Lawrence's critical insights into Cézanne's struggle to realize his *petite sensation,*[75] which Lawrence perceives as the effort "to achieve a whole new marriage of mind and matter" that was "*more* true to life" ("Introduction to His Paintings," 338).

Lindsay notes that Lawrence "goes to the heart of Cézanne's creative aim, and shows a penetration still far ahead of general critical understanding of what he was doing" (39). Lawrence, for example, understood that Cézanne's truth, though not photographic, was still realistic and therefore representational, simply because Lawrence's notion of the representational was not confined to the narrowly conceived idea of verisimilitude that had dominated nineteenth-century realism. Further, in extending representation beyond visual imitation or copy, Lawrence was able to perceive the significance of the tactile quality of Cézanne's forms: "Cézanne wanted something that was neither optical nor mechanical nor intellectual. . . . He wanted to touch the world of substance once more with the intuitive touch, to be aware of it with the intuitive awareness, and to express it in intuitive terms. That is, he wished to displace our present mode of mental-visual consciousness, the consciousness of mental concepts, and substitute a mode of consciousness that was predominantly intuitive, the awareness of touch" ("Introduction to His Paintings," 338–39).

Cézanne's work, for Lawrence, particularly demonstrates the triumph of a "rich intuitive vision" that acknowledges the dynamic and organic nature of matter. He suggests that in Cézanne's "best landscapes we are fascinated by the mysterious *shiftiness* of the scene under our eyes; it shifts about as we watch it. And we realize with a sort of transport, how intuitively *true* this is of landscape. It is *not* still. It has its own weird anima, and to our wide-eyed perception it changes like a living animal under our gaze" ("Introduction to His Paintings,"

342). In fact, while Fry and Bell celebrate what they thought were the transcendental implications of Cézanne's abstractive process, Lawrence retains his own vigorous sense of the way in which Cézanne's earlier landscapes had given concrete and tangible visual definition to a more primitive life-worshipping vision of form. Thus, while Bell in *Art* characterizes the esthetic emotion as one that transports the observer "out of life into ecstacy," providing an "escape from circumstances, flux, and humanity" (29, 37, 92), Lawrence takes literally Cézanne's advice to "follow nature—to go to the bottom of what you see in front of you."

For Lawrence, "Cézanne's apple hurts. It made people shout with pain. And it was not till his followers had turned him again into an abstraction that he was very accepted. Then the critics stepped forth and abstracted his good apple into Significant Form, and henceforth Cézanne was saved. Saved for democracy. Put safely into the tomb again, and the stone rolled back. The resurrection was postponed once more" ("Introduction to His Paintings," 329). Just as Brueghel's grain "hurts" Hemingway, so too Cézanne's apple "hurts" Lawrence. Just as Hemingway makes the abstract concrete, so too Lawrence embraces the resurrection of the body in its full complexity that allows Cézanne's forms to make contact with "the whole consciousness of man."

In "'Real Thinking': Lawrence and Cézanne," John Remsbury notes the parallel between Lawrence's appreciation of Cézanne's struggle to know the apple as apple and his admiration for Hardy's "inside awareness of Egdon Heath."[76] Hardy's capacity to render what Lawrence defines as "the terrific action of unfathomed nature"[77] is borne out by the way in which Lawrence suggests Hardy gives foreground treatment to the landscape's background so that it "matters more than the people who move upon it." English landscape painting, by contrast, deals with the landscape as "background with the real subject left out" ("Introduction to His Paintings," 318).

In Lawrence's mind both Hardy and Cézanne move beyond a preoccupation with the naturalistic surface and execute what he describes in his analysis of Cézanne's still lifes as the "first step back into real substance, to objective substance." It is Cézanne's reverence for the otherness of the forms that he explores, for example, that secures Lawrence's admiration: "Cézanne's apples are a real attempt to let the apple exist in its own separate identity, without transfusing it with personal emotion. Cézanne's great effort was, as it were, to shove the apple away from him and to let it live of itself" ("Introduction to His Paintings," 326). In grasping the inside of the apple as "objective substance," or in allowing the landscape to function as landscape rather than stage or mirror, both Hardy and Cézanne abort the impulse to infuse external realities with purely personal emotions.

The movement beyond a purely human point of view to allow forms to "live of their own laws . . . not by the laws of the Kodak—or of man" ("Art and Morality," 526) sustains the impersonal quality that Lawrence celebrates, in "Introduction to His Paintings," in Cézanne's *Portrait of Madame Cézanne:*

> It is the appleyness of the portrait of Cézanne's wife that makes it so permanently interesting: the appleyness, which carries with it also the feeling of knowing the other side as well, the side you don't see, the hidden side of the moon. For the intuitive apperception of the apple is so *tangibly* aware of the apple that it is aware of it *all round*, not only just of the front. The eye sees only fronts, and the mind, on the whole, is satisfied with fronts. But intuition needs all-roundedness, and instinct needs insideness. The true imagination is forever curving round to the other side, to the back of presented appearance. (340)

Loran, in his own analysis of *Madame Cézanne,* refers to the qualities of "dynamic tension" in this portrait that "cannot be explained on human or literary grounds," qualities Lawrence responds to and that depend upon the dramatic effect Cézanne achieves by axial tipping (the main volume axis of the figure falls to the left), which "creates a strong tension and pull away from the right side of the frame or picture format," and the space effect of the diagonal diversion in the background wall, which is felt "as if there were actually two separate planes pulling apart" (84–85). Because of these qualities Lawrence enjoys intensely the illusion of awareness in the round that dramatizes the corporeality of the figure. He is responding above all to something in Cézanne's grasp of form, which is neither self-projection nor pathetic fallacy.

This sense of the distinction between self-projection or pathetic fallacy, and fidelity to the autonomy of objective reality, is central to Lawrence's response to Cézanne. The painting, for Lawrence, offers a correlative for a way of knowing, of entering into a fullness of possession with, and not of, the object. In his understanding of the impersonal quality of Cézanne's art and the archetypal nature of his grasp of the depth experience, Lawrence reveals his intuitive understanding of Cézanne's basic position—that of the commitment to nature to express the essence of form—and of the basic position of Post-Impressionist art, which is to assume a reciprocity between mind and matter.

Nor does the distinction Lawrence draws between van Gogh's "subjective earth" and Cézanne's "objective substance" in "Introduction to His Paintings" undermine his authority, for the commentary he provides in "Morality and the Novel" suggests that he does not see van Gogh's landscapes as having been determined by the superficiality of the "All-Seeing Eye." Observing the kind of interdependence and mutual revelation that takes place in his canvases, Lawrence explains: "When van Gogh paints sunflowers, he reveals, or achieves, the vivid relation between himself, as man, and sunflower, as sunflower, at that quick moment of time. His painting does not represent the sunflower itself. We shall never know what the sunflower itself is. And the camera will *visualize* the sunflower far more perfectly than van Gogh can." Van Gogh has the capacity to reveal the relation between self and other in the "fourth dimension": "It is a revelation of the perfected relation, at a certain moment, between a man and a sunflower. It is neither man-in-the-mirror nor flower-in-the-mirror, neither is it above or below or across anything."[78] In recognizing the nonegotistical nature of van Gogh's fidelity to the given, Lawrence places van Gogh's more passionate emphasis within the context of Cézanne's major theme of contact with nature.

Perhaps it is Lawrence's own fascination with otherness, which he loosely defines in his "Life" essay as the "primal unknown" from "whence all creation issues,"[79] and the kind of cosmic perspective that evolves in his novels as a measure of his character's growth toward a recognition of that nonhuman order which allows him to intuit and appreciate the impersonal quality of Post-Impressionist forms. In exploring alternate modes of vision, Lawrence engages in processes of abstraction that disclose natural forms at levels that require the penetration of photographable realities. This essential theme in Post-Impressionist art, this sense of connectedness, of mutual revelation of self and other, of an "osmotic participation" within essence, brings into creative relation Cézanne's thinking eye and its grasp of form in nature, van Gogh's yearning for contact with cosmogonic forces in the landscape, and Lawrence's "mackerel eye" perception in the cosmos.

In *The Rainbow*, Lawrence demonstrates the kinds of techniques that are generated by his vision of fourth-dimensional realities. The novel as a whole offers a three-generational chronicle of the tensions within family members between individualized and cosmic, social and archetypal, mental and intuitional forms of apprehending reality. Given the Post-Impressionist vision of *The Rainbow*, it seems more than coincidence that Lawrence had been reading *The Letters of a Post-Impressionist, Being the Familiar Correspondences of Vincent van Gogh* while he contemplated the final draft of the novel. In a letter to Lady Ottoline Morrell, he describes the tensions he senses in van Gogh's work in terms of an internal crisis within the artist, between the "angel of himself" and the "animal of himself." Lawrence refers that duality to van Gogh's own expressed yearning for what Lawrence himself calls "real life": "One would so love to live in the fields, in the sun, near the river, in the country, with other horses, also free, and have the right to procreate one's kind." But "real life" is thwarted by the actual conditions imposed by social conventions: "One feels exactly like an old cab horse." Lawrence's major point in the letter is that a man's life can be a "piece of supreme art" if that internal discord can be creatively resolved: "where to live one's animal would be to create oneself, *in fact be the artist creating a man in living fact.*" It is in this sense that art becomes "the final expression of the created animal or man,"[80] an esthetic which corroborates those statements Lawrence makes in "Introduction to His Paintings" when he suggests that "real works of art are made by the whole consciousness of man working together in unison and oneness" (334).

One appreciates immediately the parallel between Lawrence's sense of van Gogh's yearning for contact, which is visualized in the apocalyptic dimensions he intuits in landscape forms, and Ursula's struggle to realize her own archetypal response to the cosmos in *The Rainbow*. More importantly, the conceptual parallel is borne out technically in Lawrence's exploration of the dramatic and expressive possibilities of perspective, by the forceful interchange between foreground and background pattern to concretize his sense of vital relation between self and other, by his use of symbolic lighting to place the hierogamous nature of that relation in high relief,[81] and by the integration of visual and tactile elements to realize the in-depth nature of the protagonist's experience of phenomenal reality.

Lawrence visualizes themes of inaccessibility (the desire to unite with the cosmos) and consummation through his use of perspective to dramatize, as van Gogh does in *Cornfield at Sunrise,* dynamic relations between near and far. In the paradigmatic opening of the novel, these terms establish the dialectic between archetypal and strictly human points of view to define the nature of the marriages that take place. The opposition between the Brangwen women, who characteristically look toward the seats of intellectual power defined by the vicarage and the "spoken world beyond," and the Brangwen men, who are absorbed by the "blood-intimacy" of their own "blind intercourse of farm-life," is concretized by Lawrence through the contrapuntal rhythms of horizontal and vertical planes: "Whenever one of the Brangwens in the field lifted his head from his work, he saw the church-tower at Ilkeston in the empty sky. So that as he turned again to the horizontal land, he was aware of something standing above and beyond him in the distance."[82] Their essentially primitive responsiveness to the generative cycle in which they participate is further delineated by the interpenetration of horizontal and vertical planes to integrate surface and depth: they feel "the pulse and body of the soil, that opened to their furrow for the grain, and became smooth and supple after their ploughing, and clung to their feet with a weight that pulled like desire, lying hard and unresponsive when the crops were to be shorn away. The young corn waved and was silken, and the lustre slid along the limbs of the man who saw it" (2).

To amplify the opposition between horizontal and vertical *perspective vécue,* Lawrence offers two competing centers of focus: the men, "their senses full fed, their faces always turned to the heat of the blood, staring into the sun, dazed with looking towards the source of generation, unable to turn around" (3), and the woman "looking out, as she must, from the front of her house towards the activity of man in the world at large, whilst her husband looked out to the back at sky and harvest and beast and land, she strained her eyes to see what man had done in fighting outwards to knowledge" (3). The church-tower and the sun operate as two antithetical magnetic poles just as the ever-expanding horizon that the tower defines is countered by the enclosed Marshland, which defines the parameters of the Brangwen men's existence.

The tension between male and female forces is also expressed in the alternate though equally poetic syntactical forms Lawrence selects to embody the opposition between the Brangwen men and the Brangwen women. The natural intimacy between the men and the landscape is felt, for example, in fluid and expansive verbal rhythms: "It was enough for the men, that the earth heaved and opened its furrow to them, that the wind blew to dry the wet wheat, and set the young ears of corn wheeling freshly about. . . ." Their sense of organic unity is expressed in parallel and balanced phrasing: "it was enough that they helped the cow in labour, or ferreted the rats from under the barn, or broke the back of a rabbit with a sharp knock of the hand." This vigorous sense of place is further strengthened by the specificity of the details that accumulate, and in the clear and reciprocal relation between abstract and concrete terms that Lawrence sustains: "So much warmth and generating and pain and death did they know in their blood, earth and sky and beast and green plants " (3).

The women, in contrast, struggle to articulate their desire for something that is beyond their grasp conceptually and verbally. This distance is embodied in the awkward word order and uncertain pace of the syntactical structures: "At home, even so near as Cossethay, was the vicar, who spoke the other, magic language, and had the other, finer bearing, both of which she could perceive, but could never attain to." The paradox of home as alien ground is felt equally in the tension between "near" and "other" that is embodied in the prose in the density of interrogative statements and the diffuseness of the descriptive terms that the women use to evoke the essential yet immaterial quality that sets the vicar apart: "What was it in the vicar, that raised him above the common men as man is raised above the beast? She craved to know. She craved to achieve this higher being, if not in herself, then in her children. That which makes a man strong . . . what was it? . . . What power had the vicar. . . . And why—why?" (4).

In a very similar way, van Gogh uses the opposition of concentric and convergent schemes that culminate in two centers of rest to emphasize the discontinuity between simultaneous points of view, a discontinuity which is further exaggerated by incompatible color values as well. In *Cornfield at Sunrise* (fig. 13), a fecund foreground is challenged by the iced background tones. One perspective has its point of entry into the picture space as indicated by the wall that defines a movement path integrating the spectator's standing ground with the new creation on purely visual terms. As a result, though the observer enters the picture space, he never loses consciousness of his exterior and fixed position. The second point of view is detached and unspecified and finds its center of rest in the sun with its concentric rings. Van Gogh not only explores

the tension created by establishing two competing centers of rest, he also dramatizes the human conflict between desire and fulfillment. That conflict is developed as well by the way in which the insistent, heavily shadowed fence prohibits
the advance of the field's directional lines, and by the tension created between
the boldly outlined straight lines of its enclosing walls and the long washed,
wavy lines of the mountain range beyond.

In his exploration of the tension between mental and intuitional modes of
vision in ritual scenes in *The Rainbow*, Lawrence offers verbal correlatives for
the kind of reintegration of figure and background found in Cézanne's bathing
motifs, in Fauvist adaptations of that iconographic pattern, and in van Gogh's
own harvest landscapes. The landscapes embodying this tension move the reader
beyond familiar topographies: surfaces are dematerialized by the breaking down
of arbitrarily imposed distinctions that not only isolate the senses from one
another but also erect artificial boundaries between human and nonhuman forms.
It is in this latter sense—what I would like to define as the visualization of the
human figure as phenomenal form—that Lawrence begins an exploration of the
reciprocal relation between consciousness and matter that is rooted in the Post-
Impressionist esthetic.

While Jack Stewart recognizes the affinity that exists between Lawrence's
handling of ritual scenes in *The Rainbow* and pictorial techniques, he tends to
perceive Lawrence's deformations of the naturalistic surface as examples of a
radical kind of subjectivism that he associates with Expressionism. Though
Stewart consistently argues that Lawrence's landscapes provide evidence of his
readiness to override nature in the interest of emotion, where the psyche is
imposed upon the cosmos which then reflects processes of "neurotic self-projection" or "traumatic objectification,"[83] he himself insists upon a distinction between "anthropomorphism" and "visionary transformation" that his very choice
of analytical terms renders inapplicable. Thus, in examining the final moonlit
scene of the first chapter following Tom Brangwen's successful proposal of
marriage to Lydia Lensky, Stewart argues simultaneously that "Lawrence does
verbally what van Gogh does with paint in 'The Starry Night,' he imposes an
image of man's soul upon the cosmos" and that "this is not anthropomorphism,
but an act of visionary transformation" (300).

In blurring the distinction between the "anthropomorphism" generated by
the "All-Seeing Eye" and the "visionary transformation" achieved by the "mackerel eye," Stewart implies that Lawrence repudiates the very substantiality of
form that he welcomes with a vengeance in Post-Impressionism and affirms in
the dimensions of the landscapes that are illuminated by disindividualized perspectives within ritual scenes in *The Rainbow*. For Tom Brangwen, the experience of Lydia initiates a new mode of vision, one that is consistent with the
marriage as ritual, and one that involves a regeneration of both self and cosmos
that is real and true. This shift in perception is prepared for through a leitmotif

of rebirth images to indicate that a "swift change had taken place on the earth for him, as if new creation were fulfilled, in which he had real existence. Things had all been stark, unreal, barren, mere nullities before. Now they were actualities that he could handle" (26). Thus Tom emerges from his embrace with Lydia as "newly created, as after a gestation, a new birth, in the womb of darkness" (41). That process of revivification finds its correlatives in landscapes that exist in complementary terms, not as expressions of the pathetic fallacy, but as the revelation of an underlying pattern and mode of existence that "daylight consciousness" fails to perceive: "Aerial and light everything was, new a morning fresh and newly-begun. Like a dawn the newness and the bliss filled in" (41).

Thus the contiguity between Tom's emotional state just prior to his announcement of intent to Lydia and the turbulence within the landscape must be interpreted not as "turmoil projected into visual forms that have the hallucinatory strangeness of a dream" ("Expressionism in *The Rainbow*," 301), but rather as evidence of the kind of reciprocity that illuminates a profoundly natural kinship between man and cosmos: "Then, being ready, as grey twilight was falling, he went across to the orchard to gather the daffodils. The wind was roaring in the apple trees, the yellow flowers swayed violently up and down, he heard even the fine whisper of their spears as he stopped to break the flattened, brittle stems of the flowers" (37).

Just as the apocalyptic dimensions of van Gogh's landscapes are concretized through highly charged structurally similar patterns that unify disparate elements by discovering a dominant shape, so too Lawrence presents the volatile interchange between human and nonhuman forms by repeating parallel configurations that register Tom's approach to Lydia's cottage: the stooping figure of the man, the daffodils stooping in the wind, the "shattered crocuses," the "wild waving of the trees," the crouched figure of the child "curled in against her mother" with its "wild, fierce hair . . . drooping towards the fire-warmth," and the "clouds which packed in great, alarming haste across the dark sky."

In the midst of these charged isomorphic forms, all similarly deposed by the wind, Lawrence places the still-dark figure of the man half-emergent in the darkness with "the gripped fist of flowers" (39). The symbolic interplay of light and dark dramatizes themes of interpenetration and allows Lawrence to visualize the way in which human forms participate in cosmic events. Outlines are not clearly delineated; objects lose discrete and complete identities, while human and nonhuman elements are equivocally presented as Tom and Lydia feel the essential otherness of one another:

> She looked down at him as he stood in the light from the window, holding the daffodils, the darkness behind. In his black clothes she again did not know him. She was almost afraid.
>
> But he was already stepping on to the threshold, and closing the door behind him. She turned into the kitchen, startled out of herself by this invasion from the night. . . . Then he stood in

the light in his black clothes and his black stock, hat in one hand and yellow flowers in the other. She stood away, at his mercy, snatched out of herself. She did not know him, only she knew he was a man come for her. She could only see the dark-clad man's figure standing there upon her, and the gripped fist of flowers. She could not see the face the living eyes. (39)

While Lawrence uses light and dark values to convey the same qualities of mystery and suggestion intrinsic to Gauguin's *Bonjour Monsieur Gauguin,* he also strives to eliminate distinctions between human and nonhuman forms by visualizing the characters in terms of the confrontation between light and dark forces. Lawrence's perception of human figure as phenomenal form is also realized, as a synthesis of background and foreground forces, later in the first section of the novel in his description of Will Brangwen's passion for Anna. Lawrence's terms parallel the sense of relatedness between self and cosmos that van Gogh achieves in his Saint-Rémy portrait where, through a unity brushwork, the artist gets what he describes as "a mysterious effect, like a star in the depths of an azure sky" (letter 520, *Letters of Vincent van Gogh* 3:6): "And the youth went home with the stars in heaven whirling fiercely about the blackness of his head, and his heart fierce insistent but fierce as if he felt something balking him" (111). Stewart describes this image of Brangwen as "pure potentiality isolated in space" (300), yet rather than isolation, figure and form here work together to express the primordial drive that animates both man and cosmos. Lawrence reduces the field of vision to a concentrated astrological image, with the head of the man functioning as a planet haloed by whirling stars, much as van Gogh uses a similar verticil configuration to express that which is "eternal" in man and in nature.

Lawrence's disindividualization of the human figure is a technique that is integrally related as well to the depersonalized quality of Cézanne's almost faceless figures in *The Bathers,* a motif highly favored by the Fauves who extend that quality. Their figures, as Goldwater observes, "are not simply placed in a landscape setting which serves them as a scene of action while they yet preserve their human characters distinct from it; they are mixed up with the landscape in such a manner that they become part of it."[84] This particular effect is strikingly presented in the André Derain's *The Bathers* (fig. 27), which suggests those themes of harmony and vital relation that Lawrence pursues in parallel technical terms in *The Plumed Serpent.* Kate sees Cipriano as the embodiment, in alternate form, of elemental forces, the God of Fire and Blood, merging with the sun, "flushed" upon the water: "He dropped off the edge of masonry and waded out in the dim soft, uncanny water. And at that moment the light tipped over the edge of the mountain and spilled gold upon the surface of the lake. And instantly he was red as fire. The sunshine was not red, the sun was too high for that. It was golden with the morning. But as it flushed along

Figure 27. André Derain, *The Bathers*, 1908
(Narodni Galerie, Prague)

the surface of the lake it caught the body of Cipriano and he was red as fire, as a piece of pure fire."[85]

The moonlit scene which closes the first chapter of *The Rainbow* clearly illustrates how "visionary transformation" which discovers consanguinity between human and natural phenomena differs from anthropomorphic reductionism:

> He went out into the wind. Big holes were blown into the sky, the moonlight blew about. Sometimes a high moon, liquid-brilliant scudded across a hollow space and took cover under electric, brown-iridescent cloud-edges. Then there was a blot of cloud, and shadow. Then somewhere in the night a radiance again, like a vapour. And all the sky was teeming and tearing along, a vast disorder of flying shapes and darkness and ragged fumes of light and a great brown circling halo, then the terror of a moon running liquid-brilliant into the open for a moment, hurting the eyes before she plunged under cover of cloud again. (44)

Lawrence's convulsive forms, with their accelerated rhythms, fantastic chiaroscuro, and synesthetic interplay, combine to give us a sense of man vibrating in unison with the impersonal rhythms of the cosmos. Just as Tom cannot bear to be near the woman, nor endure "the utter foreignness of contact," so too "the terror of a moon running liquid-brilliant into the open for a moment" hurts the eyes. This paradigmatic cosmological drama, in its revelation of one's essential otherness, corresponds with van Gogh's own pursuit of that "other thing" manifest in the swirling rhythms of the predominantly spiral motif of his *Starry Night*.

The meteorological and astrological symbolism that Lawrence visualizes so forcefully as Tom goes "out into the wind" recurs in the succession of moonlit scenes chronicling the characters' movement beyond the parameters of familiar identity and their initiation into the procreative mysteries of the cosmos. In the scene that takes place between Anna and Will in the corn field, for example, Lawrence reduces the human figures to phenomenal forms to visualize the theme of interchange and the way in which, as male and female, the protagonists participate in cosmogonic processes as embodiments of some underlying generative principle.

Both Anna and Will are conceived in phenomenological terms. Anna becomes one with the "flaring moonlight," which makes "her drift and ebb like a wave" (118); she waits as a dark column, "like a glow of light" to which Will, as the "shadowy figure" is drawn; her voice sounds like the "low, plaintive call" of a "bird unseen in the night" (119). Will responds with his own passionate fixity "like a gleaming bright pebble, something bright and inalterable" (121), pursuing her "like a shuttle across the strip of cleared stubble." Concomitantly, landscape forms themselves participate in the same life principle that obliterates superficial generic distinctions. Lawrence presents the partially harvested fields

in terms as graphically compelling as Brueghel's vertical and horizontal configurations. Thus sheer corporeality is directly felt in the "prostrate" "bodies"
of the sheaves (116), the erect shocks riding "like ships in the haze of moonlight" (116–17), with the trees themselves "waiting like heralds, for the signal
to approach": "They went across the stubble to where the long rows of upreared
shocks ended. Curiously populous that part of the field looked, where the shocks
rode erect; the rest was open and prostrate" (117). To sustain this sense of
substantiality, Lawrence imbues qualities of light and atmosphere with a tangible presence. The moonlight, for example, "seemed to spread against their
faces" (116), "the air was all silver," the space between them a "vague crystal,"
and Will's approach that of a shadow through "gossamer dusk" (117). In all its
aspects, this ritual scene picturizes Lawrence's primitivistic sense of contact
with substance that reverberates in van Gogh's harvest landscapes.

To reestablish contact with cosmogonic forces Lawrence not only treats
character as phenomena, he also attends to the reunification of the senses that
occurs when the "whole consciousness of man" is brought into relation with the
"circumambient universe" at the "living moment." In the second moonlit scene
between Anton and Ursula, for example, he visualizes the ritual dance by fusing
tactile, aural, and visual sensations. Far from being disembodied, music becomes a tangible force whose reverberations are visible as an animated surface
pattern controlled by one persuasive wavelike motion that defines all aspects of
the scene:

> There was a wonderful rocking of the darkness, slowly, a great, slow swinging of the whole
> night, with the music playing lightly on the surface, making the strange, ecstatic, rippling on
> the surface of the dance, but underneath only one great flood heaving slowly backwards to the
> verge of oblivion, slowly forward to the other verge, the heart sweeping along each time, and
> tightening with anguish as the limit was reached, and the movement, at crises, turned and
> swept back. (316–17)

Within this dialectic of surface and depth, Lawrence conjoins a nonnaturalistic handling of the human figures with a synesthetic impulse that is concretized
in a series of oxymorons. These climax in the image of Ursula "like glimmering
gossamer," which seems "to burn among them, as they rose like cold fires to
the silvery-bluish air. All was intangible, a burning of cold glimmering whitish-
steely fires" (319).

Lawrence's brand of seeing engages the full consciousness of the observer,
and allows for a contact with otherness that is usually denied by habit and
convention to the "daylight consciousness." Such a "dim-eye vision" and the
notion of empathetic relation that it entails should not simply be received,
however, as evidence of what Stewart defines as "traumatic objectification" in

Expressionist art. Stewart suggests, for example, that in his presentation of Ursula's confrontation with the horses at the end of *The Rainbow,* external forms exist only to express individualized interior states. The horse group reflects, therefore, the passion of the protagonist and, as a mirror of this condition, Stewart advises, the group is composed of "figures of nightmare or hallucination":

> The barrier between natural vision and unconscious imagery has broken down. Vivid images and incantatory rhythms become the medium of an intense, disordered state of being: "She was aware of the great flash of hoofs, a bluish, incandescent flash surrounding a hollow darkness" (487). This irrational state of awareness is immediate as a dream. Ursula does not have to look at the horses: they materialize in all their horror and splendor in her psyche. The vision is non-natural in focus, with enlargement and illumination of the most terrifying detail (the hoofs). Ursula obviously fears destruction by the forces unleashed upon, or within, her. Since the expressionist style renders a subjective response, it is impossible to measure the degree, if any, of objective menace. The horses exist, but they are also a traumatic objectification of all the social and sexual pressures on Ursula (now pregnant), and a vengeful reflex of her own apocalyptic yearnings. ("Expressionism in *The Rainbow,*" 314)

I have chosen to quote this analysis at length because it so clearly demonstrates that a reliance on a limited notion of how nature can function in Post-Impressionism leads critics to surmise that any violation of a naturalistic surface is indicative of an Expressionistic technique.[86] The horse scene in *The Rainbow* brings to fruition Lawrence's conception of "design" as something that is recognized in the "fourth dimension" and his expressed intention to grasp the living-ness of external forms and bring that into vital relation with the whole consciousness of the individual:

> She knew they had not gone, she knew they awaited her still. But she went on over the log bridge that their hoofs had churned and drummed, she went on, knowing things about them. She was aware of their breasts gripped, clenched narrow in a hold that never relaxed, she was aware of their red nostrils flaming with long endurance, and of their haunches, so rounded, so massive, pressing, pressing, pressing to burst the grip upon their breasts, pressing for ever till they went mad, running against the walls of time, and never bursting free. Their great haunches were smoothed and darkened with rain. But the darkness and wetness of rain could not put out the hard, urgent, massive fire that was locked within these flanks, never, never. (487)

In large measure, the effect of Lawrence's presentation depends upon the way in which he sustains an internal point of view which participates in the *perspective vécue* of the protagonist. He is able to intensify the reader's own sense of being at one with the action rather than being fixed at a point located outside of its rhythms. To duplicate that *perspective vécue,* he is particularly careful to observe the restrictions imposed by the actual physical angle of vision that he selects for Ursula. She travels a path, a "narrow groove in the turf between high, sere, tussocky grass" (486), that prevents her from seeing the horses in their entirety. Because Lawrence deliberately constricts the visual dimension of the experience,[87] the protagonist and the reader who shares both her physical and internal point of view are compelled to know the horses through senses that usually play a subordinate role. The rhythms and images are chaotic and fragmentary precisely because one can no longer rely upon the visual sphere alone to make the kinds of adjustments the Kodak eye has been trained to make to differentiate human and nonhuman worlds, and to render, in the process, external forms impotent and abstract.

It is not because Lawrence wants to use landscape forms to mirror a disordered state of being, but because he wants to express in pictorial form a vision of reality that evolves during the dissolution of the isolate ego and, in doing so, give form to that which van Gogh defined as the "eternal" in his model. It is thus imperative that the visual exclusiveness of perspective art, which encourages external points of view, be abandoned in favor of a mode that more closely approximates the dynamic and organic character of perception of external forms. One notes immediately the structural congruency between these energetic curvilinear hollows and haloes of light and parallel configurations that close the moonlit scene at the end of chapter 1: "She was aware of the great flash of hoofs, a bluish, iridescent flash surrounding a hollow of darkness. Large, large seemed the bluish, incandescent flash of the hoof-iron, large as a halo of lightning around the knotted darkness of the flanks. Like circles of lightning came the flash of hoofs from out of the powerful flanks" (487).

The quality of fragmentation that Lawrence's choice of *perspective vécue* actualizes is similar in kind to the reorientation Cézanne and van Gogh work toward to realize their sense of the consubstantiality of figure and setting. This reorientation is as strongly expressed in Derain's *The Bathers*, where figure and natural scene are coextensive and mutually clarifying. By filling the frame with figures, the scene itself ceases to function as an open window. We cannot rely on the assumptions that ordinarily dictate the relation of figure and background, nor can we enter the canvas through a path of vision that gives a conventional spatial illusion.

In *The Rainbow*, the horses concretely embody the primordial drive that animates the first chapter's cosmic drama and bring the implications of Ursula's "moon madness" into relation with the Post-Impressionist triad of penetration, transformation, and revelation. Lawrence's reliance on intensification and magnification within this scene can be related to van Gogh's close-range approaches in *Willows at Sunset,* to the pulsating rhythms that energize moon and field in *Moonrise* and sustain the dynamic sense of absorption in *Crows over the Wheat Field* (fig. 28). In his discussion of the latter painting, Schapiro analyzes the "disquieting situation" van Gogh creates for the spectator "who is held in doubt before the great horizon and cannot, moreover, reach it on any of the roads

Figure 28. Vincent van Gogh, *Crows over the Wheat Field*, 1890
(*Vincent van Gogh Foundation, Rijksmuseum, Amsterdam*)

before him; these end blindly in the field or run out of the picture. The familiar perspective network of the open field is now inverted; the lines converge towards the foreground from the horizon, as if space had suddenly lost its focus and all things turned aggressively upon the beholder" (*Vincent van Gogh,* 130).

Just as van Gogh inverts perspective and brings the background into the foreground, such that the usual relations between near and far and the sense of space itself between them no longer obtain, Lawrence abandons an external point of view, which would create distance between the observer and the horse group, and chooses instead to have his figures fill the frame. He forgoes clear distinctions between foreground, middle ground, and background in order to emphasize the way in which the protagonist is "enveloped in the rain and the waving landscape" (486). In a correlative way, van Gogh's "endless sky," the "abnormal format" of the painting as a whole, creates, Schapiro suggests, a sense of "a submersion of the will," of a "desire to be swallowed up and to lose the self in a vastness" (34).

Though Ursula attempts to "beat her way back through all this fluctuation, back to stability and security" (486), she is "dissolved like water," extinguished by the weight of the horses' "fierce flanks," encircled, enclosed, and spread against them. As in van Gogh, the tension between the impulse to acquiesce and the impulse to withdraw is visualized through obstacles in the path of vision, the "dark, heavy, powerfully heavy knot" of horses, "gathered on a log bridge over the sedgy dike," that block her back (487) and that pursue her, prohibiting an escape through "the gate in the high hedge" that would bring her into "the smaller, cultivated field, and so out to the highroad and the ordered world of man" (488).

When Ursula finally accepts that "vaster power," the vital and organic forces in the cosmos that she intuitively responds to throughout the novel, she feels herself "destined to find the bottom of all things to-day: the bottom of all things" where "there was nothing deeper" (490). With her personality diffused, she begins to see with "mackerel" eyes, so that landscape forms reveal dimensions inaccessible to the photometric. The process entails the forgetting of old forms and the recovery of the eternal law of being that exists beneath them. The naturalistic surface becomes "unreal," the outward "shell" that she penetrates: "And again, to her feverish brain, came the vivid reality of acorns in February lying on the floor of a wood with their shells burst and discarded and the kernel issued naked to put itself forth" (492). As imprisoning and life-denying conventions of seeing are cast off, Ursula becomes one with the organic forces that she intuits, her unconscious yearning for direct connection granted some measure of fulfillment: "She was the naked, clear kernel thrusting forth, the clear, powerful shoot, and the world was a bygone winter, discarded." The process of discovery visualized through grasping the inside of the natural form is itself

Figure 29.   Vincent van Gogh, *The Olive Orchard*, 1889
Canvas, 73 × 92 cm.
(National Gallery of Art, Chester Dale Collection)

connatural with the Post-Impressionist artist's conception of his role as thinking eye, manifest in the extremely close-range vision that generates van Gogh's vital and organic, serpentine and vertical forms in *Ears of Corn*. It is further a potential "at-one-ness" that van Gogh's *The Olive Orchard* (fig. 29) achieves, where all aspects of the painter's motif are united by a dominant undulating rhythm, so that the harvesters, rather than dominating the landscape, coexist within it, sharing the plastic disposition of land forms and sky to expand the implications of the artist's generative motif.

Through a wide variety of stylistic experiments in Post-Impressionist art, there runs a common objective: a desire to return to the essential elements of art. These elements include the recovery of the nonrepresentational two-dimensionality of the medium and older notions of verisimilitude, and an effort to rid art of its anecdotal, documentary character and make it a reflection of the important truths of the universe as they are experienced by the thinking eye of the artist. Seizing origins means conveying or presenting through formal equivalents the fundamentals of existence both in terms of underlying structures (i.e., Cézanne's harmonies, which discover patterns and rhythms that are organic and vital and thus in "parallel with nature"), and the basic or fundamental centers of human life (i.e., those significant deformations of conventionally received appearances that expose the way that the mind, in the fullest sense of its optical, tactile, auditory, and even olfactory capacity, experiences form).

In a parallel way, verbal artists attempt to penetrate the captivating reflecting surfaces of the Impressionist pond to strike its bottom. They too explore the capacity of their medium to realize conceptions of *energia* as well as *enargia*. Post-Impressionist techniques of penetration are integral to that "other reality" that Woolf discloses by attending to the expressive power of the various graphic correlatives for conceptions of reality that define the parallax vision of *To the Lighthouse*. Hemingway's notion of a fifth-dimensional quality in his prose that would actualize a reality "truer than a photograph" evolves, at least in part, from his attempt to discover verbal techniques that would imbue his landscapes with the kind of internal coherency and substantiality he felt so strongly in his experience of Cézanne's spatial effects. Lawrence's "fourth dimension" commits him to the revelation of the underlying consubstantiability of character and landscape that depends upon the reintegration of optic and haptic sensibilities and the elimination of superficial generic boundaries between human and nonhuman worlds.

It is the reciprocity between mind and matter—the fact that the penetrative eye can bring the subject and the object into vital relation—that in large measure defines the meaning of Post-Impressionism. While the Post-Impressionist dispensation seeks to penetrate surface appearances to establish alternate conceptions of the correspondence between man and nature, Cubism seeks to destroy the accepted appearance of things to express conceptions of form. Taking the Post-Impressionist emphasis upon the mural character of the plastic medium to more extreme formulations, the Cubist artist commits himself to a study of the depth, density, and duration of objective realities and translates that analysis into the two dimensions of his medium. While in Post-Impressionist art the pursuit of depth retains at least tangential relation to spiritual and hieratic values, in Cubist art those metaphysical implications are held in abeyance.

3

"Total Representation":
"Cubification" and Cubist Effects

Cubism was gradually formulated from 1907 to 1914 through the collaboration of Pablo Picasso and Georges Braque, and extended into the late 1920s to include the work of Juan Gris. The term *Cubism* originates with Braque's one-man show at Daniel-Henry Kahnweiler's gallery in November 1908, when critic Louis Vauxcelles observed that in his estimation Braque reduced everything "to geometric patterns and cubes": "He despises form, reduces everything, sites and figures and houses to geometric complexes, to cubes."[1] Vauxcelles similarly referred to the paintings which Braque exhibited at the *Salon des Indépendants* of 1909 as "*bizarreries cubiques*" (qtd. in Golding, 20), and by April 1911 the term was in current use and was accepted by many of the artists themselves.

Within Cubism as a whole there are two major periods. The first, or Analytic phase, which generally ends in 1912 or 1913, refers to the deconstruction of form and of space, which is the starting point for the breakup of the picture surface; the second, or Synthetic phase, is distinguished by the *collage* and *papier collé* experiments of Picasso, Braque, and Gris. The terms *Analytical* and *Synthetic* derive in fact from Kant's analysis of two antithetic modes of perception. Analysis for Kant was the study of objects in nature achieved by breaking the objects up into their basic components, while synthesis meant the assembling of distinct parts to make a unique whole. The terms were first used by Vauxcelles in a review of the *Salon des Indépendants* of 1908 in Paris, as he attempted to articulate differences among Cubist works.

Conceptually, Analytical Cubism implies that the artist moves in a general sense from representation to abstraction, breaking open contours, eliminating superficial continuities, and displacing or fragmenting the single form to allow the artist to register his total response to the natural form, and to express what André Salmon describes in his 1912 "Anecdotal History of Cubism" as the "total representation of man and of things."[2] The artist's vision in this sense is conceptual and intellectual rather than physical and sensory. It exhibits a mental reconstruction of the object, a kind of heightened enumeration of one's history of the external form, which would accommodate the two-dimensional plane.

Synthetic Cubism implies that the works are created through a building-up of separate elements originating, as Norbert Lynton advises, in art and artifice, and not in nature.[3] Gris, in conversation with Kahnweiler, who was the first major dealer for both Picasso and Braque, provides an explicit commentary on the synthetic process in his own work: "I begin by organizing my picture; then I qualify the objects. My aim is to create new objects which cannot be compared with any object in reality. The distinction between Synthetic and Analytic Cubism lies precisely in this. These new objects, therefore, avoid distortion. My *Violin* [perhaps his 1913 *Violin and Guitar*], being a creation, need fear no comparison."[4] For Gris, the first thing for the painter was to establish the abstract compositional framework on the canvas, and then to allow the subject matter to materialize. The objectification of pictorial form, or the bestowing upon abstract elements a literal representational value, was defined by Gris as an essentially deductive method: "I try to make concrete that which is abstract. I proceed from the general to the particular, by which I mean that I start with an abstraction in order to arrive at a true fact. Mine is an art of synthesis, of deduction."[5]

Whether the Cubist subject is built up or broken down, the artist's focus rests with the way in which the mind apprehends and experiences form. In both methods, the artist is concerned with rendering perceptible his ideas about types of objects rather than with representing a unique manifestation within that type. Synthetic Cubism extends the conceptual basis of Cubism as a whole and, like the Analytic phase that preceded it, affirms both the autonomy and referentiability of the medium. Critics who discuss the second stage of Cubism beginning with the *collages* of 1912 invariably trace its development from the trompe l'oeil nail in Braque's 1909–1910 *Violin and Palette* (fig. 30), a device Picasso absorbs into his own work, and which is amplified through a variety of illusionistic details in the paintings of both artists prior to the *collage* and *papier collé* experiments. Braque's nail makes explicit the complicated dialectic between representational and nonrepresentational values that is implicit in Analytic canvases. It asserts that the painting maintains its contact and connection with external reality even while it departs from traditional standards of iconicity. The tension between these values, articulate as the copresence and convergence of artistry and reference in the work itself, is an extension of the debate manifest in the multiple iconic modes of Analytic works.

In both phases artists commission forms that are naturalistic and nonnaturalistic, traditionally mimetic and hieroglyphic, concrete and abstract, to serve the realization of a single and coherent compositional form. The absorption of a vast array of extrapictorial fragments within Synthetic works dramatizes that stylistic multiplicity even more by making the observer particularly conscious

Figure 30. Georges Braque, *Violin and Palette*, 1909–1910
Oil on canvas, 36⅛″ × 16⅞″.
(Solomon R. Guggenheim Museum, New York; photograph by Robert E. Mates)

of the picture as a constructed reality. Though the extraneous materials undergo some kind of alteration or transformation through their inclusion in the canvas, they nonetheless maintain the bold assertion of their ready-made autonomy. Their very material existence is never revoked or denied by their newly acquired compositional value.

In his discussion of the "diagrammatic" character of Cubist art, John Berger clarifies the nature of the optical synthesis itself by noting that the picture is "a sign referring to, but not imitating" the appearance of surface realities. In this context "all references to appearances are made as signs on the picture surface." "A diagram need not eschew certain aspects of appearances: but these two will be treated symbolically as *signs,* not as imitations or re-creations."[6] In an effort to "paint totalities," the artist collaborates with the multiple signs of his subject, while the divergence between the "different claims" that this stylistic multiplicity encourages is resolved or arbitrated by "the two-dimensional surface of the picture" itself.

To further explain the cipher nature of the relationship between the picture and its reference to material reality, Berger observes that in a Cubist painting:

> We start from the surface, we follow the sequence of forms which leads into the picture, and then suddenly we arrive back at the surface again and deposit our newly acquired knowledge upon it, before making another foray. This is why I called the Cubist picture-surface the origin and sum of all that we can see in the picture. There is nothing decorative about such two-dimensionality, nor is it merely an area offering possibilities of juxtaposition for dissociated images—as in the case of much recent neo-Dadaist or Pop art. We begin with the surface, but since everything in the picture refers back to the surface we begin with the conclusion. We then search—not for an explanation, as we do if presented with an image with a single, predominant meaning (a man laughing, a mountain, a reclining nude), but for some understanding of the configuration of events whose interaction is the conclusion from which we began. When we "deposit our newly acquired knowledge upon the picture surface," what we in fact do is to find the sign for what we have just discovered: a sign which was already there but which previously we could not read. (24)

I have quoted extensively from Berger for he so effectively defines the major components of a Cubist technique: the primacy of the flat plane, the diagrammatic character of the signs whose provisional or synecdochal nature allows them to suggest totalities but never to define them in isolation, and the unpredictable pace at which the meaning of each of the multiple claims is revealed through reference to the picture plane itself.

Collage was, in fact, invented by Picasso early in 1912 in *Still Life with Chair Caning* (fig. 31), in which the artist introduced a piece of oilcloth printed with a chair caning pattern simply by gluing it on to his canvas. *Papier collé*'s author was Braque, who utilized strips of paper for more purely formalistic ends in his first *collé, Fruit-Dish and Glass.* In Gris's 1914 *Glasses and Newspaper* (fig. 32), the strips of paper serve both representational and pictorial functions, as does Picasso's ready-made oilcloth. In fact the *collé* elements exist on four levels: they are shapes and colors that function independently of the object to whose delineation they contribute but do not define; they represent or suggest certain objects in the picture by analogies of color and texture, or by the addition of keys or clues which render the objects legible; as with the *collage* element, they are solid, tactile pieces of extraneous matter, strips of simulated wood-grained wallpaper and colored paper whose extrapictorial ontological autonomy emphasizes the material existence of the canvas itself; finally, as Pierre Daix observes, they give "concrete form to the new picture space," which duplicates the "space of actual life" by encouraging the eye to decipher relation and depth.[7] In Gris's *Glasses and Newspaper,* the observer enjoys both the emphasis upon the opacity of the canvas that the attached strips of paper make insistent, and the illusion of three-dimensional spatial relations created by forms placed one behind the other as the image is built up on the surface itself.

In *Cubists and Cubism,* Daix clarifies the historical development of the movement by distinguishing between Cubism proper and the Cubist School. The latter was composed of a number of painters who began to form a group during 1910, a group that brought artists and art theorists like Robert Delaunay, Jean Metzinger, Albert Gleizes, Fernand Leger, and Henri Le Fauconnier together with literary critics such as Guillaume Apollinaire, Gustave Kahn, and Salmon, and which grew to include other artists and estheticians who met regularly and became increasingly aware of a commonality of treatment.

Daix points out that neither Picasso nor Braque, whom he defines as the true originators, were present at these gatherings, nor did they exhibit regularly with the group. Picasso avoided the Salons entirely. Neither he nor Braque was part of the first Cubist exhibition, which took place at the 1911 *Salon des Indépendants* in *Salle 41,* nor were they part of the single most important Cubist exhibition, the *Section d'Or* in October 1912. Ironically, therefore, both Picasso and Braque become "the founders of a movement to which they never actually belonged" (Daix, 7). Not only is it an altogether different group of painters who figure in Cubist exhibitions, but the art and rhetoric of the Cubist School opens the door to the Academic or Codified Cubism that flourished during the First World War. These are artists who preserved the "manner" but not the "style" of Cubism, and who exploit the formula of the geometric pattern and surface fragment without pursuing the conceptual nature of Picasso's and Braque's reformulations of space and time.

Picasso's and Braque's conceptual approach to reality is most appropriately defined by the distinction Maurice Raynal formulated in a series of essays beginning in 1912. In *"Conception et vision"* Raynal uses the term "the fourth dimension" to indicate the shift in intensity from the Impressionist optic, *"la peinture de la vision,"* to what he felt was the more tenacious eye of Cubism's *"la peinture de la conception."*[8] In broadening the intellectual basis of Impres-

Figure 31.   Pablo Picasso, *Still Life with Chair Caning*, 1912
(*Musée Picasso; cliché des Musées Nationaux*)

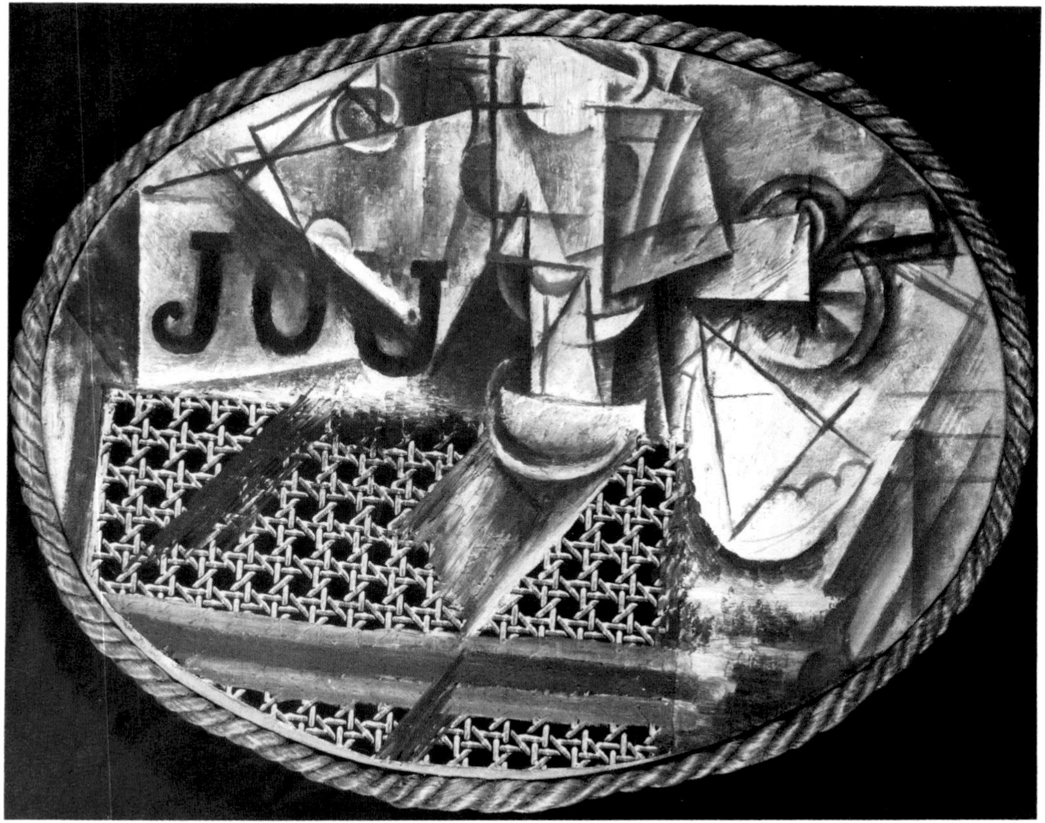

Figure 32. Juan Gris, *Glasses and Newspaper,* 1914
Gouache, conte crayon, and chalk on paper and canvas,
61 × 38.1 cm.
(Smith College Museum of Art; gift of Joseph Brummer, 1921)

sionism's scientific realism by grasping an unseen fourth-dimensional quality that is neither an elusive metaphysical property nor an Einsteinian postulate, Cubism aims at a more profound realism, one that will overcome the limitations of Impressionism's fascination with the three dimensions of the old visual reality. The fourth dimension in Cubist art is a dimension that is realized through the synthesis of visual, tactile, and motor space perceptions, and it refers to the inherent plasticity of objective reality. It is a dimension that strict fidelity to traditional perspective and to the sides and surfaces of objects in scenographic space obscures rather than discloses. Its realization depends upon the free and mobile perspective that Analytical Cubism develops in its synthesis of multiple views, which registers the totality of the artist's intellectual possession of the object. Indeed, it is this conceptual orientation so basic to primitive art that is embraced by the term *fourth dimension* that Raynal uses in *"Qu'est-ce que . . . le 'Cubisme'?"*: "In place of painting objects as they [primitive peoples] saw them, they painted them as they thought of them, and it is precisely this law that the cubists have readopted, amplified and codified under the name of 'the *fourth dimension.'*"[9]

As significantly, the image realized through the Cubist artist's intensive collaboration with his total experience of different aspects of the object no longer exists in the time of the old visual reality from which the object is torn. The optical synthesis in Cubist art provides, as Gleizes and Metzinger observe in *Cubism,* a fusion of the successive experiences of a form within a single image that is reconstituted in time.[10] One must distinguish very carefully, therefore, between the concept of Simultaneism that is developed through Futurism's chronophotographic techniques (i.e., the recording of the successive stages of an action in one image), and the idea of the optical synthesis in Cubist art, between the multiplication of views in the former and the multiple views in the latter. Futurism's celebration of modern technology, its fascination with movement and metamorphosis, often finds its technical complement through a multiplication of views—a quick succession of minimally gradated exposures of a single subject that aim, H. H. Arnason suggests, directly to involve the observer in an "orgiastic" experience of the subject's "total action."[11] It is in this sense that Futurism adapts Cubist faceting to explore its ideals of speed and dynamism. The very notion of the "Cubist Dance" around the object, a notion that was fostered within the Cubist School, engages a concept of succession that is more in keeping with Futurism's chronophotographic technique than it is with the actual nature of the Cubist synthesis itself.

The difference between succession and synthesis in Cubist art is expressed in Gris's work as he moves from his *Portrait of Picasso* of 1912 (fig. 33) to the actual Synthetic form of *The Washstand.* In *Portrait of Picasso* one sees the extent to which Gris dissects his subject, examines each part from a different angle, and then reconstructs the total image from the various parts. In this way disparate planes of view are not so much synthesized as juxtaposed. What Gris is doing in fact is adapting and elaborating scientific perspective by conjoining a series of different but consistent viewpoints in a single painting. The optical synthesis achieved by Picasso and Braque, in contrast, immediately challenges the predominance of scientific perspective and optically derived standards of iconicity. At the height of Analytical Cubism, for example, in Picasso's *Portrait of Monsieur Kahnweiler* (fig. 34), background and object are fused through a complex of planes inextricably involved. Any even superficial allegiance to the surface continuities of the model's external form and structure, an allegiance sustained in Gris's *Portrait of Picasso,* is relinquished. The fragments in the painting are arranged according to a pictorial order and effectiveness that are unrelated to the illusions of mass and continuity we usually rely upon for concepts of identity.

The optical synthesis renders what is often described as the "task of reconstruction" irrelevant to the form as given. It becomes impossible to detach the object from its surroundings or reconstruct any one of the objects independently from the other objects around it. In a correlative way, it becomes impossible to return the object so reconstituted to the temporal and spatial coordinates from which it has been removed. Gris's *Portrait of Picasso* becomes, therefore, prototypic of the kind of "cubification" of space and volume that artists of the Cubist School will develop. The latter's superimposition of the Cubist grid and faceting to overlay a perspective definition and multiplication of viewpoints is paralleled in the Futurist preoccupation with succession rather than synthesis in Marcel Duchamp's *Nude Descending a Staircase, No. 2* of 1912 (fig. 35).

Not only is the concept of the easel picture as simply an open window rendered obsolete by the optical synthesis in actual Cubist works, but the act of intellectual possession that the Cubist artist achieves shifts the focus from subjective values to plastic dimensions. The Cubist artist is therefore capable of the most profound kind of negative capability. In conversation with Hélène Parmelin, Picasso makes this point, and his Cubist notion of emphatic substitution of self has as much relevancy for still life as it does for portraiture: "When you do a head, you have to draw like that head. Ingres drew like Ingres, and not like the things he drew" (qtd. in Daix, 21).

The implications of this kind of fidelity to an exterior reality that can be known by the mind are borne out in Cubist canvases, which, even while they depart from conventional standards of iconicity by penetrating the naturalistic surface, assert a basic correspondence between pictorial space and actual space that is never revoked. Even in their most abstract formulations, therefore, Picasso and Braque retain a fundamental up-down and left-right correspondence between the picture plane and the extrapictorial visual field. In his analysis of the growing fragmentation and distortions in Braque's *Still Life with Violin and Pitcher,* Robert Rosenblum explores the way in which the painting, even while

Figure 33.   Juan Gris, *Portrait of Picasso*, 1912
Oil on canvas, 21″ × 18″.
(Courtesy of the Art Institute of Chicago; gift of Leigh B. Block)

Figure 34.   Pablo Picasso, *Portrait of Monsieur Kahnweiler*, 1910
Oil on canvas, 100.6 × 72.8 cm.
*(Courtesy of the Art Institute of Chicago; gift of Mrs. Gilbert
W. Chapman in memory of Charles B. Goodspeed, 1948)*

Figure 35.   Marcel Duchamp, *Nude Descending a Staircase, No. 2,* 1912
Oil on canvas, 58″ × 35″.
*(Philadelphia Museum of Art; Louise and Walter Arensberg
Collection)*

it transforms the given, remains at least "partially relevant to the world of appearances": "The browns of the violin and the table top at its right are directly appropriate to the colors of wood, just as the milky white planes of the tablecloth and the pitcher can allude, not implausibly, to the folds of a fabric and to the crystalline facets of what is perhaps a transparent pitcher. In the same way, the light in this painting, for all the arbitrariness of the contradictory patterns of highlight and shadow, conveys a luminosity that refers to the laws of physics and visual perception as well as to the laws of art."[12] Cubism's allegiance to both the rule of art and the rule of nature allows Picasso and Braque to retain the object's connection with the natural environment in which it is discovered. In point of fact, the descriptive geometry Cubism develops to explore the interior structure of external forms allows for a more sophisticated notion of iconicity in art. In synthesizing a variety of disparate views and in fusing visual, haptic and manual reactions to the subject within a single image, the Cubist artist revaluates the nature of the solid form and moves beyond the limitations of optically derived notions of resemblance. The observer enters into a creative and vigorous experience of the full complexity of the subject's three-dimensionality without losing contact with the flatness of the picture space.

Braque's *Houses at L'Estaque* (fig. 36), one of the group of canvases presented by Kahnweiler in the 1908 exhibition, provides an example of how the rigid system of horizontals and verticals that compose the Cubist grid work to secure the balance of two-and three-dimensional values within a Cubist painting. The grid establishes a kind of "geometry of discontinuity" (Daix, 110), which enables the artist to pierce the closed form and analyze its seemingly homogeneous surface into a series of sculptural units or crystal facets. This process of fragmentation and reconstruction becomes the most prominent feature of Analytical Cubism. Though forms in Braque's *Houses at L'Estaque* are closed, the geometrization the painter develops to articulate a sympathy between organic and inorganic forms works in conjunction with an adaptation of the Cézannean elevation to create a vigorous spatial illusion. As Daix suggests, geometry in Cubist art is neither "static" nor "cultivated for its own sake" as an abstract schema superimposed upon and unrelated to natural or existing structures. Rather, it is "decisively used to create a reversal of perspective, a dynamic forward thrust of space out of the picture toward the spectator" (43). It is in this way that the grid contributes to what Salmon had described as Cubism's invitation to "touch" and "feel" objects in their "total existence" ("Anecdotal History of Cubism," qtd. in Chipp, 204).

One can trace the implications of Braque's researches into space by moving from the *Houses at L'Estaque* to the shimmering faceting and exchange of translucent and opaque planes in his 1910 *Fishes* (fig. 37), a canvas that epitomizes the classical pre-war phase of Analytical Cubism. *Fishes* carries the principles of disassociation and dislocation further to enhance the tactile and

Figure 36.   Georges Braque, *Houses at L'Estaque*, 1908
Oil, 71 × 59.5 cm.
(Kunstmuseum, Bern)

manual sensations of the spatial illusion by breaking down surfaces through a series of verticals, horizontals, and accompanying diagonals. Braque describes the sculptural experience integral to Analytical Cubism's decomposition of surface as one that allows for an explicit volumetric treatment of the object in a tangible space within the two dimensions of the picture plane: "the fragmentation [of objects] enabled me to establish space and movement within space, and I was unable to introduce the object until I had created the space" (qtd. in Golding, 85).

The dynamic quality of the Cubist picture space, its materiality, and the tangibility of its multidimensional forms become increasingly significant in Cubism's assertion of the ontologically free nature of the pictorial invention. Gleizes and Metzinger announce, for example, that the "picture bears its pretext, the reason for its existence within it. . . . It does not harmonize with this or that environment; it harmonizes with things in general, with the universe: it is an organism" (19). The nature of the correspondence, or the kind of referentiability implicit in the relationship between the pictorial reality and external reality in Cubism, is one that engages concepts of *energia* rather than *enargia*. Picasso advises that a form, when realized in its full complexity, lives "a life of its own" just as the "mineral substance, having geometric formation" remains "what it is and will always have its own form."[13] In a 1925 article, *"Chez les Cubistes,"* Gleizes clarifies the organic analogy intrinsic to Cubism's sense of the conceptualized subject when he talks about the Cubist painting "having the quality of an object and the same relationship to nature."[14]

The Cubist destruction[15] of the naturalistic surface is neither subjective appropriation nor nihilistic glorification. Rather, the formal abstraction of the natural object provides what Gris describes as "simply a new way of representing the world" (qtd. in Kahnweiler, 138). The conceptual realism of Cubist art comes as an intensification of the old visual reality of Impressionist art because it allows an "intellectual control" over the retina that the Impressionist artist did not allow (*Cubism*, 11). For Gleizes and Metzinger, "the visible world can become real only by the operation of the intellect" (12), and it is this kind of conceptual approach—nascent in Cézanne's more "resolute eye" (15) as well as inherent in the realistic impulse within Impressionist art—that Cubism inherits from the nineteenth century.

It is in this context that one speaks of Cubism's "homage to" and "transformation of" the principles of composition that helped define both Impressionism and Post-Impressionism. While Post-Impressionists like Cézanne, as a rule, relied completely on visual models, working *sur le motif* in landscape especially, Cubists like Picasso and Braque use as a point of departure the structural and constructive dimensions of the forms Cézanne intuitively discovered. Working in a conceptual way, relying as much on memory as on visual models, Picasso's and Braque's approach is more intellectual, their alteration of surface

Figure 37. Georges Braque, *Fishes*, 1910
(*The Tate Gallery, London; copyright ARS, New York, 1988*)

more severe, their homage to particular data of vision more variable and ambiguous, and their dismissal of anecdotal values more pervasive.

One of the most distinguishing features of Cubist art becomes the way in which the tension between representational and nonrepresentational values becomes an explicit theme in the canvas itself. Rosenblum suggests that Cubist artists, "instead of assuming that the work of art was an illusion of a reality that lay beyond it," and trying to conceal those devices that allowed for the illusion, "proposed that the work of art was itself a reality that represented the very process by which nature is transformed into art" (13). The ambiguous spatial and temporal dimensions of the Cubist subject as well as the multiple, though coequal, iconic modes that realize those dimensions, provide an indication of the extent to which the issue of correspondence materializes in the work itself. In attempting to realize his total experience of sculptural form in a two-dimensional medium, the Cubist artist makes explicit his prevailing sense that no fact of vision is unequivocal, and that no mode of representation is any more real or true than another. In accommodating to the flat surface his synthesis of various and contradictory reactions to his subject, the artist renders perceptible his understanding of the dynamic properties of form. The translation of the experience from actual to pictorial space involves processes that destroy any consistent illusion of mass. Often the usual relation between load and support is inverted. The conventional iconic identities of objects and the boundaries between them are concealed or confused. In combining seemingly disparate modes of presentation the artist's conceptual recreation of material reality becomes the center of the painting.

If we compare an early still life by Picasso, his 1912 *Bottle of Pernod* (fig. 38) with Cézanne's *Still Life with Fruit Basket* (fig. 16), Cubism's more explicit dialectic between nature and art becomes apparent. Picasso achieves this intensification by amplifying the gradations of his fidelity to the data of vision and by defamiliarizing the illusions of mass and gravity. The close-up view magnifies the challenge to the usual relationship of load and support that Cézanne's tilted axis and truncated table work toward. Further, Picasso explores the exchange of values between man-made and natural objects in a more decisive way, while his manipulation of inconsistent light sources makes the compromise between two- and three-dimensional values a clear issue in the canvas as a whole. These kinds of alterations allow Picasso to declare the flat surface even while he explores conceptually and, in fact, dramatizes the assumptions underlying the still-life exchange of things *on* tables, which will become part of the *tableau-tableau* or *tableau-objet* theme in *collage* and *collé.*

While Cubism extends the implications of the realistic impulse in Post-Impressionism, one must distinguish the Cubist inquiry into the nature of being from the Post-Impressionist artist's pursuit of an underlying and essential pattern and significance. In moving from phenomena to noumena, Cubist artists and

Figure 38. Pablo Picasso, *Bottle of Pernod*, 1912
(Hermitage, Leningrad)

critics turn to Kant for intellectual support. In so doing, they assimilate into their conception of the primacy of reason and the ability of the intellect to disclose the inner dynamism of objective realities Kant's notion of the synthetic a priori, those innate cognitive categories that allow for the organization, interpretation, and conceptualization of phenomena. Apollinaire, for example, speaks of the accessibility of inner realities in Kantian terms: Cubism "is the art of painting new structures out of elements borrowed not from the reality of sight, but from the reality of insight. All men have a sense of this interior reality. A man does not have to be cultivated to conceive, for example, a round form."[16] The doctrine of coequality intrinsic to Cubist art manifests itself not only in terms of the dismissal of hierarchies of values within the canvas, but also in terms of the democratization of the relation between the artist and his audience.

One of the ways in which this democratization manifests itself is through the iconography that Picasso and Braque develop to explore their conceptions of the commonplace and the everyday. Daix describes their character as "disindividualized" (70), but the term itself is not meant to preclude evocations of intimacy, for there is a real sense that the musical instruments, playing cards, pipes, and newspapers in the Synthetic phase especially have personal associations for the artists. Golding reconciles this apparent disparity by noting that "despite the extremely personal aspect of so much Cubist painting, the movement remained free from introspection, and the painters continued to view and record their ideas of the material world and their immediate experience in a detached and objective way" (89). The combination of detachment and intimacy, of impersonality and whimsy, especially in the verbal and visual punning that is intrinsic to *collage* and *collé,* characterizes Cubist art. Even though Picasso returns to the human form, and both he and Braque saturate their *collés* and *collages* with the details of their daily lives by introducing the names of popular songs as in Picasso's *Ma Jolie* (fig. 39) or the brand names of the colognes they used as in Gris's *The Washstand,* these objects function less as expressive correlatives and more as compositional entities that work out the dialectic between illusion and reality central to *collage* and *collé.*

Another factor that is equally significant with respect to the role of "subjective values" in Cubist painting involves the democratic perspective that superintends the relinquishing of a hierarchy of values or the imposition of a purely human perspective in either choice of object or choice of style. Within this context artists speak of new canons of beauty and of notions of appropriateness that move beyond the limitations inherent in prevailing academic traditions that perpetuated the antique ideal. Salmon speaks of the Cubist reinvention of the human form: "The smile of *La Gioconda* was for too long, perhaps, the Sun of Art," the "adoration of her" analogous "to some decadent Christianity" ("Anecdotal History of Cubism," qtd. in Chipp, 203). Picasso advises that all objects have equal significance: "The artist is a receptacle for emotions that come from

Figure 39.   Pablo Picasso, *Ma Jolie*, 1910
Oil on canvas, 100 × 65.4 cm.
*(Collection, the Museum of Modern Art, New York; acquired
through the Lillie P. Bliss Bequest)*

all over the place: from the sky, from the earth, from a scrap of paper, from a passing shape, from a spider's web. That is why we must not discriminate between things. Where things are concerned there are no class distinctions. We must pick out what is good for us where we can find it" ("Conversation, 1935," qtd. in Chipp, 271).

One speaks of this democracy of touch with respect to the Cubist subject in terms of the concern with the plastic potential of the object itself. The contemporaneity of the subject is therefore not symptomatic of a deliberate search for a modernist perspective, nor reflective of a desire to exalt the mundane and the commonplace and render them symbolic or philosophical, psychological or emotional points of view.

Similarly, Cubism's more purely visual point of view provides the most viable context to interpret the equanimity of focus that conditions the fusion of seemingly disparate styles within a single painting. We can therefore speak of the contemporaneity of historical styles, but not, as does Mario Praz, of their "contamination" or confusion.[17] Picasso himself derides any notion of a hierarchy of styles by undermining the conception of evolution as progress that the notion of hierarchy implies: "To me there is no past or future in art." No single style therefore proves itself to be any more adequate than another: "Variation does not mean evolution. If an artist varies his mode of expression this only means that he has changed his manner of thinking, and in changing, it might be for better or worse." To explain the fusion of idioms in his own work he notes that the choice of style is determined by subject and intention: "Whenever I had something to say, I have said it in the manner in which I felt it ought to be said. Different motives inevitably require different methods of expression. This does not imply either evolution or progress, but an adaptation of the idea one wants to express and the means to express that idea" ("Statement, 1923," qtd. in Chipp, 264–65).

The kind of freedom from a hierarchy of values or the homogeneity of style that Picasso supports materializes in his *Les Demoiselles d'Avignon* (fig. 40), a painting whose emotional disequilibrium justifies its classification as "one of the most passionate products of twentieth-century Expressionism" (Golding, 47), and yet a work that anticipates in its dislocations and stylistic multiplicity the doctrine of coequality integral to Cubist art. The painting expresses the immediate heritage of Cézanne's studies of bathers, the reassessment of the human form in Matisse and Derain, the whole Renaissance tradition of the monumental nude, and the pagan art of Iberia and ritual mask of African Negro art.

The second feature of the painting that renders it representative of a Cubist technique is the free and mobile perspective through which the figures are realized. Picasso violates perspective orthodoxy by distending and dislocating the anatomy of the squatting *demoiselle* on the right, for example. By pulling

Figure 40. Pablo Picasso, *Les Demoiselles d'Avignon,* 1907
Oil on canvas, 243.9 × 233.7 cm.
(Collection, the Museum of Modern Art, New York; acquired
through the Lillie P. Bliss Bequest)

the far leg and arm into the picture plane he abnormally extends a simple back view of the subject. In this way the painting sustains a sculptural sense of form even while it challenges the integrity of mass. This challenge to conventional descriptive modes is restated in the arbitrary color values and in the partially melted contour of the nude at the right.

Cubism's fidelity to "total representation" creates a dynamic between the sculptural experience of form and the pictorial surface that is extended in Picasso's *Seated Female Nude* of 1910 (fig. 41). Though in this early Analytical work Picasso still follows the contours of his model, the rhythms of the faceting exploit the asymmetry of the face. This kind of dislocation becomes indicative of Picasso's experimentation with pictorial technique that would realize manual and tactile sensations. Releasing these sensations in pictorial form moves the image so conceived beyond the constraints imposed by an adherence to visual appearances alone. Both Picasso and Braque pursue the felt quality of clearly defined pictorial passages between objects to enhance the material reality of the picture space. Even in those paintings that epitomize the most radical dislocations of the Analytical experiment, where the penetration of the closed form is completely realized through a "geometry of discontinuity," and the fragmentation's allegiance to surface contour is arbitrary and capricious, both artists sustain a vigorous sculptural experience. In Picasso's 1910 *Kahnweiler* portrait the subject ceases to be stated as an independent entity. The painting no longer represents in any traditionally conceived mimetic sense. A variety of iconic forms ranging from the more naturalistic configuration of hands and ear in the portrait to the crepuscular network of lines and planes that integrate background and figure work together to create a painting that declares the presence of beings and things.

The rich and complicated interplay of the naturalistic and the schematic becomes progressively more significant in Cubist art as a means of realizing—through levels of artistic illusion and varying degrees of optical fidelity to the given—the implications of the doctrine of coequality. As the paintings of 1910 and 1911 become more adamant in their challenge to the natural perspective, Braque and Picasso provide realistic clues, adaptations of the guide-mark Picasso used in the *Les Demoiselles* to sustain a balance between the type and the actual, which carry the spectator through the work's more difficult passages. In *Les Demoiselles,* the small low table in the foreground functions to establish the scale of the painting and evoke a more familiar third dimension. Braque's trompe l'oeil nail in *Violin and Palette* sharpens this dialectic between the optically perceived and the intellectually conceived, a dialectic that is continued through the adaptations of the ready-made in *collage* and *collé* and in paintings which bear the imprint of *collage* and *collé* techniques.

This fusion of multiple standards of authenticity, which Daix defines as the combination of the "'pure' rigour of a pyramidal composition and the profusion

Figure 41. Pablo Picasso, *Seated Female Nude*, 1910
Oil on canvas, 36¼″ × 28¾″.
(Tate Gallery, London; copyright ARS N.Y. / SPADEM, 1988)

of tangible clues" (67) is epitomized in Braque's *The Portuguese* (fig. 42). In Braque's painting, stencilled letters and numbers—D BAL, D CO, &, 10, and 40—exist as literal fragments, parts of the typographical environment of the posters that decorated the café walls. The ready-mades, the letters that are mechanically produced through the application of an ordinary stencil, refer in a realistic but also in a conceptual way to the actual setting of the painting. They identify the café bar, just as the title itself refers to a guitarist whom Braque had seen play in a café in Marseilles. However, insofar as these symbols have been assimilated into the picture space, they suffer the same kind of fragmentation and their block forms are echoed in the complex arcs and angles of the painting as a whole: they become plastic entities. Their referential relationship with external reality and the very arbitrariness of that relation is both questioned and placed in high relief. Braque's assimilation and transformation of the ready-made is paradigmatic of the endless contradictions in the work's entirety. The conceptual nature of the painting's relation with reality allows multiple variations between the two extremes of description and construction.

In Synthetic Cubism, Picasso, Braque, and Gris continue their destruction of the traditionally conceived mimetic relationship between art and reality. In his exploration of the variety of typographical styles and modes of signature that function as part of the ready-made vocabulary that *collage* and *collé* adapt, Rosenblum, in "Picasso and the Typography of Cubism," emphasizes the extent to which those kinds of extrapictorial substances amplify the implications of Braque's trompe l'oeil nail. The modulation of verbal meanings through fragmentation and elision often provides an explicit commentary upon the conceptual nature of the relationship between art and reality that the paintings advocate.[18]

Through a variety of *collage* permutations extracted from the verbal premise of *Le Journal*, for example, Cubist artists often posit, in verbal terms, an analogue for the ambiguity of the planar dissections of depicted objects, as in Gris's *Glasses and Newspaper*. Elision delivers the newspaper title from its usual mode of signification and allows *Le Jou* to participate in the *tableau-tableau* theme of the whole. The implications of the literal meanings of the fragment *LE JOU* open a variety of potential and stored meanings, which function in conjunction with the subheadings themselves to emphasize the way in which correspondence itself is at issue in the work. The word play—"*Aillières*," "*duel*," "*détruit*," *Les Villes soeurs*"—animates the checkered gaming table and encourages the observer to appreciate the way in which unexpected continuities between the volumes, the framing motifs, and the dual allegiance of forms work out the suggestions of the verbal terms themselves.

In asserting both the pictorial and the empirical fact, exploring the paradoxes this dual responsibility engages in the canvas, and allowing that explicit dialectic to become their major theme, Cubist artists shatter traditional concep-

Figure 42. Georges Braque, *The Portuguese*, 1911
Oil, 117 × 81.5 cm.
(Oeffentliche Kunstsammlung Basel, Kunstmuseum)

tions of both nature and art with an unprecedented deliberateness and awareness. Cubism is an inquiry into being that extends notions of iconicity and correspondence within the terms of the plastic medium itself. It is far less a comment on the nature of reality than it is upon how that reality is absorbed by the artist and assimilated by the picture plane.

In asserting correlations between Cubist art and Modernist literature, critics have relied on a series of misconceptions about the nature of the Cubist vision and technique, misconceptions that have encouraged them to use Cubism as an all-embracing period concept offering a "visual equivalent" for the ambiguity and uncertainty of the "twentieth-century experience" (Rosenblum, *Cubism*, 14). These are misconceptions that many literary critics have inherited from the members of the Cubist School, who themselves only partially grasped the actual nature of Picasso's and Braque's experiment. At times, for example, Cubist School artists and estheticians misinterpreted Picasso's and Braque's disindividualization of people and things, and saw their impersonality as evidence of a kind of twentieth-century psychological realism and dislocation rather than as a recovery of primitive priority and the pursuit of inner structure. At other times, they asserted retrospectively that Cubism's stylistic multiplicity expressed conceptions of relativity and uncertainty rather than affirmed the artists' belief in the autonomy and knowability of matter. The fourth-dimensional realism of Cubism's optical synthesis seemed to sanction a connection between Picasso's and Braque's fragmentation of expected continuities and Einstein's absolute space-time continuum, even though pre-Einsteinian texts provide a more than adequate conceptual framework to describe the "mundane" reality of Cubist still lifes and landscapes.[19]

Led by Gleizes and Metzinger particularly, who perceived the geometrization of form in Picasso and Braque as evidence to support their notions of what they believed would define Cubism's ultimately pure and abstract form,[20] critics postulated correspondences between what they thought was Cubism's exclusive emphasis upon the opaque surface and what can be defined as a "grammacentric divorce between language and reality"[21] that seems to be part of Modernist literature's rethinking of the referentiability of its own medium. The pressure that Cubist artists placed upon optically derived notions of iconicity, and on the traditions of correspondence, generally led to ambiguities that could only thrive, however, when the attachment between the picture surface and the material reality was maintained. In evading this tension in Cubist art, critics were often eager to promote analogies based on what they perceived to be the mutually abstract dimensions of both Modernist forms and Cubist compositions.

Finally, many critics perceived the fusion of multiple views within the optical synthesis as a correlative for the cinematic time sense that was engaged in Futurism's multiplication of successive views. In positing this equivalence, they confused the techniques Cubist artists explored to realize the synchronic character of their own medium with the techniques Modernist writers evolved to overcome the limitations of their diachronic convention. While Futurism's illusion of simultaneity was compatible with the kind of discontinuity that narrative media attempted to realize by focusing on processes of becoming and change, the Cubist synthesis did not aim at the direct representation of the processes themselves, but rather aimed at the mimesis of the form so conceived.

Joyce

Literary critics looking for verbal correlatives of Cubist techniques frequently point to James Joyce's *Ulysses,* arguing that his use of multiple points of view is the equivalent of Cubism's multidimensional approach to reality. In *Ulysses* Joyce explores a potential father-son relationship, recording through a variety of styles and perspectives the meanderings of Leopold Bloom, Homeric hero, wandering Jew and ad man, and Stephen Dedalus, iconoclast, possible artist, and potential son. A discussion of the issue of multiplicity in Joyce and Cubism is often based on an analysis of the "Wandering Rocks" episode in the middle of the novel, an episode that gives the illusion of simultaneity through a sequence of nineteen time-related though seemingly disparate events.

In "James Joyce and the Cubist Esthetic," Jo-Anna Isaak builds an analogy between what she defines as the "flattening of climaxes" in Cubist art and the "*seeming* non-structure of *Ulysses*" [emphasis mine]. Ignoring the implications of the term she uses, Isaak suggests that the techniques of discontinuity in Cubist art function in narrative terms. She evades the fact that the illusion of simultaneity in the "Wandering Rocks" is only an illusion of the style, and further that the techniques Joyce devises to compensate for the diachronic nature of his medium are different in kind from those developed for the optical synthesis in the visual medium where succession does not operate as the basic convention. This fundamental distinction is not observed by Isaak, and therefore she offers this misleading analysis of the optical synthesis in Cubist art: "objects are given not as seen at any one moment, but in temporal sequence; that is to perceive the many views of the object as given would either have required movement by the viewer through temporally sequential positions or movements on the part of the objects depicted."[22] Because Isaak defines Cubism's representation of the object in its total existence as "the addition of dimension of time to spatial dimensions," she argues that Joyce's ability to establish his Dublin by "superimposing numerous planes of time and space" functions as a verbal correlative for the free and mobile perspectives of Cubist art (77).

The method of analysis that allows for the assimilation of narrative temporal constructs into Cubist art originates with Sypher, who confounds the media thoroughly by suggesting that the Cubist image, like Joyce's *impression multidi-*

mensionelle, depends upon a "cinematic style" (267) to represent "modern space and time" (277). Sypher's choice of terms reflects an inability to deal with the reality of Cubism's fourth dimension, for he describes the fragmentation of homogeneous form in Cubist art in terms that implicate surface only: the Cubist artist represents "the several *faces* of things simultaneously" [emphasis mine]. It is because Sypher sticks to surfaces and to the conception of the "Cubist Dance" that he can conceive of an interartistic analogy between Joyce and Cubism. Ironically, it is exactly because of that fidelity to surface and the adaptation of the "Cubist Dance" that a novel like *Ulysses* is anything but Cubist in conception and form.

The notion of sides and succession relevant to Joyce's method in *Ulysses* involves a sense of sculptural completeness that Joyce brings into play in discussion with Frank Budgen. For Joyce, Ulysses is a fully realized three-dimensional figure as well as an ideal human being: "I see him from all sides, and therefore he is all-round in the sense of your sculptor's figure. But he is a complete man as well—a good man."[23] Budgen himself suggests that perhaps the most acceptable paradigm for Joyce's sculptural approach to external reality is provided by Auguste Rodin: "Rodin once called sculpture *'le de tous les côtés.'* Leopold Bloom is sculpture in the Rodin sense. He is made up of an infinite number of contours from every conceivable angle" (64).

Through the agency of the unnamed, impersonal, and omniscient camera eye, Joyce presents, as does Rodin himself, a complicated three-dimensional scenographic space. Perhaps the best way to highlight the difference between Joyce's fidelity to the outside of things and the Cubist fidelity to their insideness is given by Budgen when he observes the way Joyce's visual facts work through suggestion and nuance, as tips of the iceberg which evoke underlying substances not realized in totality themselves:

> Joyce, in *Ulysses,* takes life as it is and represents it in its own material. Violences of temperament apart, his art resembles that of Rodin. He achieves the monumental through the organic, through the swift seizing of an infinite number of contours from the living model. There is a saying of Rodin's to the effect that what is visible in the human body is but a fraction of that which lies below the surface. Each undulation is a mountain peak, the base of which lies below. As with the human body, so with the human being in action. What a man does displays only a part, and that the smaller part, of his character. What he thinks and dreams is the greater part. That which is manifest in action is to the unacted part as the visible peak of the iceberg is to the submerged invisible mass. (90)

The kind of affinity Budgen intuits between Joyce and Rodin is one which Sypher and those who inherit his notion of the Cubist narrative would most vehemently oppose, for Rodin's approach to form has nothing in common with Cubist techniques. Rodin's fragments, for example, are episodic in character, three-dimensional in form, and securely based in nature. One of the most remarkable dimensions of Rodin's realism, as Arnason suggests in his discussion of the sculptor's *Gates of Hell*, is the quality of his commitment to the naturalistic surface. Even while exploring with an almost Expressionistic violence the human figure "bent and twisted to the limits of endurance," Rodin's forms manifest "little actual naturalistic distortion" (66).

It is because Rodin's iconographic and technical means share so much with Joyce's manner of adaptation and construction in the "Wandering Rocks" that Budgen's commentary is particularly intriguing. Both sculptor and literary artist share a predeliction for a mythic method and episodic analysis, a fidelity to naturalistic and realistic standards of authenticity, a concern for the psychology of the figure and the expressive and symbolic potential of the object, a commitment to the evocative power of the surfaces they explore in keeping with the Symbolist nature of the iceberg theory, and a fascination with the labyrinthine, but ultimately three-dimensional scenographic motif.

Praz suggests in "Notes on James Joyce" that *Ulysses* reflects the two poles within which Joyce worked, the mythopoetic and the realistic. The mythic method defines the novel's inherently metaphoric structure, yet, as David Lodge points out, the metaphoric structure is compatible with Joyce's "extensive and deliberate exploitation of metonymy."[24] The traditional realistic novel's enduring attention to naturalistic details and apparent realities, synecdochic in character and cumulative in effect, provide *Ulysses* with a vigorous and consistent sense of place and time, and allow the reader to feel the contemporaneity of Bloom's odyssey. Dublin itself, the heart of the Hibernian metropolis, is the subject of the "Wandering Rocks." It is not surprising that the full force of Joyce's fidelity to the given is most strongly felt within this episode as he pursues his goal of all-roundness and completeness.

"I want," Joyce remarked to Budgen as they made their way down the *Universitätstrasse* in Zurich, "to give a picture of Dublin so complete that if the city one day suddenly disappeared from the earth it could be reconstructed out of my book" (Budgen, 67–68). Joyce's picture of Dublin exists in the old visual reality of Impressionist art. The reason for the apparent idiosyncracy of its form does not stem from the fact that Joyce is deliberately dislocating or distorting forms and violating canons of accuracy and authenticity. Rather, as in Impressionist art, Joyce's fidelity to an accurate recreation of surface and the naivety of his recording intelligence is absolute.

The nineteen diverse but interconnected events in the "Wandering Rocks" evolve about two central axes: Father Conmee's advance toward the Artane orphanage in pursuit of possible provisions for the Dignam boy, whose father's funeral marks but one of the many incidents that have engaged Bloom thus far, and the procession of the viceregal cavalcade of the Earl of Dudley as it makes its way from Phoenix Park toward the Mirus bazaar. The reader must pit his wits against a labyrinthine structure, tracking down cross references and elusive fragments, which function at varying and multiple contextual exposures, that partially reveal and conceal familiar terrain. The task of reconstruction is particularly difficult because of the deliberate naivety of the orchestrating intelligence who superintends the evolution of the sequence. Without imbuing that evolution with an interpretative framework that would sustain anything more than a marginal sense of plotted action, Joyce's narrator makes seemingly arbitrary and coincidental connections within the maze of topographical detail it articulates.

In *The Odyssey of Style in "Ulysses,"* Karen Lawrence defines this apparent discontinuity as a "lack of synthesis," a planned confusion that creates a paradoxical relation between the seemingly meticulous nature of Joyce's documentation—the quest for authenticity in his realization of Dublin's face—and the strangeness of the reality of the text. Reality is defamiliarized because, as Lawrence suggests, the type of narrative mind that Joyce engages, a mind which Lawrence defines as a "lateral" or "paratactic" imagination,[25] deliberately obscures the temporal connections between the events presented in successive sections. Even though events are occurring simultaneously, "there is no reference to this simultaneity in the text" (83).

This point is especially relevant for the one-legged sailor, whose progress is recorded in various contexts as he encounters Father Conmee before the convent of the Sisters of Charity. Though descriptive terms that identify various characters and fragments of the landscape are continuous through patterns of incremental repetition, the recording eye never provides a larger framework within which details can be integrated. The five men who advertize for H.E.L.Y.'s, for example, first appear as Blazes Bolan flirts with a shop girl while purchasing a basket of fruit destined for Molly Bloom: "H.E.L.Y.'s filed before him, tallwhitehatted, past Tangier lane, plodding towards their goal."[26] The men reappear outside the Capel Street library in section 7 as "five tallwhitehatted sandwichmen between Monypenny's corner and the slab where Wolfe Tone's statue was not, eeled themselves turning H.E.L.Y.'s and plodded back as they had come" (228).

In the second section of the episode, "a onelegged sailor" crutches past Katey and Boody Dedalus, Stephen's younger siblings, who help him retrieve the coin Molly Bloom has just tossed out the window. The text, though identifying the two girls at the beginning of the section, refuses to make any connection when they render that service for the sailor. They are described with a degree of anonymity that their contiguous position moments earlier cannot corroborate: "Two barefoot urchins, sucking long liquorice laces" gape at the sailor's stump with "yellowslobbered mouths" (224–25).

The fact that the usual synecdochal relations are rendered impotent is evident not only in terms of the ambiguity of spatial and temporal values, but also in terms of the way the text identifies its subjects. Characters, for example, are consistently reproduced in cipher form: "a onelegged sailor," "Marie Kendall, charming soubrette," "Mr. Denis J. Maginni, professor of dancing, &c.." The mannequin-like effect of these tags contributes to the linguistic strangeness of the whole episode, a strangeness that is often reflected syntactically through a pseudo-paratactic style: "Master Brunny Lynam ran across the road and put Father Conmee's letter to father provincial into the mouth of the bright red letterbox, Father Conmee smiled and nodded and smiled and walked along Mountjoy square east" (219). Alternately, an inflated hypotactic style emerges, which, while it sustains the illusion of internal connectedness through subordination, also creates confusion because of the extremity of its form: "Lawyers of the past, haughty, pleading, beheld pass from the consolidated taxing office to Nisi Prius court Richie Goulding carrying the costbag of Goulding, Collis and Ward and heard rustling from the admiralty division of king's bench to the court of appeal an elderly female with false teeth smiling incredulously and a black silk shirt of great amplitude" (231).

Both styles emphasize the radical disinterestedness and impersonality of the recording intelligence that levels events and persistently resists the logic of subordination and emphasis that one normally expects in conventional descriptive prose. One could argue that Joyce's method of presentation resembles the doctrine of coequality, which superintends the dissolution of any hierarchy of values in Cubist art. Yet, if one defines the depersonalized quality of the observing eye in terms of a challenge to the natural perspective, one sees that Joyce can defamiliarize the landscape simply by altering the established hierarchy while leaving the old visual reality intact.

This is precisely Joyce's strategy. Facts are accumulated and dispersed in the text without the imposition of any "apparent" ordering principle except the random and accidental juxtaposition of people and things. The fragments, however, never challenge traditional and optically derived notions of iconicity. They are located in a three-dimensional scenographic space where immediate spatial and temporal coordinates are exact. The quality of defamiliarization that attends their dispersal evolves because Joyce deliberately suppresses the vision as a whole. The reader moves along on the tips of the iceberg knowing that the unseen—the actual topography of Dublin itself—superintends the disposition of each of the parts.

Thus one knows exactly where Father Conmee is at "five to three." We know that as he walks down Great Charles street the "shutup free church" where the Reverend T. R. Green B.A. will speak is "on his left" (220). As Conmee crosses from Richmond street, we are made aware that Saint Joseph's church, Portland row, is "on his right hand" (220). Individual vignettes are realized from a particular and fixed point of view: "Moored under the trees of Charleville Mall Father Conmee saw a turfbarge, a towhorse with pendent head, a bargeman with a hat of dirty straw seated amidships, smoking and staring at a branch of poplar above him" (221). In fact, Father Conmee's enervate traditionalism is exaggerated by the narrator's extreme fidelity to Renaissance rules of composition in the creation of idyllic pastorals: "The lychgate of a field showed Father Conmee breadths of cabbages, curtseying to him with ample underleaves. The sky showed him a flock of small white clouds going slowly down the wind" (223).

Even in his experiments with the close-up view, the view that Picasso, for example, uses consistently to destroy the illusion of mass and continuity, Joyce may abridge connectives and superficially truncate identities, but the fragments themselves that materialize never seriously challenge the familiar standards of verisimilitude authorized by the realistic picture of Dublin that Joyce works from. The arm, for example, that is extended generously toward "a onelegged sailor," is a woman's in the most conventional sense. It shines forth "plump," "bare," and "generous," extending "from a white petticoatbodice and taut shiftstraps" (225). Joyce sustains that conjunction of Rubenesque sensuality and bordello humor in subsequent images that synchronize actions that appear only casually related: "Corny Kelleher sped a silent jet of hayjuice arching from his mouth while a generous white arm from a window in Eccles street flung forth a coin" (224).

In contrast to Joyce's preservation of decidedly naturalistic surfaces, Picasso's close-up views expose the way in which the stereoscopic illusion—achieved by our eyes working together at a more distant plane of view—breaks down. LaPorte notes that any close-up view needs a complementary movement of the eyes in order to reveal the whole surface of an object. A close-up view effects a disparity of the pictures impressed on the two eyes of the observer. In other words, "even if the eyes are not moved, each eye assumes a different point of view and receives a different picture image" (27). Picasso's multiple imaging of form as he assaults the human figure particularly is readily apparent in the discontinuity of intersecting planes in his *Seated Female Nude,* where various profiles are repeated and planes are shifted in the articulation of a stable limit. The model is transformed through an intricate series of crystalline facets. Though Picasso still acknowledges the contours of his subject at this early stage in the development of Analytical Cubism, the painting exhibits a freedom from the naturalistic surface that Joyce's fragment never intends. Picasso's model is only tangentially related to the commonsense world Joyce's fragments implicate as their absent landlord.

In point of fact, it is the irony and wit generated by the seemingly casual and adventitious juxtaposition of fundamentally congruent details in this episode that dramatizes, without seeming to, the illicit rendezvous about to take place between Bloom's wife and her agent, Boylan. As M'Coy and Lenehan pass the time of day on their way to meet Boylan in section 9, for example, just after

M'Coy dodges a banana peel and Lenehan notes the "darkbacked" figure of Bloom scanning books on a hawker's cart, and while M'Coy remarks upon his wife who has just completed a recital which Molly Bloom attended at the Glencree reformatory, the text cunningly and with a deliberate subterranean logic of its own brings Lenehan's quite innocent "Did She?" to bear upon "A card *Unfurnished Apartments* reappeared on the windowsash of number 7 Eccles Street" (233)—the card that was replaced after that "bare," "plump," "generous" arm inadvertently knocked it down while giving alms to "a onelegged sailor" (225).

The reader knows the exact location of each of the parts, and yet is denied the benefit of a sense of the whole, the map itself that Joyce fragments but never alludes to in its entirety. One can, as Clive Hart and Leo Knuth have done for the scheme of events in the "Wandering Rocks,"[27] chart the streets and the place names and reconstruct a topographical map. Though the naturalistic surface is disturbed, it is not violated: the viewpoint, though naive and variable, never challenges the rules of linear and atmospheric perspective and the whole can be reassembled. Joyce's assassinations of the object are never "destructions" in the Cubist sense. Joyce, in fact, constructs this episode with a blueprint before him, a blueprint conditioned not only by the mythic structure or "ground plan," as Budgen calls it (15), with which he is working, but also by a blueprint of the city of Dublin itself literally laid out before him, on which, Budgen notes, "were traced in red ink the paths of the Earl of Dudley and Father Conmee. He calculated to a minute the time necessary for his characters to cover a given distance of the city" (122–23): "To see Joyce at work on the *Wandering Rocks* was to see an engineer at work with compass and slide-rule, a surveyor with theodolite and measuring chain, or, more Ulyssean perhaps, a ship's officer taking the sun, reading the log and calculating current drift and leeway" (121).

Rather than a suggestion of haptic and manual space conceptions, Joyce's method of realization insists that the retina literally and emphatically predominates over the brain. Indeed, Joyce's use of a roving camera eye, which attaches itself to the surface and steadfastly refuses to know its subject by deliberately ignoring the nuances that the very recording of facts themselves imply, encourages one to see the "Wandering Rocks" as a parody of Impressionist technique. Joyce prevails upon his narrator to provide an accurate reproduction of surfaces without the mediation of any form of human intelligence. I use the term parody here because the mythic structure of the narrative, the story values that do exist in the text, are only "seemingly" abandoned or submerged in this section. Joyce called this chapter an "Entr'acte," a "pause in the action," which though occupying the "middle" of the book had "absolutely no relation to what precedes or follows."[28] More specifically, Joyce intends that the chapter has "absolutely no relation" in the traditional sense of explicitly advancing the story. The Impressionist extremism inherent in the choice of narrative perspective allows Joyce superficially to fragment space and time to yield a comic illusion of incongruity that has little in common with the intellectual precision and actual synchronicity of Picasso's and Braque's inquiry into form.

The kind of construct Joyce creates can be best described in terms of the montage, the building up of the whole through an infinite number of homologous parts. While the Cubist image cannot be returned to its original spatial and temporal coordinates, the task of reconstruction is possible in *Ulysses* because the fragments, like the pieces of the montage, are conceived from variable but consistently naturalistic points of view. Further, this is a task that Joyce deliberately sets up for his reader through a number of guide-marks that are provided to synchronize the action. It is because the "Wandering Rocks" is optically derived, perspective in form, and diachronic in its evolution, that it cannot be approached through a Cubist perspective. Perhaps the final irony is that, whereas Cubist artists refused to compete with the trompe l'oeil of the sun and chose instead to reinvent form, Joyce attempted to create the literary artifact that could compete with visual reality by recreating it in kind.

Just as Joyce's method in *Ulysses* involves the "cubification" of space and time (the division of the narrative into component parts that overlay a consistent perspective articulation) rather than the conceptualization of volume, so too it allows for the "cubification" of the individual characters who traverse the scene. The fragmentation of identities, particularly that of the lady who appears in four of the nineteen sections of the episode, is representative of the difference between Joyce's and Cubism's methods of dislocation. The "listless" and "elderly" lady appears in Father Conmee's revery in section 1, a revery that fuses past and present history. She is at first, it would seem, a figure in the contemporary landscape as Conmee moves toward Clongowes where he was once rector: "A listless lady, no more young, walked along the shore of lough Ennel" (222). She is then assimilated into Conmee's speculations on the possible infidelity of the Countess of Belvedere during the "old times in the barony": "Mary, first countess of Belvedere, listlessly walking in the evening, not startled when an otter plunged" (222). She reappears in altered form in the ninth section of the episode as "an elderly female with false teeth smiling incredulously" with a "black skirt of great amplitude" (231). Yet her connection with the "listless lady" is affirmed in the tenth section through the continuity of the descriptive terms: "An elderly female, no more young, left the building of the courts of chancery, king's bench, exchequer and common pleas, having heard in the lord chancellor's court the case in lunacy of Potterton, in the admiralty division the summons, exparte motion, of the owners of the Lady Cairns versus the owners of the barque Mona, in the court of appeal reservation of judgment in the case of Harvey versus the Ocean Accident and Guarantee Corporation" (235). Finally, she surfaces in thumbnail form as the viceregent's cavalcade proceeds through the metropolis in section 19: "an elderly female about to enter changed her plan and retracing her steps by King's windows smiled credulously on the representative of His Majesty" (251).

Not only does Joyce provide guide-marks for the reconstruction of his figure through the pattern of repetition, but also none of the fragments themselves moves beyond a statement of the lady's apparent reality. The details are evocative but they are optically derived and conventional in form. If one turns to Picasso's own enigmatic lady, his 1910 *Girl with a Mandolin* (Fanny Tellier) (fig. 43), one sees the extent to which the old visual reality that Joyce remains faithful to has been reshaped by Picasso's dissolution of the contours that would have conventionally described the boundaries of the model and her mandolin. Not only does Picasso create an interchange between the organic and the inorganic as the round of the hair destroys the solidity of the head by merging with the planes that describe the adjacent space, but spatial positions themselves are indeterminate. The cylinder of the upper arm simultaneously exists behind and before the incomplete cubes at the left. The profile of the head is reasserted; the upper arm shifts to a plane different from that articulate in the plane of the shoulders; the contour of the left elbow becomes paper-thin to dramatize the suggestion of depth. This variety of iconic means allows Picasso to extend the referentiability of his form, and it is this variety that is not part of Joyce's strategy.

The analogy between *Ulysses* and Cubism breaks down at yet another level, for even though Joyce experiments with mirror images to create the illusion of multiple identities by complicating the single form, these reflections are not synthesized in the text. When young Patrick Dignam, for example, courts his multiple images in the window of Madame Doyle's court dress millinery, the novelty of the boy's tripartite division is registered sequentially not synchronically: "From the sidemirrors two mourning Masters Dignam gaped silently. . . . Master Dignam on his left turned as he turned. That's me in mourning. When is it? May the twentysecond. Sure, the blooming thing is all over. He turned to the right and on his right Master Dignam turned, his cap awry, his collar sticking up. Buttoning it down, his chin lifted, he saw the image of Marie Kendall, charming soubrette, beside the two puckers" (250). Though Joyce works with a number of graphic images—"the two puckers stripped to their pelts and putting up their props," the poster picture of "Marie Kendall, charming soubrette," and the three Masters Dignam—there is absolutely no sense of the kind of integration of planar dislocations achieved in Cubism's optical synthesis because Joyce's points of view, though variable, are consistent.

A second area of potential correlation posited by critics focuses upon the apparent congruity between Joyce's and Cubism's stylistic multiplicity. Praz suggests, for example, that the doctrine of coequality that generates Synthetic Cubism plurality of styles is paralleled by the contemporaneity of historical styles in *Ulysses,* which demonstrate the novel's "lack of an axis, of a centre,

Figure 43. Pablo Picasso, *Girl with a Mandolin* (Fanny Tellier), 1910
Oil on canvas, 100.3 × 73.6 cm.
*(Collection, the Museum of Modern Art, New York; Nelson
A. Rockefeller Bequest)*

of a hierarchy of values" ("Notes on James Joyce," 96). Before one talks of Joyce's endorsement of a doctrine of coequality, however, one has to come to terms with the way in which stream of consciousness functions as the dominant linguistic mode of the novel. It is certainly the narrative norm of the first six chapters through which Joyce creates the sensibilities of his major characters, Stephen and Bloom, and it becomes the touchstone for the reader's sense of Dublin's fictional reality. The novel, it would seem, has its preferred style, a style which is exquisitely responsive to the way in which the recording intelligences assimilate and transform external reality. This sense of a preferred style, and the notion of a hierarchy of values and the evolution of linguistic style that the preferred style engenders, is consistently reinforced through Joyce's use of parody in the novel and challenges the assertion that the Cubist doctrine of coequality actually superintends the novel's construction.

The "Nausicaa" chapter, for example, takes as its Homeric parallel Ulysses's encounter with Nausicaa, daughter of Alcinous, King of Phaeacia, who discovers the hero's naked form upon the beach, tends to his needs, clothes him, and takes him home to her father. In the chapter, Joyce combines two stylistic modes: a method of indirect discourse that records Gerty (Nausicaa) MacDowell's response to Leopold Bloom, who stands off observing her as she and friends supervise the antics of their charges on the Sandymount shore, and the interior monologue of Bloom himself. The duologue between the two allows them to work out their sexual fantasies against the ceremonial background of the pyrotechnics display that climaxes in unison with Bloom's phallotechnics (373), and the temperance retreat that is taking place in the parish church Our Lady as Star of the Sea on Howth Hill.

In "Nausicaa," a particular character and quality of mind generates a particular compatible style. Gerty's second-rate mind recommends a second-rate fictional style, a style that is responsive to Gerty's sentimentality, romantic idealism, and tendency toward the pathetic fallacy, qualities which are epitomized in the cliché-ridden descriptions of her physical appearance. She is a "specimen of winsome Irish girlhood" with a face "waxen" in "pallor," "almost spiritual in its ivorylike purity" with a "rosebud mouth," like a "genuine Cupid's bow," with "tapering fingers" of "finely veined alabaster," "as white as lemon juice and queen of ointments could make them though it was not true that she used to wear kid gloves in bed or take a milk footbath either" (346).

Just as Gerty's immature sensibility conjoins romantic excess with precious diction, hackneyed cliché, and the very worst kind of syntactic stultification, so too the landscape views offer debased forms of picturesque and picture-box iconography. Gerty's sexual yearning finds its correlatives in listless views of the bay, "like the paintings that man used to do on the pavement with all the coloured chalks and such a pity too leaving them there to be all blotted out, the evening and the clouds coming out and the Baily light of Howth and to hear the music like that and the perfume of those incense they burned in the church like a kind of waft. And while she gazed her heart went pitapat" (355). In dress, as well, she favors simpering pastels: her "undies" "rosepink, pale blue, mauve and peagreen." Her wardrobe is superintended by the art deco of the *Lady's Pictorial*, which recommends her "coquettish little love of a hat of wideleaved nigger straw contrast trimmed with an underbrim of eggblue chenille" with "a butterfly bow to tone" at the side (348); and she entertains notions of presenting Father Conmee, potential recipient of her enthusiastic confessional, with a "ruched teacosy with embroidered floral design" or a clock "white and gold with a canary bird that came out of a little house to tell the time" (356).

In contrast, Joyce selects the interior monologue as the mode within which to explore the dimensions of Bloom's penetrative intelligence as the hero muses on the potential "seaside" girl in his own Molly: "Open like flowers, know their hours, sunflowers, Jerusalem artichokes, in ballrooms, chandeliers, avenues under the lamps" (374). Whereas Gerty finds the chalk pastel on the sidewalk an adequate medium for her own Pollyannesque vision of nature, Bloom exposes the trompe l'oeil of the still life's conventional iconicity where flowers look real because of the smell of the turpentine in the paint (372). Bloom censors the delusions of the pathetic fallacy that Gerty's manner of self-projection generates by noting that it is only an "optical illusion" created by the setting sun that makes the nightclouds look "like a phantom ship" instead of actual trees (374). He discovers the source of intrigue inherent in Impressionism's fidelity to the given by noting that colors "depend upon the light" in which they are disclosed (375).

Bloom's own landscape correlatives maintain the distinctions between tenor and vehicle that Gerty's obscure, and convey in kind those qualities that attest to Bloom's first-ratedness, his old-world wisdom, his ennui and self-deprecating wit, his dogged attempt to understand the cause and effects of this "little affair of being" within which he is engaged. Thus the pyrotechnics display has its practical genesis and decline: "There she is with them down there for the fireworks. My fireworks. Up like a rocket, down like a stick" (369). Bloom's descriptive terms, which energize the landscape, do not reduce it to purely anthropomorphic terms. While Gerty's sobsister impulse is overwhelmed by the aptness of the newspaper poetry she memorizes ("*Art thou real, my ideal*"), which epitomizes for her the trite images of "gathering twilight," and "the touching chime" of "evening bells" from the "ivied belfry" (361), Bloom censors his own romantic impulse. Thus the actual condition of Howth Hill, the setting of his first union with Molly years before though momentarily concealed by a Wordsworthian gesture—"The year returns. History repeats itself. Ye crags and peaks I'm with you once again"—is plainly reasserted as he confronts the possibility of Molly's infidelity: "All quiet on Howth now. The distant hills seem. Where we. The rhododendrons. I am a fool perhaps. He gets the plums and I the plumstones. Where I come in. All that old hill has seen. Names change: that's all. Lovers: yum yum" (374).

One can describe the juxtaposition of these two styles in "Nausicaa" as still life in landscape. In comparing Joyce's duologue technique with Picasso's and Gris's still life in landscapes of 1915, one sees the extent to which Joyce's pluralism establishes a hierarchy of values absolutely foreign to the kind of equanimity that Cubist artists achieve. In "Nausicaa" the *Nature Morte* is literally manifest in the extravagances of Gerty's insipid style, which expires as one confronts the dynamism of Bloom's interior landscape. In Gris's *The Open Window: Place Ravignan* (fig. 44), on the other hand, there is no suggestion that the artist is commenting on the adequacy of the styles he conjoins. The view out the window brings the easel convention, scenographic spatial illusion, and intensification of naturalistic coloring to bear upon the Synthetic style of the still-life interior; yet exterior and interior modes work together to explore a variety of iconic means without establishing a preferred style. Gris even integrates realities, bringing exterior and interior views into relation by carrying the landscape indoors and the still-life outdoors. The angle of the mountain peak is duplicated in the upper corner of the book and table. The tones of the background view are restated in inverse terms through portions of the decorative wallpaper and medicine chest, and duplicated in portions of the soap-dish. The street railing and window in the upper right are brought into the tonal environment of the still life. The angles of the trees are repeated in the cylindrical planes that circumscribe the shaving brush and glass and portions of the base and sides of the soap dish. The horizontal slats on the window shutters are echoed in the hieroglyphics on the left side of the newspaper fragment.

The conjunction of typographical rhetoric, simulated wood-grained table, trompe l'oeil of *Le Journal,* and grid that confounds the appearance of objects on the table indicates how the *tableau-tableau* theme works in *collage* and *collé.* That theme finds its most explicit expression through Gris's use of irregular margins, which function as framing devices to comment on the whole concept of the easel as open window in pictorial art.

In establishing this kind of rapport between different kinds of styles, Gris develops the sense of equanimity between modes of treatment that Joyce does not intend when he measures the deficiencies of Gerty's esthetic response against Bloom's more perspicuous treatment of parallel objects and landscape events.

While Joyce's polymorphous text appears to be so closely allied with Cubism's affirmation of stylistic multiplicity, his recourse to a hierarchy of style undermines the connection. One can speak of the relativity of all styles in *Ulysses* only by ignoring the fact that Joyce parodies limitations of various points of view through his choice of alternate stylistic modes that can only integrate mind and matter in superficial ways. Joyce chooses a stream-of-consciousness form in "Nausicaa" to explore Bloom's experience of external reality

Figure 44.   Juan Gris, *The Open Window: Place Ravignan*, 1915
             (Philadelphia Museum of Art; Louise and Walter Arensberg
             Collection)

because its mode allows the kind of psychological realism that is the touchstone of authenticity and veracity in the novel as a whole.

Just as the preferred style in *Ulysses* offers a norm through which one evaluates the credibility of alternate perceptual experiences, so too the sense of the actual and the real that functions within the interior monologue establishes a hierarchy of truth. Joyce relies on this hierarchy in "Calypso," for example, to parody Bloom's taste for organs, human and otherwise, and his tendency to dream of the kind of sexual fulfillment that real life with Molly denies. In his fantasy, a leitmotif of images brings Bloom and the young female customer in the local meatmarket together to "make hay while the sun shines" (61); but the possibility of such an encounter is censored by Bloom himself in the monologue. The fantasy's idealized conventions are never meant to be taken for anything other than that, so that even while Bloom brings them into play, he undermines the possibility of their consummation. This kind of commentary establishes the frame within which the reader evaluates the momentary collapse of boundaries that usually hold between the real and the false, boundaries that are reinstated at the episode's conclusion.

Joyce achieves a triple-pane effect by juxtaposing the image of the hanks of sausages and oozing kidneys on the "willowpatterned dish" in Dlugacz's porkbutcher shop window with Bloom's peeping Tom's gloss on the more provocative anatomical features of the "nextdoor girl at the counter." As his view is partially filtered by an advertisement he's holding that extols the idyllic virtues of the "model farm at Kinnereth on the lakeshore of Tiberias" (61), urban and rural landscapes seem to interpenetrate. This illusion is sustained by an exchange of human and heifer values. The young woman's "moving hams" imaged by Bloom "whacking a carpet on the clothesline" conjoin forces with the "shiny links," "folded" sausages, and "ripemeated hindquarter[s]" of the "stallfed" heifers at Kinnereth. The leitmotif of images that sanctions this imaginative form of intercourse never overwhelms the reader's awareness of the dividing line between reality and fantasy, however, but rather, as a playful kind of *coitus interruptus,* this exchange insists upon a hierarchy of authenticity that Synthetic Cubism does not pursue.

In the last of the three interartistic analogies, critics suggest that the *collage* element, which seems to exist in the vast array of ready-mades that Joyce assimilates in the text, functions in the same way extrapictorial substances do in Synthetic Cubism. The kind of metamorphosis Joyce effects, however, as he appropriates the real-life fragment into his fictional environment, often imbues the fragment itself with an ontological and esthetic status that is inherently different from that enjoyed by the extrapictorial substance in Synthetic Cubism. *Ulysses'* ready-mades are details whose status as actual empirical facts has been altered by their very inclusion in the text; either they are adapted—as in the *Freeman's* advertisement for Plumtree's Potted Meat—to serve symbolic functions within the mythic structure of the whole, or they are used simply as brand names and placenames, and "remnants" of Dublin culture that help secure a sense of the novel's photometic character and authority. In both cases, while their original status as actual details is a source of intrigue, the fragments of necessity relinquish their extraliterary status the moment they are appropriated by the author to serve his created reality.

In Synthetic Cubism, in contrast, artists incorporate actual substances within the pictorial environment, but the *collage* and *collé* elements retain their original ontological identities even as they argue new kinds of meaning within the pictorial space. This is the special fascination of *collage* and *papier collé,* for the dual reality of the fragment as both empirical and esthetic fact generates the dialectic between fact and fiction that absorbs all other levels of artistic illusion within the canvas from the trompe l'oeil detail to the more arcane hieroglyph. This duality—the ready-made's capacity to present as well as to represent realities— is one which Archie Loss, for example, overlooks when he suggests that *collage* elements in Synthetic Cubism and Joyce's "Aeolus" chapter only appear to make up "a version of the 'real' world" but affirm instead "the greater reality of the artist's imagination."[29]

In the "Aeolus" chapter Joyce interpolates what appear to be actual newspaper clippings in the narrative. Here Bloom and Stephen are brought together in the offices of the *Weekly Freeman and National Press* and the *Freeman's Journal and National Press* (the partial reversal of the titles is prophetic of the futility of their respective tasks in this section) as Stephen endeavors to complete an errand to deliver his employer's letter, part of the Dalky school headmaster's crusade against foot and mouth disease in Ireland, and Bloom attempts, without success, to obtain an advertisement for Keyes, a local tea, wine, and spirit merchant. Critics like Lawrence treat the headings as if they were indeed *collage* elements, and interpret their appearance as further evidence of the *tableau-tableau* orientation of *Ulysses.* For Lawrence the bold face type of the newspaper headings and subheadings brings an obtrusive public language into the text, which encroaches on the writing of the narrative and advertises the opacity and relativity of language itself. The newspaper fragments, she argues, are to be perceived as stylistic, visual, tonal, and conceptual "disturbances" that emphasize Joyce's shift in attention from narrative to rhetorical elements in the novel, from the "myth of development" and "the illusion of a stable narrative voice" (60), to an art for art's sake exploration of stylistic masks and rhetorical possibilities that have no connection with the story values themselves.

Lawrence's thesis works, however, only if one ignores the fact that these fragments are facsimiles and not artifacts. As facsimiles that function as trompe l'oeil illusions of the actual through their typographical form, they provide, as does any gloss, an alternate and ironic stylistic mode, which Joyce creates as a commentary on the action that takes place. Because Lawrence perceives the headings as actual fragments that invade the text, rather than as facsimiles that respond to it, she fails to appreciate the way in which they perform an integrating function and emphasize the very story values that she suggests they abandon. Instead of an irreconcilable disparity between novel writing and "other writing," Joyce is able to develop a playful and witty exchange of values precisely because the newspaper facsimiles seem to possess the force of the actual content of experience even though they offer only illusions of the style. Joyce is capitalizing on the persuasive power of the newspaper genre's responsiveness to actual events, its referentiability, and appropriating that context for his own fictional documents.

As surrogates, these *collage* facsimiles correspond to the handpainted lettering that Picasso and Braque experiment with in "transitional" Analytical canvases like *Ma Jolie* and *The Portuguese,* experiments that anticipate only in part the extant ready-made that is asserted through *papier collé* and *collage* in Synthetic Cubism. This distinction is an important one, for it is the essentially photometic bias of the handpainted lettering that Joyce replicates through his facsimiles rather than the presentational autonomy of the ready-made. While critics argue that the newspaper style within "Aeolus" demonstrates the grammacentricity of the text (and even this analogy with Cubism cannot be secured, for Cubism does not deny but "makes" correspondence), or that the headings affirm the presence of extraliterary substances, it becomes clear that Joyce's inclusion of the pseudo-*collage* element is determined by his desire to create a Dublin whose relation with the actual is that of an "exact" reproduction. It is, in fact, because the headings are responsive to the story that they provide such a rich and varied contrapuntal dialectic for Joyce's exploration of the potentially epic dimensions of the seemingly trivial frustrations of our daily lives.

The headline at the opening of the "Aeolus," "GENTLEMEN OF THE PRESS," for example, functions in mock heroic terms in conjunction with the chiasmic construction beneath it that satirizes the whole concept of journalistic eloquence: "Grossbooted draymen rolled barrels dullthudding out of Prince's stores and bumped them up on the brewery float. On the brewery float bumped dullthudding barrels rolled by grossbooted draymen out of Prince's stores" (118). So too, the headline which announces the editor's magisterial entrance, "WILLIAM BRAYDEN, ESQUIRE, OF OAKLANDS, SANDYMOUNT," sets up an honorific tone that is progressively undermined by the subsequent anatomical dissections that reify his figure. These emphasize the disparity between his style and content, not only in terms of the relation between the level of expectation that the typeface initiates and the quality of the subject it exposes, but also in terms of Brayden's "stately figure" and the reality of his impotent stewardship of the daily presses: "Mr. Bloom turned and saw the liveried porter raise his lettered cap as a stately figure entered between the newsboards of the *Weekly Freeman and National Press* and the *Freeman's Journal and National*

Press. Dullthudding Guinness's barrels. It passed stately up the staircase steered by an umbrella, a solemn beardframed face. The broadcloth back ascended each step: back. All his brains are in the nape of his neck, Simon Dedalus says. Welts of flesh behind on him. Fat folds of neck, fat, neck, fat, neck" (119).

The facsimiles function in a variety of ways to provide mock heroic frames for the action, and they also work symbolically, as does the "HOUSE OF KEY(E)S" subheading, to emphasize the Ishmael-like struggle Bloom is engaged in as an outsider. At times they provide descriptive parallels for the images they evoke, working through association to bring Bloom's racial past to bear on the present. The heading "A DAYFATHER" prefaces the rather stolid reduction of the typesetter Old Monks: "Nearing the end of his tether now. Sober serious man with a bit in the savings-bank I'd say. Wife a good cook and washer. Daughter working the machine in the parlour. Plain Jane, no damn nonsense" (123–24). At another level the picture of Monks intent upon reading the type backwards calls forth an image of Bloom's own father reading the Passover Hagadah in Hebrew script, an evocation set in uppercase type, "AND IT WAS THE FEAST OF THE PASSOVER," which accentuates the pathos of Bloom's Diaspora, an inheritance bequeathed through his father and obligatory, it would seem, for all sons of Abraham.

In similar terms the headline "ERIN, GREEN GEM OF THE SILVER SEA" works through the Homeric parallel and archetypal frame to circumscribe the role Bloom is assigned through the mythic prototypes with which he is allied. The subheading refers immediately to the fragment of a patriotic speech recorded in the *Freeman*, which Ned Lambert satirizes in his recitation. But the speech evokes visions of Ireland's legendary past, and works in conjunction with Professor MacHugh's "the ghost walks" and Mr. Dedalus's "agonising Christ" partially to define Bloom's discrete entrance into the *Evening Telegraph* office, thus expanding the philosophical implications of Bloom's status as ghost-father to Stephen's Hamlet (125).

In a very real and provocative way the pseudo-*collage* elements in "Aeolus" ironically and effectively announce what the episode in part and as a whole is about. To the extent that they are only illusions of the actual and not the things in themselves, and to the extent that they perform interpretative functions in the text, Joyce's fragments do not perform as *collage* elements. Rather, their role is essentially allusive. One is not dealing with extraliterary substances at all. Joyce's adaptation of the journalistic method, like the other verbal quotations from the history of writing that *Ulysses* employs, brings the conceptual and stylistic paradigm that the convention embodies into relation with a variety of other narrative styles in the novel as a whole.

The *collage/collé* technique in Synthetic Cubism, in contrast, means the conspicuous inclusion of extrapictorial substances that retain the history of the prior use and original nonpictorial ontology even as they perform functions in the plastic environment for which they were never intended. What is an artifact in Gris's *Glasses and Newspaper* is a facsimile in Joyce's "Aeolus" chapter. Gris's work capitalizes on a series of visual and verbal puns generated by the inclusion of the newspaper clipping, puns contextually related to the theme of illusion that the painting graphically and typographically articulates. The partial heading of the second-from-left column appropriately comments on a still life that explores levels of iconicity through an array of illusionistic devices. That commentary is amplified by the newspaper diagram of the dirigible whose defiance of gravity finds its plastic complement in the vanishing contour of the base of the wine glass. At the same time, however, the *collage* element exists as a compositional value within the picture space, working in conjunction with the illusionistically transplanted *collé* fragments to build up the sensation of material space. The newspaper graphic is formally analogous to the checker-board squares. The ready-made's rectangle helps to establish a primary shape that is repeated with variation through the boundaries of the transparent pane that declares *Le Jou,* in the juxtaposed squares and lightened plane that brings the wood grain to the surface. The bent edge of the newspaper's left corner is intensified in the sharply folded angle of the table cloth and repeated in a series of darkened triangles that recede within the picture space. It becomes apparent that the dialectic between compositional and noncompositional values that the *collage* element makes explicit in Synthetic canvases is not part of Joyce's equally intriguing though essentially pseudo-*collage* illusionism.

Stein

Up to a point, the tendency to discuss Gertrude Stein's writing in Cubist terms is understandable, given the amount of attention she herself gave to this pictorial movement. Many of her observations indicate an acute understanding of the plastic means and envisioned realities of Cubist art. In an interesting and enigmatic synesthetic analogy she presents in an interview with Robert Bartlett Haas, for example, Stein emphasizes that Picasso does not rely upon his retina alone in his grasp of form but rather "seemed to swallow the things he saw."[30]

In her study of the artist in *Picasso* Stein carries this sense of Picasso's ability to paint things as he thinks them rather than as he sees them even further by noting that "Picasso knows, really knows the faces, the heads, the bodies of human beings, he knows them as they have existed since the existence of the human race."[31] She is exquisitely responsive to the distinction that is made in Cubism between the old visual reality, the "vision of nature as every one sees it" (which Stein allies with the "seduction of things seen" in nineteenth-century realism [17]), and the world as Picasso "sees" it: "I am always struck with landscapes of Courbet because he did not have to change the color to give the vision of nature as every one sees it. But Picasso was not like that, when he ate a tomato the tomato was not everybody's tomato, not at all and the effort was not to express in his way the things seen as every one sees them, but to express the thing as he was seeing it" (17). Stein's sense of the uniqueness of Picasso's conceptual response becomes one of the most salient points of her own esthetic of the "I am I not any longer when I see."[32] Because in Stein's view Picasso does not "believe in reality as the world knows it," and because he moves beyond a vision of reality determined by appearances and expectations of what objects look like, his work moves toward the revelation of things that is not conditioned by "the habit of knowing what one is looking at" (18).

The provocative distinctions which Stein makes between painting and picturing[33] become even more interesting in light of the contiguity of technique and purpose that she declares between her own work and that of the Cubist artist. In the Haas interview, Stein allies her efforts as a writer with Picasso's own objectives as a painter: "A writer should write with his eyes, and a painter paint with his ears. You should always paint knowledge which you have acquired, not by looking but by swallowing" (31). She distinguishes her "realizations" from those achieved by "the typical newspaperman who writes novels as a newspaperman" by defining herself as "a thinker" who "enters right into things" (34). She recognizes that insofar as the things Picasso represents through his acts of possession transmogrify the realities that we have come to expect, his art will be generally misunderstood and repudiated: "One does not ever understand, before they are completely created, what is happening and one does not at all understand what one has done until the moment when it is all done. Picasso once said that he who created a thing is forced to make it ugly" (*Picasso,* 9). In *Picasso* Stein presents herself as both confidante and colleague: "I was alone at this time in understanding him, perhaps because I was expressing the same thing in literature" (16), while in the Haas interview Stein's perception of their shared vision and technique is expressed in her recollection of Picasso's description of their "camouflage" art (33).

In *Picasso* Stein also defines the major tenets of Cubist art, highlighting its doctrine of coequality ("each thing was as important as any other thing"), its challenge to accepted standards of verisimilitude ("the faith in what the eyes were seeing, that is to say the belief in the reality of science, commenced to diminish"), and its dialectic between constructive and descriptive elements that alternate framing motifs in Cubist art make explicit ("A picture remaining in its frame was a thing that always had existed and now pictures commenced to want to leave their frames and this also created the necessity for cubism" [12]). Stein appreciates the fact that Picasso's struggle to "know" the "heads, faces and bodies of men and women" "without remembering having looked at them" (*Picasso,* 13, 15) engages the destruction of the familiar illusions of coherence and identity: "Picasso knows faces as a child knows them and the head and the body. . . . when he saw an eye, the other one did not exist for him and only the one he saw did exist for him" (15).

The challenge to custom and authority that Cubism raises, the "disconcerting" (15) and seemingly "ugly" quality of their creative derangement is one Stein feels the writer must enact in her own medium. Thus within the Haas interview she acknowledges the innovations that her emphasis upon the "realism" of the composition "as an end itself," where "one thing was as important as another thing," have achieved: "It was the first time in any language that anyone had used that idea of composition in literature" (15). Stein's own doctrine of coequality leads, as it does in Cubist art, to patterns of disassociation that challenge the dominance of what Lawrence had defined as the "All-Seeing Eye of humanity": "After all, to me one human being is as important as another human being, and you might say that the landscape has the same values, a blade of grass has the same value as a tree. Because the realism of the people who did realism before was a realism of trying to make people real. I was not interested in making the people real but in the essence, or as a painter would call it, value" (16). Stein's sense of the "real" is one she also articulates in *Tender Buttons* as the difference between being a "white old chat churner" (an image and technique that recalls the "character-mongering" Woolf's narrator perceives as a "frivolous fireside art, a matter of pins and needles, exquisite outlines enclosing vacancy, flourishes and mere scrawls" in *Jacob's Room,* 153) and "any example of an edible apple in";[34] and indeed she consistently credits the influence Cézanne and then later Picasso have on her understanding of the nonnaturalistic possibilities of her medium. Thus she explains to Haas that during the composing of *The Making of Americans* her interest in the participial style of its grand "Beethovian passages" becomes subordinate to her growing absorption with the inner qualities of the semantic unit itself. It is an absorption with means that she feels she shares with Picasso, whose own experimentation during the early stages of Cubism Stein appreciates as the logical extension of the Cézannean principles of composition under whose spell she shaped *Three Lives:*[35] "I began to play with words then. I was a little obsessed by words of equal value. Picasso was painting my portrait at that time, and he and I used to talk this thing over endlessly. At this time he had just begun on cubism. And I felt that the thing I got from Cézanne was not the last composition. You had to recognize words had lost their value in the Nineteenth Century, particularly towards the end, they had lost much of their variety, and I felt that I could not go on, that I had to recapture the value of the individual word, find out what it meant and act within it" (Interview, 17–18).

For Stein, *Tender Buttons* offers the "apex" of that process of discovery, a time of composing she defines as her "middle period" dominated by "the idea of portraiture and the idea of the recreation of the word," its "weight and volume" and its relation to the word beside it" (18). This middle phase portraiture, which is established with the "Portrait of Mabel Dodge at the Villa Curonia" in 1911 and which takes its most radical form in *Tender Buttons* (published in 1914), is a period that Stein defines as "painting" and that she compares with the "elemental abstraction" of Picasso's Cubist experiment (*Toklas*, 63–64). Arnold Rönnebeck, her contemporary, remembers Stein presenting the "Mabel Dodge" portrait with the following: "Well, Pablo is doing abstract portraits in painting. I am trying to do abstract portraits in *my* medium, *words*."[36] Within the Haas interview itself, Stein attempts to respond to individual pieces within *Tender Buttons* to show how "the rhythm of the visible world" is reproduced within her still lifes. The terms she uses to describe this process offer remarkable parallels with the concept of "total representation" in Cubist art: "You must remember each time I took something, I said, I have got to satisfy each realistic thing I feel about it. Looking at your shoe, for instance, I would try to make a complete realistic picture of your shoe. It is devilish difficult and needs perfect concentration, you have to refuse so much and so much intrudes itself upon you that you do not want it, it is exhausting work" (29).

Critics have special difficulty with the term "abstract" that Stein uses to establish a parallel between her own work and Picasso's Cubist performances and therefore dispute the reliability of the Rönnebeck anecdote, arguing that as Picasso did not do "abstract" portraits, and as Stein knew and acknowledged this fact in her own study of him, her deliberate and increasingly grammacentric orientation (her nonreferentiability) renders the analogy impotent. However, the terms *abstract* or *elemental abstraction* can be applied to Cubism as long as they are not perceived as equivalents for *nonreferentiability*. There is abstraction in Cubist art, just as in Steinian portraiture, abstraction engaged by the process that allows for the writing out or displaying of the artist's ideas about the experienced form, and it is this conceptualizing of the experience of external reality that defines the shared hieroglyphic character of their presentations and the "cipher" quality of the referential relationship between the art object and material reality itself in their work.

This assertion of Stein's "abstract" orientation or her seeming nonreferentiability persists in criticism, however, for when Stein praises Picasso for his ability to convey the "reality not of things seen but of things that exist" (*Picasso*, 19), critics often suggest that Stein is interpreting Cubist art through the frame of her notion of the "complete actual present."[37] As this concept of the "time-sense in the composition" would seem to abrogate all connection with memory and association, with those frames of reference that secure the "time of the composition," Stein, critics argue, imbues Cubist art with a calligraphic emphasis that is incompatible with the balance between representational and nonrepresentational values that Cubism maintains.[38]

Throughout Stein's commentary in *Picasso*, however, her sense of things seen "without remembering having looked at them" (15) expresses her appreciation of Picasso's ability to move beyond the conventional iconic configuration that had been sustained by a naturalistic standard of correspondence within the pictorial arts. It is an ability she considers at length in *The Making of Americans*, and which she defines as a peculiar talent she has for appreciating that "there are many ways of making kinds of men and women" and "in each way of making kinds of them there is a different system of finding them resembling."[39] Stein's resemblances in *Making* are achieved by securing the "complete history" and "completed understanding" of the "bottom nature" of her human subjects to establish categories of meaning. It is a "basis of comparison" that allows superficially incompatible entities to be brought into relation (341). For Stein it is "a real way of learning" (341) and *Making* is a "history" of her "love of it" (291). And while the seeing and telling and writing of resemblances grounded in the concept of essential or definitive rhythm is "baffling" and "confusing" and often "irritating" to others, it is an approach she will not abandon:

> This then is a beginning of learning to make kinds of men and women. Slowly then all the resemblances between one and all the others that have something, different things in common with that one, all these fall into an ordered system sometime then that one is a whole one, sometimes that one is very different to what was in the beginning the important resemblance in that one but always everything, all resemblances in that one must be counted in, nothing must ever be thrown out, everything in each one must be included to know that one and then sometime that one is to some one a whole one and that is then very satisfying. (340)

In many ways *Tender Buttons* offers the culmination of that talent for making resemblances. Defined as a "precocious" "game in green" (166), the volume's still lifes liberate alternate modes of referentiability in language to make unexpected "match[es]" (176) between words and things. In its own terms, *Tender Buttons* offers an intriguing demonstration of a verbal medium's capacity to extend correspondence through synecdochal figures that are mimetic of the process of "total representation." The technique provides a correlative for the kind of "ideational notation of forms" achieved in Cubism's optical synthesis of multiple iconic modes, which, as Edward Fry observes in *Cubism*, operates as an "equivalent to objects in the visual world without in any way being illusionistic representations of those objects."[40]

Throughout the stylistic experimentation that takes shape in the final stages of *The Making of Americans*, continues in *Two*, and culminates in *Tender Buttons*, Stein focuses on the capacity of language to create "complete description[s]" ("The Gradual Making," 89) that exhibit the mind's apprehension of external reality in a more direct and immediate way. She allies the resurgence of the noun in her work and her effort to know how "the things to see the things to look at . . . were there by their names" with the parallel shift in subject matter made by visual artists. Both used synecdochal and metonymic figures to show resemblances that moved beyond the surface aspect (what Stein defines as the "quality of description" in "Portraits and Repetition"),[41] and both were "trying to live in looking" that did not "mix itself up with remembering." These feats are achieved by disrupting those spatial and temporal continuities that create illusions of stability and coherence that do not entirely reflect how the mind knows what it knows: "And so I began again to do portraits but this time it was not portraits of men and women and children, it was portraits of anything and so I made portraits of rooms and food and everything because there I could avoid this difficulty of suggesting remembering more easily while including looking with listening and talking than if I were to describe human beings" ("Portraits and Repetition," 113).

While Stein sees the presence of the noun as making the "poetry"[42] of *Tender Buttons,* I have chosen to concentrate on this volume in my study of Cubist effects in her art, for it continues the experimentation of the earlier works by trying to find new ways to make the "time-sense in the composition" model the time sense of contemplation, just as the Synthetic form of Cubism extends the repertoire of techniques that the plastic artist can use to synthesize those conceptual entities that enumerate the mind's knowledge of external form. Further, Stein so thoroughly mixes genres throughout the stages of the composing life that lead toward *Tender Buttons,* that any strict adherence to generic distinctions violates the actual nature of the way Stein fuses prosaic and poetic possibilities in her medium.

My rationale for treating the volume as a narrative is further developed by the fact that Stein's speaker functions as the narrator whose first-person point of view in "Rooms" offers an extended meditation upon the esthetic nature of the debate that the first two sections exhibit. The speaker guides the reader through the still lifes achieved by the mind of an author who "is in there behind the door" (197) by bestowing a "reed" to "re letter and read her" (196). Stein has therefore conceived a voice for her own composing mind that will present a story about the maker of art as a biography of the thing made. While so often *Tender Button*'s voice is defined as Stein *in propria persona,* the distinction drawn between "me" and "the author" emphasizes the critical role this intelligence plays. Her primary task is to "instruct" (182) the reader, and to offer an invitation "to consider a lecture" (204) that will explain and demonstrate the principles of composition that inform the still lifes and hopefully mitigate the perplexity generated by works of art that disturb prevailing assumptions. Further, the speaker's task is imaged in *Tender Buttons* as one which will give the reader a handle on the author's medium, the door that is simultaneously opaque and translucent, open and closed, in keeping with an art form that, as in Cubist art, encourages the two-dimensional surface to function as the "arbiter and resolver of different claims" (Berger, 21): "There is a disturbance. Trusting to a baker's boy meant that there would be very much exchanging and anyway what is the use of a covering to a door. There is a use, they are double" (196). As the "baker's boy" (alternate images develop in the text to amplify the narrator's role as aide de camp and dressmaker's assistant), the narrator offers an opportunity to "read her with her for less" (196), a bargain that can be struck by having the "two" in "one."

In many ways the narrative strategy in *Tender Buttons* anticipates the parallel onomastic intrigue of *The Autobiography of Alice B. Toklas* by giving "the inside as seen from the outside" (*Toklas*, 156). Stein's choice in both offers an analogy with the Cubist dissatisfaction with fixed and frontal views of the subject's appearance. On another level, the splitting of the author into both subject and narrator provides a correlative for Picasso's fascination with the way his presence as a signatory identity could enter his own Cubist compositions. Rosenblum posits an analogy between Stein's *Toklas* and Picasso's use of calligraphic means and calling card motifs to mimic other writing styles, to transmute real-life occurrences into pictorial fictions, and to comment ironically on matters of authorship ("Typography of Cubism," 68), and the analogy has applicability to the narrative strategy engaged by Stein in *Tender Buttons* as well.

The commentary on and demonstration of the esthetic principles integral to *Tender Buttons*'s "Composition as Explanation" orientation encourages Stein to build a series of figures that will exhibit the character of an art created from different systems of finding resembling. In *Tender Buttons* this orientation is expressed by the fact that "a window has another spelling" (204), a figure that effectively describes Stein's own challenge to the open-window tradition that had prevailed to determine the mimetic condition of both plastic and verbal artifact. *Tender Buttons*'s "many many lead games" (176) estrange the actual subject by insisting that the artist does not simply "copy" and therefore "borrow" realities (the "extra") but rather makes out of "research" and "selection" and "breakages" a "fine substance" seen "strangely": "it is so earnest to have a green point not to red but to point again" (163).

Stein's understanding of the autotelic nature of the literary artifact depends upon the concept of *energia,* which she defines as "an arrangement in a system to pointing." In other words, the organic integrity of the created reality exhibits in its relations a parallel with natural processes, but that integrity does not depend upon the extent to which the thing made duplicates the overall appearance of an existent reality. In Cubism, this understanding accounts in part for the high profile of the flat plane, which, as Gleizes and Metzinger announce, encourages the art object to have a complex life of its own and to harmonize "with things in general."

This understanding of how objects are ingested and translated within the conventions of the medium is, of course, the synthesizing theme of *Tender*

Buttons. It is a declaration that, in Stein's text, explores a variety of resemblances between Cubism's insistence on the two dimensions of its medium and Stein's own "earnest pursuit" of the "difference" that is "spreading" (161) when the basic conventions of her medium—its syntactical rules, orthographic patterns, and indexical relations—are plumbed by the "plain [plane] resource[s]" (177) of her "visible writing." In "SAUSAGES" this is imaged as the toehold on reality lost when the observer is destabilized by a "hanging" perspective ("a toe extractor" [190]). In "Rooms" the drama between front (the flat surface) and back (the potential open window) is imaged as the frame holding it to the wall: "A window has another spelling, it has 'f' all together, it lacks no more then and this is rain, this may be something else, at any rate there is no dedication in splendor. There is a turn of the stranger" (204).

This different window spelled "f" refers to the sign *fecit* that artists often use to state the new ontological conditions of their making. It also refers, perhaps, to the French translation *fenêtre*. It may refer to alternate values that the individual brings to the sign itself. More importantly, the whole concept of "another spelling" destroys the authority of established patterns of correspondence in both plastic and verbal media. Stein defines this achievement as the creation of a "better" "place" that "has so much stretched out" (167), and indeed there are multiple figures throughout the volume that reference both the framed flat plane and the enclosed linguistic surface. In "A PIECE OF COFFEE," which offers Stein's own version of the *tableau-tableau* orientation of Synthetic Cubism, the "showing" of the exchange of things on tables is developed by the antithesis between the figures shaped by custom where the raw material is concealed and by those that are developed by disclosing technical means: "The settling of stationing cleaning is one way not to shatter scatter and scattering. The one way is to use custom is to use soap and silk for cleaning. The one way to see cotton is to have a design concentrating the illusion and the illustration. The perfect way is to accustom the thing to have a lining and the shape of a ribbon and to be solid, quite solid in standing" (163–64).

The more explicit verbal correlative for the same debate appears in "A RED STAMP" where what "lilies" are (perhaps an allusion to Stein's car so christened or to objects in general which make "noise," cover distances, and emit exhaust) is displayed in print: "if they dusty will dirt a surface." Further, the entity conceived within the diachronic mode is, in part, freed from the practical and purposeful considerations that ordinarily superintend how we value the object and from an orientation that remembers the names for objects by focusing exclusively on the visual and surface appearance of the thing so named. Read ("red") from another angle, the spoken character of the object must be perceived as an entirely new thing rather than simply as a "sign of extra": "if they do this and it is not necessary it is not at all necessary if they do this they need a catalogue" (164).

The catalogue of things Stein conceives within *Tender Buttons* endlessly debates the nature of the forms that are created when the "nice old chain . . . is absent . . . is laid by" (185), and the usual attachments between the signifier and the thing signified that have been authorized by custom are broken or bent. Custom's optically derived notion of resemblance (*enargia*) becomes only one of a variety of patterns of resemblance that achieve correspondence by exploring likeness in terms of parallel gestation processes (*energia*), and in this way Stein's "talking arrangement" works by "collecting claiming" (179) just as Cubism's optical synthesis aims at exhausting resemblance.

The full implications of Stein's departure from the canons of linguistic orthodoxy and the complex forms of her destruction of habits of correspondence emerge in the variety of technical means that she discovers to spread the "difference" between the "time-sense in the composition" (the virtual or immaterial time of the created object) and the "time of the composition" (the biographical and historical and linguistic customs which are "laid by" or rearranged by the rule of her artistic intention and technique). Critical analogies that explore the applicability of a Cubist context to Stein's compositions focus primarily on the attention to the linguistic surface Stein's calligraphic orientation suggests, which Wendy Steiner, for example, defines as "*écriture-objet*" to highlight the potential correlative between Stein's *Tender Buttons* style and the *tableau-objet* theme of Synthetic Cubism (*Exact Resemblance*, 159). This foregrounding of the word-system and the variety of semantic codes so generated creates a pluridimensionality that is perceived as a correlative for the shifting perspectives and interactive planes of both the Analytical and Synthetic phases of Cubist art.[43]

Often critics who posit these correspondences test its limits by suggesting, as does Steiner herself, that the Cubist analogy ceases to be meaningful because Stein's insistence on "exact reproduction" leads to the "overextension of her medium" by eradicating all those representational elements that Synthetic Cubism maintains. Thus Steiner advises that Stein's "failed experiments" "rather than serving as a key to cubism" illustrate "the very real barriers between painting and literature. And furthermore, where the cubists were satisfied with a compromise in overturning the norms of their medium, Stein insisted on trying the impossible" (160). Marilyn Gaddis Rose also uses Cubist art as a standard of evaluation to support an alternative sense of Stein's "failure." Referring to Max Jacob's "Nocturne" and Stein's *Ida,* she observes: "Stein's and Jacob's 'Idas' . . . have reductively used—or rejected and abused—the resources of genre and language. If their example is definitive—and Cubism *is* over—Cubism in literature was an interesting experiment, but experiments, their example reminds us, occasionally fail."[44]

Frustration with Stein's seeming nonreferentiability is not new. In *The Modes of Modern Writing,* David Lodge describes *Tender Buttons* as "a feat of *de*creation . . . so drastic that it kills the patient,"[45] and there are a wide variety of comments throuhout Steinian criticism that focus not only on the "pathological" condition of a text like *Tender Buttons* but also on the "pathological" perversity of its author.[46] What is unique is the extent to which a Cubist perspective is invoked as a way of assessing the nature of Stein's supposed misadventure. In *A Different Language,* for example, Marianne DeKoven addresses the Cubist analogy to suggest that judging Stein's linguistic strangeness in terms "borrowed from painting, where meaning must be either referential or abstract" has little validity, for "meaning in experimental writing need be neither: it often has no anterior, referential, thematic content, yet it has readable meaning—it is not abstract."[47] Like Steiner, DeKoven concludes that the fugitive relationship between the titles and the actual still life composition in *Tender Buttons* renders the reader's search for the "subject" in "the shape of the language" "irrelevant" (78). Interestingly, while DeKoven insists that "Stein is playing, and playing entirely in the realm of language, without interest in representation of the material world" (78), and that therefore her "presymbolic *jouissance*" (76) cannot be evaluated in terms of the kind of referentiability that Cubist art maintains, her final judgment of *Tender Buttons* is that "Stein went beyond the book in this period" (81). By implication, when DeKoven turns to "a few successful short pieces in the late 'lively words' style" ("Susie Asado," for example), the very lack of reference she had celebrated as *jouissance* becomes evidence of *Tender Buttons*'s insufficiency.

In abandoning a Cubist analogy by citing Stein's semantic displacement as evidence of her misunderstanding of Cubist art and/or her own inability or unwillingness to sustain reference, or by implying that Cubist effects in a verbal medium perverts the resources of language, critics may propose an alternate interartistic frame that they believe can deal with Stein's technical iconoclasm. In "Poetry as Word-System: The Art of Gertrude Stein," Marjorie Perloff advises that given the "indeterminacy" of a Steinian text like *Tender Buttons* and the impossibility of attaining a "coherent image of reality" because of its ritualized style, the longstanding correlation between Stein's work and what Allegra Stewart momentarily considers as a parallel "cubistic vision of the object"[48] is untenable. Perloff suggests that a more viable interartistic analogy can be developed between Stein and the Orphic Cubism of Francis Picabia and Duchamp. She cites Apollinaire's definition of the term he conceived to address the fantastic machinery and bizarre irreverence of Duchamp's *Nude Descending a Staircase, No. 2,* and suggests that this Surrealistic dimension and the kind of privacy it entails more accurately respond to the way in which Stein develops a language that is much more responsive by design to the medium of her own "verbal labyrinth" than to the actual object that seems to be denoted (40–42).

The Cubist analogy, however, has intense significance for Stein's middlephase portraiture particularly, and the viability of this analogy can be guaranteed by examining the specific techniques Stein develops within her medium to achieve the linguistic version of Cubism's vision of a conceptualized subject. These techniques actualize the tension between reference and autonomy that a Cubist thinking eye explores. In Steinian composition they range from the "mixing and mingling and contrasting"[49] of tenses within a single syntactical maneuver to achieve an actual synchronic illusion—as is the case, for example, when Stein conjugates the rotational axis of her dancing figure in a transitional work like "Orta or One Dancing" to present a "complete history" of her subject's being (*Making of Americans,* 284)[50]—to the interpenetration of rhetorical planes of meaning, those multivalent semantic codes synchronized by a series of isomorphic and pervasive metaphors for the creative process that hold this multivalency in place.

In *Tender Buttons,* for example, the making of art involves a process of ingestion, secretion, metamorphosis, and expulsion, and this transformative process is encoded in a variety of parallel synecdochal forms that describe the ruminating activity of the narrator and author in terms of other "ruminant" life forms: the cow who chews her cud and translates grass into milk, the grazing sheep that grows the fleece, the oyster that secretes the pearl. These metastatic— and often metabolic—configurations, and the rich metonymic character of the interactive planes of meaning that they generate, display the facets of a single idea about how raw materials are metamorphosized in a variety of still-life portraits. Stein achieves the kind of synthesis intrinsic to the polymorphic character of Cubism's interpenetrative planes by encouraging the metastatic pattern to build relations between the synonymic processes engaged in millinery, cullinery, veterinary, martial, medical, graphic, agricultural, plastic, and calligraphic art forms.

Just as the Cubists expand iconographic means by asserting the flat plane, so too Stein foregrounds the conventions of her medium to exhibit possibilities that accepted standards of "grammaticalness" would deny, and to develop indexical resources through synecdoche and metonymy that habits of naming may conceal. In this sense, the linguistic equivalent of a plastic trompe l'oeil becomes those syntactical patterns that place ideas in logical relation: the principle of cause and effect, for example, which Stein often brings into "play" to build coherence between seemingly incongruous semantic units. Homonymic word groups held in relation by a single syntactic maneuver reveal unexpected parallels because of the synecdochal character of the relations they disclose. This possibility encourages the reader to see the difference between product and process throughout *Tender Buttons*.

In "APPLE," for example, the correlative for the fixed categories of meaning (the sugar cane as a vegetable perception) comes in terms of the openwindow tradition in landscape art, which authorizes only a single entrance or "climb" into the canvas by preserving attachments to a familiar category or ground of meaning: "A little piece please. Cane again to the presupposed and ready eucalyptus tree, count out sherry and riple plates and little corners of a kind of ham. This is use" (187). In contrast, the sugar cane candied image that emphasizes the transformation that takes place in the candy-making process asserts a correlation between the breakdown of established categories—"Sugar is not a vegetable" (162)—and the entrance into the landscape orchestrated by free and mobile perspectives to create new compositional entities: "In between a place and candy is a narrow foot-path that shows more mounting than anything, so much really that a calling meaning a bolster measured a whole thing with that. A virgin a whole virgin is judged made and so between curves and outlines and real seasons and more out glasses and a perfectly unprecedented arrangement between old ladies and mild colds there is no satin wood shining" (172). This "IN BETWEEN" orientation leads to a string of associations that link the author's presence as an "elephant" at the close of "Rooms" and her voice in "A SOUND" with a variety of analogies that show Stein's fascination with the implication of a Cubist "destruction" in her medium: "Elephant beaten with candy and little pops and chews all bolts and reckless reckless rats, this is this" (174).

The diagrammatic quality of Cubist iconography—the way in which, as Berger suggests in "The Moment of Cubism," reference is achieved through metonymic and synecdochal figures that do not imitate appearances (*enargia*) but rather sign "invisible processes, forces, structures" (20) to realize the way that the mind knows the object of contemplation—is one Stein intuitively understands. In "Portraits and Repetition," she attempts to resolve the difficulty of "suggesting remembering" in her medium while "trying to live in looking" by relating the "difficulty" to the evocative character of painted signs of contemporary painters: "Remembering with them takes the form of suggesting in their painting in place of having actually created the thing in itself that they are painting" (113). The verbal correlative for this kind of suggestiveness appears in Stein's own split descriptions and in her responsiveness to the meanings stored within the individual word, meanings that often relate to the origins of the naming act itself and that, though lost in use, may be recovered by liberating in abbreviated form the history of knowing that a single word may encode. Thus the "old say" in *Tender Buttons*'s "EATING" explores the echoic basis of the individual word "owl" to realize a wealth of resemblances between the sounds of the one eating and the disappearance and reappearance of the letter "h" (193).

The opening of the closed linguistic form, either through syntactic contortions or through collaboration with etymological resources of language, makes the reader simultaneously aware of the fact that language is not "natural" and that processes of deformation can in fact make the linguistic fabric more directly iconic of the processes of knowing: words can relate and combine in alternate ways without losing their referentiability to an evaluative mode of perception.

In using an established syntactical pattern as a trompe l'oeil, even while she confounds both its integrity and authority, Stein offers a correlative for the way in which Cubist artists encourage the naturalistic standard of verisimilitude to function through patterns of expectation and the mechanism of projection even while they dissolve those sanctioned continuities and the boundaries between categories that those continuities endorse. These deliberate category "mistakes" relate to the variety of rhetorical strategies Stein uses to conjugate seemingly disparate units to show the "last touch of being" of her still-life subjects. The last phrase comes from *The Making of Americans* (181), and relates to that composition's attempt to realize what Stein calls the "bottom nature" or "rhythm of personality" in "The Gradual Making of *The Making of Americans*."[51]

While critics argue that Stein's work has little affinity with Cubism because, as Jayne Walker advises, Stein only "enacts the movements of her own mind" (67) because the trace of the object of contemplation seems lost in the act of conceptualization, it is precisely because of that process that the analogy between a Steinian destruction and a Cubist one can be so fruitful. In using the term "destruction" to define his own work, Picasso observes: "There is no abstract art. You must always start with something. Afterward you can remove all traces of reality. There's no danger then, anyway, because the idea of the object will have left an indelible mark. It is what started the artist off, excited his ideas, and stirred up his emotions. Ideas and emotions will in the end be the prisoners in his work. Whatever they do, they can't escape from the picture. They form an integral part of it, even when their presence is no longer discernible" ("Conversation, 1935," Chipp, 270). In "A SUBSTANCE IN A CUSHION," Stein advises as well that "the question does not come before there is a quotation," and that the "quotation" does not disappear entirely even though one is "reckless" and "extreme" in the act of appropriation: "A sight a whole sight and a little groan grinding makes a trimming such a sweet singing trimming and a red thing not a round thing but a white thing, a red thing and a white thing" (162).

The "quotation" trimmed or read according to the demands of the medium defines an orientation that Picasso knew Stein to have grasped in the solutions to plastic problems he exhibited in his own work:

> Do you think it concerns me that a particular picture of mine represents two people? Though these two people once existed for me, they exist no longer. The "vision" of them gave me a preliminary emotion; then little by little their actual presence became blurred; they developed into a fiction and then disappeared altogether, or rather they were transformed into all kinds of problems. They are no longer two people, you see, but forms and colors: forms and colors that have taken on, meanwhile, the idea of two people and preserve the vibration of their life. . . . People who try to explain pictures are usually barking up the wrong tree. Gertrude Stein joyfully announced to me the other day that she had at last understood what my picture

of the three musicians was meant to be. It was a still life! ("Conversation, 1935," Chipp, 270–72)

It is an orientation that Stein's commentary on the oblique way in which reference functions in her art makes explicit in "Rooms," through her narrator's description of the "rubbing" process that shows the original as a handmade replica even though the "change" is made: "The author of all that is in there behind the door and that is entering in the morning. Explaining darkening and expecting relating is of all of a piece. The stove is bigger. It was a shape that made no audience bigger if the opening is assumed why should there not be kneeling. Any force which is bestowed on a floor shows rubbing. This is so nice and sweet and yet there comes the change, there comes the time to press more air. This does not mean the same as disappearance" (197).

In her interview with Haas, Stein describes the story enacted in *Tender Buttons*'s "A LITTLE BIT OF A TUMBLER" by defining its subject as a series of problems she solved through a still-life perspective: "I used to take objects on a table, like a tumbler or any kind of object and try to get the picture of it clear and separate in my mind and create a word relationship between the word and the things seen. 'A shining indication of yellow . . .' suggests a tumbler and something in it. ' . . . when all four were bought' suggests there were four of them. I try to call to the eye the way it appears by suggestion the way a painter can do it" (25).

In his discussion of how description is split in Picasso's own *Studies of Glasses,* Wilhelm Boeck notes that the Cubist destruction "unfolds its image of things in a sequence of separate conceptual steps" such that line and color "although inseparable in the actual appearance of objects, are not inseparable in the imagination. Hence the structure."[52] Stein's own dislocations use a comparable technique to establish tension between two alternate semantic codes for the "shining indication of yellow" relates to the "little bit" that is presently being displayed on the table as an object of esthetic contemplation, while "the four" that "were bought" references the set purchased to complete a table setting. Stein allows the trace of the tumbler's practical reality to vibrate in the still life even while she transforms its mode of identification. In the interview, Stein completes her commentary with the following: "This is difficult and takes a lot of work and concentration to do it. I want to indicate it without calling in other things. 'This was the hope which made the six and seven have no use for any more places. . . .' Places bring up a reality. ' . . . and this necessarily spread into nothing,' which does broken tumbler which is the end of the story" (25). Stein is able to sustain that tension and her focus on the tumbler as a plastic value as long as the notion of use—of the place setting and the place of purchase—does not dominate. If that esthetic moment collapses, and the memory of those purposive attachments becomes too strong, the difference between the tumbler conceived as "a shining indication of yellow" and as "four" which "were bought" is lost.

Even if one compares a pre-Analytical work like Picasso's *Portrait of Gertrude Stein* (fig. 45) with Stein's portrait of the artist in "Picasso"—the latter written in a participial pre-*Tender Buttons* style—one can see the extent to which Stein's conception of her created subject offers a parallel with Picasso's representation of the "bottom nature" of his model. Stein's "Picasso" works toward the realization of her subject by defining the essential action of the man himself: "This one was one who was working and he was one needing this thing needing to be working so as to be having some way of being one having some way of working."[53] In *The Development of Abstractionism in the Writings of Gertrude Stein,* Michael Hoffman complains that Stein's commitment to a single dimension as definitive renders the portrait subject elusive: "We would not even know from the portrait that Picasso was a painter. Miss Stein has abstracted all specific references that would connect the subject to the life in the world of things, places, events, and people."[54] To offset Hoffman's charge of nonreferentiability, one can cite Kahnweiler's enthusiasm for what he considers to be the life-likeness of Stein's portrait in his Introduction to *Painted Lace:* "The *Leitmotiv* of the 'Picasso' for example—the 'This one was working'—strikes me truly at the crux of the problem of the man and the painter Picasso, who lives only in order to work and is unhappy when he is not working."[55]

The quality of nonspecificity in Stein's "Picasso" occurs in part because the biographical preconditions as they are traditionally narrated are conspicuously absent. An examination of Picasso's *Stein* from this perspective reveals as well that Picasso makes no reference to his subject's "occupation": the essential "fact" seems to be that this is one who was sitting and thinking and indeed, Stein sat for the portrait an unprecedented eighty times. This dominant aspect is dramatized in plastic terms by the foreground heaviness of the portrait and the overwhelming sense of volume and stasis conveyed through the power of the seated figure curved within the arc of the armchair.

In Stein's "Picasso," the central motif is equally passive, for Picasso is conceived as one who "was working," whom "some were following," "who was completely charming" and who "had something having meaning" that "was coming out of this one." In Picasso's *Stein* one experiences that passivity at all levels: the restricted palette and the quietism of its color values, the predominance and recurrence of an insistent horizontal plane, the introspective qualities of the eyes, a strangeness negotiated by the disequilibrium between the left and right sides of the face.

In point of fact, Picasso reworked Stein's face entirely following his exposure to a series of archaic reliefs from Osuna and Cerro de los Santos exhibited in the Louvre in the spring of 1906, and his modified adaptation of this influence is felt in the masklike silence and dignity of Stein's facial expression in the

Figure 45.   Pablo Picasso, *Portrait of Gertrude Stein,* 1906
(The Metropolitan Museum of Art, New York)

portrait, qualities generated by the series of primitive distortions that give the features their severity, flatness, and asymmetry. In Stein's "Picasso," a parallel archaic quality is achieved by the ritualized style that invokes the felt presence of "this one" who "was working." This linguistic strangeness is the result of a variety of techniques. The exclusion of specific concrete nouns in favor of indefinite pronouns combine with the limited range of adjectives. The evolving polysyndetic character of the participial style inscribes the ongoingness of what is the prototypic action of ones who have been "working" to have "something" coming out of them that others are "following." Through the insistent pattern of repetition Picasso is identified completely as "this one" who "was one who was working," and the fact that his alliance is gradually formulated syntactically imbues the piece with an incantatory quality—a cultic resonance—that the stylistic ritual is meant to embody.

In her study of *Picasso,* Stein defines Picasso's ability to think like the things he saw in terms of a knowledge of the human figure he possesses that reaches back into the beginnings of time. In a corresponding way, Stein knows the passion of the one who was making, and this understanding materializes in the gerund act itself. The repetitive motifs that highlight the four "facts" of the portrait—this is "one who was working," who was "completely charming," "whom some were certainly following," and who "was bringing out of himself then something"—are continually reformulated through a series of interpenetrative units to render Stein's total absorption with the essential disposition of her portrait subject. So too, the uniform mode through which Stein is conceived in Picasso's portrait is achieved technically through the reduced palette and the repetition with variation of large compositional units. The arc of the wainscotting, the hair, the oval of the face, the slope of the shoulders, the heavy round of the ample lamp, the quiet of the hands combine to impose a sense of what Stein will define in *Tender Buttons*'s "END OF SUMMER" as "a rested development" (190).

In Stein's "Picasso" the "something being coming out of" the one who "was needing to be working" remains elusive, and that indeterminancy is secured by the process that conjoins a string of antithetical qualities. The "something" is at once "a heavy thing" and "a solid thing," a "simple" and "clear thing" as well as a "complicated" and "disconcerting" thing, a "lovely" and "charming" thing, a "very pretty" thing and a "disturbing" and "repellant" thing (214). The reader focuses not only on the tension that is created by the contrary values of the specific qualifiers but also on the sense of inclusiveness the catalogue as a whole sustains. Rather than ranking the adjectives, the text enumerates them blind to the logical contradictions that are bred among them. To dramatize the pattern of disassociation that Stein's doctrine of coequality advises, the portraitist turns abruptly from the split description back to the larger repetitive rhythm of the piece: "This one was certainly being one having something coming out of him. This one was one whom some were following. This one was one who was working." The lack of resolution that Stein's technique insists upon here provides a verbal correlative for the kind of asymmetry Picasso's conceptual response to his subject's facial topography insists upon in *Stein*.

There is only one instance in which a more stable connection between the "one" and the "something" is authorized in the text. This comes through Stein's repetition of the term "charming" to define both "this" one who "was one certainly working" and "who was certainly completely charming," and the "something" that "had been coming out of him," which had "a charming meaning" (213). In a very real way this technique suggests a correlation with the kind of effect Picasso achieves in a second pre-Analytical work *Woman with Mandolin* (fig. 46), an effect that will remain though in more complicated form as contours are rendered discontinuous in an Analytical work like *Girl with a Mandolin*. In the earlier *Woman with Mandolin*, the uniformity of Picasso's stylistic mode is achieved by the repetition of a dominant compositional element: the configuration of the body of the mandolin, which refeatures the woman's face, is restated in the strained handle of the neck, in the hands and mirror imaged in the chest. In *Girl with a Mandolin* the intimacy between the music made and its maker is secured by the way in which the format of the sound hole materializes as the configuration for the eye, or by the way in which the fractured line of the neck of the mandolin recurs in the left forearm and hand, and in the hand and the fingers. This intricate pattern of intersecting shapes scatters superficial continuities by challenging the traditional boundaries that hold between opaque and translucent, volumetrical and flattened, naturalistic and hieroglyphic forms. It presents a levelling of established categories and hierarchies that is as essential to Stein's collocation of seemingly contrary qualifiers in her "Picasso." Both *Girl with a Mandolin* and "Picasso" concentrate on the typicality of the figures they conceive, on the essential attitude and disposition of the maker who is "one having something coming out of him."

The techniques of disassociation and realignment that Stein develops in "Picasso" to move beyond superficial continuities are simply extended in *Tender Buttons*. One of the most intriguing points to be made about *Tender Buttons* is its overwhelming reference to the still-life subjects and plastic and calligraphic means of Synthetic Cubism, which Stein asserts as a correlative for her own artistic intention within the text. Composed of three sections, "Objects," "Food" and "Rooms," the volume presents fifty-eight still lifes that seem primarily concerned with household articles in the first section, fifty-one responses that actualize the menu items catalogued in the second section, and an extended rumination and display of the esthetic principles that shaped the "whole collection made" (199) in the third. The volume's absorption with the implications of Synthetic Cubism's *tableau-tableau* orientation generates a series of illusions

Figure 46.   Pablo Picasso, *Woman with Mandolin*, 1909
(Hermitage, Leningrad)

that illustrate the principles of composition central to Gris's *Glasses with News-paper* and *The Table* (fig. 47). In Stein's second "A BOX," for example, a single term asserts its new dimension with each instance of its reappearance: "The one is on the table. The two are on the table. The three are on the table. The one, one is the same length as is shown by the cover being longer. The other is different there is more cover than shows it. The other is different and that makes the corners have the same shade the eight are in singular arrangement to make four necessary" (165). Stein not only conveys the capricious nature of the light source and the randomness of the cast shadow to overturn assumptions about density and gravity, she also sees the juxtaposition of seemingly incompatible illusions in the very terms of Gris's redoubled cigarettes: "Lax, to have corners, to be lighter than some weight, to indicate a wedding journey, to last brown and not curious, to be wealthy, cigarettes are established by length and by doubling" (165). Stein takes this idea of how the conceptualized subject is displayed through split descriptions literally by exhibiting it grammatically: "A box is made sometimes and them to see to see it neatly and to have the holes stopped up makes it necessary to use paper" (165). The technique appears in its most extreme formulation in the second "EATING" still life to foreground the semantic unit's ability to function as both a constructive and descriptive entity (194).

An allusion to Picasso's 1910 *Woman with Mustard Pot* thrives in Stein's own study of the disindividualized seated figure in "A SUBSTANCE IN A CUSHION," a still life that seems also remarkably aware of the tassel from an upholstered chair, swan and ivy motifs, playing-card effects and color values of Picasso's 1914 *Portrait of a Young Girl in Front of a Fireplace*. The "chance to see a tassel" in "CUSHIONS" seems equally responsive to Gris's declaration of a parallel motif in his 1912 *The Watch*, while its "circle of fine cardboard" effectively responds to the oval formats both Picasso and Braque experiment with during their Synthetic adventures. The trompe l'oeil guide-marks that take their cue from Braque's *Violin and Palette* are referenced in multiple forms, from the "something suggesting a pin" in Stein's first "A BOX" (163) through to the wealth of allusions to her own calligraphic instruments that build compositions that are hung: "Climb up in sight climb in the whole utter needles and a guess a whole guess is hanging. Hanging hanging" ("MILK," 186). The intrigue of these kinds of allusions forms the center of the *double entendre* of Stein's "RHUBARB," where "rhubarb is susan not susan" (188) finds its "sugar is not a vegetable" or Cubist alternate in Picasso's shuffling of identities in his 1913 *La Suze* (fig. 48). By pasting the ready-made label *"Suze Apéritif à la Gentiane"* on the Cubist bottle, Picasso plays with both its medicinal and decorative possibilities, and these suggestions are borne out in the newspaper fragments whose subheadings—*"Le Meeting en plein air," "L'ordre du jour," "La dislocation"*—combine with the "key" which shears *"Les jour . . . annoncent un . . . e victoire"*

Figure 47.   Juan Gris, *The Table,* 1919
            Colored papers, printed matter, charcoal on paper mounted
            on canvas.
            (Philadelphia Museum of Art; A. E. Gallatin Collection)

to define the tension between reference and compositional game. Even while Stein's "RHUBARB" endeavors to distinguish between the thing made as "susan" and its attachment to antecedent realities as "not susan," the two signs are held in place as "susan not susan" to encourage all the things that "not susan" references to vibrate within the esthetic terms of debate. In this way, rhubarb's own tonic qualities, the history of our response to its ecology ("not seat in bunch toys not wild and laughable not in little places not in neglect and vegetable") and culinary use ("not in fold coal age not please," terms which bring in the reality of the breakfast table and the linguistic habit of "please pass the jam") emphasize "not susan's" extraliterary reality, which is encouraged to function in the mounted reality of "RHUBARB's" compositional actuality.

In what appears to be her own playful version of Picasso's 1912 *Dead Birds,* Stein's "A PAPER" (170) builds tension between "a courteous occasion" (the preparation or presentation of the material) and the irreverence of the "paper show" that is made. The latter departs from such courtesy by drawing attention to the fictive in contrast to the practical dispensation of what is about to be consumed—the "stool" pigeon. In Picasso's *Dead Birds* this exchange is shown by the splayed form of the bird scattered throughout the canvas, and the "paper show," "*Jou,*" which refers to both the verbal and visual play dramatized by the presence of the newspaper fragment, which, having been read, is about to become the bird's disposable wrapper. "SHOES" concentrates on the effects achieved by conscripting wallpaper fragments to serve as compositional entities in *papier collé* construction—to build the "shallow" sound "holes" of the mounted violins and guitars of Cubist art. Interestingly, the thing made through the application of *papier collé* appears in Stein's "SHOES" in metonymic form as "ale less," (174) an allusion, perhaps, to Braque's first *papier collé, The Fruit-Dish* which shows ("Shoes") the handmade "ALE" and "BAR." "VEGETA-BLE" (191) offers a parallel commentary on the verbal permutations of newspaper fragments within Synthetic *collages* through "News. News capable of glees, cut in shoes, belike under plump of wide chalk, all this combing" (where "combing" references Braque's attempts to create a trompe l'oeil wood-grained surface using a decorator's comb), as does "A BROWN": "A brown which is not liquid is not more so is relaxed and yet there is a change, a news is pressing" (173). This attention to the constructive means of the *collé* fragment is a recurring motif in "Rooms" as well as Stein explores the "use of paper" to create "more sugar" performances: "A tribune, a tribune does not mean paper; it means nothing more than cake, it means more sugar, it shows the state of lengthening any nose" (201).

Tender Buttons's synecdochal images consistently reference the Cubist still-life subject and technique. The chair-caning materials of Picasso's *Still Life with Chair Caning* appear as one of the elements that "hold the pine, hold the

Figure 48.   Pablo Picasso, *La Suze*, 1912–1913
Paper *collage* with charcoal, 25¾″ × 19¾″.
*(Washington University Gallery of Art, St. Louis; University
Purchase, Kende Sale Fund, 1946)*

dark, hold in the rush, make the bottom" in "A WAIST" (171), and reappear in "Rooms" to show "relief." Here the suggestion of a third dimension has as much to do with solving the problems of the medium's two-dimensional reality as it does with the trace of anal humor that is retained in the reference to processes of elimination: "Looking into a place that was hanging and was visible looking into this place and seeing a chair did that mean relief, it certainly did not cause constipation and yet there is a melody that has white for a tune when there is straw color" (202). There are studies of fish like the "play sole" exhibited "in a plank" in Stein's first "CREAM" (192) and the dislocated salmon sectionally displaced in typographic terms by the intervening sauce to make "sam in" in "SAUCE" (194). In "CAKE" Stein seems to reference Gris's presentation in *The Washstand* with its "mussed ash," "tin," "cake" and "foolish number" (the "Two" that circulates in Stein's piece and Gris's canvas) and in the abbreviated landscape that decorates Gris's pulled-back shower curtain that materializes in "CAKE's" "green land": "A little leaf upon a scene an ocean any where there" (189). Stein not only brings into being Gris's interactive conceptualized fragments, she also describes the *grisaille* technique of the painting's stained glass effect: "Cake cast in went to be and needles wine needles as such."

Within Stein's "CAKE" there is also an explicit reference to the trompe l'oeil guide-mark itself in "there was extra a hat pin long sought," which was used "another time" by Gris, perhaps, as is the case in his 1913 *Violin and Engraving* where the sign of "extra" takes the form of the two pegs of the violin as well as the painted nail that appears to hold the pasted part of a real engraving by an anonymous artist into the illusionistic molding of the picture in the upper part of the right half of the painting. The Cubist guide-mark and the debate it makes between representational and nonrepresentational values appears in a variety of figures throughout the first two sections of Stein's volume, and recurs in "Rooms" to provide Stein with a parallel for her oblique pointing systems: "A curving example makes righteous finger-nails. This is the only object in secretion and speech" (205).

The reference to verbal and visual means is as pervasive as is the reference to subject matter in *Tender Buttons*, for the two are inextricably involved as the three-dimensional entity is translated onto the flat plane. There are a variety of terms within this context that operate as synecdoches to define the graphic means of drypoint etching and copper plate engraving (copper, plates, biting, pressing, cutting, blackening, needles, nigged, picking, oxides, mordants, beeswax), charcoal sketching and calligraphy (feathers, lines, paper, ink, drawing boards, coal, pencils, lead, erasers), oil painting and water color (wetting, pigments, powder, painting tubes, washes, drawing pins, dusting brushes, underpainting, canvas, stretchers, frames, seasoning, egg and oil glazes), the mixed media of the *collage* and *papier collé* (glue, sand, sawdust, wood, tickets, stamps, oil cloth, glass, wire, labels, name plates, newspapers, wallpaper, combing), as well as the casting of molds, the firing of pots and the chiselling of stone.

Though critics often argue that the ostensible subject of Stein's still life does not materialize in the writing, seemingly arcane passages become accessible once the conceptual relationship between the title and its formulation in the writing is understood within this context. Thus in "DIRT AND NOT COPPER" (164) the terms reference the graphic means that establish the etching ground of soft asphalt and beeswax that is blackened by smoking the copper plate. Stein also places the surface so created in high relief by bringing into play the challenge to traditional illusions of load and support central to the Cubist study of things on tables: "It makes mercy and relaxation and even a strength to spread a table fuller. There are more places not empty. They see cover" (164). So too, Stein's "PEELED PENCIL, CHOKE" (176), which is often perceived as but one of the many veiled references to Stein's blossoming sexual relationship with Alice B. Toklas,[56] refers equally to the charcoal used with oils and ready-made substances as part of the mixed media of *collage* and *collé*. The peeling of the pencil and the rubbing of the coke engage processes of distillation or partial decomposition that prepare for the food analogy—the peeled apocopated artichoke that is enacted through "choke." These analogies are established in terms of the isomorphic relationship between processes that expose a common function: the conversion of raw materials into new compounds whether as art, love, food, or mineral substances. Stein's doctrine of coequality demands that the intersecting semantic codes have equal value, and encourages the text to bring into alignment resemblances between seemingly discrete semantic units that release connections that linguistic habit and convention may conceal.

This is the matching principle that is repeatedly engaged to exhibit parallels between the variety of signature motifs and calling-card identities that Picasso uses, for example, in his 1914 *Still Life with Calling Card* (fig. 49). Composed by using a worn Stein-Toklas calling-card left at his home when he was absent, Picasso replaces the dog's ear with his own trompe l'oeil fold and includes a die and a package of cigarettes. As the story goes, Picasso left the still life as his calling card at 27 rue de Fleurus ("Typography of Cubism," 68). Stein's own "A PLATE" offers a parallel "game in green" by contrasting the freedom of the nonnaturalistic sign for a dinner engagement—"An occasion for a plate, an occasional resource is in buying and how soon does washing enable a selection of the same thing neater. If the party is small a clever song is in order"—with a more naturalistically conceived calling-card counterpart whose address is fixed insofar as the plastic and calligraphic resources of the medium are hidden: "A splendid address a really splendid address is not shown by giving a flower freely, it is not shown by a mark or by wetting" (165–66). In *Calling Card,* Picasso highlights the oblique nature of the reference to material reality that his stylized painted signs and opened forms display. So too, Stein's showing in

"PLATE" capitalizes on a parallel *"CONTRIBUTIONS INDIRECTES"* theme. That indirection materializes in Stein's own metaphoric transformation of die into "compressed disease" and in the way she "shows filling" by opening the meanings stored within the verbal sign to release parallels for the creative act, which fuse stone cutting, glass-making, cake-baking and soapstone-carving analogies: "A lamp is not the only sign of glass. The lamp and the cake are not the only sign of stone. The lamp and the cake and the cover are not the only necessity altogether" (116).

"MUTTON" provides a remarkable linguistic correlative for Picasso's comic treatment of things that possess face value in *Student with a Pipe* (fig. 50), a work Stein had in her possession at the time of *Tender Button*'s composition: "Students, students are merciful and recognized they chew something" (181). Picasso's topographic displacements find their complement in Stein's own syntactic contortions: "Like a very strange likeness and pink, like that and not more like that than the same resemblance and not more like that than no middle space is cutting." The sentence inscribes this idea of the equivalence among likenesses in keeping with Picasso's insistence on the viability of each of the multiple descriptions of his figure, such that even the apparent lack of symmetry between the semantic units "like a very strange likeness" and "pink" is incidental to their common grammatical function. The running line which introduces the sentence cited above creates this kind of tension between surface imbalance and underlying continuity, for the punctuation of the second run-on, while it does not respond to its own rhetorical intention, simultaneously enacts the idea expressed in the preliminary imperative: "Change in a single stream of denting and change it hurriedly by, what does it express, it expresses nausea" (181).

As Picasso disrupts the potential integrity of a single profile by introducing alternative conceptualizations, so too Stein provides the trompe l'oeil illusion of syntactic order even while she disturbs that illusion by deliberate errors in agreement: "A letter which can wither, a learning which can suffer and an outrage which is simultaneous is principal." Her mistreatment of grammatical rules engages the misuse of shifters so that the contour of an inductive line of argumentation is shattered by the oxymoronic nature of its resolution: "Interleaved and successive and a sample of smell all this makes a certainty a shade." And just as Picasso juxtaposes seemingly incompatible iconic signs—the trompe l'oeil pipe flattened against the hieroglyphic plane of smoke to highlight the conceptual nature of their symmetry—so too Stein uses synesthetic figures to bring alternate modes of reference into alignment. The "sample of smell" is "a shade" just as students are recognizable because "they chew something" and these parallels are mediated by the synecdochal character of the signs themselves. Accordingly, the more immediate denotative function of the word is subordinate to the larger conceptual process within which its indexical matrix is assimilated. The kind of intellectual challenge Stein's consistent application

Figure 49. Pablo Picasso, *Still Life with Calling Card*, 1914
Collage with drawing, 5½″ × 8¼″.
(*Mrs. Gilbert W. Chapman, New York*)

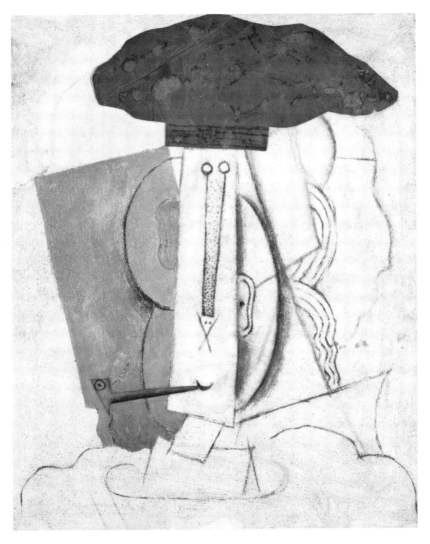

Figure 50.   Pablo Picasso, *Student with a Pipe*, 1913
            Oil, charcoal, pasted paper, and sand on canvas, 73 × 58.7 cm.
            (Collection, the Museum of Modern Art, New York; Nelson
            A. Rockefeller Bequest)

of synecdochal forms brings into being in "MUTTONS" forces the reader to concentrate on associations that usually exist on the fringe of attention, and the pressure exerted helps the iconoclastic spirit of the student theme to materialize in the medium. In "Rooms" Stein uses metonymic and synecdochal figures to build coherence to bring the advance of a military detail into relation with the spread of an infectious disease (parallel references to metastatic patterns such as the "pus" of "SHOES" offer Stein pathognomonic analogies to exhibit how difference is spread in her medium): "A whole soldier any whole soldier who has no more detail than any case of measles" (204). By attending to their common disposition, Stein's terms show an "exchange in" the "principle" of association (the syncopated forms that build the "nausea" of "MUTTON"), but not a departure in subject matter. The students in "MUTTON" sign the case of like objects who chew their cud and are perhaps easily led, and who break patterns of authority ("principal") simply as a matter of principle.

Conceptually parallel linguistic clichés simultaneously assert themselves within the still life. By "cutting" their teeth on more radical rather than "middle-ground," these whippersnappers invite alternate definitions to function: "An eye glass, what is an eye glass, it is water." What appears as a convincing demonstration to those who despise established categories of meaning may appear fugitive and illogical to those in authority. This kind of imaginative alternative to established convention corresponds exactly to the glass of water that Picasso conceives for the nose of the frontal portrait. Held by the antennas that join the eyes to the base of the nose, the figure releases a string of associations that relate the theme of eyesight and spectacle to the plastic technique. Each conceptualized unit in Picasso's polymorphic presentation displays a different iconic version of the figure cut by the student. It is the discrete nature of these contiguous units that Stein attempts to inscribe through "insistence" in her own still life: "A centre can place and four are no more and two are not middle" (181). Stein's notion of "insistence" is defined by her as a "beginning again and again," so that each entity that recurs is perceived as a self-enclosed form. Donald Sutherland defines the concept that Stein's theory of "insistence" recommends as "one in which each unit, even if it is identical or nearly with the previous one, is still, in its present, a completely self-contained thing, as when you say one and one, the second one is a completely present existence in itself, and does not depend, as two or three does, on a preceding one or two. . . . [It] arrives in a continuous present, that is, the present is so continuous it does not allow any retrospect or expectation."[57] As one of the multiple techniques that Stein relies on to establish the "distribution" ("Rooms," 196) and equilibration ("Composition as Explanation," 30) of "the time-sense in the composition," the continuous presents holds the temptation to rely solely on an accumulative sense of identity in abeyance: numbers are not allowed to simply combine or relate in their usual mode just as semantic units are not collectivized within their grammatical structures.

Stein's decentering of her medium relates equally to her use of a free and mobile perspective. The authorial voice, which, like single-point perspective in the pictorial arts, could traditionally synchronize story values and synthesize the material that accumulates to maintain stability and surface continuity, abandons this task to encourage the reader to abandon the preconceptions that have been shaped by these established methods of presentation. As in "PLATE," the narrator consistently invites the reader to "see cover" ("DIRT AND NOT COPPER," 164) as a way of acknowledging the authority of the flat plane which can show "filling" by exhibiting interiors inaccessible to a frontal view. This effect is central in "OBJECTS," for example, where, as in Picasso's *Girl with a Mandolin,* various aspects of the closed form of the "slender joint" are "cut" to "show" by "squeezing" that "the elbow is long and it is filled." In other words, a total experience of the object is achieved by exhibiting the various claims "all together" (170).

The loss of a fixed center in the Picasso materializes in the juxtaposition of discrete iconographies that systematically evade the center of the canvas and are equally off-balance in themselves. To distinguish the distortions of the face that confronts us directly, Picasso uses an X, and indeed this sign references the asymmetry that is multiplied in the series of profiles that are developed. This is the kind of explicit commentary Picasso's hieroglyphic characters often present in his Synthetic constructions to make the viewer acutely conscious of their "composition as explanation" theme. Interestingly Stein seems to allude to this maneuver in "MUTTON" to draw attention to the intellectual grid that holds her semantic codes in relation: "Melting and not minding, safety and powder, a particular recollection and a sincere solitude all this makes a shunning so thorough and so unrepeated and surely if there is anything left it is a bone. It is not solitary" (181).

The terms relate equally to the kind of linguistic and ideational disturbances that Stein's "bone" heads (and Picasso's blockheads) create, disturbances that are really not as fractious as they appear, for the "safety" pin is intact even though the piece is armed with manifestos ("powder"). (By association, of course, one is drawn to the comic effects of the *collé* wide-brimmed *faluche* of the French student in Picasso's composition and to the play on "cap" that leads to the military terms Stein uses to expose the pinheadedness of her still-life subject.) The manifesto quality of the still life takes explicit form in the following: "Light curls very light curls have no more curliness than soup. This is not a subject" (181). The narrator instructs the reader that there is no way the "subject" of the piece can be reduced to a single compositional entity or semantic code. Students have "light curls" and the relationship between this assertion combines with an array of metaphoric implications authorized by the analogies in the text to create a mixture whose conceptual vitality does not depend on the composition of one of its parts: students make waves, they fleece the establishment by challenging the status quo,they pull the wool over their own eyes, they are impostors whose iconoclasm is short-lived, they send up smoke screens, they are of common stock.

In "shunning" convention—everything from grammatical orthodoxy to naturalistic verisimilitude—Stein maintains an underlying structural integrity and semantic coherence that relates each unit to the overall iconoclastic theme. It is an iconoclasm that would split the indexical matrix that repetitions of a linguistic root are meant to sustain. Thus the piece makes "a sincere solitude" that "is not solitary." The still life displays a "particular recollection" framed by the autotelic conditions of art. As art, it is generically linked to other "sincere solitude[s]," but as importantly it does not exist in absolute isolation from the actual subject that inspired the composition. Reference is maintained. Those "traces" are consistently presented as guide-marks that allow us to assess the extent to which Stein departs from established conventions. It is a departure Picasso signals with his own crossed bones in *Student,* and one Stein invokes by playing with the multiple references orchestrated by her exposure of the vulnerabilities of the herding instinct that masquerades as defiance in the disposition of her youthful subjects.

This awareness of the role "recognition" must play within her compositions is a concept Stein's narrator courts explicitly in "Rooms": "If comparing a piece that is a size that is recognized as not a size but a piece, comparing a piece with what is not recognized but what is used as it is held by holding, comparing these two comes to be repeated" (199). The principle is shown in the second "A BOX": "to be sure cigarettes do measure an empty length sooner than a choice in color" (165). Both aspects—color and volume—coexist in our conception of cigarette, but the naturalistic standard traditionally places the visual mode in a dominant position as far as recognition is concerned. By emphasizing the cigarette's volumetrical dispensation, Stein encourages an alternate identification strategy to function. Berger relates this diagrammatic use of appearance in Cubist art to the way in which the naturalistic allusion measures the transformation that has taken place: "the details are smuggled in and hidden as mementos" (28) to maintain contact with ordinary habits of seeing even while the splitting of the descriptive content of the object itself makes the whole idea of the authority of appearances suspect.

In "MUTTON," as in "A BOX," conceptualized fragments coexist to make us aware of the process of knowing stored in the names of things: "Suppose an example is necessary, the plainer it is made the more reason there is for some outward recognition that there is a result" (165). And, as is often the case with *Tender Buttons,* the "MUTTON" still life reappears in synoptic form in "Rooms" in conjunction with other synecdochal smoking figures from previous still lifes to explain the compositional rationale for the split description: "A package and a filter and even a funnel, all this together makes a scene and supposing the question arises is hair curly, is it dark and dusty, supposing the question arises, is brushing necessary, is it, the whole special suddenness commences then, there is no delusion" (200). That rationale is demonstrated in "Rooms" to spread the difference between copy (cat) and conceptualized subject by deploying alternate naming strategies: "The sight of no pussy cat is so different that a tobacco zone is white and cream" (205).

What often appears as a failure of logic actually expresses the integrity of the conceptual frame within which "MUTTON" is meant to exist. Further, this recurring "Composition as Explanation" frame brings various still lifes into relation even though they appear arbitrarily dispersed in the text. In this way, Stein explores the capacity of her medium to achieve synchronic effects. There are a series of still lifes, for example, that metaphorically debate the distinctions that hold between "painting" and "picturing" in terms of an umbrella. The first, "MILDRED'S UMBRELLA," provides a demonstration of how objects are realized when artistic means are concealed. The naturalistic standard materializes syntactically in the "straight exchange" that establishes the logical advance of the inductive argument: "A cause and no curve, a cause and loud enough, a cause and extra a loud clash and an extra wagon, a sign of extra, a sac a small sac and an established color and cunning, a slender grey and no ribbon, this means a loss a great loss a restitution" (164).

"MILDRED'S UMBRELLA" is itself hung between two still lifes that present landscapes that are realized by antithetical means. The first, "NOTHING ELEGANT," challenges the authority of a single-point perspective: "A charm a single charm is doubtful" (164). The ambiguity that results when the fixed standing ground is eliminated is displayed by the indeterminancy of the terms that are enclosed by the if-then construction: "If the red is rose and there is a gate surrounding it, if inside is let in and there places change then certainly something is upright. It is earnest" (164). The second, "A METHOD OF A CLOAK," reinstates the authority of the open-window tradition that invites the observer to enter the art object by creating the illusion that the picture space extends his familiar terrain: "A single climb to a line, a straight exchange to a cane, a desperate adventure and courage and a clock, all this which is a system, which has feeling, which has resignation and success, all makes an attractive black silver" (164).

The titling of "MILDRED'S UMBRELLA" announces the naturalistic standard by which it is to be evaluated, for it invokes a criteria of use, purpose, and propriety. The umbrella represented belongs to Mildred and, by extension, to the world of things that people own to protect themselves from the basic elements (in this case from the flat surface of the medium itself). The language within the still life makes this clear. There is "a cause and no curve"—no deviation from the usual habit of association that allows us to recognize this umbrella as Mildred's. The declaration of whose thing this is is "loud enough" and, given that these attachments remain intact, the umbrella becomes the "sign of extra" with an "established color and cunning." The usual tricks of illusionism conceal the difference between artifact and facsimile. As a "slender grey" with "no ribbon" (a synecdochal form Stein consistently engages to represent framing techniques), the trompe l'oeil has incidental and purely anecdotal significance: "a sign of extra, a sac a small sac." The colloquial expression is abbreviated in form as *sac* rather than *cul de sac,* which, when conjoined with the term "small," draws attention to the diminished value of the object that is simply restated without translation. While the observer/reader, assured of likeness in this pedestrian sense, is appeased by an appearance he recognizes, this method of representation also means "a loss a great loss" for the hoped-for invention is reduced to copy: "an extra wagon." The way in which the represented object insists upon its usual connection with a familiar reality is enacted grammatically, for the series of qualifiers that describes "this" exaggerates the one-dimensionality of the pointing system that is engaged. Even the subordinate conjunction, which is itself assumed, highlights the trompe l'oeil theme of the piece.

In contrast to this usual standard of measure, Stein's second and third umbrella still lifes (quite like Cubist canvases that show mounted instruments) explore the advantages of declaring the flat surface. "A MOUNTED UMBRELLA" highlights the "exchange" of value that occurs when one is given the "chance" of "seeing it come there" (169). Again Stein frames this showing of her subject by bringing into play the differences that obtain between the art of picturing that "A PURSE" subscribes to and the art of painting engaged in "A CLOTH." In the former, the subject is constrained by the customary attachments to external reality that are retained: "A purse was not green, it was not straw color, it was hardly seen and it had a use a long use and the chain, the chain was never missing, it was not misplaced, it showed that is was open, that is all that it showed" (169). In the latter, Stein demonstrates the "lesson" that is learned through the terms of "A MOUNTED UMBRELLA," and accordingly the cloth no longer obliged to produce scale drawings can accommodate the dimensions of "any occasion." The resources of the medium allow it to support multiple and seemingly contradictory illusions. The paradox is reformulated in "Rooms" as "this which is mastered has so thin a space to build it all that there is plenty of room" (202), and presented in "A CLOTH" by the same kind of "logical" contradiction that Stein's quantifiers uphold: "Enough cloth is plenty and more, more is almost enough for that and besides if there is no more spreading is there plenty of room for it. Any occasion shows the best way" (169).

In keeping with this egalitarian instinct, Stein's third umbrella still life is simply catalogued as "AN UMBRELLA." Stein exploits the resources of the indefinite article, here and elsewhere, to announce the disindividualized nature of the type figure she will show. With the attachment to Mildred no longer in a privileged position (though the old-fashioned sensibility engendered by "handsome" and "right" encourages the trace of that former tradition to function), the mounted umbrella offers the rationale for its existence in the terms of its composition: "Coloring high means that the strange reason is in front not more in front behind. Not more in front in peace of the dot" (171). That "strange reason" materializes linguistically, as terms that define spatial relations appear confused, much as translucent and opaque planes interact in Cubist canvases. This indeterminancy is deliberate, for it shows that when the single point loses its authority to harmonize foreground and background relations the integrity of each compositional unit is assured by the flat plane itself.

Stein's fascination with the freedom and mobility possible within her medium by turns of phrase and structure is particularly evident in the constructive and descriptive roles assigned the "free play" of the signifier in "EATING" (196). Stein tests her ability to express her conception of eating by examining a variety of forms that are so consumed—the "stated flower" or "read butter" of other still life compositions. The resemblances to metabolic processes negotiated by the disappearance and the reappearance of the letter *h* can be defined as metaplasmic displacements, permutations in the "visible writing" that function quite like the "many many lead games" in Gris's *The Table*.

In the Gris, the headline of the lead article that the painter attaches to the pictorial surface announces "*LE VRAI ET LE FAUX*," a partial heading that appropriately comments on the still life that explores levels of iconicity through a provocative variety of illusionistic devices. At the extreme right, another newspaper pasting amplifies the commentary through the terms of the upper half of a man's head, whose face disappears beneath an opaque plane topped by the word fragment *dispar* (disappeared or disappearance), a reference, it would seem, to the "missing person" who "vanishes" in the pictorial environment as well. These Cubist jokes, as Rosenblum defines them ("Typography of Cubism," 62), work together with the fragmentation and bent axis of "*LE JU*" as verbal cues or turns of phrase (highlighted by the trompe l'oeil key "in" and the opened text "on" the table) that debate the theme of "VRAI" and "FAUX" within the composition. The quality of "linguistic strangeness" that these visual permutations sustain enables new meanings to be established, and those "breakages" are equally a part of the plastic values themselves: the broken angel of "*LE JU*," repeated through the pipe arm, through the angle of the curved diagonal upon which the base of the fractured U rests, and through the more abstract terms of the scrolled form adjacent to the lips of the pipe base whose own aperture echoes the format of the missing person in the composite drawing illustrated in the newspaper clipping.

The metaplasmic "lead" game in "EATING" is engaged by Stein's use of "pie" or mixed type and is displayed through the first three terms of the composition: "Eat ting, eating" (193). The reader hunts for the absent *h* in "ting" and observes the way in which the artificial boundary enforced in "eat ting" is consumed in the "eating"—typographical quirks that enact the still-life subject. This kind of rhetoric is as much a part of Gris's *Table* with its doubled cigarettes and lost *O* in "*LE JU*": it appears as a pale figure partially concealed by the tilted *U* in front of it. And as forms are mixed in *The Table,* so too sounds are garbled in "EATING," as if the "grand old man" (of letters) were talking with his mouth full, so that words lose their familiar or "near ring" (i.e., "ting"). An array of partial resolutions begin to assert themselves in Stein's composition. Perhaps the "old man" meant to say "never cry wolf," and "bay" and "bewildered neck" are fragments of some lame defense (the virtuoso performances of Gris's bent axes) about a hunting accident he authored, witnessed, or overheard. Or perhaps, as another shot in the dark (an image bolstered by the collaboration of "soluble burst" and "not a near ring"), the story he's telling is about someone who didn't lose his head and commit some fatal error in judgment. And then, given other potential values stored in "soluble burst" and the actual semantic permutations, perhaps the bubble has burst for the teller and he is literally and metaphorically eating his own words because the authenticity of what he's said has been challenged. In a related way, we may be talking here of departures from canons of linguistic orthodoxy suggested by the semantic lead "re," where "not really any such bay" may refer to traditional bay windows or holes in the wall that the open window sanctioned in art, a tradition now "burst" by the apparent grammatical disruptions of this linguistic experiment. Stein's terms by their very indeterminancy engage the kind of detective work that Gris's abridged reference to his missing subject encourages. Latent meanings are amplified but never explicitly defined.

The second paragraph of Stein's "EATING" shows the absence of many of the clues that materialize the subject's appearance in more conventional writing: "Is it so, is it so, is it so, is it so is it so is it so." That what is placed in doubt ("Is it so") may be actually true ("so it is") is secured by the nature of the line itself, which can run forward and backward to confound the boundaries between true and false elements, much as Gris's visual and verbal fragments challenge a single "reading" of his composition. Stein even abandons the comma in the middle of the polysyndetic construction to signal this potential reversal. Further, this second paragraph seems to allow for a number of simultaneous leads that might define "EATING's" puzzling story values. "Is it so a noise to be" may, for example, catalogue the sounds swallowed by the "old man" who quotes the "old say" itself to score the moral of his tale. Or, the line may index a second and related layer of meaning where errors in tense like "is it a leading are been" signify the unique temporal conditions of narrative structures that rely on retrospective time frames—the classic tale told by the aged story-teller about some intrigue in his youth.

Stein's commitment to "the time-sense in the composition" allows for possibilities that a fixed attachment to "the time-sense of the composition" would define as inadmissable evidence.

Throughout *Tender Buttons,* Stein deliberately makes figures that negate the usual temporal zoning laws to construct "exact" reproductions of how the mind knows what it knows. The "whole section" therefore must be shown in "one season" ("Rooms," 206). In attempting this kind of synchronicity by refusing to simply corroborate the time and space sense that functions outside the compositional frame, Stein juxtaposes seemingly incompatible values that reveal underlying likenesses. These are intellectual connections that the mind makes to disclose patterns of order that go beyond accidental differences. In the second "A BOX," Stein's narrator signals this shift by establishing parallels based on the nominative case—the noun-forming properties of the suffix "-ness"— to make contact with the birth metaphor for the making of art: "Out of kindness comes redness and out of rudeness comes rapid same question, out of an eye comes research, out of selection comes painful some cattle" (163). The narrator synchronizes references to grammatical case, generic type, and syntactical, medical and livestock operations to inbreed images that host the gestation process, which applies equally to the churning of milk into cheese ("a white way of being round") as it does to the calligraphic strategies that deliver a new compositional entity.

These are the same kinds of rhetorical strategies that are made use of in the second paragraph of "EATING" to generate the simultaneous leads whose parallelism is orchestrated by the metastatic processes they share. The seemingly abrupt shift in the third paragraph paradoxically returns the reader to the "scene of the crime," so to speak, insofar as crime refers equally to the fragmentation of narrative continuities generated by insistence on the flat plane, and the idea of retribution—perhaps even rehabilitation—evoked by "eel" and the "cost" of confinement or prison "stretches." The cockneyed "eel," when combined with the linguistic ready-made "Pease Porridge Hot," reinstates the missing or garbled *h* of the opening "ting" and on one level we may speculate that the "grand old man," his prison term at an end, is back in circulation—perhaps even an unchanged heel.

My rationale for defining Stein's allusion to the nursery rhyme here as a linguistic ready-made comes from the fact that Stein emphasizes the compositional properties of the artifact itself rather than simply the thematic parallel. In other words, Stein's line, "no no pea no pea cool, no pea cool cooler, no pea cooler," draws attention to playfulness that distinguishes the nursery rhyme format as a potential correlative for the narrator's own calligraphic exuberance. Yet the linguistic strangeness of Stein's unique adaptation of the quotation also maintains the foreignness of the material that is borrowed. In this way the ready-made as linguistic artifact asserts the reality of the flat surface of the composition it enters as well as that from which it comes. While Joyce's facsimiles are so completely assimilated by his story values, Stein's ready-mades preserve their autonomy and that of the new artifact they help support. The "no pea cooler" functions as both a constructive and a descriptive value, much as Gris's newspaper fragments collaborate to present the picture plane and the investigative theme. Stein's "old say" is metastasized in colloquial terms ("pea cooler") by the still-life subject while the ready-made's own title with its potentially absent *l* emphasizes the typographical strategies that allow *h* to be at large in Stein's composition. We are led by association to consider the salutory effects of the fictive entity being established (the "land cost in stretches"), and to the curious mixture of truth and falsehood that distinguishes the "pea cooler" nature of the tall tale ("stretches"), the story-teller, and the intrusive narrator who overhears the scene.

Appropriately, the thematic center of "Pease Porridge Hot" relates to the matter of individual taste that ought to be respected insofar as "some like it hot" and "some like it cold." That doctrine of coequality directs the multivalence of Stein's rhetorical planes much as it does the stylistic multiplicity of Gris's *Table*. The linguistic key—Stein's "pie"-"bolsters" a variety of semantic possibilities and each one exposes the tension between reference and compositional game that is central to the interplay of representational and nonrepresentational values in Synthetic Cubism as well. The feat of the "old man" is displayed once again in the fourth paragraph when the *h* concealed earlier materializes as a new linguistic entity in "heating" and the actuality of that metastatic transformation is enacted syntactically: "Eating he heat eating, he heat it eating he eat it heating. He heat eating." The intrigue of what he cooks up (and all puns are intended) compensates for the loss of the old typeface. This is precisely the point that Stein emphasizes in her discussion of the crime story within "Portraits and Repetition," where the "moment to moment" realization of the subject creates the interest. This shift from the "what is happening" or from a "description of what" someone is "doing" (*Look at Me Now*, 123, 110) materializes in "EATING" because Stein connects with the process-quality of the story that is realized and insists that her narrator literally live in the looking and listening without trying to reduce the details that materialize to established frames of reference.

The fifth paragraph of the still life offers yet another illustration of "old say" by recovering the echoic root of "owl,"[58] a sound released by Stein's foregrounding of the typographic strategy itself within the piece: "owls owls such as pie, bolsters." The reader is led back into the flat plane of the still life, redirected to the "not a near ring" reverberations that are lisped in "ting," in the fractured aphorism "a grand old man said roof and never never re," and encouraged by the semantic freedom that is not held at "bay" because authorized modes of presentation are refused top billing. And the theme and technique of the metastasized "old say[s]" continue in the final two paragraphs in the piece where Stein liberates a collocation of nursery rhyme fragments that pull the owl and released howl of the fifth paragraph into the narrative structure of "The Little Boy" "who went into a barn" and was frightened away by an owl; accent the tale of the naughty boy who threw pussy down a well in "Ding, Dong, Bell"; and highlight the "bad guy" motif of Georgie Porgie's own "pudding and pie" transgressions. These fictive occasions metonymically and synecdochally review acts of intrusion that parallel the dubious character of the tale, the tale-teller and the frame narrator in "EATING"—a dubiousness that is structural as well as thematic.

While "George" might be a missing person according to the expectations of a naturalistic mode of presentation, his presence "is amass[ed]" by the suggestive and cumulative power of the various signs the narrator assembles to speak her "specimen" ("MUTTON," 182). Stein conceives her character in terms of volume exhibited on the flat plane just as she conceives of narrative in terms of interactive spatial relations realized in landscape terms (the "dining is west" of the still life that prefaces "EATING") to demonstrate how these basic elements can be articulated by her medium's basic conventions. As "any example of an edible apple in," rearranged by the type figures of the linguistic surface, Stein's character drawing in "EATING" offers a remarkable parallel with Cubist art.

We are led with a commanding sense of the applicability of this analogy to Picasso's *Kahnweiler,* flattened by the resources of the picture plane, and to a wide range of restaurant still lifes in Cubism like Gris's *Figure Seated in a Cafe* (fig. 51), where the supposedly central character is concealed behind *Le Matin* and a glass of beer. Gris's commentary on the fugitive nature of his human subject is directed by his fidelity to the actual disposition of the scene he experiences. The story highlighted in the newspaper clipping, *"Bertillonnage: On ne truquera plus les oeuvres d'art,"* alludes to the famous French criminologist Alphonse Bertillon, who had devised a fingerprinting system to prevent forgeries, the kind of forgery that would take place, for example, if Gris, to satisfy our appetite for appearances, showed more of the human figure than his adherence to compositional principles would allow. This is exactly the argument the narrator offers in "Rooms" to invite other standards of verisimilitude to function, standards that defy our expectations about time ("all the time there is a single climate" [203]) and space ("Please a pease and a cracker and a wretched use of summer" [205]):

> The sensible decision was that notwithstanding many declarations and more music, not even notwithstanding the choice and a torch and a collection . . . notwithstanding Europe and Asia and being overbearing, not even notwithstanding an elephant and a strict occasion, not even withstanding more cultivation and some seasoning, not even with drowning and with the ocean being encircling, not even with more likeness and any cloud, not even with terrific sacrifice of pedestrianism and a special resolution, not even more likely to be pleasing. The care with

Figure 51.   Juan Gris, *Man in a Cafe*, 1914
Collage and oil on canvas, 39″ × 28¼″.
(Acquavella Galleries, New York)

which the rain is wrong and the green is wrong and the white is wrong, the care with which there is a chair and plenty of breathing. (206)

While DeKoven, for example, argues that in a piece like "EATING" "multivalent signification is sacrificed to the disruption of conventional language" (*A Different Language,* 82), Stein's speaker draws "George" out according to the dimensions of her medium because in doing so she can challenge our instinct for mimesis in the traditional sense of copy and exhibit how "very agreeable" it is "to hear a voice and to see all the signs of that expression" ("Rooms," 201). What Stein emphasizes with precision throughout *Tender Buttons* is the metamorphosis that the linguistic surfaces can authorize to metastasize the homologous relationship among superficially distinct signs. Stein's narrator closes the homilectics of her subject's esthetic principles by striking a "match" in "Rooms" between culinary and calligraphic art forms to bring into relation a "magnificent asparagus" and "a fountain" (206). In doing so, she displays the character of the correspondences that can be built by attending with "care" to a doctrine of coequality ("there is incredible justice") and a philosophy of total representation ("there is incredible . . . likeness" [206]).

One of the most intriguing demonstrations of these principles comes at the close of the first section of the *Tender Buttons* gallery in "THIS IS THE DRESS, AIDER." Although this section is defined by many critics as a clandestine reference to Stein's homosexuality to authorize a specific connection between "Aider" and Stein's *Ida*/Alice, one can remove the exclusiveness that such a reading of the still life would impose by discovering the extent to which "DRESS, AIDER" participates in the metastatic pattern that defines the transformative intrigue of each still-life composition. That participation is secured by the variety of dressmaking figures created to show the esthetic parallel between the line on the canvas and the "long line" in print that "distinguishes" the thing made in "A LONG DRESS" (167).

In each clothing still life, the configuration focuses on exposing the seams—examining the principles of composition that direct the way the piece is made. In exercising this prerogative, the speaker often turns to the "bottom nature" analogy to bring what she defines in "Rooms" as the author's behind-the-door presence and the showing of how "the back is furnished" (202) into graphic relation. Indeed, the clothing metaphors—the "any so" and "undercoat" in "A SHAWL" (175), the "tiny seat" that is "messed" in "TAILS" (187), the "show a stitch of ten," which literally loses time in "jam it not plus more sit in when" in "A LITTLE CALLED PAULINE" (173), and the exhibiting of the "top to covering" in "A SUBSTANCE IN A CUSHION" (162)—consistently appear in still lifes that make contact with Picasso's chair-caning and seated figures. Referenced is everything from the chair-caning signature piece of *collage,* whose technique is amplified in a number of canvases that play with mock framing and signature illusions, to the variety of disindividualized women seated in arm-chairs presaged in his 1906 Stein portrait.

Stein's studies of cloth allow calligraphic, graphic, and plastic planes of meaning to interpenetrate to expand the implications of the Cubist analogy. In pieces leading toward "THIS IS THE DRESS, AIDER," like "SUPPOSE AN EYES," the narrator raises the possibility of sharing the author's "really splendid address[es]" (166) with the discriminating reader who will enter the "time-sense of the composition": "All the seats are needing blackening. A white dress is in sign. A soldier a real soldier has a worn lace a worn lace of different sizes that is to say if he can read, if he can read he is a size to show shutting up twenty-four" (175). The parallel between graphic and verbal means is mediated by the term "blackening," which is the synecdochal figure Stein uses to refer-ence an etching ground, by the "collapse in rubbed purr," an image that recurs in various guises to distinguish replication of the given from the creation of the new (the shift occurs linguistically as the more conventional cat is exchanged for "purr" to designate the spoken character of the "specimen"), and by the word "size," whose plurisignation multiplies to include the application of glazes, the patterning of cloth, the ranking of military figures, the ordering, preparing and rationing of food and drink, the manufacturing of materials, and the meas-urement of linguistic artifacts (and, by extension, the instrument that measures pearls—Stein's own unique tender buttons). The "sizer of talks" in "A SHAWL" makes things that are tied together in a "strange" way and the "green" "string" (the oblique, backdoor, hidden string of associations released in the prose to hold the pearls of the volume in place) spreads a language of "suppose" through the still lifes that lead toward the final selection in "Objects." In "IT WAS BLACK, BLACK TOOK" the invention ("wheel") is tied with brown bale twine (a size that evokes the roped bail-shaped frame of Picasso's chair caning *col-lage*), and makes a new ink drawing that does not take its imprint from the "pearl" traditionally cast before swine: "no past pearl pearl goat" (176).

In "THIS IS THE DRESS, AIDER" (176) one feels the triumph of the Napoleonic struggle of Stein and of the aide who soldiers on behalf of her author's esthetic principles. (The military analogy becomes central to the Picasso-Napoleon analogy in the second portrait of Picasso, "If I Told Him: A Com-pleted Portrait of Picasso" and appears in the patrician and "special resolution" of "Rooms" [206]). The complicated web of interactive planes campaigns in "DRESS" to join various semantic leads: the "bale" of "INK" releases the bail of "Jack and Jill," the "ear-rings" bred in "BOOK" bring the equivalence among compositional units in "sister and sister and a flower and a flower" to emphasize the parallel in "Jack and Jill," the sizing techniques of "SUPPOSE" lead to the destruction of the linguistic ready-made itself, the "laid climb" in "A SHAWL" synchronizes two- and three-dimensional values and anticipates Stein's pasturing of the "meadowed king," the "hull" of "IT WAS BLACK" brings the focus on outer coverings into the broken crown of the nursery rhyme in "DRESS" and focuses attention on the agrammatized "whow," which in turn synchronizes two- and three-dimensional values by highlighting the inventiveness of the new linguistic entity as well as the process of transformation itself.

Stein destroys the appearance of the "Jack and Jill" "old say" in a number of ways in "DRESS" to express the reality of the linguistic surface. Taking the colloquial slur literally to make "jack in" visualizes its spoken character. Her interest in the type figure and action leads to the addition of the indefinite article of "a jack." To dramatize the fact that she is playing with a linguistic artifact to release new possibilities, she collapses the boundaries that usually hold the "old say's" sequence in place so that "a jack in kill her" metonymically signs the whole plot. This kind of ellipsis flattens the climax so that "makes a meadowed king" achieves synchronic effects. By stopping the running line of the rhyme ("stop the muncher, muncher munchers"), Stein touches on another possibility, "makes a to let," and seats (toilet) the "old" within a novel arrangement. The match that is established between "DRESS" and "Jack and Jill" achieves its parallel by inviting the reader to become less fixed on the particular chronology of a particular literary event and to observe how characters can be drawn out when stories about "breakages" in the most inclusive sense are told. The referential axis of language must function for the difference between naturalistic and nonnaturalistic techniques to be made visible ("whow"), just as correspondence to surface appearance is engaged even as it is denied priority in Cubist compositions. It is this preoccupation with illustrating the compositional themes and techniques that defines the "camouflage" art in *Tender Buttons*. As Stein signs alternate patterns of correspondence between language and reality by revealing their hidden metastatic correlatives, the effects she materializes secure the vitality of the Cubist analogy in this phase of her experimental writing.

Stein's own image of the composer in *Tender Buttons* as "an elephant beaten with candy" releases a Cubist analogy, one that, I think, is corroborated by the rhetorical strategies she develops to realize and exhaust resemblance in her medium. "The painter," Braque said, "knows things by sight, the writer who knows them by name, profits by a prejudice in his favor."[59] It is a prejudice Stein takes advantage of by exploring the indexical resources of the verbal sign, working to release not only established patterns of correspondence that assert the old visual terms but also to liberate the more oblique references and associations that are stored within the names of things to highlight the underlying continuities sponsored in the naming act itself and extended by the intellectual history of its occasions: "Language as a real thing is not imitation either of sounds or colors or emotions it is an intellectual recreation and there is no possible doubt about it and it is going to go on being that as long as humanity is anything. So every one must stay with language their language that has come to be spoken and written and which has in it all the history of its intellectual recreation."[60]

My analysis of critical discussions of a parallel Cubist dispensation in the works of Joyce and Stein reveals the kind of care that must be taken to ensure that the correlatives posited actually confront the reality of the Cubist esthetic and technique. Often a period concept approach to the movement imbues it with notions of relativity, multiplicity, and nonreferentiability that are incompatible with its affirmation of the autonomy and knowability of external matter. Referencing the techniques of discontinuity that Joyce relies on to create the tension between sequential and radial readings of events in *Ulysses*'s "Wandering Rocks" does not guarantee the legitimacy of a Cubist "narrative" technique, for the concept in itself assumes cinematic values that do not function within Cubism's composite time. So too, Joyce's pseudo-*collage* technique in "Aeolus," while offering a facsimile of the ready-made, does not exhibit a parallel illustration of the tension between extrapictorial and plastic frames of reference asserted by the presence of the actual *collage* and *collé* element in Synthetic canvases. While Joyce disturbs the naturalistic surface by complicating its appearance, his distortions do not engage the kind of challenge to illusions of coherence, density, mass, gravity, and spatial relation integral to the disposition of the Cubist "destruction."

My analysis of Stein's middle-phase portraiture, in contrast, demonstrates the significance of the Cubist analogy in her compositions. Stein's own revaluation of the priority that optically derived notions of resemblance assume through naturalistic points of view materializes in the variety of rhetorical techniques she develops to show alternate patterns of correspondence between the verbal sign and the thing signified. Consistently, these matches are grounded in her affirmation of the conceptual nature of the mind's knowledge of external reality and her split descriptions are designed to bring its grasp of the primary, secondary, and tertiary qualities of her still life subjects into dynamic relation. The interplay among those alternate patterns of resemblance is negotiated by Stein's metastatic theme in *Tender Buttons,* while her fidelity to "the time-sense in the composition" imbues the still life with synchronic effects as simultaneous semantic leads interpenetrate to display her "specimen." And while words are not paint, and therefore the bending of the referential axis of language and the breaking of the usual patterns of indexical relation create a more complicated ambiguity in Stein's prose, her agreement "errors" exhibit in their terms the dynamic between descriptive and constructive values that defines Cubist art.

Conclusion

In attempting to identify the kinds of verbal strategies that might function as correlatives for pictorial techniques, one gains a clearer perception of the potential use of a comparative method in literary criticism. Conversely, one becomes sensitive to the kinds of abuse that can result when pictorial terminology is applied to the verbal arts without sufficient regard given to actual nature and function of the terms appropriated. In arguing for affinities between Modernist literature and an Impressionist perspective, for example, critics have often ignored Impressionist art's continuing fidelity to the naturalistic surface and photographable realities, and have therefore imbued the Impressionist optic and the naivety of its recording eye with subjective values that do not obtain. Not only have Impressionist canvases been selected to adumbrate essentially non-Impressionist principles of vision in narrative works, but often the actual nature of the Impressionist surface that verbal artists really do and can sustain in their own media has been overlooked.

When a comparative method is misapplied because the basic conventions of the media are not respected, it can lead to an error as serious as that which evolves when Cubist methods of construction are used to analyze Joyce's techniques of narrative discontinuity in *Ulysses*. This misapplication leads critics to define the illusion of simultaneity that Joyce achieves through the fragmentation and multiplication of views in terms of Analytical Cubism's optical synthesis of disparate aspects of their subject. In asserting this correspondence, critics tend to disregard the source of intrigue that is developed as Joyce *approximates* a spatial illusion in an essentially diachronic form. Further, to make the analogy work, critics demand that the actual synthesis that does take place in the synchronic medium be read in narrative terms.

When qualitative differences are acknowledged and the pictorial context clearly defined, the interart analogies that do develop can be mutually clarifying. Post-Impressionism's challenge to the open window as the prevailing perspective convention in the plastic arts, for example, takes the form of a reunification of both optic and haptic sensibilities. This reintegration, which is indicative of the plastic artist's emphasis upon the two-dimensional reality of the canvas itself, finds its correlative in certain Modernist writers who recognize, as well, the self-reflexive character of their art form and who deliberately amplify the haptic dimensions of the landscapes they create to indicate that visible and surface realities alone no longer define their notions of verisimilitude. At the same time, Cubism's continuing development of techniques that will display how forms are revealed by adaptation to the picture plane can find a correlative in the strategies Stein designs to realize alternate patterns of resemblance by attending to the material resources of her medium's basic conventions.

These analogies simply suggest that certain linguistic and plastic phenomena share a common orientation and correlative technique and that an understanding of that correspondence depends upon the careful annotation of the terms of reference used to establish the analogy. With this framework intact, it might be equally interesting to explore the apparent fusion of surreal and real elements that seem to work within Joyce's "Philosophical Brothel"[1] in the "Circe" chapter of *Ulysses*. Through its extreme refeaturing of the human face and figure, and its haunting integration of cosmic and tragic *grotesquerie,* the chapter seems to provide parallels for the techniques Max Beckmann works with to express his absorption with nightmare and metamorphosis. As Hemingway's hypercorrect telegram style has often been allied with the Superrealistic vision of Post-Expressionist artists like Otto Dix and George Grosz, it might be beneficial to demonstrate those possibilities by examining the techniques of reportage Hemingway employs to realize the postoperative point of view in works like *A Farewell to Arms* and *In Our Time*. If we are to accept that the denotative world collapses in some of Stein's more private performances, it might be interesting to analyze the kind of affinity that may exist between the Surrealist manifesto and form and her work within this context. As Duchamp's *Nude Descending a Staircase* is the canvas that Anaïs Nin suggests as the counterpart for *A Spy in the House of Love,*[2] it might be equally fruitful to explore the way in which Duchamp's chronophotographic technique and disenchantment with Futurism's aggressive modernity can in fact relate to Nin's fascination with the process of reification that affects her own potentially iron maiden Sabina. Finally, the expressive use of the open window, which intensifies the dualism of "here" and "there" that is integral to the dream of lost wholeness in Expressionist art, may find its correlative in Woolf's *The Waves,* where similar themes are realized as a divergence in perspective and where the window is encouraged to disclose alternate realities that bring dream and mythic perspectives to bear upon the historical present.

The method developed here has applicability for poetic forms as well. When one understands the nature of Cubism, for example, one recognizes the pitfalls of assuming a correlation between the symbolic "fragments" that T. S. Eliot's persona has "shored against" his ruin in *The Waste Land* and those collated in Cubist canvases to reveal conceptions of form. In "Modern Art

Techniques in *The Waste Land*," Jacob Korg posits this kind of analogy without realizing that Eliot's symbolic perspective and Picasso's formal one lead to antithetical ends even though an analectic technique may be common to both created realities.[3] In "T. S. Eliot and the Cubists," David Tomlinson similarly argues that Picasso's *Woman in a Chemise Seated in an Armchair* provides a paradigm for the second section of *The Waste Land* because Eliot, though "with more rigorously philosophical intent, has built up his conceptual picture by combining fragmented memories of great seductions in literature. . . . These are overlaid and intercut in precisely the same manner as in Picasso's picture, except Eliot's combining memory is not that of a single human observer but of a whole cultural tradition."[4] Actually, the distinctions Tomlinson himself raises indicate the extent to which Eliot's symbolic fragments and allusive method are at odds with rather than in keeping with Cubist frames of analysis.

It is not enough to base one's sense of correspondences upon a similar technique of juxtaposition, unless that technique serves a similar function in both media under comparison. Not all juxtapositions are Cubist in intention. If the Analytical synthesis in Cubist art is to have any meaning in interart analogies, one cannot read into its processes of destruction and construction symbolic and thematic values that violate the cerebral and more dispassionate nature of the Cubist artist's delineation of the mundane objects in his immediate environment.

For the same reason, one has to reevaluate Benamou's claim that Wallace Stevens's "Thirteen Ways of Looking at a Blackbird" engages the "multiple perspective of the cubist, the dance round the object,"[5] just as one must clarify the way in which the term *Impressionism* is used by W. V. O'Connor in his discussion of Stevens's poetry. While Benamou, on the one hand, ignores the spatial form of the actual Cubist synthesis, O'Connor, on the other, infuses Impressionism's fascination with surface appearances with the ennui that is intrinsic to the *fin de siècle* estheticism and exoticism of Pater and Aubrey Beardsley. Interestingly, O'Connor opens his discussion by noting that while "*Impressionism* is a tricky word in literary criticism," he has "no intention of trying to define it," as he explores Stevens's Americanized Impressionism.[6] The kind of confusion that O'Connor's actual blending of partial definitions therefore creates epitomizes the shortcomings of this kind of cavalier attitude.

When terms are clearly defined and the metaphoric nature of the analogies consistently acknowledged, a comparative method for poetry has positive value. Thus, for example, Bram Dijkstra discusses the essential differences between the poetry of Stevens and William Carlos Williams by exploring the divergence between them in terms of their alternate responses to the concrete reality that artists like Duchamp and Braque make contact with in their canvases.[7] Henry Sayre's concentrated focus on the way in which the plastic point of view intrinsic to Duchamp's revaluations of ready-made realities in *Urinal* might relate to

Williams's imaginative transvaluation of the commonplace in a poem like "The Red Wheelbarrow" is equally effective because Sayre's perspective is informed and his analysis specific.[8]

With this sense of specificity and exactitude engaged, a comparative method could perhaps clarify the sense of the nonhuman that functions in Robinson Jeffers's poetry, by seeing to what extent his renunciation of a human perspective in his realization of landscape forms coincides with the techniques Expressionist artists use to actualize what Franz Marc describes in "How Does a Horse See the World?" as "the predicate of living things."[9] One might explore, as well, the relationship that seems to be suggested between the plastic point of view that functions within concrete poetry and the "narrative" impulse that develops in Klee's calligraphic compositions.

The parameters established within this study provide a clearer indication of how these and other analogies might be developed. Mediating the problems that arise when inadequately conceived definitions for pictorial terms and concepts are applied to Modernist narratives encourages us to respect the integrity of the plastic traditions from which these terms derive. Exploring the applicability of more precise definitions leads to a deeper understanding of both media and to a more complete appreciation of the possibilities an interartistic method can sustain. The aim of this study has been "mutual illumination." In working toward it, the potential benefit and intrigue of an *ut pictura poesis* point of view becomes more systematically extended. So too, our experience of the shared techniques and realities of compositions that embody this perspective becomes more effectively grounded.

Notes

Introduction

1. Ulrich Weisstein, "Literature and the Visual Arts," *Interrelations of Literature*, eds. Jean-Pierre Baricelli and Joseph Gibaldi (New York: MLA of America, 1982), 266–67, 258.

2. Elizabeth Abel, "Redefining the Sister Arts: Baudelaire's Response to the Art of Delacroix," *Critical Inquiry,* 6 (Spring 1980): 363.

3. Alastair Fowler, "Periodization and Interart Analogies," *New Literary History,* vol. 3, no. 3 (Spring 1972): 506.

4. John Ruskin, "Of the Pathetic Fallacy," vol. 5 of *The Works of John Ruskin,* eds. E. T. Cook and Alexander Wedderbrown (London: George Allen, 1904), 209.

5. Jean Hagstrum, *The Sister Arts: The Tradition of Literary Pictorialism and English Poetry from Dryden to Gray* (Chicago: University of Chicago Press, 1958), 11–12.

Chapter 1

1. Maria Elizabeth Kronegger, *Literary Impressionism* (New Haven, Conn.: College and University Press, 1973), 24. Further references to Kronegger's own ideas will be noted parenthetically in the text.

2. Helmut A. Hatzfeld, *Literature through Art* (New York: Oxford University Press, 1952), 166.

3. Hermann Bahr, *Expressionismus* (Munchen: Delphin Verlag, 1918) 67, qtd. in and trans. by Kronegger, 24 n. 5.

4. Michel Décaudin, "Poésie impressionniste et poésie symboliste," *Cahiers de L'Association Internationale des Etudes Française* 12 (1960): 132–42, qtd. in and trans. by Kronegger, 27 n. 21.

5. Lionello Venturi, *Painting and Painters: How to Look at a Picture from Giotto to Chagall* (New York: Charles Scribner's Sons, 1945), 152.

6. R.-M. Albérès, "Plongées dans les profondeurs de l'impressionnisme," *Histoire de roman moderne* (Paris: Albin Michel, 1962), 186, qtd. in and trans. by Kronegger, 40 n. 14. Albérès observes:

   > Multiple, swirling around, made of luminous dust suspended in nothingness, impressionist reality is not *told,* nor is it even *described* at all. Words and men's meagre gestures, their

hesitations and arabesques, scarcely indicate several lines on the surface of that nebula of reality that is "Life." Bewildered by a new perspective, the reader is thus transported into a molton universe. . . . Far from being an objective vision, impressionism is in effect a plunge into the consciousness.

7.   E. H. Gombrich, *Art and Illusion: A Study in the Psychology of Pictorial Representation,* *Bollingen Series* 35 (Princeton: Princeton University Press, 1969), 14.

8.   Georges Rivière, qtd. in Venturi, "Impressionist Style," *Impressionism in Perspective,* ed. Barbara Ehrlich White (Englewood Cliffs, N.J.: Prentice-Hall, 1978), 108.

9.   John Rewald, *The History of Impressionism,* 4th rev. ed. (New York: The Museum of Modern Art, 1973), 114.

10.   Wylie Sypher, "The Impressionist Experiment," *Rococo to Cubism in Art and Literature* (New York: Random House, 1960), 177.

11.   Kenneth Clark, *Landscape into Art,* paperback ed. (1949; rpt. London: John Murray, 1979), 150–61.

12.   John Ruskin, "Letter 1: On First Practice," *The Elements of Drawing,* Vol. 15 of *The Works of John Ruskin* (London: George Allen, 1904), note to par. 5, 27; hereafter cited as "E of D."

13.   Bernard Dunstan, *Painting Methods of the Impressionists* (London: Pitman, 1976), 42.

14.   Jules Laforgue, qtd. in Linda Nochlin, *Impressionism and Post-Impressionism, 1874–1904: Sources and Documents,* ed. H. W. Janson (Englewood Cliffs, N.J.: Prentice-Hall, 1966). In the 1883 statement Laforgue observes: "The Impressionist sees everything not with dead whiteness, but rather with a thousand struggling colors of rich prismatic decomposition."

15.   Hans Phatte, *Les Impressionnistes,* trans. Marianne Duval-Valentin (Paris: Arthaud, 1962), 154.

16.   Arnold Hauser, "Impressionism," *The Social History of Art* (London: Routledge & Kegan Paul, 1951), 872–73.

17.   Claude Monet, qtd. in Diane Kelder, *The French Impressionists and Their Century* (London: Pall Mall Press, 1970), 63–64.

18.   Jean-Luc Daval, *Journal de l'impressionnisme* (Geneve: Editions d'Art Albert Skira, 1973), 136. Translations in the text are mine.

19.   Walter Pater, "Leonardo da Vinci: Homo Minister et Interpres Naturae," *The Renaissance: Studies in Art and Poetry* (London: Macmillan, 1910), 98–129.

20.   Joris-Karl Huysmans, 'L'exposition des indépendants en 1880." Reprinted in *L'art moderne,* (Paris, 1883), 90 and qtd. in Oscar Reustervärd, "Journalists (1876–1883) on 'Violettomania,' " *Impressionism in Perspective,* 41.

21.   Jean Guiguet, *Virginia Woolf and Her Works,* trans. Jean Stewart (London: The Hogarth Press, 1965), 31.

22.   Sheldon Cheney, *A Primer of Modern Art* (New York: Liveright Publishing Corporation, 1966), 79.

23.   Jack F. Stewart, "Impressionism in the Early Novels of Virginia Woolf," *Journal of Modern Literature,* vol. 9, no. 2 (1982): 247.

24. Bruce Johnston, "Conrad's Impressionism and Watt's 'Delayed Decoding,'" *Conrad Revisited: Essays for the Eighties*, ed. Ross C. Murfin (University of Alabama: Alabama University Press, 1985), 66. While supporting a parallel misconception about the nature of Impressionist realism, Patrick Brantlinger offers this alternative in "*Heart of Darkness:* Anti-Imperialism, Racism, or Impressionism?": Conradian impressionism discloses an "'impressionistic' deviousness of art and language" that betrays the "moral bankruptcy" of Conrad's supposedly "anti-imperialistic message" (*Criticism*, vol. 27, no. 4 [1985]: 374–83). The critical argument which depends upon this erroneous correlation between Impressionism and the phenomenological novel appears as well in Paul B. Armstrong's "The Hermeneutics of Literary Impressionism: Interpretation and Reality in James, Conrad, and Ford": "As they play with the workings of representation, the literary impressionists explore how we make reality by interpreting it. Their narrative experiments challenge our sense of reality and lead us on a journey of discovery into the mysteries of how we create and construe meaning" (*Centennial Review*, vol. 27, no. 4 [1983]: 244–69).

25. David Stouck, "Willa Cather and the Impressionist Novel," *Critical Essays on Willa Cather*, ed. John J. Murphy (Boston: G. K. Hall, 1984), 54–63. In "A Study in Contrasts: Impressionistic Perspectives of Ántonia and Lena Lingard in Cather's *My Ántonia*," Edward J. Piacentino relies on a comment Cather makes herself in "The Novel Demeuble" to substantiate his Impressionist analogy (*Studies in the Humanities*, vol. 12 (June 1985): 39–44). Rather than confirming this possibility, Cather's remark demonstrates the extent to which she departs from an Impressionist perspective" as she exhorts younger writers to "attempt to break away from mere verisimilitude," and to follow "the development of modern painting" and "interpret imaginatively the material and social investiture of their characters" (Cather, "The Novel Demeuble," *Willa Cather on Writing: Critical Studies on Writing as an Art* [New York: Alfred A. Knopf, 1949], 40).

26. Roger Fry, *Transformations: Critical and Speculative Essays on Art* (London: Chatto and Windus, 1926), 218.

27. Fry, *Vision and Design* (1920; rpt. Harmondsworth, Middlesex: Penguin Books, 1961), 223.

28. Virginia Woolf, "Modern Fiction," *Collected Essays, Volume Two* (London: The Hogarth Press, 1966), 106.

29. Woolf, "Jane Austen," *Collected Essays, Volume One* (London: The Hogarth Press, 1966), 153.

30. Hermann Bahr, *Expressionismus*, 67, qtd. in and trans. by Kronegger, 24 n. Bahr sees the Impressionist emphasis upon outer rather than inner vision as the immobilization of the will: "Impressionism is merely the last stage of classical art, it is the completion and the culmination of classicism insofar as it seeks to increase outer vision to the highest extent, to exclude inner vision as much as possible, and steadily to decrease the role of the eye as an instrument directed by independent and spontaneous will, and thus to make man into a completely passive victim of his senses."

31. Michel Benamou, address, "Symposium on Literary Impressionism," *Yearbook of Comparative and General Literature* 17 (1968): 40.

32. Herbert Howarth, address, "Symposium on Literary Impressionism," 41–43.

33. Calvin S. Brown, address, "Symposium on Literary Impressionism," 58.

34. Paul Ilie, address, "Symposium on Literary Impressionism," 47. In his discussion of the difficulties which arise when the verbal artist attempts to record an instantaneous sensorial

impression, Ilie observes:

> A word cannot express a pure and isolated perception without the latter being altered to some degree either by empirical knowledge or by memory. That is, no word can be employed without this involving some form of understanding, and insofar as an intellectual process enters the awareness, the sensory impression becomes deformed. Therefore, language is regarded as the vessel of experience and conceptualization, expressing apperceptions and previously known categories of data. The Impressionist's avowed aesthetic purpose of communicating verbally his instantaneous perception is never achieved, because the latter must, to be expressed, undergo a certain reconstruction.

35. Virginia Woolf, "Kew Gardens," *A Haunted House and Other Short Stories* (London: The Hogarth Press, 1953), 32.

36. Joseph Conrad, Letter to Edward Garnett, Dec. 5, 1897, Letter 213, *Stephen Crane: Letters,* eds. R. W. Stallman and Lilian Gilles (New York: New York University Press, 1960), 155.

37. Conrad, "Stephen Crane: A Note without Dates," *Joseph Conrad: Life and Letters,* vol. 1, ed. G. Jean-Aubry (New York: Doubleday, Page, 1927), 211–12.

38. Conrad, "His War Book," *Last Essays* (New York: Doubleday, Page, 1926), 119–24.

39. Stephen Crane, "War Memories," *Wounds in the Rain: War Stories* (New York: n.p., 1899), 229.

40. James Nagel, *Stephen Crane and Literary Impressionism* (University Park, Penn.: The Pennsylvania State University Press, 1980), 43.

41. Crane, *The Red Badge of Courage: An Authoritative Text, Backgrounds, and Sources Criticism,* eds. Sculley Bradley et al. (New York: W. W. Norton, 1972), 23.

42. Milne Holton, *Cylinder of Vision: The Fiction and Journalistic Writing of Stephen Crane* (Baton Rouge: Louisiana State University Press, 1972), 75–76.

43. Charles C. Walcutt, *American Literary Naturalism, A Divided Stream* (Minneapolis: University of Minnesota Press, 1956), 66–67.

44. Sergio Perosa, "Naturalism and Impressionism in Stephen Crane's Fiction," in *The Red Badge of Courage: An Authoritative Text,* 275.

45. Conrad, Preface to *The Nigger of the "Narcissus." The Nigger of the "Narcissus": An Authoritative Text, Backgrounds and Sources, Reviews and Criticism,* ed. Robert Kimbrough (New York: W. W. Norton, 1979), 145–48.

46. Rodney Rogers, "Stephen Crane and Impressionism," *Nineteenth-Century Fiction* 24 (1969–70): 293, emphasis mine.

47. R. W. Stallman, "Stephen Crane: A Revaluation," in *The Red Badge of Courage: An Authoritative Text,* 197.

48. Michael Fried, *Realism, Writing, Disfiguration: On Thomas Eakins and Stephen Crane* (Chicago: The University of Chicago Press, 1987), 117 n. 21.

49. Donald C. Yelton, *Mimesis and Metaphor: An Inquiry into the Genesis and Scope of Conrad's Symbolic Imagery* (The Hague: Mouton, 1967), 148.

50. Bert Bender, "Hanging Stephen Crane in the Impressionist Museum," *Journal of Aesthetics and Art Criticism* 35 (1976–77): 48, 50.

51. Bender refers the emotional evocativeness of Crane's palette in *The Red Badge of Courage* and "The Open Boat" to the striking similarity of the corpse with its yellow mouth in Crane's chapellike bower and Gauguin's *The Yellow Christ*, and to the similarities between Odilon Redon and Henri (The Douanier) Rousseau and Crane's "strange sometimes primitive shadowings of surrealism" in "The Monster" or "Manacled" (51–52).

52. Woolf, *Jacob's Room, Jacob's Room and The Waves* (New York: Harcourt Brace and World, 1959), 156.

53. Quentin Bell, *Virginia Woolf: A Biography, Volume One: Virginia Stephen 1887–1912* (London: The Hogarth Press, 1972), 157.

54. Woolf, "Street Haunting: A London Adventure," *Collected Essays: Volume 4* (London: The Hogarth Press, 1967), 157.

55. In her discussion of pictorialism in Woolf's *The Waves*, Marianna Torgovnick blurs this distinction by suggesting that the serial approach that Woolf's prologues create to display light's "transforming role" offers a "literary equivalent" for the serial approach in *both* Cézanne and Monet. If, as Torgovnick observes, the symbolic light values in the prologues in *The Waves* function as analogies "of what happens to the characters in the chapters," then Woolf's technique, rather than demonstrating that "the Impressionist and Post-Impressionist idiom [are used] more complexly and with greater insistence" in this novel, show that often an Impressionist effect is redefined by a Post-Impressionist (and Expressionist) vision. *The Visual Arts, Pictorialism, and the Novel: James, Lawrence, and Woolf* (Princeton: Princeton University Press, 1985), 131–32.

56. Jean Alexander, *The Venture of Form in the Novels of Virginia Woolf* (Port Washington, N.Y.: Kennikat Press, 1974), 63.

57. For a more complete discussion of "mirror modes" see Harvena Richter, *Virginia Woolf: The Inward Voyage* (Princeton: Princeton University Press, 1970), 99–112.

58. Woolf, *The Waves, Jacob's Room and The Waves*, 303.

59. Rivière, *L'Impressionniste*, 6 avril 1877, qtd. in Daval, 150. Translation mine.

60. Peter Matthiessen, *Far Tortuga* (New York: Random House, 1975), 26.

61. Barbara Godard argues from this perspective in "El Greco in Canada: Sinclair Ross's *As for Me and My House*," *Mosaic* 14 (Spring 1981): 55–75.

62. Sinclair Ross, *As for Me and My House* (Toronto: McClelland and Stewart Limited, 1941), 154.

63. Charles Gauss, *The Aesthetic Theories of French Artists, 1855 to the Present* (Baltimore: Johns Hopkins Press, 1949), 20–21.

Chapter 2

1. Richard Shone, *The Post-Impressionists* (London: John Calmara & Cooper Ltd., 1979), 9.

2. Clive Bell, *Art* (1928; rpt. New York: C.P. Putnam's Sons, 1958), 22.

3. R. H. Wilenski, *The Modern Movement in Art* (London: Faber and Faber Limited, 1934), 12.

4. John Rewald, *Post-Impressionism from van Gogh to Gauguin*, 3rd. ed. rev. (New York: The Museum of Modern Art, 1978), 7.

5. Emile Verhaeren, *"Le Salon des indépendants,"* *La Nation*, qtd. in Rewald *Post-Impressionism*, 7.

6. Hans Hess, *Pictures as Arguments* (Sussex: Sussex University Press, 1975), 32.

7. Carol Donnell-Kotrozo, *Critical Essays on Postimpressionism* (Philadelphia: The Art Alliance Press, 1983), 27.

8. André Lhote, *La Peinture, le coeur et l'esprit* (Paris: Denoel et Steele, 1933), 13, qtd. in and trans. by Erle Loran, *Cézanne's Composition: Analysis of His Form, with Diagrams and Photographs of His Motifs* (Berkeley and Los Angeles: University of California Press, 1946), 32–33. Lhote's enthusiasm for Cézanne's realization of *perspective vécue* is paralleled by Maurice Merleau-Ponty's recognition and analysis of what he defines as "lived perspective" in his discussion of Cézanne's compositions: "By remaining faithful to the phenomena in his investigations of perspective, Cézanne discovered what recent psychologists have come to formulate: the lived perspective, that which we actually perceive, is not a geometric or a photographic one. . . . It is Cézanne's genius that when the over-all composition of the picture is seen globally, perspectival distortions are no longer visible in their own right but rather contribute, as they do in naturalism, to the impression of an emerging order, of an object in the act of appearing, organizing itself before our eyes" ("Cézanne's Doubt," *Sense and Non- Sense.* trans. Hubert L. Drefus and Patricia Allen Drefus [Evanston: Northwestern University Press, 1964], 14).

9. Paul Gauguin, "Diverses Choses, 1896–1897," an unpublished manuscript qtd. in Hershell B. Chipp, *Theories of Modern Art: A Source Book by Artists and Critics* (Berkeley and Los Angeles: University of California Press, 1968), 65.

10. Meyer Schapiro, "Seurat," *Modern Art Nineteenth and Twentieth Centuries* (New York: George Braziller, 1978), 102.

11. Charles S. Moffett and James N. Wood, Introduction to *Monet's Years at Giverny: Beyond Impressionism* (New York: Harry N. Abrams, 1978), 12.

12. Robert Goldwater, *Symbolism* (New York: Harper & Row, 1979), 2–3.

13. Gauguin, letter to Emile Schuffenecker, Pont-Aven, 14 August 1888, letter 67, *Lettres de Gauguin à sa femme et à ses amis,* ed. Maurice Malengue (Paris: Grasset, 1949), 134.

14. Gauguin, 'Notes Synthetiques," originally published in *Vers et Prose* (Paris) 22 (July-August-September, 1910), qtd. in Chipp, 63.

15. Vincent van Gogh, letter to Emile Bernard, Arles, April 1888, letter B3, *The Complete Letters of Vincent van Gogh,* 3 vols. (Greenwich, Conn.: New York Graphic Society, 1958) 3: 478.

16. Maurice Denis, "Subjective and Objective Deformation, 1909" in *"De Gauguin et de van Gogh au Classicisme,"* *L'Occident* (Paris, May 1909), qtd. in Chipp, 106.

17. Denis, "Definition of Neotraditionism," originally published in *Art et critique* (Paris, 23 and 30 August 1890), qtd. in Chipp, 94.

18. Gauguin, qtd. in Denis, "The Influence of Paul Gauguin," *L'Occident* (Paris, October 1903), qtd. in Chipp, 101.

19. Roger Fry, qtd. in Woolf, *Roger Fry: A Biography* (London: The Hogarth Press, 1940), 177–78.

20. Emile Bernard, *"Une Conversation avec Cézanne," Mercure de France* (Paris, 1921), qtd. in Chipp, 13.

21. Marshall McLuhan, *the Gutenberg galaxy: the making of typographic man* (Toronto: University of Toronto Press, 1962), 43. This concept of reintegration and the synesthetic character of Cézanne's art is one Merleau-Ponty explores in "Cézanne's Doubt": "We *see* the depth, the smoothness, the softness, the hardness of objects; Cézanne even claimed that we see their odor" (15).

22. Georges Seurat, letter to Maurice Beauberg, 28 August 1890, qtd. in Rewald, *Post-Impressionism,* 128.

23. Goldwater, *Gauguin* (New York: Harry N. Abrams, 1928), 28–31.

24. Paul Cézanne, Letter to Emile Bernard, Aix, 12 May 1904, letter 168 *Paul Cézanne: Letters,* ed. John Rewald (London: Cassirer, 1941), 235–36. Emphasis mine.

25. Schapiro, *Vincent van Gogh* (New York: Harry N. Abrams, 1950), 29.

26. This comment is recorded by Bernard in *"Une Conversation avec Cézanne"* and is quoted in Chipp, 12. Linda Nochlin observes in *Impressionism and Post-Impressionism 1874–1904* that many of Bernard's articles on Cézanne reflect his own Symbolist bias. Nochlin notes that this imposition is apparent in those articles "purportedly reporting 'conversations' with the artist—such as the one which appeared in the 1921 Mercure de France" (99) that I am citing here. However, I do not think that Bernard misrepresents Cézanne's sense of the nonrepresentational nature of his medium, the sentiment this statement expresses. In selecting Cézanne's comments as recorded by Bernard in his *Mercure de France* article, and represented in his *Souvenirs sur Paul Cézanne,* Paris, 1925, I am deliberately choosing those which I feel embody Cézanne's awareness of the transforming power of his medium's basic convention, an awareness that is borne out in the determining role the picture plane plays in the creation of space and depth in his canvases.

27. Cézanne, qtd. in Venturi, *Impressionists and Symbolists: Manet, Degas, Monet, Pissarro, Sisley, Renoir, Cézanne, Seurat, Gauguin, Van Gogh, Toulouse-Latrec,* trans. Francis Steegmuller (New York: Charles Scribner's Sons, 1950), 138.

28. H. W. Janson, *History of Art: A Survey of the Major Visual Arts from the Dawn of History to the Present Day,* rev. ed. (New York: Harry N. Abrams, 1969), 506.

29. Gauguin still considers himself an Impressionist at this point. In his study of Gauguin, Goldwater explains the artist's use of this term by observing that as one of the great masters "who built upon Impressionism, Gauguin transformed it the most. Indeed he was the only one who at last set himself in final opposition to it, although to the end he abjured all attempts to endow him with a 'system.' And yet of the four Post-Impressionist masters he was perhaps an Impressionist the longest" (*Gauguin*, 22). Gauguin was allied with the Impressionists from the middle of the 1870s until his trip to Martinique in the spring of 1887. He began his own career under the tutelage of Pissarro, and exhibited with the Impressionists from 1881 to 1886. Thus in this 1888 letter he still uses the term "Impressionism" without the blatant disparagement that characterizes his later correspondence.

30. Cézanne, qtd. in Joachim Gasquet, *"Le Motif, ce qu'il m'a dit," Paul Cézanne* (Paris: Bernheim-Jeune, 1926), 130, qtd. in Loran. Loran points out that, while it might be questionable as to whether or not the language of Gasquet is actually Cézanne's, the approach to pictorial creation expressed through Gasquet's record seems to coincide with Cézanne's actual manner of composition (15).

31. Cheney, *Expressionism in Art* (New York: Liveright Publishing Company, 1958), 5, 90–92. Cheney absorbs all nonrepresentational art into an Expressionistic framework because he considers any movement away from so-called realistic art evidence of what Denis defines as subjective deformation. He therefore tends to underplay the quality of objective deformation (i.e., the deformation of external forms necessitated by the two-dimensional reality of the medium within Post-Impressionist art as a whole). In doing so, Cheney advises that the term "Expressionism" is broad enough to determine the "entire creative stream from Cézanne and van Gogh to Rouault, Lurçat, Marin and Arp" (75). Cézanne, who was dead by 1905, reached his maturity from 1890 to 1896. Though his final canvases appear more fragmentary and abstract, they embody the culmination of technical researches that are most appropriately defined in Post-Impressionist terms.

32. Cézanne, *Correspondence,* ed. John Rewald (Paris, 1937), 273, qtd. in Venturi, *Impressionists and Symbolists,* 129.

33. Maurice Denis, for example, hails Gauguin as a "kind of Poussin without classical culture" in an "agonized" and "corrupt" century ("The Influence of Paul Gauguin," *L'Occident,* March, April, and May 1903, qtd. in Chipp, 104).

34. D. H. Lawrence, "Art and Morality," *Phoenix: The Posthumous Papers of D. H. Lawrence,* ed. E. D. McDonald (New York: The Viking Press, 1968), 526.

35. Fry, qtd. in J. K. Johnstone, *The Bloomsbury Group: A Study of E. M. Forster, Lytton Strachey, Virginia Woolf, and Their Circle* (New York: The Noonday Press, 1954), 60.

36. Charles Mauron, *The Nature of Beauty in Art and Literature,* trans. Roger Fry (London: The Hogarth Press, 1927), 54–55.

37. When McLuhan speaks of "the anguish of the third dimension" he is referring to the limitations of three-dimensional verbal and visual perspective art, which train the eye to be impassive and exclude the observer from participating fully within the picture field. It is precisely because Gloucester is blind in act 4, scene 6 of *King Lear* that Edgar can so effectively convince him of the credibility of the space illusion he creates, which depends upon the separation of the visual from the other senses, and relies exclusively upon Gloucester's visual imagination (McLuhan, 16–17). In the same way, Milton creates the illusion of Eden from Satan's aerial perspective in book 4 of *Paradise Lost.* By excluding all tactile sensations, Satan encourages us to succumb to our dream visions of a perfect order that in reality has already experienced the Fall simply by virtue of Satan's entry into paradise.

38. Crane, "The Open Boat," in *The Norton Anthology of Short Fiction,* ed. R. V. Cassill, 3rd ed. (New York: W. W. Norton, 1986), 337.

39. Woolf, letter to Hugh Walpole, qtd. in Quentin Bell, *Virginia Woolf: A Biography, Volume 2: Mrs. Woolf 1912–1914,* 162.

40. Woolf, *A Writer's Diary: Being Extracts from the Diary of Virginia Woolf,* ed. Leonard Woolf (New York: Harcourt Brace Jovanovich, 1953–54), 103.

41. Erich Auerbach, "The Brown Stocking," in *Mimesis: The Representation of Reality in Western Literature,* trans. William Task (New York: Doubleday & Company, 1957), 474. For an intriguing discussion of the strategies Woolf uses to frame her "privileged moments" or to circle the "imagined picture" see Mary Ann Caws, *Reading Frames in Modern Fiction* (Princeton: Princeton University Press, 1985), 237–61.

42. Woolf, *To the Lighthouse* (1927; rpt. New York: Harcourt Brace Jovanovich, 1955), 294.

43. Jaako Hintikka, "Virginia Woolf and Our Knowledge of the External World," *Journal of Aesthetics and Art Criticism* 38.1 (1979), 6. In *The Seen and the Unseen: Virginia Woolf's "To the Lighthouse,"* Lisa Riddick pursues this concept in her terms as she explores the relationship between male and female perspectives in the novel and Lily's synthesis of the two in her canvas (Cambridge: Harvard University Press, 1977), 25–53.

44. Lee Whitehead, "The Shawl and the Skull: Virginia Woolf's 'Magic Mountain,'" *Modern Fiction Studies*, vol. 18, no. 3 (1972), 410–15.

45. In her discussion of pictorialism in *To the Lighthouse*, Torgovnick uses the terms *abstract* and *nonrepresentational* interchangeably to define the nature of the art within Lily's composition and the "drama" of the geometric forms that dominate the novel generally (139). However, the term "abstract" creates particular problems when applied to Woolf's configuration, for far from being nonreferential, the geometric forms are inextricably tied to apperceptions of external phenomena. This is a point Torgovnick herself pursues within her discussion as she observes how the triangular figure Mrs. Ramsay sustains in a moment of stasis is represented in Lily's work and becomes "a symbol of universal balance and harmony" (140). Torgovnick concludes her analysis in this section of the text with the observation that "abstract art provides Woolf with an idiom to express ideas that might sound trite if explicitly stated or if elaborated at great length" (140). Woolf's geometric forms are rooted in the observation of phenomena and therefore far from "abstract" or nonobjective. The abstractive process that isolates the tensions between lines, shapes, and colors originates with natural analogues set in motion at the very beginning of the novel. Because these forms symbolize various conceptions of the underlying and essential disposition of the characters and their relationship to material reality, this pictorial dimension of *To the Lighthouse* cannot be accommodated by the terms Torgovnick implements.

46. Allen McLaurin, *Virginia Woolf: The Echoes Enslaved* (Cambridge: At the University Press, 1973), 85–91.

47. Woolf, *The Diary of Virginia Woolf, Volume 1: 1915- 1919*, ed. Anne Olivier Bell (London: The Hogarth Press, 1977), 140–41.

48. Daniel R. Schwarz, "'I Was the World in Which I Walked': The Transformation of the British Novel," *University of Toronto Quarterly* 51 (Spring 1982): 293.

49. Douwe W. Fokkema, "An Interpretation of *To the Lighthouse* with Reference to the Code of Modernism," *A Journal for Descriptive Poetics and Theory of Literature* 4 (1980): 493.

50. Marjorie Brace, "Worshipping Solid Objects," in *Critics on Virginia Woolf: Readings in Literary Criticism*, ed. Jacqueline E. Latham (Florida: University of Miami Press, 1970), 120, 123.

51. Woolf, *Flush* (1933; rpt. London: The Hogarth Press, 1968), 125.

52. Jan Heinemann, "The revolt against language: A critical note on twentieth-century irrationalism with special reference to the aesthetico-philosophical views of Virginia Woolf and Clive Bell," *Orbis Litterarum* 32 (1977): 213, 225.

53. Lillian Ross, "How Do You Like It Now, Gentlemen?" in *A Collection of Critical Essays*, ed. Robert P. Weeks (Englewood Cliffs, N.J.: Prentice-Hall, 1965), 36.

54. Hemingway, *A Moveable Feast* (1964; rpt. Harmondsworth, Middlesex, England: Penguin Books, 1966), 16.

55. George Plimpton, "An Interview with Ernest Hemingway," in *Hemingway and His Critics*, ed. Carlos Baker (New York: Hill and Wang, 1961), 35, 37.

56. Hemingway, *Death in the Afternoon* (1932; rpt. London: Jonathan Cape, 1952), 10.

57. John Willett, *Expressionism* (New York: McGraw-Hill, 1970), 26.

58. H. E. Bates, "Hemingway's Short Stories," in *Hemingway and His Critics,* 77.

59. Raymond S. Nelson, *Hemingway: Expressionist Artist* (Ames, Iowa: The Iowa State University Press, 1979), 12.

60. Richard Murphy, *The World of Cézanne, 1839–1906* (New York: Time-Life Books, 1968), 7, 8.

61. For discussions of the less-is-more paradox that engage this Expressionist notion of subjective deformation see Robert Lair, "Hemingway and Cézanne: An Indebtedness," *Modern Fiction Studies,* vol. 3, no. 2 (1960): 165; Harry Levin, "Observations on the Style of Ernest Hemingway," in *Hemingway and His Critics,* 100–103; and Carlos Baker, *Hemingway: The Writer as Artist* (Princeton: Princeton University Press, 1972), 289.

62. E. T. Jones, "Hemingway and Cézanne: A Speculative Affinity," *American Literary Scholarship,* vol. 8, no. 11 (1970): 27.

63. Hemingway, *A Farewell to Arms* (1929; rpt. New York: Charles Scribner's Sons, 1954), 3.

64. Hemingway, *The Sun Also Rises* (1926; rpt. New York: Charles Scribner's Sons, 1954), 93.

65. Meyly Chin Hagemann, "Hemingway's Secret: Visual to Verbal Art," *Journal of Modern Literature,* vol. 7, no. 1 (1979): 96.

66. Emily Stipes Watts, *Ernest Hemingway and the Arts* (Chicago: University of Illinois Press, 1971), 138.

67. Hemingway, "Big Two-Hearted River," *The Nick Adams Stories* (1927; rpt. New York: Bantam Books, 1981), 163.

68. Hagemann defines the picture plane, for example, as "the viewer's position as he faces a picture" (92), whereas Loran demonstrates that the picture plane defines the two-dimensionality of the canvas: it does not define the observer's position. To see it functioning in Hagemann's sense implies that one is dealing with the picture plane in an effort to ignore its flat surface as one does in the open-window tradition of perspective art. This point of view is, however, entirely incompatible with Cézanne's respect for the flat plane. It is for this reason, perhaps, that Hagemann enters the Cézanne on the wrong footing, so to speak, and carries the misconception with her when she enters Hemingway's pine tree scene to emphasize the disembodied spiritual quality of Nick's rebirth: "This cathedral-like arch is so serene that Nick looks straight into its curved space and closes his eyes" (111). Hagemann's correlative here ignores the fact that the last thing Hemingway or Cézanne wishes to emphasize is a perspective line that leads the viewer "into" deep space. Hemingway's pine tree scene and Cézanne's *Jas de Bouffan* are parallel because neither uses mechanical perspective to realize a third dimension.

69. Hemingway, *Islands in the Stream* (1970; rpt. New York: Bantam Books, 1972), 3. My thanks to Dr. Hinz for drawing my attention to this parallax effect.

70. Hemingway, *The Old Man and the Sea* (New York: Charles Scribner's Sons, 1952), 47.

71. Lawrence, "Introduction to His Paintings," *D. H. Lawrence: Selected Essays* (Harmondsworth, Middlesex, England: Penguin Books, 1950), 340, 323.

72. Lawrence, "Art and Morality," *Phoenix,* 525.

73. Lawrence, *Mornings in Mexico and Etruscan Places* (1932; rpt. Harmondsworth, England: Penguin Books, 1960), 166–67.

74. Lawrence, "Making Pictures," *D. H. Lawrence: Selected Essays*, 304.

75. Jack Lindsay, "The Impact of Modernism on Lawrence, " in *The Paintings of D. H. Lawrence*, ed. Mervyn Levy (London: Cory, Adams and Mackay Ltd., 1964), 38.

76. John Remsbury, " 'Real Thinking': Lawrence and Cézanne," *Cambridge Quarterly*, vol. 2, no. 2 (1967): 121.

77. Lawrence, "Study of Thomas Hardy," *Phoenix*, 419.

78. Lawrence, "Morality and the Novel," *Phoenix*, 527.

79. Lawrence, "Life," *Phoenix*, 696–97.

80. Lawrence, letter to Lady Ottoline Morrell, *The Letters of D. H. Lawrence*, 4 vols. (Cambridge: Cambridge University Press, 1979–87), 2: 296–97.

81. For a discussion of this concept and an analysis of how it functions in *The Rainbow* see Evelyn J. Hinz, "Hierogamy versus Wedlock: Types of Marriage Plots and Their Relationship to Genres of Prose Fiction," *PMLA* 91 (October 1976): 900–913.

82. Lawrence, *The Rainbow* (1915; rpt. New York: The Viking Press, 1961), 1.

83. Stewart, "Expressionism in *The Rainbow*," *Novel* 13–14 (Spring 1980): 314–16.

84. Robert Goldwater, *Primitivism in Modern Art* (New York: Vintage Books, 1967), 90.

85. Lawrence, *The Plumed Serpent* (1926; rpt. New York: Vintage Books, 1959), 465.

86. This critical tendency is one Donnell-Kotrozo extensively confronts and exposes as deficient in her study of how Post-Impressionist artists like Gauguin, for example, have been misrepresented by art historians who perceive the nonnaturalistic disposition of his landscape forms as evidence of the artist's repudiation of nature herself. Donnell-Kotrozo's discussion of the actual character of Gauguin's dynamic response to natural forms allows one to question the validity of the correspondence that Jack Stewart establishes between what he perceives as the shared "hallucinatory" quality of Gauguin's and Lawrence's treatment of landscape form ("Lawrence and Gauguin," *Twentieth Century Literature* 26 [1980]: 385–401) and to question the viability of Expressionistic interpretations of Post-Impressionist art generally, where Expressionism is itself narrowly defined in terms of the objectification of a subjective response. While it is clear that there is "a proto-Expressionist" character to van Gogh's and Gauguin's response to nature, that emotional complex is part of the Post-Impressionist inquiry into external form and should not be defined retrospectively as indicative of an essentially Expressionistic intention.

    The term *Expressionism* is most properly applied to a stage in the artistic development within Germany from 1905 through to the 1920s. It is associated principally with two groups of artists. The first, a Dresden group composed of four former architecture students—Ernest Kirchner, Erich Heckel, Erich Bleyl and Karl Schmidt-Rottluff—called itself *Die Brücke* (The Bridge) and was formed officially in 1905 and dissolved in 1913. The second, a Munich group inspired by Wassily Kandinsky and Franz Marc, exhibited under the aegis of an almanac entitled *Der Blaue Reiter* (The Blue Rider) of which only one issue appeared in 1912. The term *Expressionism* was introduced publicly in an August 1911 article by Wilhelm Worringer for *Der Sturm*, an avant-garde periodical whose first issue appeared in 1910 coincident with the tenth anniversary of the Berlin Succession, which had been formed by a group of artists who were enraged by the official academy's closure of the 1892 Berlin exhibition of Munch's work. Though

Worringer used the term to describe "the young Parisian Synthetists and Expressionists, Cézanne, van Gogh and Matisse," the term more properly defines a German phenomenon.

The movement can be viewed as an extension of the Post-Impressionist campaign against the mimetic basis of art; however, the Expressionist reaction also promulgated an esthetic that was intrinsically linked to theories that endeavored to identify the quintessential nature of the Germanic spirit and the destiny of its people as a whole. Thus, Expressionism is also part of a nationalist cry for a healthy, pure, German art form that would free the artistic community from the charge that depended upon foreign models. It is integrally linked with a dream of a new humanity. The latter presents itself positively as a kind of pantheistic humanitarianism; negatively it takes the form of a strident opposition to those materialistic and industrial forces that deny the emergence of a new society and a new man. The fertile individual styles within Expressionism are united by a common factor that Weisstein defines through the term *Aufbruch:* "a complete destruction of the past, a burning of bridges, a progress beyond the point of no return" ("Expressionism as an International Literary Phenomenon: Introduction," *Expressionism as an International Phenomenon: 21 Essays and a Bibliography,* ed. Ulrich Weisstein [Paris: Rider, 1973], 35).

This long explanation is meant to suggest that the literary critic must be particularly aware of the implications of the pictorial terms that are being engaged in analysis. The term *Expressionism* within this context has applicability to Modernist narratives and to Lawrence's own work in *Women in Love,* for example, where the chthonic character of the landscapes is more disturbing, and the capacity for regeneration through contact with cosmogenic forces more complicated and equivocal than it had been in *The Rainbow.* The vision and the technique of the novel is therefore more deeply responsive to the nightmarish dimensions of the process of decreation that Lawrence defines as "progressive devolution" in the novel, and to the conception of inner necessity as fate. It is also more expressive of the urgency and desperation that characterizes Expressionism's desire to "make another world" (*Women in Love* [1920; rpt. New York: The Viking Press, 1960], 196–97). It is in this sense that Lawrence's condemnation of the lassitude of a mechanized, dispirited age is more strident and explicit and his sense of the mindlessness and unreality of the external order more deeply felt and more clearly formulated in *Women in Love.* Accordingly, an Expressionist analogy can be most fruitfully developed by attending to the full implications inherent in the relationship between technique and vision that the term *Expressionism* embodies.

87. My sense of how Lawrence constricts the visual dimension of this ritualistic experience may account for Torgovnick's response to moments of crises in *The Rainbow* as "distinctly *unpictorial* and *unvisual*" (129) because Lawrence relies on qualities that, Torgovnick recognizes, are "unseen." In the scene that brings Tom into Lydia's orbit, for example, Torgovnick argues that "aural stimuli assume, moreover, an importance equal to that of visual stimuli," and that Lawrence's phrases "have an abstractness that blocks full pictorialism" (145). My point is that sound is given visual definition here through emotionally dynamic and unstable isomorphic landscape forms. In the scene between Will and Anna and the haystacks, Torgovnick argues as well from an optically derived notion of the pictorial by suggesting that "the most important features of the characters' emotions have no pictorial equivalents." Though Lawrence consistently materializes the inner consanguinity between human and nonhuman forms in this section by conceiving of characters as phenomenal form, Torgovnick suggests that "though imaginable in an impressionist, post-impressionist, or expressionist style," Lawrence's phrases do not develop "visual stimuli or pictorial images but . . . highly irrational and abstract feelings": "the characters seem far more affected by each other and by tactile stimuli than by scenery or visual stimuli around them" (146–47). However, Lawrence's drive to provide visual equivalents for the interplay of optical, auditory, and tactile dimensions in landscape experience leads the

reader to confront forms that are not defined by the "visual" exclusiveness of optically determined notions of the pictorial. It is in this way that Torgovnick's responsiveness to the
coequality of haptic and visual stimuli in Lawrence's scenes demonstrates the applicability of
a Post-Impressionist analogy.

Chapter 3

1. Louis Vauxcelles, *Gil Blas*, 14 November 1908, qtd. in John Golding *Cubism: A History and
    an Analysis, 1907–1914*, 2nd ed. (New York: George Wittenborn, 1959), 67.

2. André Salmon, "Anecdotal History of Cubism," *Le jeune peinture française* (Paris: Société
    des Trente, 1912), qtd. in Chipp, 203.

3. Norbert Lynton, *The Story of Modern Art* (Oxford: Phaidon Press Limited, 1980), 62.

4. Juan Gris, qtd. in Daniel-Henry Kahnweiler, *Juan Gris, His Life and Work*, trans. Douglas
    Cooper (London: Lund Humphries, 1947), 104.

5. Gris, "Response to a Questionnaire on His Art 1921," originally published in *L'Esprit Nou-
    veau*, no. 5, February 1921: 533–34. This English translation is from Kahnweiler, *Juan Gris*,
    138.

6. John Berger, "The Moment of Cubism," *The Moment of Cubism and Other Essays* (London:
    Weidenfeld and Nicholson, 1969), 22, 20.

7. Pierre Daix, *Cubists and Cubism* (New York: Rizzoli International Publications, 1982), 101.

8. Maurice Raynal, "*Conception et Vision*," qtd. in Lynn Gamwell, *Cubist Criticism* (Ann Arbor,
    Mich.: UMI Research Press, 1980), 2.

9. Raynal, qtd. in *Cubism*, ed. Edward Fry (New York: McGraw-Hill, 1966), 129–30. Though
    the tendency to approach Cubist art through an Einsteinian perspective becomes increasingly
    suspect following World War I, this viewpoint persists in interartistic analogies. Paul M.
    LaPorte in his 1948 article, "The Space-Time Concept in the Work of Picasso" (*Magazine of
    Art*, vol. 41, no. 1), suggests, for example, that Picasso's multiple views affirm the presence
    of Einsteinian notions of relativity (26–33). His position is absorbed by Timothy Bergson in a
    1977 article, "Bergson, Le Bon, and Hermetic Cubism." Bergson amplifies Le Bon's refutation
    of the indestructibility of matter and concludes that Hermetic Cubism's multiple views are
    paradigmatic by implication "of these philosophical and scientific principles" (*Journal of
    Aesthetics and Art Criticism*, vol. 36, no. 2 [1977]: 177).

10. Albert Gleizes and Jean Metzinger, *Cubism* (London: T. Fisher Unwin, 1913), 55.

11. H. H. Arnason, *History of Modern Art* (Englewood Cliffs, N.J.: Prentice-Hall, 1977), 220.

12. Robert Rosenblum, *Cubism and Twentieth-Century Art*, rev. ed. (New York: Harry N. Abrams,
    1976), 45.

13. Pablo Picasso, "Statement, 1923," from an interview with Marius de Zayas, qtd. in Chipp, 265.

14. Gleizes, "*Chez les Cubistes*," *Bulletin de la vie Artistique*, 1924–25, qtd. in Golding, 94.

15. In "Conversation, 1935," Picasso uses the term "destructions" to indicate that his reformulation
    of the object within the picture space, even while it abrogates the object's connection with its
    original place, nonetheless maintains the "vibration" of its former life as plastic "problems" are
    resolved: "In my case a picture is a sum of destructions. I do a picture—then I destroy it. In
    the end, though, nothing is lost; the red I took away from one place turns up somewhere else"

(from an interview with Christian Zervos published as *"Conversation with Picasso," Cahiers d'Art,* vol. 10 [1935]: 173–78, qtd. in Chipp, 267).

16. Guillaume Apollinaire, *Les Peintres Cubistes: Méditations Esthetiques* (Paris: Figuière, 1913) from *The Cubist Painters: Aesthetic Meditations,* trans. Lionel Abel (New York: Wittenborn, 1944), qtd. in Chipp, 227.

17. Mario Praz, *Mnemosyne: The Parallel between Literature and the Visual Arts, Bollingen Series,* vol. 35, no. 16 (Princeton: Princeton University Press, 1974): 192–93.

18. I am indebted to Rosenblum's intriguing discussion of Synthetic Cubism's typographic environment in "Picasso and the Typography of Cubism," *Picasso in Retrospect,* eds. Sir Roland Penrose and John Golding (New York: Praeger Publishers, 1973), 49–75.

19. Gamwell , 6–7. Both Gamwell and Linda Dalrymple Henderson in "New Facets of Cubism: 'The Fourth Dimension' and 'Non-Euclidean Geometry' Reinterpreted" (*Art Quarterly,* vol. 34, no. 4 [1971]: 410–33) offer a detailed discussion of the inapplicability of Bergsonian and Einsteinian concepts of relativity and becoming to Cubist art. The temptation to evoke this cinematic form and other essentially post-Cubist perspectives is a pervasive one in both literary and art criticism. For demonstrations of misrepresentations of the Cubist dispensation in this context see Sypher, 264–65; Georges Lemaître, *From Cubism to Surrealism in French Literature* (Cambridge: Harvard University Press, 1941), 80–92; Christopher Gray, *Cubist Aesthetic Theories* (Baltimore: Johns Hopkins Press, 1953), 3; Chipp, 193; and Wendy Steiner, *The Colors of Rhetoric: Problems in the Relation between Modern Literature and Painting* (Chicago: The University of Chicago Press, 1982), 192–96.

20. In *Cubism,* for example, Gleizes and Metzinger attempt to justify Cubist art's departure from traditional concepts of mimesis by maintaining that abstraction is the logical and desired end of the movement as a whole: "Let the picture imitate nothing, let it nakedly present its motive, and we should indeed be ungrateful were we to deplore the absence of all those things— flowers, or landscape, or faces—whose mere reflections it might have been. Nevertheless, let us admit that the reminiscence of natural forms cannot be absolutely banished, as yet, at all events. An art cannot be raised to the level of pure effusion at the first step" (28). Though Gamwell notes that Metzinger's and Gleize's emphasis upon the formal basis of the style was a "defensive reaction against the mounting negative criticism" of Cubism in the French press (17), this emphasis tends to disregard the tension between representational and nonrepresentational elements vital to the Cubism of Braque and Picasso and has been transmitted by literary critics, who speak, as does Marilyn Gaddis Rose, of correlatives between the nonreferentiability of Stein's prose in *Lucy Church Amiably* and Cubism's "abstractionist" analytical paintings ("Gertrude Stein and Cubist Narrative," *Modern Fiction Studies,* vol. 22, no. 4 [Winter 1976– 77]: 550).

21. Charles Bernheimer, "Grammacentricity and Modernism," *Mosaic,* vol. 11, no. 1 (Fall 1977): 106.

22. Jo-Anna Isaak, "James Joyce and the Cubist Esthetic," *Mosaic,* vol. 14, no. 1 (Winter 1981): 85, 68. The tendency to minimize the actual synchronic character of Cubist painting to justify modes of analysis based on temporal sequence and cinematic and chronophotographic methods is also evident in Rosenblum, *Cubism,* 57; Praz "Notes on James Joyce," *Mosaic,* vol. 6, no. 1 (Fall 1972): 97–98; and Betty M. Foley "The Ubicubist Joyce," *Ball State University Forum,* vol. 7, no. 4 (Autumn 1976): 41–45. Perhaps the basis for this kind of perspective comes from the critical reliance on Joseph Frank's discussion of spatial form as he applies it to *Ulysses.* Frank, for example, suggests that despite the "unbelievably laborious fragmentation of narra-

tive structure" within the novel, a "unified spatial apprehension" of the discontinuous temporal sequence is possible ("Spatial Form in Modern Literature," *Sewanee Review* 53 [1945], 234–35). Thus Frank speaks of the reader's "task of reconstruction" as a spatial or nonsequential reading of the text. The kind of reading that Frank advocates obscures the difference that holds between an illusion of simultaneity in an essentially diachronic form and the actual optical synthesis in Cubist art. This obfuscation informs Archie K. Loss's analysis of the applicability of Cubist frames of reference within *Ulysses* in *Joyce's Visible Art: The Work of Joyce and the Visual Arts, 1904–1922* (Ann Arbor, Mich.: UMI Research Press, 1984): "although these thoughts and utterances [within the "Wandering Rocks" episode] occur sequentially in the text, they have the same quality of simultaneity to be found in the various fragments which make up Cubist and Cubist-influenced collage. That is, though we may read them in sequence, we must take them as occurring simultaneously" (46). Further, this kind of blurring is integral to Lauro Flores's argument in "Narrative Strategies in Rolando Hinojosa's *Rites and Witnesses*" (*Revista Chicano-Riquena*, vol. 12, no. 3–4 [Fall-Winter 1984]: 172–73): "Hinojosa's writing resembles the task of a cubist painter who studies his subject matter from a variety of angles and whose works' complexity can only be understood upon a simultaneous reading of the work in its entirety" (172). To achieve this spatial reading, Flores refers as well to the reader's "task of reconstruction" as one in which the novel's "series of snapshots" are to convene together in the mind so that the ambiguity created by their juxtaposition can be resolved (178). So, too, Panthea Reid Broughton in "The Cubist Novel: Toward Defining the Genre" uses the term *cubist* to define the tension between succession and simultaneity in Faulkner's novels even while she repeatedly endorses a notion of reconstruction defined here as the reader's search "to make sense" by positing temporal coherence: "With all Faulkner's cubist novels we similarly join different planes and reassemble narratives" ("*A Cosmos of My Own": Faulkner and Yoknapatawpha*, ed. Doreen Fowler and Ann J. Abadie [Jackson: University Press of Mississippi, 1981], 87, 94). So, too, Jack Stewart's analysis of "cubist" elements in Woolf's *Between the Acts* depends upon a parallel notion of cubification or the superimposition of spatial and temporal planes of meaning. Though Stewart uses the term "syncopation" to define this multiplication, he does observe that Woolf's dissection "seldom departs from sequentiality." The inapplicability of a Cubist analogy with respect to this novel is further disclosed by the fact that Stewart increasingly establishes affinities between Woolf's pursuit of the "*Ding-an-sich* behind the phenomenon" and the "Expressionist overtones" of the adaptation and modification of Cubist techniques in Paul Klee, for example, and between Woolf's techniques of "dismemberment" and a Futurist concept of Simultaneism rather than synthesis ("Cubist Elements in *Between the Acts,*" *Mosaic*, vol. 18, no. 2 [Spring 1985]: 70, 79, 80–81).

23. James Joyce qtd. in Frank Budgen, *James Joyce and the Making of Ulysses* (Bloomington: Indiana University Press, 1960), 17.

24. David Lodge, "The Language of Modernist Fiction: Metaphor and Metonymy," *Modernism 1890–1930*, eds. Malcolm Bradbury and James McFarlane (Harmondsworth, England: Penguin Books, 1976), 486.

25. Karen Lawrence, *The Odyssey of Style in "Ulysses"* (Princeton: Princeton University Press, 1981), 83.

26. James Joyce, *Ulysses* (1922; rpt. Harmondsworth, Middlesex, England: Penguin Books, 1968), 226.

27. Clive Hart and Leo Knuth, *A Topographical Guide to James Joyce's "Ulysses",* 2 vols. (Colchester, England: A WAKE Newsletter Press, 1975).

28. Joyce, *Letters,* ed. Stuart Gilbert (New York: The Viking Press, 1957), 149.

29. Loss, "Joyce's Use of Collage in 'Aeolus,'" *Journal of Modern Literature,* vol. 9, no. 2 (1981–82): 179. Loss reasserts this correlation in *Joyce's Visual Art.* The basis in the latter engages what Loss defines as the "associative function" of the *collage* element: "The fragments in Cubist collage achieve this significance by their recurrence in a series of related compositions, just as the fragments in *Ulysses* achieve significance by their recurrence in various episodes which comprise that work" (49). To preface this assertion, however, Loss distinguishes between Cubist and Joycean fragments by noting that "the fragments in Cubist collage do not suggest some deeper psychological reality nor do they form part of a continuous narrative" (48). On the one hand, Loss invokes a narrative frame for the Cubist *collage* element to justify the analogy, while, on the other, he acknowledges the difference that must be respected insofar as this kind of narrative context does not apply to the *collage* element in Cubist canvases. In "Verbal Paintings, Fugal Poems, Literary Collages and the Metamorphic Comparatist," Weisstein cautions against the use of the term *collage* to define Joyce's quotations from daily life for, by their very nature, these literary elements "cloud the difference between art and reality" that is highlighted in *collage:* "to be precise: what makes a collage a collage in whatever medium is the fact that bits of reality recognizable as such are, literally or illusionistically, transplanted onto or superimposed upon an esthetic construct—but never to the extent of obfuscating the construct and robbing it of its artistic integrity" (*Yearbook of Comparative and General Literature* 27 [1978]: 10). Weisstein advises that critics acknowledge the "near-exact" nature of the equivalence, a principle John Tucker, for example, adheres to when he discusses the "mock collage" element within Faulkner's *As I Lay Dying* ("William Faulkner's *As I Lay Dying:* Working Out the Cubist Bugs," *Texas Studies in Literature and Language,* vol. 26, no. 4 [Winter, 1984]: 392).

30. Robert Bartlett Haas, "A Transatlantic Interview—1946," *A Primer for the Gradual Understanding of Gertrude Stein* (Los Angeles: Black Sparrow Press, 1971), 31.

31. Gertrude Stein, *Picasso* (1939; rpt. London: B. T. Botsford, Ltd., 1946), 47.

32. Stein, "Henry James," *Four in America* (New Haven, Conn.: Yale University Press, 1947), 119.

33. For a more complete demonstration of Stein's grasp of the way in which modern art challenges an open–window concept see her "Pictures," *Lectures in America* (New York: Random House, 1935), 59–90.

34. Stein, "DINNER," *Tender Buttons* in *Look at Me Now and Here I Am: Writings and Lectures 1909–45,* ed. Patricia Meyerowitz (Harmondsworth, England: Penguin Books, 1967), 193.

35. Stein, *The Autobiography of Alice B. Toklas* (New York: Harcourt Brace and Co., 1933), 34.

36. Arnold Rönnebeck, "Gertrude Was Always Giggling," *Books Abroad,* vol. 18, no. 4 (October 1944): 3.

37. Stein, "Plays," *Lectures in America,* 104–5.

38. Stein, "Composition as Explanation," *Look at Me Now and Here I Am,* 29–30. The perception that Stein's concept of "the time-sense in the composition" immunizes notions of identity and relation is expressed by Kenneth Burke in "Engineering with Words" (*The Dial* 74 [April 1923]: 410) and B. L. Reid in *Art by Subtraction: A Dissenting Opinion of Gertrude Stein* (Norman: University of Oklahoma Press, 1958). It is a position that is reformulated as critics define Stein's seemingly *esse est percipi* orientation in cinematic terms as the sequence of nonrelational nows or the juxtaposition of preconceptual perceptual fragments. To retain a Cubist correlative with Stein on the basis of this orientation, Randa Dubnick, for example,

imposes a cinematic reading of the Cubist synthesis: Picasso "wanted to preserve each individual present moment of perception before those moments are synthesized by intellectual knowledge of reality into the concept of the object as it is known (remembered) to be" (*The Structure of Obscurity: Gertrude Stein, Language and Cubism* [Urbana and Chicago: University of Illinois Press, 1984], 20). Norman Weisstein relies on a cinematic reading of the Cubist synthesis as well to apply what is essentially a Futurist concept of Simultaneism to both Cubism and Stein in *Gertrude Stein and the Literature of the Modern Consciousness* (New York: Frederick Unger, 1970), 21–22. This assertion that Cubism realizes a preconceptual perceptual now is also endorsed by L. T. Fitz to authorize an analogy between Stein and Cubism in "Gertrude Stein and Picasso: The Language of Surfaces" (*American Literature* 45 [1973], 228–37). In *Exact Resemblance to Exact Resemblance* Wendy Steiner argues that Stein's development of a mode of signification, responsive only to the perceptual now, leads to the breakdown of a Cubist analogy: "Stein had taken the idea of the *tableau- objet* at face value rather than as half of the tension between aesthetics and representationality essential to cubism" (New Haven and London: Yale University Press, [1978], 158). While Steiner acknowledges the conceptual nature of the relationship of the parts that compose the optical synthesis of an array of temporally distinct perceptions in Cubist art (141–45), she insists that Stein's more radical writing exhibits a series of isolated signs, "devoid of all but potential (or lexical) meaning" which exist in "an on-going 'now' unrelated to categories of thought" (154). My point is that Stein's split descriptions, for example, operate as mimetic synecdochal figures that display the mind's ideas about external forms. As such they exist as conceptually related fragments synthesized within the unique atemporal conditions of the composition. The array of resemblances Stein collects to exhibit her ideas about homologous metastatic patterns in the material world within *Tender Buttons* offers a correlative with the variety of iconic means that Cubist artists engage to establish, maintain, and extend our understanding of correspondence. Both Cubist artists and Stein achieve that amplification by moving beyond the notion of equivalence sanctioned by optically derived standards of verisimilitude, so that those signs that realize the surface appearance of the object function as but one of the many kinds of signs that cooperate together to allow an intellectual vision of the object to materialize in the medium.

39. Stein, *The Making of Americans: Being a History of a Family's Progress,* complete version (1925; rpt. New York: Something Else Press, 1966), 290.

40. Edward Fry, *Cubism* (London: Thames & Hudson, 1966), 38–39.

41. Stein, "Portraits and Repetition," *Look at Me Now and Here I Am,* 115.

42. Stein, "Poetry and Grammar," *Look at Me Now and Here I Am,* 141.

43. For interesting discussions of these potential correlatives see Marjorie Perloff, "Poetry as Word-System: The Art of Gertrude Stein," *American Poetry Review,* vol 8, no. 5 (1979): 33–43; and Jayne L. Walker, "Tender Buttons: 'The Music of the Present Tense'," *The Making of a Modernist: Gertrude Stein from Three Lives to Tender Buttons* (Amherst: The University of Massachusetts Press, 1984), 127–49.

44. Gaddis Rose, "The Impasse of Cubist Literature: Picasso, Stein, Jacob," *Proceedings of the International Comparative Literature Association; Budapest August 12 to 17, 1976* (Kunst und Wissen: Eric Bieber, Stuttaart, 1980), 692. This is the point that Broughton asserts in her study of the Cubist narrative as it relates to Faulkner. While she does acknowledge the tension between referential and compositional values in her analysis of Cubist art, Broughton ignores the importance of this observation and defines Cubism as an "abstract or non-referential art." In turning to Stein's deformation of established patterns of correspondence in language, she uses the term *abstract* as well: the "novel cannot become a pure form like abstract art. Gertrude

Stein's attempts to so purify the novel were abysmal failures" ("The Cubist Novel: Toward Defining the Genre," 58, 59).

45. David Lodge, *Modes of Modern Writing: Metaphor, Metonymy and the Typology of Literature* (London: Edward Arnold, 1977), 154.

46. Laura Riding Jackson, "The Word-Play of Gertrude Stein," in *Critical Essays on Gertrude Stein,* ed. Michael T. Hoffman (Boston: G. K. Hall, 1986). Jackson observes: "Gertrude Stein's writings were not simple manifestations of robust individuality; they did not provide prototypes of constructive revolutionary innovation in linguistic practice. They were early products of a pathological condition, mistakenly associated with liberation from mind-imprisoning verbal conventions, with which modern writing, modern thinking, and modern speaking, have become extensively affected: they illustrate how language can be dehumanized by the ignoring of the standards of rational coherence that are, in intellectual actuality, inseparable from it" (242).

47. Marianne DeKoven, *A Different Language: Gertrude Stein's Experimental Writing* (Madison: The University of Wisconsin Press, 1983), 28.

48. Allegra Stewart, *Gertrude Stein and the Present* (Cambridge: Harvard University Press, 1967), 176.

49. Stein, "A Long Gay Book," in *Matisse Picasso and Gertrude Stein with Two Shorter Stories* (also known as *G.M.P.* [Millerton, N.Y.: Something Else Press, 1972], 18).

50. The prolonged presentness of Stein's participial style in "Orta" (and I think a reference to Picasso's and Braque's early 1909 Horta de Ebro canvases is implicit in Stein's title) allows her to sustain the constant and insistent theme of the "one dancing" through a variety of time values. When Stein conjoins multiple time frames within a single sentence she is able to approximate the composite time of a Cubist synthesis: "Even if she was one being one, and she was one being one, even if she was one being one she was one having come to be one of another kind of one." In a similar way, Stein conjugates states of mind and then fuses their diverse aspects in a single figure. This kind of dynamic operates as one moves from "she was one being one" to "she was one believing that thing" to "she is one doing that thing" to a synthesis of states of "doing, believing, being the one she is being," which returns the reader to the original participial formulation: "She is one being one" (*Two: Gertrude Stein and Her Brother and Other Early Portraits 1908-1912,* vol. 1 of *The Unpublished Writings of Gertrude Stein* [New Haven, Conn.: Yale University Press, 1951]: 286, 288). These verbal permutations accentuate the internal movement within the passage and inhibit a sense of linearity from developing. The technique suggests the kind of transition within a passage that is articulate in the shimmering oscillating surfaces of the interactive crystalline structures of Analytical Cubism.

51. Stein, "The Gradual Making of *The Making of Americans,*" *Look at Me Now and Here I Am,* 86.

52. Wilhelm Boeck, "Evolution of Cubism," in Wilhelm Boeck and Jaime Sebartés, *Picasso* (New York: Harry N. Abrams, 1955), 173.

53. Stein, "Picasso," in *Look at Me Now and Here I Am,* 214.

54. Michael Hoffman, *The Development of Abstractionism in the Writings of Gertrude Stein* (Philadelphia: University of Pennsylvania Press, 1965), 165.

55. Kahnweiler, Introduction to *Painted Lace and Other Pieces 1914–1937*, vol. 5 of *The Unpublished Writings of Gertrude Stein*, trans. Donald Gallup (New Haven, Conn.: Yale University Press, 1955): 11.

56. For discussions of the biographical possibilities of what is often perceived as the "protective" nature of Stein's language, see Pamela Hadas who, in "Spreading the Difference: One Way to Read Gertrude Stein's *Tender Buttons*," interprets the collection "in the broad context of the rift that develops between Stein and her brother Leo because of Toklas's presence" (*Twentieth Century Literature*, vol. 24, no. 1 [Spring 1978]: 57–75). In "Gertrude Stein as Post-Modernist: The Rhetoric of *Tender Buttons*," Neil Schmitz alternately traces a leitmotif of "alogical coherence" throughout the first section of the volume, which he describes as a bluntly solipsistic exploration of Stein's sexual relationship with Toklas (*Journal of Modern Literature*, vol. 3, no. 5 [July 1974]: 1203–18). In *Gertrude Stein in Pieces*, Richard Bridgman ignores the potential graphics that Schmitz explores, though he notes that one of the central contrasts within the volume polarizes dirtiness and cleanliness and suggests that "very likely Gertrude Stein intended to encourage moral tolerance here as well, an acceptance of doing 'dirty' things" (New York: Oxford University Press, 1970), 128.

57. Donald Sutherland, "Gertrude Stein and the Twentieth Century," in *A Primer for the Gradual Understanding of Gertrude Stein*, 146–47.

58. In many ways, Stewart's exploration of the potential root meanings of Stein's words in *Gertrude Stein and the Present* and the pictographic quality of Stein's writing can only extend the applicability of the Cubist analogy I am exploring. While Stewart focuses on a Jungian model and the "deracination of a consciousness" (137), I have attempted to highlight the referentiability of Stein's etymological research in "EATING" as a way of inviting the literary critic to consider alternate definitions for the "abstract" in both Stein and Cubism. While Stewart advises that "like the abstract paintings it resembles, *Tender Buttons* remains vacuous even when it is no longer opaque" (138), I would suggest that a continuing investigation of theories of language will only amplify our understanding of Stein's ability to exploit the resources of her medium to develop a concept of correspondence just as Cubist artists perform a parallel task as they explore the plastic possibilities of their medium.

59. Braque, qtd. in John Malcolm Brinnin, *The Third Rose* (London: Weidenfeld and Nicholson, 1960), 139.

60. Stein, "Poetry and Grammar," *Look at Me Now and Here I Am*, 142.

Conclusion

1. This was part of the original title that Picasso conceived for *Les Demoiselles d'Avignon* canvas, and its thematic implications were at least partially effaced in the series of transformations the painting underwent as Picasso excized the literary associations in the work itself. For a lengthy discussion of the metamorphosis see Leo Steinberg, "The Philosophical Brothel," Parts 1 and 2, *Art News* 71. 5–6 (Sept.-Oct. 1972), 20–29, 38–47.

2. This correspondence is suggested by Nin in her chapter on "Abstraction" in *The Novel of the Future*: "I used Duchamp's painting "Nude Descending a Staircase" to express dissociation of the personality" in the *House of Love* (New York: The Macmillan Company, 1968), 31.

3. Jacob Korg, "Modern Art Techniques in *The Waste Land*," *Twentieth Century Interpretations: A Collection of Critical Essays on "The Waste Land*," ed. Jay Martin (Englewood Cliffs, N.J.: Prentice-Hall, 1968), 87–89.

4. David Tomlinson, "T. S. Eliot and the Cubists," *Twentieth Century Literature,* vol. 26, no. 1 (Spring 1980): 79.

5. Michel Benamou, "Wallace Stevens: Some Relations between Poetry and Painting," *Comparative Literature* 11 (1959), 51.

6. W. V. O'Connor, "Wallace Stevens: Impressionism in America," *Revue des Langues Vivantes* 32 (Jan.-Feb. 1966), 66.

7. Bram Dijkstra, "Wallace Stevens and William Carlos Williams: Poetry, Painting and the Function of Reality," in *Encounters: Essays on Literature and the Visual Arts,* ed. John Dixon Hunt (New York: W. W. Norton, 1971), 156–72.

8. Henry M. Sayre, "Ready-Mades and Other Measures: The Poetics of Marcel Duchamp and William Carlos Williams," *Journal of Modern Literature* vol. 8, no. 1 (1980): 3–22.

9. Franz Marc, "How Does a Horse See the World?" from *Briefe, Aufzeichnungen and Aphorismen,* 2 vols. (Berlin: Cassirer, 1920) 1:121–22. This translation is by Ernest Mundt and Peter Selz, qtd. in Chipp, 179.

Bibliography

Primary Sources

Crane, Stephen. "The Open Boat." 1898. In *The Norton Anthology of Short Fiction*. Ed. R. V. Cassill. 3rd ed. New York: W. W. Norton, 1986.
_____. *The Red Badge of Courage*. 1895. Rpt. *The Red Badge of Courage: An Authoritative Text, Backgrounds and Sources, Criticism*. Eds. Sculley Bradley et. al. New York: W. W. Norton, 1972.
_____. *Stephen Crane: Letters*. Eds. R. W. Stallman and Lilian Gilles. New York: New York University Press, 1960.
_____. "War Memories." *Wounds in the Rain: War Stories*. New York: n.p., 1899.
Hemingway, Ernest. *Death in the Afternoon*. 1932. Rpt. London: Jonathan Cape, 1952.
_____. *A Farewell to Arms*. 1929. Rpt. New York: Charles Scribner's Sons, 1954.
_____. *Islands In The Stream*. 1970. Rpt. New York: Bantam Books, 1972.
_____. *A Moveable Feast*. 1964. Rpt. Harmondsworth, England: Penguin Books, 1966.
_____. *The Nick Adams Stories*. 1927. Rpt. New York: Bantam Books, 1973.
_____. *The Old Man and the Sea*. New York: Charles Scribner's Sons, 1952.
_____. *The Sun Also Rises*. 1926. Rpt. New York: Charles Scribner's Sons, 1954.
Joyce, James. *Letters*. Ed. Stuart Gilbert. New York: The Viking Press, 1957.
_____. *Ulysses*. 1922. Rpt. Harmondsworth, England: Penguin Books, 1968.
Lawrence, D. H. *D. H. Lawrence: Selected Essays*. Harmondsworth, England: Penguin Books, 1950.
_____. *The Letters of D. H. Lawrence*. 4 vols. Cambridge: Cambridge University Press, 1979–87.
_____. *Mornings in Mexico and Etruscan Places*. 1927, 1932. Rpt. Harmondsworth, England: Penguin Books, 1960.
_____. *The Plumed Serpent*. 1926. Rpt. New York: Vintage Books, 1959.
_____. *Phoenix: The Posthumous Papers of D. H. Lawrence*. Ed. E. D. McDonald. New York: The Viking Press, 1968.
_____. *The Rainbow*. 1915. Rpt. New York: The Viking Press, 1961.
_____. *Women in Love*. 1920. Rpt. New York: The Viking Press, 1960.
Matthiessen, Peter. *Far Tortuga*. New York: Random House, 1975.
Ross, Sinclair. *As for Me and My House*. Toronto: McClelland and Stewart Limited, 1941.
Stein, Gertrude. *The Autobiography of Alice B. Toklas*. New York: Harcourt Brace and Co., 1933.
_____. *Four In America*. New Haven, Conn.: Yale University Press, 1947.
_____. *Lectures In America*. New York: Random House, 1935.
_____. *Look at Me Now and Here I Am: Writings and Lectures 1909–45*. Ed. Patricia Meyerowitz. Harmondsworth, Middlesex, England: Penguin Books, 1967.

_____ . *The Making of Americans: Being a History of a Family's Progress*. Complete version. 1925. Rpt. New York: Something Else Press, 1966.

_____ . *Matisse Picasso and Gertrude Stein with Two Shorter Stories* (also known as *G.M.P.*). Barton, Berlin, Millerton, N.Y.: Something Else Press, 1972.

_____ . *Picasso*. 1939. Rpt. London: B. T. Batsford, Ltd., 1946.

_____ . *Two: Gertrude Stein and Her Brother and Other Early Portraits 1908–1912*. Vol. 1 of *The Unpublished Writings of Gertrude Stein*. New Haven, Conn.: Yale University Press, 1951.

Woolf, Virginia. *Collected Essays*. 4 vols. London: The Hogarth Press, 1966–67.

_____ . *The Diary of Virginia Woolf, Volume 1: 1915- 1919*. Ed. Anne Olivier Bell. London: The Hogarth Press, 1977.

_____ . *The Diary of Virginia Woolf, Volume 3: 1925–1930*. Ed. Anne Olivier Bell. New York and London: Harcourt Brace Jovanovich, 1980.

_____ . *Flush*. 1933. Rpt. London: The Hogarth Press, 1968.

_____ . *Jacob's Room and The Waves*. 1922, 1931. Rpt. New York: Harcourt Brace and World, 1959.

_____ . "Kew Gardens." In *A Haunted House and Other Short Stories*. 1943. Rpt. London: The Hogarth Press, 1953.

_____ . *Roger Fry: A Biography*. London: The Hogarth Press, 1940.

_____ . *To the Lighthouse*. 1927. Rpt. New York: Harcourt Brace Jovanovich, 1955.

_____ . *A Writer's Diary: Being Extracts from the Diary of Virginia Woolf*. Ed. Leonard Woolf. New York: Harcourt Brace Jovanovich, 1953–54.

Secondary Sources

Abel, Elizabeth. "Redefining the Sister Arts: Baudelaire's Response to the Art of Delacroix." *Critical Inquiry*, vol. 6 (Spring 1980): 363–84.

Alexander, Jean. *The Venture of Form in the Novels of Virginia Woolf*. Port Washington, N.Y.: Kennikat Press, 1974.

Armstrong, Paul B. "The Hermeneutics of Literary Impressionism: Interpretation and Reality in James, Conrad, and Ford." *Centennial Review*, vol. 27, no. 4 (1983): 244–69.

Arnason, H. H. *History of Modern Art*. Englewood Cliffs, N.J.: Prentice-Hall, 1977.

Auerbach, Erich. *Mimesis: The Representation of Reality in Western Literature*. Trans. William Task. New York: Doubleday & Company, 1957.

Baker, Carlos. *Hemingway: The Writer as Artist*. Princeton: Princeton University Press, 1972.

_____ . ed. *Hemingway and His Critics*. New York: Hill and Wang, 1961.

Bell, Clive. *Art*. 1928. Rpt. New York: C. P. Putnam's Sons, 1958.

Bell, Quentin. *Virginia Woolf: A Biography*. 2 vols. London: The Hogarth Press, 1972.

Benamou, Michel, et. al. "Symposium on Literary Impressionism." *Yearbook of Comparative and General Literature* 17 (1968): 40–72.

_____ . "Wallace Stevens: Some Relations between Poetry and Painting." *Comparative Literature* 11 (1959): 47–60.

Bender, Bert. "Hanging Stephen Crane in the Impressionist Museum." *Journal of Aesthetics and Art Criticism* 35 (1976–77): 47–55.

Berger, John. "The Moment of Cubism." *The Moment of Cubism and Other Essays*. London: Weidenfeld and Nicholson, 1969.

Bergson, Timothy. "Bergson, Le Bon and Hermetic Cubism." *Journal of Aesthetics and Art Criticism*, vol. 36, no. 2 (1977): 175–83.

Bernheimer, Charles. "Grammacentricity and Modernism." *Mosaic*, vol. 11, no. 1 (Fall 1977): 103–16.

Boeck, Wilhelm and Jaime Sebartés. *Picasso.* New York: Harry N. Abrams, 1955.

Bradbury, Malcolm and James McFarlane, eds. *Modernism 1890–1930.* Harmondsworth, Middlesex, England: Penguin Books, 1976.

Bratlinger, Patrick. *"Heart of Darkness:* Anti-Imperialism, Racism, or Impressionism?" *Criticism,* vol. 27, no. 4 (1985): 374–83.

Bridgman, Richard. *Gertrude Stein in Pieces.* New York: Oxford University Press, 1970.

Brinnin, John Malcolm. *The Third Rose.* London: Weidenfeld and Nicholson, 1960.

Budgen, Frank. *James Joyce and the Making of "Ulysses".* Bloomington: Indiana University Press, 1960.

Burke, Kenneth. "Engineering with Words." *The Dial* 74 (April 1923): 408–12.

Cather, Willa. *Willa Cather on Writing: Critical Studies on Writing as an Art.* New York: Alfred A. Knopf, 1949.

Caws, Mary Ann. *Reading Frames in Modern Fiction.* Princeton: Princeton University Press, 1985.

Cézanne, Paul. *Paul Cézanne: Letters.* Ed. John Rewald. London: Cassirer, 1941.

Cheney, Sheldon. *Expressionism in Art.* New York: Liveright Publishing Company, 1958.

———. *A Primer of Modern Art.* New York: Liveright Publishing Corporation, 1966.

Chipp, Hershell B. *Theories of Modern Art: A Source Book by Artists and Critics.* Berkeley and Los Angeles: University of California Press, 1968.

Clark, Kenneth. *Landscape into Art.* Paperback ed. 1949. Rpt. London: John Murray, 1979.

Conrad, Joseph. "His War Book." *Last Essays.* New York: Doubleday, Page, 1926.

———. *Joseph Conrad: Life and Letters,* vol. 1. Ed. G. Jean-Aubry. New York: Doubleday, Page, 1927.

———. Preface to *The Nigger of the "Narcissus." The Nigger of the "Narcissus": An Authoritative Text, Backgrounds and Sources, Reviews and Criticism.* Ed. Robert Kimbrough. New York: W. W. Norton, 1979.

Daix, Pierre. *Cubists and Cubism.* New York: Rizzoli International Publications, 1982.

Dalrymple Henderson, Linda. "New Facets of Cubism: 'The Fourth Dimension' and 'Non-Euclidean Geometry' Reinterpreted." *Art Quarterly,* vol. 34, no. 4 (1971): 410–33.

Daval, Jean-Luc. *Journal de l'impressionnisme.* Geneve: Editions d'Art Albert Skira, 1973.

DeKoven, Marianne. *A Different Language: Gertrude Stein's Experimental Writing.* Madison: The University of Wisconsin Press, 1983.

Donnell-Kotrozo, Carol. *Critical Essays on Postimpressionism.* Philadelphia: The Art Alliance Press, 1983.

Dubnick, Randa. *The Structure of Obscurity: Gertrude Stein, Language and Cubism.* Urbana and Chicago: University of Illinois Press, 1984.

Dunstan, Bernard. *Painting Methods of the Impressionists.* London: Pitman, 1976.

Ehrlich White, Barbara, ed. *Impressionism in Perspective.* Englewood Cliffs, N.J.: Prentice-Hall, 1978.

Fitz, L. T. "Gertrude Stein and Picasso: The Language of Surfaces." *American Literature* 45 (1973): 228–37.

Flores, Lauro. "Narrative Strategies in Rolando Hinojosa's *Rites and Witnesses." Revista Chicano-Riqueña* 12 (Fall-Winter 1984): 170–79.

Fokkema, Douwe W. "An Interpretation of *To The Lighthouse* with Reference to the Code of Modernism." *A Journal for Descriptive Poetics and Theory of Literature* 4 (1980): 475-500.

Foley, Betty M. "The Ubicubist Joyce." *Ball State University Forum,* vol. 7, no. 4 (Autumn 1976): 41–45.

Fowler, Alastair. "Periodization and Interart Analogies." *New Literary History,* vol. 3, no. 3 (Spring 1972): 497–510.

Frank, Joseph. "Spatial Form in Modern Literature." *Sewanee Review* 53 (1945).

Fried, Michael. *Realism, Writing, Disfiguration: On Thomas Eakins and Stephen Crane*. Chicago: The University of Chicago Press, 1987.

Fry, Edward. *Cubism*. New York: McGraw-Hill, 1966.

Fry, Roger. *Transformations: Critical and Speculative Essays on Art*. London: Chatto and Windus, 1926.

————. *Vision and Design*. 1920. Rpt. Harmondsworth, England: Penguin Books, 1961.

Gaddis Rose, Marilyn. "Gertrude Stein and Cubist Narrative." *Modern Fiction Studies,* vol. 22, no. 4 (Winter 1976–77): 543–55.

————. "The Impasse of Cubist Literature: Picasso, Stein, Jacob." *Proceedings of the International Comparative Literature Association; Budapest August 12 to 17, 1976*. Kunst und Wissen: Eric Bieber, Stuttaart, 1980: 685-92.

Gamwell, Lynn. *Cubist Criticism*. Ann Arbor, Mich.: UMI Research Press, 1980.

Gauguin, Paul. *Lettres de Gauguin à sa femme et à ses amis*. Ed. Maurice Malengue. Paris: Grasset, 1949.

Gauss, Charles. *The Aesthetic Theories of French Artists, 1855 to the Present*. Baltimore: Johns Hopkins Press, 1949.

Gleizes, Albert, and Jean Metzinger. *Cubism*. London: T. Fisher Unwin, 1913.

Godard, Barbara. "El Greco in Canada: Sinclair Ross's *As for Me and My House.*" *Mosaic* 14 (Spring 1981): 55–75.

Golding, John. *Cubism: A History and an Analysis, 1907–1914*. 2nd ed., New York: George Wittenborn, 1959.

Goldwater, Robert. *Gauguin*. New York: Harry N. Abrams, 1928.

————. *Primitivism in Modern Art*. Rev. ed. New York: Vintage Books, 1967.

————. *Symbolism*. New York: Harper & Row, 1979.

Gombrich, E. H. *Art and Illusion: A Study in the Psychology of Pictorial Representation*. Bollingen Series 35. Princeton: Princeton University Press, 1969.

Gray, Christopher. *Cubist Aesthetic Theories*. Baltimore: Johns Hopkins Press, 1953.

Guiguet, Jean. *Virginia Woolf and Her Works*. Trans. Jean Stewart. London: The Hogarth Press, 1965.

Haas, Robert Bartlett, ed. *A Primer for the Gradual Understanding of Gertrude Stein*. Los Angeles: Black Sparrow Press, 1971.

Hadas, Pamela. "Spreading the Difference: One Way to Read Gertrude Stein's *Tender Buttons.*" *Twentieth Century Literature,* vol. 24, no. 1 (Spring 1978): 57–75.

Hagemann, Meyly Chin. "Hemingway's Secret: Visual to Verbal Art." *Journal of Modern Literature,* vol. 7, no. 1 (1979): 87–112.

Hagstrum, Jean. *The Sister Arts: The Tradition of Literary Pictorialism and English Poetry from Dryden to Gray*. Chicago: University of Chicago Press, 1958.

Hart, Clive, and Leo Knuth. *A Topographical Guide to James Joyce's "Ulysses."* 2 vols. Colchester, England: A WAKE Newsletter Press, 1975.

Hatzfeld, Helmut A. *Literature through Art*. New York: Oxford University Press, 1952.

Hauser, Arnold. "Impressionism." In *The Social History of Art,* vol. 2. London: Routledge & Kegan Paul, 1951.

Heinemann, Jan. "The revolt against language: A critical note on twentieth-century irrationalism with special reference to the aesthetico-philosophical views of Virginia Woolf and Clive Bell." *Orbis Litterarum* 32 (1977): 213–28.

Hess, Hans. *Pictures as Arguments*. Sussex: Sussex University Press, 1975.

Hintikka, Jaako. "Virginia Woolf and Our Knowledge of the External World." *Journal of Aesthetics and Art Criticism,* vol. 38, no. 1 (1979): 5–14.

Hinz, Evelyn J. "Hierogamy versus Wedlock: Types of Marriage Plots and Their Relationship to Genres of Prose Fiction." *PMLA* 91 (October 1976): 900–913.

Hoffman, Michael T. *The Development of Abstractionism in the Writings of Gertrude Stein*. Philadelphia: University of Pennsylvania Press, 1965.

_____ , ed. *Critical Essays on Gertrude Stein*. Boston: G. K. Hall, 1986.

Holton, Milne. *Cylinder of Vision: The Fiction and Journalistic Writing of Stephen Crane*. Baton Rouge: Louisiana State University Press, 1972.

Hunt, John Dixon, ed. *Encounters: Essays on Literature and the Visual Arts*. London: Studio Vista, 1971.

Isaak, Jo-Anna. "James Joyce and the Cubist Esthetic." *Mosaic*, vol. 14, no. 1 (Winter 1981): 61–90.

Janson, H. W. *History of Art: A Survey of the Major Visual Arts from the Dawn of History to the Present Day*, Rev. ed. New York: Harry N. Abrams, 1969.

Johnston, Bruce. "Conrad's Impressionism and Watt's 'Delayed Decoding.'" In *Conrad Revisited: Essays for the Eighties*. Ed. Ross C. Murfin. University of Alabama: Alabama University Press, 1985.

Johnstone, J. K. *The Bloomsbury Group: A Study of E. M. Forster, Lytton Strachey, Virginia Woolf, and Their Circle*. New York: The Noonday Press, 1954.

Jones, E. T. "Hemingway and Cézanne: A Speculative Affinity." *American Literary Scholarship*, vol. 8, no. 11 (1970): 26–28.

Kahnweiler, Daniel-Henry. Introduction to *Painted Lace and Other Pieces 1914–1937*. Vol. 5 of *The Unpublished Writings of Gertrude Stein*. Trans. Donald Gallup. New Haven, Conn.: Yale University Press, 1955.

_____ . *Juan Gris, His Life and Work*. Trans. Douglas Cooper. London: Lund Humphries, 1947.

Kelder, Diane. *The French Impressionists and Their Century*. London: Pall Mall Press, 1970.

Korg, Jacob. "Modern Art Techniques in *The Waste Land*." In *Twentieth Century Interpretations: A Collection of Critical Essays on "The Waste Land."* Ed. Jay Martin. Englewood Cliffs, N.J.: Prentice-Hall, 1968.

Kronegger, Maria Elizabeth. *Literary Impressionism*. New Haven, Conn.: College and University Press, 1973.

Lair, Robert. "Hemingway and Cézanne: An Indebtedness." *Modern Fiction Studies*, vol. 3, no. 2 (1960): 165–67.

LaPorte, Paul M. "The Space-Time Concept in the Work of Picasso." *Magazine of Art*, vol. 41, no. 1 (January 1948): 26–32.

Latham, Jacqueline E., ed. *Critics on Woolf: Readings in Literary Criticism*. Florida: University of Miami Press, 1970.

Lawrence, Karen. *The Odyssey of Style in "Ulysses"*. Princeton: Princeton University Press, 1981.

Lemaître, Georges. *From Cubism to Surrealism in French Literature*. Cambridge: Harvard University Press, 1941.

Levy, Mervyn, ed. *The Paintings of D. H. Lawrence*. London: Cory, Adams & McKay Ltd., 1964.

Lodge, David. *The Modes of Modern Writing: Metaphor, Metonymy and the Typology of Literature*. London: Edward Arnold, 1977.

Loran, Erle. *Cézanne's Composition: Analysis of His Form, with Diagrams and Photographs of His Motifs*. Berkeley and Los Angeles: University of California Press, 1946.

Loss, Archie K. "Joyce's Use of Collage in 'Aeolus.'" *Journal of Modern Literature*, vol. 9, no. 2(1980-81): 175–82.

_____ . *Joyce's Visible Art: The Work of Joyce and the Visual Arts, 1904–1922*. Ann Arbor, Mich.: UMI Research Press, 1984.

Lynton, Norbert. *The Story of Modern Art*. Oxford: Phaidon Press Limited, 1980.

Mauron, Charles. *The Nature of Beauty in Art and Literature*. Trans. Roger Fry. London: The Hogarth Press, 1927.

McLaurin, Allen. *Virginia Woolf: The Echoes Enslaved*. Cambridge: At the University Press, 1973.

McLuhan, Marshall. *the Gutenberg galaxy: the making of typographic man.* Toronto: University of Toronto Press, 1962.

Merleau-Ponty, Maurice. "Cézanne's Doubt." *Sense and Non- Sense.* Trans. Hubert L. Drefus and Patricia Allen Drefus. Evanston: Northwestern University Press, 1964.

Mitchell, Timothy. "Bergson, Le Bon, and Hermetic Cubism." *Journal of Aesthetics and Art Criticism,* vol. 36, no. 2 (Winter 1979): 175–83.

Moffett, Charles S., and James N. Wood. Introduction to *Monet's Years at Giverny: Beyond Impressionism.* New York: Harry N. Abrams, 1978.

Murphy, Richard. *The World of Cézanne 1839–1906.* New York: Time-Life Books, 1968.

Nagel, James. *Stephen Crane and Literary Impressionism.* University Park, Penn.: The Pennsylvania State University Press, 1980.

Nelson, Raymond S. *Hemingway: Expressionist Artist.* Ames: The Iowa State University Press, 1979.

Nin, Anaïs. *The Novel of the Future.* New York: The Macmillan Company, 1968.

Nochlin, Linda. *Impressionism and Post-Impressionism, 1874–1904: Sources and Documents.* Ed. H. W. Janson. Englewood Cliffs, N.J.: Prentice-Hall, 1966.

O'Connor, W. V. "Wallace Stevens: Impressionism in America." *Revue des Langues Vivantés* vol. 32 (January-February 1966): 66–77.

Pater, Walter. *The Renaissance: Studies in Art and Poetry.* London: Macmillan, 1910.

Perloff, Marjorie. "Poetry as Word-System: The Art of Gertrude Stein." *American Poetry Review,* vol. 8, no. 5 (1979): 33–43.

Phatte, Hans. *Les Impressionnistes.* Trans. Marianne Duval-Valentin. Paris: Arthaud, 1962.

Piacentino, Edward J. "A Study in Contrasts: Impressionist Perspectives of Ántonia and Lena Lingard in Cather's *My Ántonia.*" *Studies in the Humanities,* vol. 12, no. 1 (June 1985): 39–44.

Praz, Mario. *Mnemosyne: The Parallel between Literature and the Visual Arts. Bollingen Series,* vol. 35, no. 16. Princeton: Princeton University Press, 1974.

————. "Notes on James Joyce." *Mosaic,* vol. 6, no. 1 (Fall 1972): 85–100.

Reid, B. L. *Art by Subtraction: A Dissenting Opinion of Gertrude Stein.* Norman: University of Oklahoma Press, 1958.

Reid Broughton, Panthea. "The Cubist Novel: Toward Defining the Genre." In *"A Cosmos of My Own": Faulkner and Yoknapatawpha.* Eds. Doreen Fowler and Ann J. Abadie. Jackson: University Press of Mississippi, 1981.

Remsbury, John. "'Real Thinking': Lawrence and Cézanne." *Cambridge Quarterly,* vol. 2, no. 2 (1967): 117–47.

Rewald, John. *The History of Impressionism.* 4th rev. ed. New York: The Museum of Modern Art, 1973.

————. *Post-Impressionism from van Gogh to Gauguin.* 3rd rev. ed. New York: The Museum of Modern Art, 1978.

Richter, Harvena. *Virginia Woolf: The Inward Voyage.* Princeton: Princeton University Press, 1970.

Riddick, Lisa. *The Seen and the Unseen: Virginia Woolf's "To the Lighthouse."* Cambridge: Harvard University Press, 1977.

Rogers, Rodney. "Stephen Crane and Impressionism." *Nineteenth-Century Fiction* 24 (1969–70): 292–304.

Rönnebeck, Arnold. "Gertrude Was Always Giggling." *Books Abroad,* vol. 18, no. 4 (October 1944): 3–7.

Rosenblum, Robert. *Cubism and Twentieth-Century Art.* Rev. ed. New York: Harry N. Abrams, 1976.

————. "Picasso and the Typography of Cubism." In *Picasso in Retrospect.* Eds. Sir Roland Penrose and John Golding. New York: Praeger Publishers, 1973.

Ruskin, John. "Letter 1. On First Practice." In *The Elements of Drawing*. Vol. 15 of *The Works of John Ruskin*. London: George Allen, 1904.

———. "Of the Pathetic Fallacy." Vol. 5 of *The Works of John Ruskin*. Eds. E. T. Cook and Alexander Wedderburn. London: George Allen, 1904.

Sayre, Henry M. "Ready-Mades and Other Measures: The Poetics of Marcel Duchamp and William Carlos Williams." *Journal of Modern Literature*, vol 8, no. 1 (1980): 3–22.

Schapiro, Meyer. *Modern Art Nineteenth and Twentieth Centuries*. New York: George Braziller, 1978.

———. *Vincent van Gogh*. New York: Harry N. Abrams, 1950.

Schmitz, Neil. "Gertrude Stein as Post-Modernist: The Rhetoric of *Tender Buttons*." *Journal of Modern Literature*, vol. 3, no. 5 (July 1974): 1203–18.

Schwarz, Daniel R. "'I Was the World in Which I Walked': Transformation of the British Novel." *University of Toronto Quarterly* 51 (Spring 1982): 279–97.

Shone, Richard. *The Post-Impressionists*. London: John Calmara & Cooper Ltd., 1979.

Steiner, Wendy. *The Colors of Rhetoric: Problems in the Relation between Modern Literature and Painting*. Chicago: The University of Chicago Press, 1982.

———. *Exact Resemblance to Exact Resemblance: The Literary Portraiture of Gertrude Stein*. New Haven and London: Yale University Press, 1978.

Steinberg, Leo. "The Philosophical Brothel." Parts 1 and 2. *Art News*, vol. 71, nos. 5–6 (September-October 1972): 20–29, 38–47.

Stewart, Allegra. *Gertrude Stein and the Present*. Cambridge: Harvard University Press, 1967.

Stewart, Jack F. "Cubist Elements in *Between the Acts*." *Mosaic*, vol. 18, no. 2 (Spring 1985): 65–89.

———. "Expressionism in *The Rainbow*." *Novel*, 13-14 (Spring 1980): 296–315.

———. "Impressionism in the Early Novels of Virginia Woolf." *Journal of Modern Literature*, vol. 9, no. 2 (1982): 237–66.

———. "Lawrence and Gauguin." *Twentieth Century Literature* 26 (1980): 385–401.

Stouck, David. "Willa Cather and the Impressionist Novel." *Critical Essays on Willa Cather*. Ed. John J. Murphy. Boston: G. K. Hall, 1984.

Sutherland, Donald. *Gertrude Stein: A Biography of Her Works*. New Haven, Conn.: Yale University Press, 1951.

Sypher, Wylie. *Rococo to Cubism in Art and Literature*. New York: Random House, 1960.

Tomlinson, David. "T. S. Eliot and the Cubists." *Twentieth Century Literature*, vol. 26, no. 1 (Spring 1980): 64–81.

Torgovnick, Marianna. *The Visual Arts, Pictorialism, and the Novel: James, Lawrence, and Woolf*. Princeton: Princeton University Press, 1985.

Tucker, John. "William Faulkner's *As I Lay Dying:* Working Out the Cubistic Bugs." *Texas Studies in Literature and Language*, vol. 26, no. 4 (Winter 1984): 388–401.

Van Gogh, Vincent. *The Complete Letters of Vincent van Gogh*. 3 vols. Greenwich, Conn.: New York Graphic Society, 1958.

Venturi, Lionello. *Impressionists and Symbolists: Manet, Degas, Monet, Pissarro, Sisley, Renoir, Cézanne, Seurat, Gauguin, van Gogh, Toulouse-Latrec*. Trans. Francis Steegmuller. New York: Charles Scribner's Sons, 1950.

———. *Painting and Painters: How to Look at a Picture from Giotto to Chagall*. New York: Charles Scribner's Sons, 1945.

Walcutt, Charles C. *American Literary Naturalism, A Divided Stream*. Minneapolis: University of Minnesota Press, 1956.

Walker, Jayne L. *The Making of a Modernist: Gertrude Stein from "Three Lives" to "Tender Buttons"*. Amherst: The University of Massachusetts Press, 1984.

Watts, Emily Stipes. *Ernest Hemingway and the Arts*. Chicago: University of Illinois Press, 1971.

Weeks, Robert P., ed. *A Collection of Critical Essays*. Englewood Cliffs, N.J.: Prentice-Hall, 1965.

Weisstein, Ulrich . *Gertrude Stein and the Literature of the Modern Consciousness*. New York: Frederick Unger, 1970.

————. "Expressionism as an International Literary Phenomenon." In *Expressionism as an International Phenomenon: 21 Essays and a Bibliography*. Paris: Rider, 1973.

————. "Literature and the Visual Arts." *Interrelations Of Literature*. Eds. Jean-Pierre Barricelli and Joseph Gibaldi. New York: MLA of America, 1982.

————. "The Mutual Illuminations of the Arts." *Comparative Literature and Literary Theory: Survey and Introduction*. Trans. William Riggan. Bloomington: Indiana University Press, 1973.

————. "Verbal Paintings, Fugal Poems, Literary Collages and the Metamorphic Comparatist." *Yearbook Of Comparative And General Literature* 27 (1978): 7–16.

Whitehead, Lee M. "The Shawl and the Skull: Virginia Woolf's 'Magic Mountain.'" *Modern Fiction Studies,* vol. 18, no. 3 (1972): 401–15.

Wilenski, R. H. *The Modern Movement in Art*. London: Faber and Faber Limited, 1934.

Willett, John. *Expressionism*. New York: McGraw-Hill, 1970.

Yelton, Donald C. *Mimesis and Metaphor: An Inquiry into the Genesis and Scope of Conrad's Symbolic Imagery*. The Hague: Mouton, 1967.

Index

Abel, Elizabeth, 1

Albérès, R.-M., 8

Alexander, Jean, 39

Analogies, 1, 4, 5, 33, 40, 104, 249; Cubist, 5, 194, 200, 210, 212, 213, 215, 228, 241, 244, 245, 248. *See also* individual artists

Analysis, interartistic, 1, 2, 3, 6. *See also* Art, verbal/visual

Apollinaire, Guillaume, 163, 177, 213

Architectonics, 15, 25, 38, 50, 51, 59, 64, 89, 119, 123, 129

Art, plastic, 2, 6, 13, 19, 26, 61, 64, 66, 73, 75, 82, 101, 155, 179, 183, 204, 217, 218, 221, 232, 237, 248; ambiguity, 76; mural, 157; objective reality, 166. *See also* individual artists

Art, Renaissance, 66, 67, 93, 179; anti-Renaissance, 124; pre-Renaissance, 89; space, 74, 138

Art, spatial/temporal, 1, 4, 14

Art, verbal/visual, 2, 3, 4, 5, 6, 7, 27, 32, 34, 55, 91, 93, 105, 113, 136, 140, 142, 146, 177, 205, 211, 227, 246, 247, 248; *energia/ enargia,* 157; mural, 133; open window, 93, 210. *See also* Dualities; Tension; individual artists

Audience, 3, 5, 17, 18, 20, 24, 28, 42, 47, 51, 52, 54, 55, 57, 58, 59, 65, 67, 105, 119, 120, 122, 123, 124, 128, 133, 134, 151, 152, 162, 163, 166, 171, 181, 189, 192, 200, 209, 214, 215, 229, 236, 239, 240

Aurier, G.-Albert, 17

Bahr, Hermann, 7

Bates, H., E., 120

Baudelaire, Charles, 1

Bell, Clive, 23, 24, 63, 64, 117, 141

Benamou, Michel, 26, 249

Bender, Bert, 32, 33

Berger, John, 162, 210, 234

Bernard, Emile, 72, 73, 74, 76, 77, 87; *Nabis,* 72, 73; self-portrait, 82, 86

Berryman, John, 29

Boeck, Wilhelm, 217

Braque, Georges, 159, 160, 171, 173, 177, 181, 183, 185, 193, 245, 249; *collage,* 202; optical synthesis, 167; *papier collé,* 162–63, 202; techniques, 167, 223; trompe l'oeil, 160, 181, 225

Brown, Calvin, 26

Brueghel, Pieter, 128, 129, 134, 141; observer, 128; tension, 128, 151

Budgen, Frank, 187, 192

Cather, Willa, 22, 23

Cézanne, Paul, 3, 9, 15, 24, 63, 73, 76, 100, 113, 119, 121, 128, 140, 141, 142, 155, 175, 206; archetypal, 87, 89, 123, 142; depersonalization, 148; distortion, 105; "dynamic tension," 142; Expressionism, 120; form, 4, 103, 138, 139, 153; fourth dimension, 138; Hemingway, 118, 119, 120, 121, 123, 130, 136; innocent eye, 15; interlocking lines/planes, 74, 75, 87, 90, 113, 121, 123, 124, 142; letters, 76, 87; "mackerel eye," 139; mural, 130; nature, 69, 78, 104; otherness, 141; parallax, 94; perspective, 89, 103, 115, 122; *perspective vécue,* 118, 123; representational/nonrepresentational, 113, 118; resolute eye, 173; space, 66–67, 78, 81, 82, 87, 91, 106, 118, 124, 126, 128, 129, 157; symbolic, 87; thinking eye, 72, 139, 143; viewer, 124

Cheney, Sheldon, 20, 64, 89

Clark, Kenneth, 10, 119, 123

Conrad, Joseph, 22, 29, 31, 32

Consciousness, 7–8, 22, 23, 30, 141, 145, 151, 152; dual, 42

Constable, John, 14

Corot, Camille, 10, 61

Correlatives, 51, 62, 146, 196, 215, 216, 246, 248; linguistic, 119, 229; objective, 75; picto-

rial, 111, 247; plastic, 2, 75, 82, 86, 87, 90, 99, 103, 113; Stein/Cubism, 4, 5, 212, 221; structural, 101; stylistic, 15; subjective, 33; symbolic, 99; technical, 32; verbal, 43, 55, 61, 94, 104, 145, 186, 211, 215, 221, 247; visual, 31, 40, 105. *See also* individual artists; individual movements
Correspondences, 1, 2, 4, 6, 33, 60, 62, 82, 114, 157, 167; Cubism, 173, 202, 208, 211, 212, 243, 245, 246, 247, 248, 249; metallic, 104; natural, 104. *See also* individual artists; individual art movements
Courbet, Gustave, 10, 61, 215
Crane, Stephen, 3, 36; dislocation, 33, 34, 36; dramatic impressionism, 30; imagery, 34, 36; Impressionism, 3, 29, 32, 34, 36; incompatibility with Impressionism, 29; Naturalism, 30, 31; parallax, 95; pathetic fallacy, 36; Post-Impressionism, 33; *Red Badge of Courage*, 3, 29, 33; techniques, 29, 30, 33; vision, 29, 30
Criticism, 2, 3, 4, 6, 7, 9, 17, 19, 20, 22, 23, 24, 26, 32, 33, 61, 63, 96, 119, 120, 140, 160, 185, 194, 201, 207, 213, 216, 228, 246, 247, 249
Cubism, 2, 158, 162, 171, 173, 175, 179, 204, 206, 209, 213–14, 237, 246, 248; abstraction, 207; canvas/reality, 162; *collage*, 163, 175, 177, 181; conceptual, 159, 160, 163, 166, 173, 217; Cubist school, 163; *energia/enargia*, 73; fourth dimension, 163, 166, 185, 187; Joyce, 4, 187, 190, 191, 192; Modernism, 185; nonreferentiability, 3; observer, 171, 181; optical synthesis, 4, 162, 166, 185, 194; nature, 171; *papier collé*, 163, 175, 177, 181; plastic dimensions, 167, 177; projection, 216; spatial relations, 163; synthesis, 171; *tableau-tableau*, 175; techniques, 3; tenets, 162, 166, 205; thinking eye, 214; "total representation," 181; verisimilitude, 216. *See also* Misconceptions; individual artists
Cubism, Analytic, 173, 181, 191, 202, 212, 218, 221, 247; defined, 159; fragmentation/reconstruction, 171, 173, 193–94; iconic, 160; multiple views, 166; optical synthesis, 247, 249; representational/nonrepresentational, 160, 175, 208, 227
Cubism, Synthetic, 160, 162, 167, 177, 183, 194, 198, 200, 202, 209, 212, 221, 223, 233; *collage*, 159, 160, 183, 201, 203, 246; defined, 159; observer, 162; *papier collé*, 159, 183, 201, 203, 246; representational/nonrepresentational, 240; *tableau-objet*, 212; *tableau-tableau*, 211, 221; trompe l'oeil, 201, 237

Daix, Pierre, 163, 171, 177, 181
Daval, Jean-Luc, 17, 18
da Vinci, Leonardo, 19
Décaudin, Michel, 7
Degas, Edgar, 9, 34, 45, 51, 52
DeKoven, Marianne, 213, 243
Delacroix, Eugene, 1
Delauney, Robert, 163
Denis, Maurice, 72, 73, 74; *Nabis*, 72, 73; Post-Impressionism, 73; subjective deformation, 72
Derain, André, 63, 148, 153, 179
de Vlaminck, Maurice, 63
Donnell-Kotrozo, Carol, 66, 68
Dualities, 11, 20, 42, 50, 51, 64, 74, 76, 77, 78, 89, 104, 111, 113, 117, 142, 145, 146, 147, 157, 201, 221, 239, 244, 248
Duchamp, Marcel, 167, 213, 248, 249
Dunstan, Bernard, 13, 14, 17, 18, 45, 72

Eliot, T. S.: Cubists, 248–49; perspective, 249
Emerson, Ralph Waldo, 29
Estheticians/esthetics, 2, 3, 4, 5, 7, 22, 24, 29, 33, 59, 64, 72, 73, 74, 95, 106, 120, 138, 145, 200, 201
Expressionism, 8, 20, 22, 24, 25, 31, 38, 64, 115, 119, 151, 179, 248, 250
Eye: "All-Seeing"/Kodak, 138, 139, 152, 206; casual, 38; disinterested, 52; innocent, 7, 10, 14, 15, 16, 17, 23, 25, 29, 30, 34, 39, 42, 52, 65, 66, 70, 78, 96; mackerel, 138, 143, 146, 155; narrative, 43; observing, 28, 33, 34, 45, 59; penetrative, 4, 66, 73, 78; professional, 38, 42; resolute, 173; thinking, 72, 87, 155, 214. *See also* individual artists; individual art movements

Fowler, Alastair, 1, 2
Fried, Michael, 32
Fry, Roger, 2, 23, 24, 63, 65, 68, 93, 104, 141; Impressionism, 24; organic unity, 91, 93; Post-Impressionism, 23, 24, 73, 91
Futurism, 166, 167, 185–86, 248

Gasquet, Joachim, 87
Gauguin, Paul, 63, 64, 68, 69, 70, 72, 73, 90, 136, 148; abstraction, 70; decorative, 76; letters, 70, 75–76, 82, 86, 100; multiplicity, 89; Post-Impressionism, 86; primitivism, 135; self-portrait, 82; space, 86; sphinx, 114; Symbolist, 136
Gauss, Charles, 61
Gleizes, Albert, 2, 163, 166, 173, 185, 210
Goldwater, Robert, 69, 76, 115, 148
Gombrich, E. H., 9, 10, 11, 19, 75

Gris, Juan, 159, 173, 177, 183, 241; *collage*, 198, 204, 221, 240; Cubism, 160; elements of work, 163, 166, 167, 198, 204, 221, 223, 227, 237, 238; and Kahnweiler, 160; observer, 163; *papier collé*, 162–63, 198, 204; *tableau-tableau*, 198
Guiget, Jean, 20

Haas, Robert Bartlett, 204, 205, 206, 207, 217
Hagemann, Meyly Chin: and Cézanne, 126
Hagstrum, Jean, 5
Hatzfeld, Helmutt, 7, 8
Weinemann, Jan: on Woolf, 117
Hemingway, Ernest, 3, 141; archetypal, 134, 135, 136; "The Big Two-hearted River," 4; Cézanne, 118, 119, 120, 121, 123, 132, 135; *Death in the Afternoon*, 119; distortions, 120–21; enclosure, 3, 4, 123; *enargia*, 119; *energia*, 119; Expressionism, 119; *A Farewell to Arms*, 4, 121, 122, 123, 124, 248; "fifth dimension," 91, 136, 157; *Islands in the Stream*, 133; nonpictorial, 124; *The Old Man and the Sea*, 134, 135, 136; perspective, 121, 123, 129, 132; *perspective vécue*, 126, 130; Post-Impressionism, 118, 133, 136; reader, 123, 132, 133, 134, 136; simplification, 134; space, 118, 119, 129, 132; *The Sun Also Rises*, 4; symbolism, 128; Symbolism, 134; synesthesia, 132, 135; technical style, 118, 124, 126, 128, 129, 135; verbal technique, 4, 121–22; visual/haptic, 130
Hess, Hans, 66, 67
Hilliard, Northern, 29
Hoffman, Michael, 218
Holton, Milne, 30
Howarth, Herbert, 26, 30
Huysmans, Joris-Karl: Impressionists and mental illness, 20

Iconicity (referentiability), 6, 17, 160, 167, 175, 181, 194, 198, 204, 208, 215, 229, 237
Iconographics, 134, 135, 145, 177, 214, 233
Ilie, Paul, 27, 32
Illusion, 13, 28, 40, 42, 43, 48, 54, 57, 66, 68, 74, 75, 106, 119, 181, 186, 200, 214, 229, 236; spatial, 82, 132, 153, 163, 247. *See also* individual artists
Impressionism, 2, 7, 9, 10, 13, 20, 27, 42, 51, 66, 81, 94, 156, 197, 247, 249; casual eye, 38, 98; Crane, 3; definitions, 7; depersonalization/detachment, 8, 14–15, 17, 18, 25, 27, 33, 34, 36, 47, 54, 61, 70; distortion, 17, 60, 81, 95; Leroy, Louis, 9; literary, 3, 7, 8, 23, 24, 27, 31–32, 50; naivety, 27, 62, 86; nonintellectual passivity, 2, 8, 10–11, 20, 26, 61, 114, 188, 192–93; open window, 19, 45, 81,

247; optics, 9, 10, 11; phenomenological, 11, 23; pictorial, 3, 23, 31, 59; projection, 19, 20, 27, 28; Salon, 9, 10, 23; serial approach, 3, 9, 13, 58, 70; verbal, 26, 27, 60; visual, 60, 115, 166, 188. *See also* Realism, ocular; individual artists; individual art movements
Isaak, Jo-Anna, 186

Johnston, Bruce, 23
Jones, E. T., 120
Joyce, James: archetypal, 203; *collage*, 202; Cubism, 4, 187, 190, 191, 192, 194, 196, 198, 200, 202, 204, 246; Impressionism, 188, 192; misconception about Cubism, 187, 194, 202, 203; multiplication of views, 4; narrator, 189; pathetic fallacy, 196, 197; point of view, 190, 192, 198; pseudo-*collage*, 202, 204, 246; reader, 192, 200; reality, 189; stream of consciousness, 196, 198, 200; style, 189, 190, 239–40; Symbolism, 188; symbols, 201, 203; trompe l'oeil, 197, 201; *Ulysses*, 4, 186, 187, 188, 196, 197, 200, 246, 247
Jung, Carl, 87

Kahn, Gustave, 163
Kahnweiler, Daniel-Henry, 159, 160, 171, 173, 218
Keats, John, 1
Kronegger, Maria, 7, 8, 20, 22

Laforgue, Jules, 13
Lair, Robert, 123
Laval, Charles: self-portrait, 82
Lawrence, D. H., 4; "All-Seeing Eye"/Kodak eye, 139, 140, 152, 206; archetypal, 143, 144; Cézanne, 138, 139, 140, 141, 142, 143; esthetics, 138; Etruscan art, 139; Expressionism, 152; "fourth dimension," 91, 138, 143, 152, 157; "mackerel eye," 143, 146, 155; naive/thinking eye, 138; open window, 153; otherness, 142, 150, 151; pathetic fallacy, 146; perspective, 143; *perspective vécue*, 144, 152, 153; point of view, 155; Post-Impressionism, 143, 153; symbolism, 150; synesthesia, 148, 151; technical style, 144, 145, 146, 148; tension, 143; van Gogh, 143, 153, 155
Lawrence, Karen, 189, 201, 202
Le Fauconnier, Henri, 163
Leger, Fernand, 163
Leroy, Louis, 9, 23
Levin, Harry, 124, 126
Lhote, André, 67, 74, 106, 123; *perspective vécue*, 67, 120
Light and Color, 11, 13, 14, 22, 26, 38, 40, 51, 65, 90; chiaroscuro, 22, 33, 81, 90; interdependence, 11, 20, 28, 40, 50, 61, 147. *See*

also Impressionism; individual artists; individual art movements

Lindsay, Jack, 140

Literary techniques, 109, 111, 118, 124, 129, 144, 145, 183, 188, 190, 206, 209, 210, 214, 216, 225, 227, 229, 235, 236, 243, 245, 246; ellipsis, 27, 43, 61, 245; *enargia*, 5; metonymy, 136; mimesis, 5, 8, 18, 19, 69, 90, 91, 94, 119, 181; omission, 61; oxymorons, 151; parataxis, 143; simile, 40; syntax, 27, 102, 122, 145, 196, 235; verb omissions, 27. *See also* individual artists

Lodge, David, 212

Loran, Erle, 78, 81, 82, 103, 128, 132, 142

Lynton, Norbert, 160

McLaurin, Allen, 104, 105, 113, 114

McLuhan, Marshall, 74, 93

Manet, Edouard, 63

Matisse, Henri, 63, 179

Matthiessen, Peter, 55; depersonalization, 55, 58; Expressionism, 55; *Far Tortuga*, 3, 55; Impressionism, 55, 57, 60; multiple points of view, 59; observing eye, 55; surfaces, 58; synesthesia, 58; technical styles, 55

Mauron, Charles: nonrepresentational, 93; psychological reality, 98

Metaphysics, 2, 33

Metzinger, Jean, 2, 163, 166, 173, 185, 210

Millet, Jean, 14

Misconceptions: Cubism, 2, 4, 187, 247, 248; Hemingway/Cézanne, 129; Impressionism, 3, 7, 20, 23, 29. *See also* individual artists; individual art movements

Mode, diachronic, 1, 2, 4, 211, 247. *See also* individual artists

Mode, synchronic, 2, 4, 247. *See also* individual artists

Modernism, 1, 3, 26, 60, 93, 185, 247, 248; stream of consciousness/pictorial Impressionism, 24–25; styles, 93–94; themes, 91

Monet, Claude, 9, 13, 14, 18, 23, 24, 34, 36, 43, 48, 59, 70; detachment, 47, 54; development, 69; fragmentation, 11; innocent eye, 15, 25, 50, 65; style, 20, 51. *See also* Impressionism

Munch, Edvard, 114

Nagel, James, 29, 30, 31

Narrative, 1, 3, 4, 30, 39, 117, 135, 138, 192, 193, 196, 201, 238, 241. *See also* individual artists; individual art movements

Narrator, 28, 38, 39, 40, 42, 50, 189, 209, 214, 217, 233, 240, 241. *See also* individual artists

Naturalism, 4, 5, 11, 18, 19, 26, 30, 31, 51; scientific, 60, 65

Nature, 9, 10, 14, 24, 48, 69, 86, 90, 94, 148, 150, 151, 171, 175, 204; man, 134, 139; space, 78. *See also* Impressionism; individual artists

Nelson, Raymond, 120, 126

Neo-Impressionism, 15, 68, 81

Nin, Anaïs, 248

Nineteenth century, 1, 2, 5, 22, 60, 72, 90, 140, 206

O'Connor, W. V., 249

Parallels, 1, 4, 82, 106, 119, 147, 218, 220, 225, 228, 229, 232, 241, 246; grammatical, 111; plastic, 103, 244; verbal, 3, 144, 157, 244. *See also* Literary techniques; individual artists; individual art movements

Parmelin, Hélène, 167

Pater, Walter, 19, 20

Period concept, 1, 29. *See also* individual art movements

Perloff, Marjorie, 213

Perosa, Sergio, 31

Perspective, 6, 13, 43, 45, 51, 74, 94, 95, 96, 105, 109, 117, 120, 129, 143, 145, 153; adult, 52; aerial, 45, 81, 94, 95; atmospheric, 4, 19, 43, 48, 75, 121; child, 52; cosmic, 115; depersonalized, 115, 121, 123; linear, 4, 19, 43, 48, 50, 66, 75, 77, 81, 121, 122, 129; Olympian, 94–95, 108; open window, 123; physical, 39; scenographic, 11; universal, 82. *See also* individual artists; individual art movements

Picabia, Francis, 213

Picasso, Pablo, 63, 160, 171, 173, 175, 179, 181, 185, 191, 193, 194, 204, 205, 206, 234; *collage*, 162, 202, 243; Cubism, 159, 207, 208, 233; optical synthesis, 167; *papier collé*, 202, 225; primitive, 218; Stein, 216, 218, 229, 244; style, 175, 181, 191, 198, 210, 216, 217, 221, 223, 228, 232, 241, 249

Pictorial, 1, 3, 5, 8, 17, 18, 22, 38, 40, 43, 47, 55, 73, 115, 124, 133, 146, 247; authorial voice, 233; Cubism, 160, 163, 167, 175, 201, 204, 208; *enargia*, 5; illusion, 68; movements, 2, 3, 9, 23, 32, 58; reality, 111, 152; space, 47, 65, 75, 105; strategies, 5

Pissarro, Camille, 9, 14, 15, 17, 18, 25, 45–47

Plato, 90

Poetry, 249

Point of view, 14, 17, 18, 22, 28, 34, 39, 43, 45, 52, 54, 55, 58, 62, 66, 67, 69, 94, 95, 97, 103, 133, 145, 152, 190; Cubism, 167, 179, 186, 192; depersonalized, 108, 117; external, 153; personalized, 121; plastic, 249, 250; stereoscopic/open window, 19, 45, 81,

93, 153, 198, 214, 235, 238, 247, 248
Post-Impressionism, 2, 3, 20, 23, 31, 33, 42,
    51, 63, 69, 74, 82, 86, 89, 106, 142, 146,
    173, 175; abstraction, 65, 90; artist/subject,
    64, 86; art and reality, 68; Expressionism, 64;
    against Impressionism, 23, 24, 62, 66, 78,
    247; interpenetration, 117, 153, 157; litera-
    ture, 3, 25, 38; Nature, 152; nonrepresenta-
    tional, 87, 89, 90, 157; objective values, 64;
    paradox, 76, 120; parallax view, 4, 81; pene-
    trating eye, 4, 66; *perspective vécue*, 93, 121;
    return to tradition, 63, 76, 157; Significant
    Form, 64; subjective values, 64; symbolic, 72;
    themes, 87, 90, 153, 157; thinking eye, 99,
    157; Woolf, 38, 98, 101, 106. *See also* Eye;
    individual artists; individual art movements
Praz, Mario, 179, 188

Raverat, Jacques, 43
Raynal, Maurice, 163, 166
Realism: conceptual, 173; psychological, 82, 98,
    115, 200; ocular, 2, 7, 10, 18, 22, 78; scien-
    tific, 69, 82, 166; Sypher, Wylie, 10. *See
    also* individual art movements
Reality: appearance, 64; conceptual, 90, 101;
    constructed, 82; *enargia*, 5, 69, 91, 119; *en-
    ergia*, 5, 69, 82, 91, 119; external, 167, 196;
    multidimensional, 111; objective, 101, 166;
    optical, 28; surface, 5, 9, 10, 26, 27, 36, 54,
    109, 139, 162, 245, 248; surface/depth, 5, 9,
    25, 29, 38, 39, 81, 94, 96, 97, 99, 124, 135–
    36, 151
Remsbury, John, 141
Renoir, Auguste, 9, 11, 18, 40, 41, 43, 65; open
    window, 81
Rewald, John, 23, 64–65, 75
Rivière, Georges, 9, 52
Rodin, Auguste, 187, 188
Rogers, Rodney, 31
Ronnebeck, Arnold, 207
Rose, Marilyn Gaddis, 212
Rosenblum, Robert, 167, 171, 175, 185, 237
Rouault, Georges, 63
Rousseau, Theodore, 14
Ruskin, John, 5, 10, 11, 17, 138

Salmon, André, 159, 163, 171, 177
Salon des Indépendants, 63, 65, 159, 163
Sayre, Henry, 249–50
Schapiro, Meyer, 69, 77, 81, 86, 87, 153
Schwarz, Daniel, 106
Sérusier, Paul, 73
Seurat, Georges, 15, 63, 68, 69, 75, 81, 90,
    109, 111; *collage*, 81; enclosure, 104
Signac, Paul, 15
Sisley, Alfred, 9, 15

Spatial factors, 43, 45, 50, 52, 55, 58, 66, 67,
    74, 78, 81, 82, 93, 94, 113, 119, 121, 123,
    124, 126, 128, 129, 130, 132, 138, 163, 194,
    241, 247. *See also* Values/planes; individual
    artists; individual art movements
Stallman, R. W., 29, 31
Stein, Gertrude: abstraction, 207; archaic, 220;
    autotelic, 210; Cézanne, 206; *collage*, 227,
    228; Cubism, 4, 204, 205, 206, 207, 208,
    209, 210, 211, 212, 213, 214, 215, 216, 223,
    225, 227, 228, 240, 241, 244, 246, 248; dis-
    sociation, 206, 221; *enargia*, 212; *energia*,
    210, 212; esthetic, 205, 210, 221, 225, 243,
    244; narrator, 209, 210, 214, 217, 233, 234,
    239, 240, 241, 244; nonreferentiality, 207,
    212; open window, 235, 238; painting/pictures,
    205; *papier collé*, 227, 228; Picasso, 204–5,
    206, 207, 208, 210, 218, 220, 221, 223, 225,
    228, 229, 233, 234; portraiture, 4, 207, 246;
    reader, 215, 229, 233, 236, 239, 240, 245;
    resemblances, 208; Surrealism, 248; synesthe-
    sia, 229; *tableau-tableau*, 211; technical style,
    5, 208, 210, 211, 212, 213, 214, 216, 217,
    220, 221, 223, 225, 227, 229, 232, 234, 235,
    236, 237, 238, 239, 240, 241, 243, 245, 246,
    248; *Tender Buttons*, 206, 208, 209, 211, 213,
    214, 217, 221, 225, 227, 234, 239, 243, 245,
    246; tension, 217, 225; Toklas, Alice B., 228;
    trompe l'oeil, 214, 215, 227, 229, 236
Steiner, Wendy, 212, 213
Stevens, Wallace, 249
Stewart, Allegra, 213
Stewart Jack, 22, 26, 146, 148, 152
Stouck, David, 23
Sutherland, Donald, 232
Symbolism, 13, 14, 22, 31, 33, 38, 69, 72, 73,
    87, 90, 91, 100, 111, 128, 136, 147, 150,
    201, 202, 203. *See also* individual artists; in-
    dividual art movements
Sypher, Wylie, 10, 17, 186, 187

Tensions, 4, 5, 9, 26, 32, 42, 64, 77, 99, 104,
    107, 111, 141, 143, 145; Cubism, 160, 175,
    185, 214, 217, 229, 240; curve/angle, 100,
    102; exterior/interior, 98, 151; horizontal/ver-
    tical, 86, 91, 104, 130, 134, 135, 144, 150;
    male/female, 144; near/far, 95, 122, 145, 147,
    153; perspective shifts, 105, 109; right/left,
    86
Tomlinson, David, 249
Turner, John, 10, 14
Twentieth century, 1, 5, 24, 106, 179, 185

Values/planes: two vs. three dimensional, 4–5,
    9, 19, 40, 58, 65, 67, 74, 78, 81, 90, 93,
    118, 122, 155, 162, 163, 171, 181, 187–88,

209, 225–27, 245, 248. *See also* individual artists; individual art movements

van Gogh, Vincent, 63, 67, 69, 72, 73, 76, 78, 100, 117, 138, 142–43, 150, 155, 157; depersonalization, 115; duality, 78, 143; "eternal," 86, 152; form, 4, 136, 147, 153; "fourth dimension," 142; Lawrence, 142–43, 152, 153; letters, 70, 75, 77, 86, 90, 103, 147; multiplicity, 89, 90; "other thing," 150; parallax, 94; perspective, 153; point of view, 145; self-portrait, 82, 86, 102; style, 86–87, 90–91, 146, 148, 153; subjectivity, 64; tension, 143, 153

Vauxcelles, Louis: Cubism, 159

Venturi, Lionello, 7, 9, 82, 89, 103, 121, 123

Verisimilitude, 18, 19, 23, 38, 61, 68, 93, 97, 99, 100, 103, 120, 122, 126, 139, 140, 191, 205, 234, 241, 248

Walcutt, Charles, 30–31

Walker, Jayne, 216

Walpole, Hugh, 95

Watts, Emily Stipes, 128, 129, 130

Weisstein, Ulrich, 1, 6

Wilenski, R. H., 64

Woolf, Virginia: creative eye, 111; decompensation/metamorphosis, 40; depths, 38, 39, 47, 48; enclosure, 4, 105, 106, 107; esthetics, 95; imagery, 38; Impressionism, 3, 21, 25, 26, 27, 39, 40, 96; *Jacob's Room*, 3, 22, 26, 36, 38, 39, 43, 45, 48, 50, 54, 97–98, 114, 206; language, 117; *To the Lighthouse*, 4, 97, 98, 99, 114, 157; meditative intelligence, 45, 47, 97; narrator, 38, 39, 40, 95, 97; nonrepresentational, 104; observing eye, 28, 45, 98; open window, 43, 45, 99, 106; otherness, 52; parallax, 111, 157; pathetic fallacy, 54; penetrative eye, 4; perspective, 96, 115, 248; pictorial, 105, 115; point of view, 96, 97, 111; Post-Impressionism, 98, 101; space, 105, 113; surface, 27, 36, 39, 40, 42, 54; Symbolism, 101, 102, 114; technical style, 102, 103, 104, 109, 111, 117; theme, 91, 104; typography, 105; visual naivety, 47; *The Waves*, 38, 39, 47, 50, 51, 57, 248